CONFESSING
ONE
FAITH

CONFESSING ONE FAITH

A Joint Commentary on the Augsburg Confession
by Lutheran and Catholic Theologians

Edited by

George Wolfgang Forell and James F. McCue

in cooperation with

Wenzel Lohff
Horst Georg Pöhlmann
Bengt Hägglund
Gerhard Müller
George A. Lindbeck
Harding Meyer
Vilmos Vajta
Holsten Fagerberg
Georg Kretschmar
Bernhard Lohse
Johannes Halkenhäuser

Walter Kasper
Karl Lehmann
Wilhelm Breuning
Vinzenz Pfnür
Avery Dulles
Heinz Schütte
Erwin Iserloh
Hans Jorissen
René Laurentin
Karl Suso Frank
Friedrich Wulf

AUGSBURG Publishing House • Minneapolis

CONFESSING ONE FAITH

Manufactured in the United States of America

Contents

Chapter 1
**The Significance of the Augsburg Confession for the Lutheran Church
and Its Relationship to the Roman Catholic Church**
by Wenzel Lohff
translated by Joan Mau

Chapter 2
The Catholic View of Confessions and Confessional Community
by Walter Kasper
translated by Omar Kaste

Chapter 3
God, Jesus Christ, and the Return of Christ
by Karl Lehmann and Horst Georg Pöhlmann
translated by Michael Rogness

Chapter 8
The Sacraments: Baptism and the Lord's Supper
by Erwin Iserloh and Vilmos Vajta
translated by Darold H. Beekmann

Chapter 9
Penance and Confession
by Holsten Fagerberg and Hans Jorissen
translated by James L. Schaaf

Chapter 10
The Cult of the Saints
by Georg Kretschmar and René Laurentin
translated by Ralph Gehrke

Chapter 11
Monasticism
by Bernhard Lohse, Karl Suso Frank,
Johannes Halkenhäuser, and Friedrich Wulf
translated by Richard W. Schoenleber

Chapter 12
Political Order and Vocation
in the Augsburg Confession
by George Wolfgang Forell and James F. McCue

Abbreviations

AAS = *Acta Apostolicae Sedis*

AE = *Luther's Works,* American Edition. J. Pelikan and H. Lehmann, gen. eds.

BC = *The Book of Concord: The Confessions of the Evangelical Lutheran Church.* Theodore G. Tappert, trans. and ed. Philadelphia: Fortress, 1959.

BSLK = *Die Bekenntnisschriften der evangelisch-lutherischen Kirche.* Göttingen: Vandenhoeck and Ruprecht, 1952.

CA = *Confessio Augustana (Augsburg Confession)*

CR = *Corpus Reformatum.*

CT = *Concordia Triglotta.* F. Bente, ed. St. Louis: Concordia, 1921.

DS = *Enchiridion Symbolorum.* H. Denzinger and A. Schönmetzer, eds. 33rd ed.

EKO = *Evangelische Kommentar*

HDG = *Handbuch der Dogmengeschichte*

Immenkötter = *Die Confutatio der Confessio Augustana vom 3. August 1530.* Herbert Immenkötter, ed. Münster: 1979.

KuD = *Kerygma und Dogma*

LThk² = *Lutherische Theologie und Kirche*

MySal = *Mysterium Salutis*

RGG³ = *Die Religion in Geschichte und Gegenwart,* 3rd ed.

RSPhTh = *Revue des Sciences Philosophiques et Théologiques*

RSR = *Recherches de Science Religieuse*

THL = *Theologische Literaturzeitung*

ThPh = *Theologie und Philosophie*

ThStKr = *Theologische Studien und Kritiken*

UR = *Unitatis Redintegratio*

ZKG = *Zeitschrift für Kirchengeschichte*

ZThK = *Zeitschrift für Theologie und Kirche*

Introduction to the American Edition

Some 450 years ago, a group of Christian laymen presented a theological document before the Hapsburg Emperor, Charles V, at the Imperial Diet at Augsburg. It was June 25, 1530. They were mostly princes and nobles, but there were a few mayors and city councils present as well. The document had been composed by Philip Melanchthon, professor at the University of Wittenberg and close associate of Martin Luther. Luther himself was under an imperial ban and was unable to be present at Augsburg. This Augsburg Confession was a summary of the faith of those Christians who, under Luther's leadership, were trying to bring about significant changes in the life and teaching of the western Christian church. They believed that they could "unite . . . in agreement on one Christian truth . . . put aside whatever may not have been rightly interpreted or treated by either side, to have all of us embrace and adhere to a single, true religion and live together in unity and in one fellowship and church, even as we are all enlisted under one Christ." [1]

This attempt to be acknowledged as teaching nothing that deviates

11

from the Catholic and even the Roman Church did not succeed, and for four and a half centuries the churches called Lutheran and Catholic have been divided. However, this concern of the Augsburg Confession to establish a basis for unity rather than division has stimulated interest in this document in an ecumenical age. The 450th anniversary of the presentation of the Confession was in itself enough to occasion an abundant literature, but a more important reason for the renewed interest in our times is its ecumenical interest. It was written to demonstrate the legitimacy of the Lutheran movement as part of the one, holy, catholic, and apostolic church; and it was to serve as a rallying point for both "Lutheran" and "Calvinist" Protestants in their struggle for legal recognition in the empire. As a confession important for the entire Protestant movement it has been studied down through the centuries. But in recent years this study has been focused in a new way. Roman Catholic and Lutheran theologians have discussed the possibility and advisability of a "recognition" of the Augsburg Confession by the Roman Catholic Church.[2] This renewed interest has led to this present commentary. The purpose has been to present a scholarly investigation of the Augsburg Confession, undertaken together by Roman Catholics and Lutherans, in order to see whether a common assessment of the Augsburg Confession has become possible. The study was to be both critical and constructive and intended to raise questions about the relevancy of the 16th-century document at the end of the 20th century. Introduced by two theological opening statements, one by a Lutheran, the other by a Roman Catholic, the commentary deals with the key issues examined by the Augsburg Confession in nine chapters, each written jointly by a Roman Catholic and Lutheran author. On the issue of monasticism a somewhat different approach has been used in order to reflect the complexity of the contemporary discussion. But even that chapter includes a common conclusion which combines the insights of the four authors.

The last chapter presents the results of a consultation of all the contributors to the book. This chapter might help the cause of reconciliation not only because of the scholarly results of the commentary but also because of the irenic spirit which helped to bring about these results. The American editors have revised the work of the various translators and must bear responsibility for whatever shortcomings may be found in the final translation. The American editors hope that this commentary may, in its English version, further contribute to mutual understanding, and thus represent a step in the pilgrimage toward the fulfillment of Jesus' high-priestly prayer (John 17:23).

George Wolfgang Forell
James F. McCue

Notes

1. Augsburg Confession, Preface (BC 25).
2. E.g. "Recognition of the Augsburg Confession by the Catholic Church," *Theology Digest* 24 (no. 1, 1976): 65-70. See also Harding Meyer, Heinz Schütte, and Hans-Joachim Mund, *"Katholische Anerkennung des Augsburgischen Bekenntnisses? Ein Vorstoss zur Einheit zwischen katholischer und lutherischer Kirche,"* Oekumenische Perspectiven, vol. 9 (Frankfurt, 1977); Heinrich Fries and others, *Confessio Augustana: Hindernis oder Hilfe?* (Regensburg, 1979).

Introduction to the German Edition

During the last several years the question of recognizing the Augsburg Confession has been discussed in numerous publications, lectures, and meetings.[1] In this discussion one thing immediately became clear: prior to any new and positive assessment of the Confessio Augustana (CA) by the Roman Catholic Church a thorough clarification of the theological issues was required, and that could be properly done only in a *common* Catholic-Lutheran effort to interpret the document. Accordingly it was proposed quite early in the discussion of the question of recognition that a common Catholic-Lutheran "commentary" on the Augsburg Confession be prepared.[2]

This proposal quickly found a positive echo. A group of two Catholic and two Lutheran theologians, whose number was soon increased by four additional theologians, in the spring of 1978 outlined a plan for such a commentary and agreed to be the editors of the planned publication.

The goal was "to determine through scholarly investigation to what extent a common Catholic-Lutheran understanding of the CA is possible." In the process, the shortcomings of the Augsburg Confession should also be noted and the questions which the CA still poses to both churches should be expressed. From the outset it was clear that this common enterprise should not be an official undertaking of the churches but should be the responsibility of the authors involved. It was hoped that in just that way the undertaking could be of service to the churches.

A series of methodological questions had to be considered:

With respect to the thematic organization of the material, it was agreed that it would not be right to limit consideration to the first part of the CA, to the "Articles of Faith and Doctrine" (CA 1-21). The second part (CA 22-28), dealing with ecclesiastical abuses, is closely connected with the first: it contains clearly theological implications relevant to the articles of faith and doctrine. Because it did not seem appropriate to treat each article separately, it was decided to identify some 10 themes that cover the basic content of the CA, combine the two parts of the confession, and in addition give adequate space to those questions which are of importance for a Catholic-Lutheran agreement (e.g. confession, veneration of saints, and monasticism). Such an organization of topics would ordinarily deal with several articles under one heading, and so there would be some overlapping; but this was seen as an advantage, since it would help to avoid isolating the individual articles and would help to clarify the connecting lines in the overall structure of the CA.

In addition to the discussion of the several topics, it seemed appropriate to have two basic chapters, one Lutheran and one Catholic, which would situate the entire work.

No less important than the problem of thematic organization was the question of the *methodological perspective* from which each topic was to be examined. It was obvious that in the end the authors themselves would have to make the decisions dictated by their subjects, but there was agreement among the editors (and in the first consultation among the authors) that certain guidelines would be followed:

● The 1530 text of the CA, in its immediate historical context (the earlier versions, the Diet, the Confutatio, the negotiations for agreement) should be at the center.

● This should not, of course, eliminate reference to the earlier history: to the early church and medieval tradition, to the Reformation, and especially to Luther's theology.

● It seems appropriate that the Apology of the CA, insofar as it is a commentary on it, be especially brought to bear in interpreting the CA.

● It was up to the authors whether to take into account the sub-sequent history of the CA; but in any event, that history was not to be used as a hermeneutical key.

● Finally, it was considered important to bring in, to the extent possible, the results of today's ecumenical developments and dialogue.

In view of the ultimate purpose of the work, it was agreed that two authors, a Lutheran and a Catholic, should work on each of the 10 topics, and in such a way that both would be responsible for the final chapter. For the same reason, the first drafts of the manuscripts were circulated among all the contributors, with the expressed request for comments and suggestions for corrections or amplifications. Two con-sultations (March and September, 1979) among the contributors furth-er served this exchange of views and consequent revisions.

In the main it worked out that each chapter, as intended, was the joint work and responsibility of a Catholic and a Lutheran author, and that each chapter was communicated to all the contributors in order to achieve the greatest possible consistency for the entire volume. How-ever, on occasion there is disagreement between a "Catholic" and a "Lutheran" view or interpretation. These differences, however, are not so substantial that they undermine the basic agreement reached.

On the question of monasticism a somewhat different procedure seemed called for. To both the Lutheran and the Catholic contribution were added a Lutheran and a Catholic response. It seemed important to reflect the rather wide variety of present-day judgment and prac-tice of monastic or community life, especially within the Lutheran church. But here too it was possible to pull together the different threads in a conclusion for which all four authors are responsible.

At the second consultation of the authors (September, 1979), it was possible to draw up a summary conclusion that was accepted by all. It is found at the end of this volume. There, and in the unanimous choice of the title for this volume, *Confessing One Faith,* one can see to what extent all the contributors were convinced that they had reached the intended goal and had arrived at a "common Catholic-Lutheran understanding of the Augsburg Confession."

This first common Catholic-Lutheran examination of the CA and its publication in the way it was planned was possible only through gen-erous financial help from the United Evangelical-Lutheran Church of Germany and the President of the German Bishops' Conference, Joseph Cardinal Höffner. In this material support, for which we express our profound thanks to the two church offices, one can see a basic affirmation of the entire undertaking and its significance for a hoped-for agreement and future fellowship of our churches.

Harding Meyer
Heinz Schütte
Strassburg/Paderborn
January, 1980

Notes

1. The literature on this question is already so extensive that we can here refer to only two collections: Harding Meyer, Heinz Schütte, and Hans-Joachim Mund, eds., *"Katholische Anerkennung des Augsburgischen Bekenntnisses? Ein Vorstoss zur Einheit zwischen katholischer und lutherischer Kirche,"* Oekumenische Perspectiven 9 (Frankfurt, 1977); Heinrich Fries and others, *Confessio Augustana: Hindernis oder Hilfe?* (Regensburg, 1979).
2. H. Schütte, in *"Katholische Anerkennung des Augsburgischen Bekenntnisses?* Ibid., p. 52.

1

The Significance of the Augsburg Confession for the Lutheran Church and Its Relationship to the Roman Catholic Church

by Wenzel Lohff

translated by Joan Mau

1. The Significance of the CA in Its Original Context

In its original context, the CA is the comprehensive account concerning the insights of the Lutheran Reformation, called for by the summons of the Diet of Augsburg of 1530, and the description of the resulting order, or new order, as it affected the teaching and life of congregations in a number of territories ("*ecclesiae apud nos*," CA 1, 1).[1]

The use of the term "*Confessio*," whose consequences for church history were unforeseeable in 1530, points to Luther. With regard to the controversies over the Lord's Supper, Luther stated at the end of his *Confession Concerning Christ's Supper* that he desired "to confess my faith before God and all the world, point by point." [2] *Confessio* also points to the necessity to state the basis of Reformation teaching before emperor and empire, before the whole church, and finally before the judgment seat of God. This is clear from Melanchthon's draft of the conclusion,[3] and later from the Preface to the *Book of Concord*.[4]

Thus, the teaching of the CA is not conceived as the dogma of a theological party or even of a new "church," but rather as the right doctrine of the one, holy, catholic, and apostolic church. Thus we read in the conclusion of the *editio princeps* regarding the intention of the confession: "Nor have we thought to injure anyone with this document; but have simply made our confession, from which can be clearly seen that in doctrine and ceremonies we hold nothing which is contrary to God's Word or the holy, universal, and catholic Christian churches. For it is manifest that we have with greatest diligence guarded against any new, unchristian doctrine being taught or received among us." [5] The issue is not a special teaching, but keeping pure the original teaching of the Christian faith.

It can indeed sound like a *captatio benevolentiae* when we read in the conclusion to the doctrinal articles, "Since this teaching is grounded clearly on the Holy Scriptures and is not contrary or opposed to that of the universal Christian church, or even of the Roman church (insofar as the latter's teaching is reflected in the writings of the Fathers), we think that our opponents cannot disagree with us in the articles set forth above." [6] But at the same time, it is against this background that we must interpret the assertion that Reformation teaching and practice were concerned only with the correction of certain abuses. It would be wrong to say that the statement *"Tota dissensio est de paucis quibusdam abusibus"* [7] is nothing but diplomatic camouflaging of a doctrinal dissension which actually existed. It is rather a compelling conclusion drawn from the basic conviction that the supporters of the CA were in agreement with the one, holy, catholic church. Even if subsequent interpretation should conclude that the differences in doctrine between the confessors of the CA and their opponents were greater than the CA itself assessed them, the following must nevertheless be noted: if the CA itself were to be understood as a fitting, albeit elementary, expression of the faith of the one, holy church, then an exclusive disagreement could only apply to the expression or shaping of the faith in which, because it corresponds to the diversity of Christian life, unity in the sense of uniformity was not compellingly necessary. It could not concern the foundation, because here any disagreement must damage the true unity of the church. It is in this sense that the article on the church (CA 7) makes a basic distinction between that which is sufficient *(satis)* for the true unity of the church, namely agreement in the right teaching of the gospel and the right administration of the sacraments, and that where uniformity is not necessary *(nec necesse):* human traditions and rites, in which the life of the church takes shape.[8]

Dissension in regard to the church's right teaching is to be avoided; this is the stated intention of the whole CA.[9]

At Augsburg the CA's authors went so far in this respect that at first they only intended to present those articles concerning church usages in which abuses, as they understood it, had been corrected (that is, the later Articles 22-28). It was only the detailed and comprehensive accusation of heresy from their opponents which necessitated the presentation of their own teaching step by step (CA 1-21). Of course, to begin with this occurred in such a spare and summary form (compare the volume of the first 21 Articles with the subsequent ones), that these articles could only be sufficient if one could assume a basic agreement with the doctrinal tradition of the church and, so to speak, only briefly note its existence. Only when it was recognized that this consensus did not exist did it become necessary to present a comprehensive and detailed exposition in doctrine as well. This purpose is served then by the Apology of the Augsburg Confession.

The short presentation of the fundamental certainties of the faith in CA 1-21 was not, as it were, improvised at the spur of the moment. It was related to a series of previous attempts.[10] At the same time, the CA stood under certain constraints derived from the specific situation. It wanted to hold fast to the whole of the universal Christian faith, and yet penetrate it anew on the basis of the fundamental Reformation insight of justification by faith. Here the CA found itself facing opposition on two fronts, resulting from the development of the decade just past. Against the accusation of false doctrine, and against the enthusiastic movements, it was necessary to substantiate agreement with right church doctrine in the central contents of the faith, without being able to achieve dogmatic completeness. Thus CA 1-21 bear the clear stamp of the ancient Christian symbols, especially the Apostles' Creed. Yet a comparison of the structure shows that the passage in the ancient Christian symbols which deals with the person and work of the Holy Spirit is enormously expanded in the CA. It already begins with CA 5—*"de ministerio ecclesiastico"* (after being set up in CA 3 and 4)—and leads through the doctrines of good works, of the church, and of the sacraments, to the last things (Article 17). This expansion is consistent with the fact that here were located the dogmatic presuppositions for the disagreement over church usages with which the remainder of the CA deals.

Again, over against the accusations of the opponents from within the established church it became necessary to assert the specific insights of the Reformation in the formulation of the common faith, and on that basis legitimate the changes in the form of the church's life which had taken place in the evangelical territories. This was done by attempting to portray the practices which had been abolished as contradicting the Reformation insight.

This twofold responsibility accounts for the specific character of the doctrinal presentation in the CA as "confession." On the one hand, the CA is clearly defined by the structure of the ancient Christian confessions, and the marks which are characteristic of early Christian confessional formulas are found again here in varied form: it is, though rarely explicitly stated, a doxological visualization of the saving event, to which the confessor turns (for example, CA 20, 24)—it is a matter of giving expression to the gathering of the one community around salvation *(consensus)*, and a matter of preserving the right content of the salvation tradition in explicit defense against errors (anti-heretical intention).[11] This can only occur in a step-by-step presentation of individual articles.

On the other hand, in the agreement with the universal Christian faith, the concern is to confess and present the Reformation insight, i.e., to witness to the gospel of justification by faith.[12] This gives to the presentation, at least from the second article on, a cohesion and systematic direction which makes it possible to assert that justification in the CA (and even more strongly in the other Reformation confessions) is not merely one article among others, but rather represents the "center and boundary" of the Reformation confession in general.[13] It is not only that the life of the believer, acting personally and in the church, is ordered by belief in the gospel of justification through Christ. Rather, it is also from this gospel that the traditional confession in its individual articles receives a new center and new power to give certainty. To be sure, the presentation of justification, which had become necessary, breaks through the closed structure of the ancient church's confessional formulas and changes them into a theological doctrinal confession no longer suited for worship purposes.[14]

Because of the challenge of the particular situation which the CA had to meet, it is understandable that its language with regard to established certainty was assertive, but that at the same time the statements of the CA were not conceived as a final doctrinal presentation which would end all further discussion concerning the truth of the faith and the right tradition. Rather, the CA, particularly in the second part (above all, CA 28), is full of appeals for continuing doctrinal discussions whose goal is agreement. Even though others, especially Luther, judged such prospects more skeptically than the CA itself,[15] this was only the expression of another (in principle fallible) historical prognosis. To end a doctrinal dispute once and for all by means of a unilateral declaration could not be the intent of the CA insofar as it referred to the right faith of the one church. It is in this sense that the appeal to a council, which is what the Preface of the CA amounts to, sets the whole document into the context of a process in which the concerns of the Reformation were to be brought to bear on the doctrinal proclamation of the whole church. Even if the appeal to a council was a politically astute move on the part of the estates advocating the CA, it must have been intended seriously, in view of the claim that the CA represented the true faith of the church.

The result of the Diet of Augsburg and the fruitlessness of the religious discussions in the years which followed, in which nontheological factors played a significant role, has placed the CA in a different context compared to the situation of 1530. The *"magnus consensus"* addressed in the CA did not become a universal consensus of the church. As a result, the ongoing reforms took separate paths in Catholic and Reformation domains, even though it is recognizable today that the development of doctrine did at first still take place in great proximity and that the schemata in which the repudiated doctrine of the opponents were portrayed were based largely on mutual lack of information. In the age of confessionalism the future belonged primarily to these schematizations—to a degree for reasons of territorial and ecclesiastical self-preservation of those areas where the Reformation had triumphed.

The fact that the champions of the CA did not succeed in winning the bishops for the Reformation's proclamation of faith (as CA 28 intended) proved to have especially important consequences. As a result, the traditional connection between the normative proclamation of faith and succession in office had to take a new shape in Reformation areas. For them the continuity and permanence of the one holy church, expressly recognized in CA 7, had to be limited to the *sucessio fidei et doctrinae evangelii*. However, the development and interpretation of the doctrine of faith to which the CA bore witness had of necessity to establish a new context of tradition, which in fact remained limited to a particular church, despite the appeal to the one holy church, which was also subsequently repeated.

From the point of view of the CA, the particular understanding of the church thus initiated could only be overcome if the intention of agreement with the one holy church—an intention also contained in the fundamental confessional norm of the CA—were brought to bear upon it once again. This required a situation of openness on the other side, in which the consensus expressed in the CA could be brought into a comprehensive consensus of the church, at least in such a way that the *consensus de doctrina evangelii* expressed in the CA would prove to be a basis for a new understanding of church fellowship.

2. The CA and Holy Scripture

In the preface to the first volume of his Latin writings in 1545, Luther named as a fundamental insight the discovery of the gospel of God's righteousness. According to his own testimony, this discovery came to him during the exegesis of Holy Scripture. Hence, above all in its beginnings, Reformation teaching, as opposed to that of the traditional theological schools, was centered in scriptural exegesis, in the writings of Luther, as well as in the first draft of Melanchthon's *Loci* of 1521. In the dispute with Erasmus, Luther appealed to the clarity of Scripture, to the evidence of the gospel to which Scripture bears witness.[16]

The church is where the gospel, as the message of the justification of the sinner for Christ's sake, finds faith. For Luther, the gospel is the true treasure of the church, her foundation and her norm.[17] Therefore the gospel found in Scripture takes on the function of a critical authority in decisions concerning doctrine. Ecclesiastical tradition, doctrine, and order may not be contrary to the gospel, but must rather conform to it.

Surprisingly, the CA contains no article on Holy Scripture and its authority. Rather, it begins with an explicit reference to the dogma of the ancient church and the antiheretical decisions arrived at in connection with that dogma (CA 1). The reasons for the reference to the decree of the Council of Nicaea (which was of significance for the law of the empire) at the beginning of the CA were surely also related to the intention of Augsburg. This was a way of consciously grounding oneself in the law of the empire. There are at the same time, however, deeper, substantive reasons hidden behind the lack of a "scriptural principle." For one thing, the appeal to Scripture as the highest authority in teaching was not a specialty of the Lutheran Reformation. Such a formal scriptural principle had been frequently expressed in past church history.[18] Secondly, it was precisely during the course of the Reformation, when groups of enthusiasts appeared, that this formal scriptural principle proved to be ambiguous and unsuitable as a proof for church doctrine. A formal, legally applied scriptural principle—that is, the deducing of legal claims from biblical statements—was among the characteristics of "enthusiastic" argumentation during the Peasants' Revolt, and at other times.[19]

By contrast, Reformation doctrine appeals to the authority of the "gospel," beginning with the early confessional formulations. Not a "scriptural principle," but the *doctrina evangelii* gained from scriptural exegesis is the critical norm for the life and teaching of the church. The central significance of the category of gospel for the whole teaching and life of the church is what is really new in the Reformation confession. The way in which the doctrinal articles are related to the gospel in the CA makes it clear that the Reformation was not concerned with the restoration of an original state of "conformity to Scripture" in church and doctrine, much less with the establishment of a new church. It is rather a matter of a new perspective.[20] No new (or "original") church of Scripture is postulated, but rather the given, existing church is critically reinterpreted in the light of the gospel.[21]

What then is the gospel? It is the promise *(promissio)* that God receives into communion sinners who have faith for Christ's sake through that faith and makes them children of God. The gospel, therefore, is not a depository of doctrinal propositions, but rather the event which takes place in proclamation and in the administration of the sacraments, the event in which God's justification in Jesus Christ is really given to a person through the Holy Spirit (cf. the interrelation of CA 4, 5, 13). All the church's teaching and formation are to serve this event. And to the extent that all doctrines and life-styles, all institutions and rites must be examined to see whether they serve the gospel or whether they obscure or even deny the complete and efficacious appropriation of salvation, the gospel also becomes the critical norm of the church's life. It is from this point of view that the ministry of the church (CA 5), the church (CA 7), the sacraments (CA 9-13), and ecclesiastical rites (CA 15) are judged. The gospel of justification is also the criterion for the changes in church usages, of which an account is rendered in CA 22-28.

The gospel of God's saving deed stands as ground and norm above the church and yet at the same time brings about the continuity of the church. This concept, substantiated in the Reformation above all by

Melanchthon's theology,[22] determines also the view of history of the subsequent confessional writings and the dogmatics of the classical period of the 16th to 18th centuries, up to the beginning of the Enlightenment. Thus the divine truth of the gospel is the ground and strength of the church through all times and the witnesses to it are to be sought in the church's tradition, as well as in the Holy Scriptures themselves. This view also determines the way the CA itself uses Scripture. It does indeed refer to specific scripture quotations as evidence, but—with the exception of CA 28—it does so relatively rarely and hardly in the sense of argumentation; and it inserts quotations from the Fathers and ecclesiastical authors into its exposition in the same way. It is precisely not a matter of a formalized scriptural principle, but of the truth of the gospel through the ages, even if one is indebted to Holy Scripture for this gospel in its fundamental and authoritative form.

It was not until the schematization and interconfessional polemics immediately following the Council of Trent that a formalized scriptural principle was more clearly developed. It was primarily the need of the developing territorial churches for doubt-free and practical foundations for doctrine and order which called for the accumulation of closed bodies of doctrine and, at the same time, the fixing of the formal authority of Scripture. But the Formula of Concord, the last of the great Lutheran confessional writings, and the only one to contain an article on the foundations of doctrine (without calculation and, in a sense, as an example),[23] still enumerates in turn the creeds of the ancient church, the CA and the other confessional writings, and beyond that other doctrinal writings, above all Luther's, as the sum of doctrine next to Holy Scripture. Here, using the picture of a court of law, in cases of doubt the "authority of the judge" does indeed belong to Scripture.[24] However, against the falsification of doctrine by heretics, the other confessions are also needed as "witnesses" to the truth in interpreting Scripture itself.[25]

The elaboration of the doctrine of the verbal inspiration of Holy Scripture took place later in the great doctrinal summations of the 17th century, in the confessional disputes as well as in defense against the rising philosophy of the Enlightenment and natural science. The Bible then became an exclusive miracle book, far removed from the church traditions derived from it. By contrast, however, the subsequent triumph of historical-critical research in Protestant theology surrendered the foundations of faith to the persuasive power of the individual biblical exegete. In neoprotestantism there arose a characteristic variety of mutually exclusive, exegetically grounded dogmas with a claim to being binding, which Martin Kähler has sarcastically called, "the learned pontificating of the historians." [26]

By contrast, the theological renewal movements of the 19th and 20th centuries and above all the experiences of the *Kirchenkampf* in Germany have brought a new recognition of the significance of the confession in view of the challenges of militant secularism. It was learned that it is only in their mutual relation to each other that the church's confession and Holy Scripture make possible a clear foundation for faith. Even the apparently exegetical and scholarly foundations for faith in neoprotestantism actually show an analogous structure: only there, instead of the church's doctrine, it is a philosophical or hermeneutical principle (idealism, existentialism, etc.) which makes the interpretation of Scripture binding.

The *magnus consensus* intended by the CA can, indeed, only be hoped for if scriptural interpretation establishes faith in the context of and in consensus with the church's doctrinal tradition and doctrinal proclamation. To be sure, this tradition requires constant reinterpretation in view of new situations if one is to arrive at certainty of faith and consensus. Thus scriptural tradition and doctrinal tradition stand in a circle in the Confession. As the source of the gospel, the tradition of Holy Scripture becomes the ground and norm of all the church's doctrinal proclamation. But the church's doctrinal proclamation points to Scripture by distinguishing a particular way of listening to the tradition of Scripture from all other conceivable ways. Thus the Confession bears witness to the gospel of Scripture and brings it to light.[27] Precisely this process of witnessing is, at the same time, unfinished, because the gospel must always be heard anew in new situations, notwithstanding the certainty gained earlier.

3. The Relationship of the CA to Other Lutheran Confessions[28]

The Preface to the CA appeals to a council. That is, it does not produce a *"magnus consensus"* for its own congregations only (CA 1), but understands itself as a statement in a process aimed at the universal consensus of the church. However, this also means that the statements of the CA itself must be open to such a consensus and able to be superseded.

The manner in which the discussion proceeded actually prevented this process in the 16th century. This, however, compelled the adherents of the CA to deepen and unfold the doctrinal consensus which had been won. This in turn created a separate body of tradition for Reformation doctrine. In addition to increasing activity in the area of theological education from a Reformation point of view, there came into being further doctrinal documents which gained the status of confessions in the congregations and territories belonging to the Reformation. Because of the need to establish valid doctrine, various collections of such writings, so-called *"Corpora Doctrinae,"* were created. Among these, the *Book of Concord* has gained the widest acceptance. Besides the "unaltered" CA of 1530, it contains the Apology of the CA by Melanchthon, the Smalcald Articles of 1537 from the pen of Luther, the Treatise on the Power and Primacy of the Pope by Melanchthon, Luther's Large and Small Catechisms (1529), and finally the Formula of Concord of 1577 in a long and a short form.

As far as the authors were concerned, the reasons for the formation of additional confessions besides the CA did not lie in the incompleteness or lack of clarity of the CA itself. Rather, subsequent historical developments posed new doctrinal challenges which could not be answered by taking recourse to the wording of the CA. In this way, already Melanchthon's Apology, with its central and extensive doctrine of justification, elucidated the doctrinal intention of the CA over against the misunderstandings of its opponents. Luther's Smalcald Articles were intended for the council anticipated in 1537. Melanchthon's Treatise, written at the same time, is to be understood as a material completion of the themes of the CA: it deals with the question of the authority of the pope. Luther's catechisms, already in use in the churches for some time, were included in the *Corpora Doctrinae* or *Book of Concord* as a summary presentation of Reformation doctrine for lay people. Finally, the Formula of Concord resolved a series of doctrinal controversies which had arisen in the Lutheran territories themselves over the interpretation of the CA. It stipulates that only the "unaltered" version of the CA of 1530 is the basis of doctrinal proclamation,[29] not the "altered" version produced by Melanchthon in 1540 (which accommodated Calvinism particularly in the doctrine of the sacraments). At the same time, the Formula of Concord established the principle that the CA is to be understood on the basis of Luther's theology. This, however, only underscored once again the fact that the CA was to be interpreted as a confession of the church. Already in

1530 it could not be understood as a private work of Melanchthon, but rather was considered as the summary of the actual result of the Reformation as a whole. As against this, the authors of the Formula of Concord now in turn expressly emphasize the fact that they do not want to make "a new confession." [30] Rather, they refer to the unaltered CA and seek to interpret it in light of the points of controversy to be answered in their own situation. In contrast to the universal creeds of the ancient church, the CA itself is qualified as a "creed of our time," [31] i.e., as a doctrinal statement called forth by the specific situation. As a whole, the relation between doctrinal tradition and doctrinal decree is seen in the Formula of Concord as follows: [32] the gospel is heard from Holy Scripture and witnessed to in the particular situation by the confessions. Return to the source and witness to the gospel in view of concrete challenges belong together. The confessions set points of orientation which must be taken into account in the continuing interpretation. Thereby the CA remains the foundation of the Reformation's doctrinal tradition and constitutes the criterion for all further confessions. The CA itself, however, points to the gospel of Holy Scripture, which has become known in the one church through the ages, for its binding character. [33]

4. The Binding Character of the CA

The binding character of the CA and the task of continuing interpretation are not mutually exclusive because the gospel must always be witnessed to anew. Here the question arises how the binding character of the CA, accepted in principle, has actually shown itself and operated in the Lutheran churches. We must distinguish here between a formal (legal) and a material (theological) aspect. [34]

Formally, the CA has received an absolute and special position over against all other doctrinal statements on the basis of its political-legal significance. It was received at Augsburg by the emperor and mentioned in the peace agreements after 1533, until it formed the basis for the imperial-legal recognition of the Reformation estates in the Peace of Augsburg of 1555. Within the churches this meant that this confession became the norm for worship and for the doctrinal commitment of the clergy. The confessionally closed territorial churches knew how to apply this authority in cases of conflict. In this sense the CA still remained binding in the Peace of Westphalia and beyond, until the end of the old empire in 1803.

As a result of the end of their imperial-legal validity and the acceptance of the concept of toleration, a new basis had to be sought for the binding character of the confessions. The confessional theology of the 19th century found it in the conception of the "confessional church," in which the confession, as a statute of church fellowship, binds its members and especially those who teach publicly.[35] In this way it was possible to preserve the confessional character of the Lutheran churches—often in opposition to the theology taught at the universities—during disputes that were in part quite protracted. To be sure, this gave rise to the danger of a self-sufficiency oriented toward the confessional status and forgetting the ecumenical intention of the CA. By contrast, the theological renewal movements of our century and the ecumenical movements have again highlighted the commitment of the confessions to the universal church. With this the CA gained anew in significance against other doctrinal norms. Against this background, the fact that not a few constitutions of Lutheran churches give special prominence to the CA as confessional basis makes good sense.

In answer to the question of how the binding character of the confessions actually shows itself in the life of the church, we must begin by saying that theological judgments of individuals cannot, in themselves, be regarded as the expression of valid church teaching any more than this is the case in any other church fellowship. Such teaching can only be derived from the effective norms, named in the church constitutions to which the clergy are committed in ordination. The test of their effectiveness is seen in cases of conflict, when doubt arises as to whether the church practice of individuals or groups corresponds to the norms. In principle, this can happen in all Christian fellowships. Today proof of the binding character of church doctrinal proclamation is exposed to increasing difficulties everywhere. The reason for this lies in the pervasive circumstance that the validity of tradition has ceased to be self-evident, resulting from the boundless idiosyncratic life experience simultaneously mirrored and produced by the modern media. This makes it more difficult to arrive at and apply an authentic interpretation of the doctrinal norms as a basis for doctrinal judgment, and this, again, is true in all confessions. However, there are also recent events—in the evaluation of the doctrine of an individual as well as in the framing of a church constitution—in which the Reformation confession was successfully activated as norm and criterion.[36] Doctrinal discussions concerning the CA can and must take place in the expectation that the participants allow themselves to be effectively regulated in faith and life by these norms.

The binding character of the CA exhibits itself differently, in the material aspect, from its formal validity. Here it could only appear from the very beginning as an abbreviation, a summary within a very much broader and deeper stream of church teaching to which the CA itself repeatedly refers. But even if the doctrinal summaries of the classical period of the 17th century appeal primarily to Holy Scripture and the whole dogmatic tradition because the stock of problems with which they deal is very much broader, nevertheless the Reformation witness to the gospel as it is fundamentally explained in the CA remains the decisive assumption from which the dogmatic teaching is developed. It was primarily about the CA that academic disputations were held, and the CA was interpreted in sermons and commentaries.

5. The CA: Sufficient Expression of the Doctrine of Faith?

What has already been said yields principles for discussing the question of in what sense the CA can or cannot be understood as sufficient expression of faith.[37] It is to be remembered that in Augsburg originally only articles concerning church usages and the correction of abuses were to be presented (CA 22-28). It is obvious that such statements alone could not be a sufficient expression of faith. Later the opponents' accusation of heresy necessitated the presentation of the faith which was the basis for the statements on church usages (CA 1-21). This presentation had the intention to articulate adequately the consensus with the faith of the one church. However, the division of the CA into these two parts was not only determined by the situation at Augsburg. Rather, it corresponds to the Reformation's fundamental distinction between those matters in which agreement is sufficient for true unity and others in which such agreement is not necessary (CA 7). The basis for unity is the consensus about the right teaching of the gospel and the right administration of the sacraments. It is in this sense that the first part of the CA had to claim to be "sufficient."

This is not to say that an exhaustive articulation of the doctrine of faith was presented. A series of controversial questions current at that time were not taken up by the CA because it apparently did not regard dogmatic pronouncements in these matters as indispensable for the unity of the church. During the Diet of Augsburg, Luther was already critical of the fact that the papacy, the veneration of the saints, and the doctrine of purgatory had not been discussed in the disputed articles.[38] Yet it was not merely political discretion involved here, but rather the conviction that, in the absence of doctrinal decrees, a consensus in these questions was still possible. It is precisely on this basis that we are to understand the fact that the CA only came to very rudimentary statements with regard to several fundamental questions, for example, the office of the ministry and ordination. A deficiency, or silence, at this point is to be understood under certain circumstances precisely as an openness to further consensus, for which agreement in the gospel would grant freedom.

Only after the failure of the discussions did a debate, going beyond the CA, of the themes of the second part of the 1530 text take place. It is in this context that the treatise on the authority of the pope and the Smalcald Articles are to be evaluated. Their sometimes sharp polemics were based on the assumption that very distinct ideas—concerning the mass or the papacy, for example—prevailed. Whether these assumptions still hold true is a question which can be discussed openly today because of the CA's distinction between sufficient agreement in the gospel and freedom in shaping the life of faith.[39]

It would, of course, be a misunderstanding of CA 7 if church orders and usages were to be regarded as matters of theological indifference and optional. Rather, the right teaching of the gospel and the right shaping of the church (and thereby also the first and second parts of the CA) are indissolubly connected, in the sense that the forms of the church's life are subordinate to the gospel as the fundamental criterion. In the historical context of the CA this statement had a primarily critical meaning; it was above all directed against the usages which appeared to deny the gospel. But this is only one side of the question. For if, according to CA 7, agreement in the administration of the gospel and the sacraments is sufficient for the unity of the church, these are the minimal conditions. The "sufficient" must not therefore be misunderstood as saying that the establishing of further agreements is no longer legitimate or desirable. If such agreements are designated as "not necessary," this is not to hinder the growth of unity in Christ in the structure of the church as well. What is true is that "we are all under one Christ and should confess and contend for Christ." [40] The constraint toward unity based on this fact is to be opened up in precisely the right manner: as an expression of faith in the gospel, which, like the works of the justified, is to follow that faith. Therefore, the "sufficient" of the CA is, according to Lutheran conviction, not opposed to the desire for the "fullness" of church life, which is often emphasized from Catholic quarters, but rather opens the way to that fullness.[41]

6. The Ecumenical Character of the CA

As a result of the situation in which it came into existence, the CA is directed toward preserving the unity of the church in the face of controversy. That unity was to show itself in listening anew to the gospel as the common confession of faith. In this sense, the CA professes the one catholic church, and its structure, content, and binding character are determined by this intention. It is concerned with unity and with renewal of the church at the same time.

The history of the CA's reception shows, to be sure, that the freedom of the gospel witnessed to in the confession did not determine the practice of the Reformation churches all that unequivocally.[42] Not only did the doctrinal discussions with the opponents fail, but the Protestant churches themselves took part in the cultivation of authority typical of their age. The established Protestant churches did not in fact grant believers the freedom to test church tradition, but often enough suppressed that very freedom. They tended to understand themselves exclusively as confessional churches. Modern Christendom, which arose from the Reformation churches in the Enlightenment, has, by contrast, conferred upon individuals and their assurance of faith a priority in principle over participation in church fellowship. But when personal assurance of faith becomes monadic and closes in on itself, the fact is forgotten that the gospel, as the message of reconciliation, establishes the gathering of the community at the same time as the freedom of the individual (CA 7). Where individual assurance is made absolute, the claim to infallibility of the devout personality easily takes the place of faith in the Spirit's power of truth in the gospel. The power of the gospel, which is the basis of the unity of the church, is thereby denied.

The present-day reflection on the original ecumenical intention of the CA does not have a restorative meaning. Rather, it is a challenge to surrender confessional self-sufficiency, also with regard to the historical shape it has taken in the doctrine of faith or the order of the church. The concentration on the one thing needful has increasingly resulted, in the Lutheran Church, in a reduction: an impoverishment in the expression of Christian life and, not infrequently, a pedantic and bureaucratic narrowing of the church's action, especially in the area of church organization.

Over against this, the intentions for the unity and the renewal of the church are linked in the CA. They are not to be separated from one another, but rather belong together. Thus, unity does not mean rigid uniformity, but rather leaves room for the renewal of the church. The efforts for church renewal based on the gospel carry in them the tendency to overcome the divisions of Christianity and to recover and deepen fellowship.

When the CA appealed to a general council at which the doctrinal differences were to be overcome, it thereby presented in its own way the model of a "conciliar" effort for church unity like the one gaining importance in ecumenical dialogs today: different doctrinal traditions meet each other as partners on the road toward the unity of the church, which is given in Jesus Christ.

By concentrating on the fundamentals of faith and of the church (Trinity, christology, soteriology, ecclesiology), the CA's point of departure also gives freedom to unfold the faith in new situations. This is significant in the current world situation, in which a great many cultural traditions are becoming conscious of their autonomy over against the western Christian tradition and are asking for indigenous structures of faith. The distinction between the agreement of the gospel and the structures of the life of faith can provide a framework for a variety of independent traditions within the unity of the church.

7. The Significance of the CA in the Catholic-Lutheran Dialog and the Problem of "Recognition"

Because of the CA's intention of reaching agreement with the one, holy, catholic, indeed Roman, church, it is understandable why the CA has taken on special significance in the Catholic-Lutheran dialog. Here the desire for greater church fellowship has repeatedly been expressed in the form of the question whether the CA could gain "recognition" as a valid expression of the faith of Christianity. How such a recognition would be realized concretely in detail cannot be discussed here. We can simply mention a few aspects for determining what significance a recognition of the CA would have for the Lutheran Church itself.[43]

To begin with, we must again take into account the fact that the CA itself originally intended such a recognition of its catholic character. But to acknowledge this declared intention does not mean the global reception of its exposition. Rather, the CA itself refers expressly to its foundation and thereby its verification in the gospel of Holy Scripture and the teaching of the ancient church. Thus the very recognition of this intention would require a binding examination, in detail, as to whether the points of controversy named there still exist in the same manner today, or whether differences in doctrine and practice still prevent church fellowship—or whether henceforth they can simply be understood as differences of theological school or ethnic or other idiosyncrasies. However, the concept of recognition would at the same time also mean the renunciation of an understanding of unity which would be determined by the notion of the absorption of one church in the other. Rather, "recognition" would mean the realization of full church fellowship, while at the same time preserving individual church identity.

Secondly, it follows from this that recognition could not refer to the CA as an isolated historical document. Ultimately it would only have significance in the church as a recognition of a church fellowship which is shaped by the CA and which is bound to continue to interpret it in its teaching and practice.

And finally, such a recognition would only be meaningful as a reciprocal process. However, this in turn poses some considerable tasks for a church determined by the CA. To be sure, it has not in principle denied the presence of the gospel and the sacraments in the Roman Catholic Church. To that extent a fundamental readiness for church fellowship can be assumed. However, there has only been a very fragmentary understanding of the continuing Roman Catholic proclamation of faith since the classical period of confessional orthodoxy, beyond traditional schematizations. Here again we can only sketch what should take place.

In view of the more extensive Roman Catholic tradition of faith, a present-day understanding could begin with the model sketched by Luther in the Smalcald Articles in conformity with CA 7.[44] There he distinguishes among three kinds of articles of faith: first, "the sublime articles of the divine majesty," i.e., the doctrine of God and the christology of the creeds of the ancient church. In these there exists no disagreement; they lie behind all others as presupposition. Second, there are articles in which "nothing can be given up or compromised." Here the Reformation understanding of justification and the resulting foundations of church teaching and practice are at stake. Finally, the third part contains a series of articles which may be discussed on the basis of what has gone before with "learned and sensible" people. These include, for all practical purposes, all the remaining articles of faith: sin, law, repentance, the gospel, Baptism, the Lord's Supper, absolution, confession, ordination, etc. Leaving aside Luther's polemics, it should be possible on the basis of this model to examine the post-Reformation doctrinal development in the Roman Church in a new, open, and sober way, to see whether it can be understood as an interpretation, an expression, of the saving event witnessed to in justification. This would at least open up an avenue of access to what is meant in the Roman Catholic doctrinal tradition by "fullness" of the universal Christian faith.

The question of recognition becomes more difficult with regard to church practice. Recognition always aims at mutual acceptance in the fellowship of faith. This is not a matter of theoretical reflection; it can only be realized in practical fellowship, and whatever shape that fellowship may take, it means the removal of past divisions. For the Roman Catholic Church, however, such fellowship includes essentially fellowship with the office of bishop in apostolic succession. In connection with the question of recognition, at least the question of the significance of this special mode of fellowship must be raised for the Lutheran churches. For the claim of the CA to stand in the authentic catholic tradition manifestly signifies that following the apostles is necessary and constitutive for the church as well as for its ministry. The authentication of apostolic following in the form of historical succession in the office of bishop was, however, called into question for the Lutherans by the fact that it was impossible to attain the desired agreement in the proclamation of the gospel. Rather, the episcopacy refused fellowship and thereby withdrew the historical succession. Thus for the Lutheran churches apostolic succession had to confine itself to the right proclamation of the gospel, to faith, and to the witness of life.

Nevertheless, over against the separate historical development, the fact remains that the CA affirmed and intended the historical continuity of the church as an expression of its unity throughout the nations and ages on the premise of the right proclamation of the gospel. For the sake of faith in the permanence of the church (CA 7), this intention cannot be invalidated, even by contravening historical experiences. It is on this basis that a Lutheran position on historical succession could be approached.

It was said earlier that the Lutheran term "sufficient" in respect to agreement in the proclamation of the gospel and the administration of the sacraments did not stand in opposition to the desire for growth into the fullness of unity, but rather opened the way. To be sure, all church order is to be measured by whether it is in accordance with the gospel. At the same time, however, this raises the question as to which form of church administration most appropriately helps the effective proclamation of the gospel. The goal of all the church's confessing is not the restoration of an ecclesiastical preserve, but rather the credible witness to the good news in the face of the challenges of this world into which Christ has sent his church. In this sense, the CA gives to the church fellowship shaped by it the freedom to raise any questions which serve that purpose, including those concerning entrance into the fellowship of the historical succession.

Notes

1. BSLK 50; CT 42.
2. AE 37, 360 (WA 26, 499ff.).
3. BSLK 136.
4. BC 9.
5. BSLK 136.
6. CA, Conclusion to Part I, 1, German (BC 47).
7. CA, Conclusion to Part I, 2 (BSLK 83; CT 58). Tappert's translation reads: "The whole dissension is concerned with a certain few abuses" (BC 47).
8. CA 7, 3-4 (BC 32).
9. CA, Introduction to Part II (BC 48-49).
10. For a summary of the CA's structure and the history of its origins cf. W. Maurer, *Historischer Kommentar zur Confessio Augustana,* vol. 1 (Gütersloh, 1976), pp. 15ff.
11. Cf. *"Thesen über das Bekenntnis,"* in *Auf dem Wege,* vol. 1, ed. by the Secretariat on Faith and Order (Zürich: 1967), p. 41.
12. The term *gospel* can have a broader and a narrower sense in Reformation usage. In the broader sense it means the whole proclamation of salvation on the basis of Holy Scriptures (e.g. Apol. 4, 62 [BC 115]; cf. below Section 2 of this chapter). In the narrower sense (in the sense of a criterion of the proclamation of salvation), *gospel* indicates the Reformation witness of justification by faith for Christ's sake (cf. also the Formula of Concord, SD 5, 3 [BC 558]).
13. E. Wolf, *"Die Rechtfertigung als Mitte und Grenze reformatorischer Theologie,"* in *Peregrinatio,* vol. 2 (Munich: 1965), pp. 11ff.
14. R. Prenter, *Creation and Redemption* (Philadelphia: Fortress, 1967), pp. 136ff.
15. WA Br 5, 495-496, no. 1657.
16. Cf. *The Bondage of the Will* (AE 33, 22ff.; WA 18, 605-606.).

17. Cf. W. Kasper, *"Die Confessio Augustana in katholischer Sicht,"* in H. Meyer, ed., *Das Augsburgische Bekenntnis im ökumenischen Kontext.* LWF Report, no. 6/7 (1979), p. 88.
18. F. Kropatschek, *Das Schriftprinzip in der Lutherischen Kirche,* vol. 1, *Die Vorgeschichte, das Erbe des Mittelalters* (Leipzig: 1904).
19. Cf. W. Elert, *The Structure of Lutheranism,* vol. 1 (St. Louis: Concordia, 1962), pp. 179ff.
20. W. Lohff, *"Die Heilige Schrift als Grundlage der Kirche,"* in *Lutherisches Bekenntnis im ökumenischen Horizont,* ed. by the *Lutherischer Kirchenamt* (1967), pp. 77ff.
21. Cf. W. Kasper, *op. cit.,* p. 7.
22. Cf. W. Maurer, *op. cit.,* p. 65. For background see P. P. Fraenkel, *Testimonia Patrum: The Function of the Patristic Argument in the Theology of Philipp Melanchthon* (Geneva: 1961), esp. pp. 52-53.
23. The Summary Formulation, Basis, Rule, and Norm, Indicating How All Doctrines Should Be Judged in Conformity with the Word of God and Errors Are to Be Explained and Decided in a Christian Way (BC 503, Solid Declaration wording; cf. BC 464 for Epitome wording).
24. Epitome, Rule and Norm, 8 (BC 465).
25. *Ibid.*
26. M. Kähler, *The So-Called Historical Jesus and the Historic Biblical Christ* (Philadelphia: Fortress, 1964), p. 73.
27. R. Prenter, *op. cit.,* pp. 115ff.
28. Cf. G. Seebass, *"Das Verhältnis der Confessio Augustana zu den anderen Bekenntnisschriften und die Veränderung in ihrer Funktion als Lehrnorm im 16. Jahrhundert und bis zur Gegenwart,"* unpublished manuscript. Already earlier: H. Asmussen, *Warum noch Lutherische Kirche? Ein Gespräch mit dem Augsburgischen Bekenntnis* (Stuttgart, 1949), above all p. 28.
29. Solid Declaration, Rule and Norm, 5 (BC 504).
30. Solid Declaration, Rule and Norm, 2 (BC 503).
31. Solid Declaration, Rule and Norm, 5 (BC 504).
32. Cf. W. Lohff, *"Konsensus und Konflikt: Zur Methode der Lehrentscheidungen der Konkordienformel,"* in: W. Lohff and L. Spitz, ed., *Widerspruch, Dialog und Einigung: Studien zur Konkordienformel der Lutherischen Reformation* (Stuttgart, 1977).
33. Solid Declaration, Rule and Norm, 5 (BC 504). See also BC 503ff. passim.
34. On the following: G. Seebass, as mentioned above in note 28.
35. W. Maurer, *"Bekenntnis rechtlich,"* in RGG [3] 1, 1006-1007. The development took a different course in those churches which connected a union of the Reformation confessions with a common constitution, often without a theological explication of the union (e.g., Prussia). Yet here, too, it was to a large extent the CA which formed the framework for the church's teaching beyond the boundaries of the confessional church. Cf. G. Seebass, as mentioned in note 28, above.
36. Cf. L. Mohaupt, *"Pastor ohne Gott? Dokumente und Erläuterungen zum Fall Schulz* (Gütersloh, 1979). In working out the constitution of the North Elbian Evangelical Lutheran Church (1976), the article concerning

the service of pastors was changed on the basis of an objection based on the CA.

37. Cf. on the following: *"Bedeutung und Funktion der Augustana heute: Bericht einer Konsultation der VELKD,"* in *Texte aus der VELKD,* no. 7 (1979).

38. AE 49, 297ff. (WA Br 5, 319-320, no. 1568) and WA Br 5, 495-496, no. 1657. Cf. W. Maurer, *op. cit.,* vol. 1, pp. 40-41.

39. Cf. W. Lohff, *"Papsttum und Kirchenspaltung,"* in *Concilium* 6 (1970), pp. 260-261.

40. CA, Preface, 11 (BC 25).

41. On this cf. the chapter by H. Meyer and H. Schütte in this volume, esp. Section 5.

42. On the following cf. W. Lohff, *"Die christliche Freiheit als Kontroverspunkt und gemeinsames Problem für Lutheraner und Katholiken heute,"* in H. Meyer, ed., *Evangelium, Welt, Kirche: Schlussbericht und Referate der Römisch-Katholischen / Evangelisch-Lutherischen Studienkommission, "Das Evangelium und die Kirche"* (Frankfurt: 1975), pp. 379ff., 386-387.

43. On the following cf. the contributions in the collection, H. Fries et al., *Confessio Augustana: Hindernis oder Hilfe?* (Regensburg: 1979).

44. SA 2, 1 (BC 292) and 3, 1 (BC 302).

2

The Catholic View of Confessions and Confessional Community

by Walter Kasper

translated by Omar Kaste

To many in our time, the current discussion about a Catholic recognition of the Augsburg Confession seems anachronistic and grotesque. They are of the opinion that there are more urgent tasks in theology and in the church than to argue about a text from the 16th century. Have not dogma and creed proved a ball and chain to ecumenical rapprochement? Do we need confessions at all? Has not the time come for a nondogmatic or metadogmatic Christianity? Voices like these are being heard today within Catholic theology as well as from liberal Protestants. There are questions and objections even from those who view confessions and dogmas as important, indispensable components of the church's life. It is pointed out that the Catholic-Protestant difference does not involve just the contents of individual dogmas and confessions, but also the authority of dogmas and confessions in general, and even the total perspective in which dogmas and confessions are understood. Therefore it is asked whether a recognition of the Augsburg Confession as Catholic would not ascribe to it a significance which is totally inappropriate to it.

The discussion of a possible Catholic recognition of another church's confession presupposes an awareness of the meaning, place, and significance of confessional formulas in the most general sense. Not until the Catholic understanding of confession and dogma is clearly in view is it possible to discuss meaningfully the relevance of the confessions of other churches, a possible future ecumenical confessional community, and so also any eventual Catholic recognition of the Augsburg Confession and the consequences which such a recognition would have for the Catholic as well as the Lutheran Church.

1. Some Historical Perspectives

1.1 The Biblical Origin and Significance of Confessions of Faith

Confessions and the formulation of confessions are basic human phenomena present from the very beginnings of human society. The one who confesses reveals what is within and makes it openly known. When one confesses in this way, one surrenders oneself and, at the same time, achieves a realization of oneself, for not until one's private, inner conviction is expressed in the realm of the corporeal and the public does it gain objective form and publicly binding validity. Conversely, publicly held systems of values can retain their concrete reality only so long as the individual members of a community, both as individuals and as a group, continue to uphold these value systems. They exist, as it were, by virtue of being put into effect. No community can long endure without a certain minimum of such unqualified statements of belief (for example, "Human life is inviolable."). For this reason, confessions and their shaping are also basic phenomena in the history of religion, especially when a certain politico-religious order which is recognized as a divine institution enters into competition with other religions. In this case confessions must preserve, by the act of confessing, the living core of that religion, and also define its uniqueness. Such confessions are not abstract doctrines; they exist rather in virtue of their cultic recitation and celebration.

All of this is true in a special and unique sense for biblical religion.[1] It is a religion of historical revelation, at the beginning and heart of which stands God's confession to his people: "I will be your God, and you shall be my people" (Lev. 26:12; Jer. 7:23). Israel's confession was a reply to God's electing word. It states what God said and did. Thus it is an acknowledgment of God's saving activity in history, a confession of the God who led them out of Egypt (Deut. 26:5-9) and who, in the fullness of time, raised Jesus from the dead

(Rom. 10:9). By telling of God's relation to human beings, the nature of God is revealed. In addition to verbal confessions of God's saving action within history (pistis-formulas), there were therefore doxological forms of confession (homologies), which say who he is by naming him: "The Lord (Yahweh) our God" (Josh. 24:17). He is the one and only God (Deut. 4:6-7), the God who makes the dead live (Rom.: 5:17; 2 Cor. 1:9). In the New Testament these naming confessional statements are, above all, markedly christological: Jesus is the Lord (Rom. 10:9; 1 Cor. 12:3; Phil. 2:11), Jesus is the Christ (Acts 5:42; 1 John 2:23; 4:15; 5:5).

The decisive result of recent biblical research is this: such credal formulas existed from the very beginning; they are even older than the biblical texts themselves. This is most clearly expressed in one of the oldest and most important texts in the entire New Testament, 1 Cor. 15:3-5, where Paul proclaims the gospel of the death and resurrection of Jesus Christ. He uses an existing formulation which had been passed on to him and which was to be passed on farther: "for above all I have delivered to you what I also received: Christ died for our sins, as the Scriptures have said, and he was buried. On the third day he was raised, as the Scriptures have said, and appeared to Cephas, then to the Twelve." On the basis of recent exegetical research, both Protestant and Catholic theologians are today coming to share the insight that such credal formulas are no later extract from the living gospel, devoid of power and life, but the foundation, essential core and center, epitome and summary of the gospel. They are the pattern, example, and norm for proclamation. This understanding is not without its irony, for thus recent exegetical study has led to a conclusion which was, for a long time, smiled at sympathetically as the last bastion of ultraconservatism. No nondogmatic Christianity has ever existed, and, for the same reason, no such thing can ever exist. Confessions of faith are an essential part of every church which appeals to the New Testament. The question, of course, is how these credal forms are understood in the Old and New Testaments. One look at the New Testament reveals that there is no uniform dogma for a universal church present there. Rather there is a great variety of differing confessional statements. The confessional forms of the Old Testament and the New Testament are therefore anything but rigid doctrinal formulas. They are Spirit-produced responses to God's saving word and work in history (see 1 Cor. 12:3). Confession therefore takes the form of acclamation (see Luke 24:34; 1 Cor. 16:22) and hymns (Phil. 2:6-11, among others). Biblical confession is, therefore, doxology. At the same time, it is always simultaneously liturgical praise of God and admission of personal sinfulness: in their confession of God, and of his Christ as the only bringer of salvation, believers also confess their own wretchedness. Assent to God is therefore also renunciation of false gods, and the confession of Jesus Christ is also repudiation of sin, the world, and Satan. Confession is a life-or-death decision (see Mark 8:38). It is both an entirely personal decision to enter Christ's company through Baptism (Rom. 6:17) and a public statement "before men," in the forum of the world and in the face of the world's opposition. Its most serious form is the *status confessionis,* in persecution and martyrdom. However, the confession of faith also came to serve increasingly as a hedge against heresy. In this sense it is called "sound doctrine" (2 Tim. 1:13; 4:3; Titus 1:9), the truth entrusted to you *(paratheke)* (1 Tim. 6:20; 2 Tim. 1:14), and a confession to hold fast (Heb. 4:14; 10:23).

The confessions of the Old and New Testaments have, therefore, a variety of settings: Baptism and baptismal instruction (the catechumenate), liturgy, sermons, exorcisms, and the combating of heresy. There is a common element expressed in all these different forms: confession is an eschatological phenomenon. It refers to God's final decision, in which those who confess their faith join their voices. The Spirit-filled liturgical doxology anticipates the God who is all in all (1 Cor. 15:28) and the judgment of the end-time. For this reason, confession leads to a decisive separation from unbelief and false teaching.

We can say in summary that confession of faith and the church belong together. The New Testament credal formulas are not yet, however, dogmas in the modern sense of the word. What we have there is a great variety of confessions related to particular proclamation situations. That means that in the New Testament we encounter a church still coming into existence and taking shape, a church which, coming into existence and taking shape in its formulation of its confession, is the continuing norm for the later church. Consequently, there is in the church not only a history of piety, liturgy, and theology, but also a history of dogma and of the changing understanding of dogma.

1.2. The Basic Form in the Ancient Church

In the church of the first centuries, we again encounter great variety and a large measure of variability in credal formulas.[2] Very soon, however, two basic types of confessions emerged on which both Catholic and Lutheran Christians agree down to the present day. First, there is the so-called Apostles' Creed, which has its roots in the Roman baptismal confession, was then finally received by all western churches, but did not receive its final form until around the year 1000. The eastern confessions, though more numerous, constitute nevertheless a unified type which underlies the confessions of the first two ecumenical councils: Nicaea (325) and Constantinople (381). While the so-called Apostles' Creed remained limited to the West, the Niceno-Constantinopolitan Creed received ecumenical acceptance in both East and West. To this day it unites all the great churches of East and West.

The transition from the New Testament to the great confessions of the ancient church has been variously judged. Traditional Catholic dogmatics saw it as a logical, straight-line or organic development, while liberal Protestant histories of dogma held the process which led to the ancient church's doctrinal statements to have been more or less an adulteration of the original gospel. Both of these views are unhistorical and fail to comprehend the essence of the gospel. For the gospel is not simply a phenomenon recorded in history. Rather, as a reality which continues to be present through the work of the Holy Spirit, it must be translated again and again; that is, it must be put into ever-new language appropriate to shifting historical situations. The history of creeds and dogmas, therefore, inherently includes both continuity and discontinuity. The continuity is not that of the individual formulations, but that of a persisting type, of a continually valid doctrinal structure and of continually valid basic motifs.[3]

This view corresponds also to current historical knowledge. Recent research on the creeds has shown that all the essential statements of the ancient church's confessions are, for the most part, rooted almost word for word in the New Testament. Even the underlying trinitarian structure of these venerable formulas of faith corresponds to the triadic or trinitarian structure of many New Testament statements (see Matt. 28:19; 1 Cor. 12:4-6; 2 Cor. 13:14, among others). On the other hand, the confessions of the ancient church are not simply the expansion and more precise formulation of the biblical credal statements. Rather, they are the ancient church's response to the new situation of the 2nd and 3rd centuries, a situation characterized by the confrontation with Gnosticism. This was probably the most serious crisis the church ever had to overcome, and in this crisis the basic structure of the ancient

church was formed. This structure is characterized by three intercon-
nected bulwarks which it raised against Gnosticism: the development
of the biblical canon, the establishment of the confession of faith, and
the doctrine of apostolic succession. All three structural elements were
characterized by apostolicity: only the writings of apostles or of their
immediate successors were received into the canon; the confession of
faith was considered to have been written by the apostles, and was
understood as the summary and hermeneutical norm of the Bible; final
authority resided in the community of those churches which were of
apostolic origin.

Thus, in its defensive struggle against Gnosticism, the church subjected itself to the norm, given once for all, of its apostolic beginnings.
At the same time, it understood itself to be the place where the truth
of the gospel is enduringly present. According to Irenaeus, the church
is the vessel in which the Holy Spirit deposited the faith of the apostles
in its youthful freshness, and where the Spirit maintains it youthfully
fresh. "Where the church is, there is also the Spirit of God, and where
the Spirit of God is, there is the church and all grace; but the Spirit is
truth."[4] Tertullian's argument, though less pneumatological than juridical, says essentially the same thing. For him it is without doubt true
that the church "possesses that which the churches received from the
apostles, the apostles from Christ, and Christ from God." For this
reason, only the church can rightfully lay claim to Scripture, for
heresies are convicted of error from the outset.[5] The church, guided by
the Holy Spirit, the Spirit of truth, is therefore the dwelling place of
truth and the universal sign of salvation.

This basic structure, which came into being in the third century,
proved broad enough to allow diverse historical transformations. The
content of the confession of faith was really not settled until the
end of the first millenium, after the acceptance of the *filioque* clause
which came to distinguish the West from the East. During the second
thousand years, however, the process of forming confessions was taken
out of the framework of the symbols of the ancient church. Already
during the First and Second Eucharistic Controversies, new confessional
formulas appeared and were confirmed by the Fourth Lateran Council
(1215, Doctrine of Transubstantiation).[6] The teaching of Thomas
Aquinas, especially, became significant, according to which articles of
faith, though immutable in their substance, could grow in their elaboration. In addition, Thomas for the first time credited to the pope
the authority to advance credal formulas.[7] In the late medieval period

there then arose the acute danger that the heart of the faith would be overgrown and obscured by secondary developments. (This danger was located less in official teaching than in popular piety and praxis.) Thus, the basic form of Catholicism, as it had been shaped in the third century, entered, at the end of the Middle Ages, a serious crisis, a crisis which neither the papacy nor the late-medieval reforming councils were able to resolve.

1.3. The Protestant Understanding of Confessions

The Reformers did not seek to establish a new church. Aware of their continuity with the ancient church, they did not wish to abandon the foundation of the ancient church's confessions.[8] The first instance of the formation of Lutheran confessions was the confession which Luther attached to his writing, "Concerning Christ's Holy Supper," in 1528. This confession adopts not only the content of the ancient church confessions, but also their trinitarian structure. The same applies also to the Augsburg Confession,[9] which states in the conclusion to both parts that it does not contain anything that contradicts either the Scripture or the *ecclesia catholica* or the *ecclesia romana,* and that the entire controversy revolves around only a number of abuses. Already at the time it was written, this statement probably represented an underestimate of the differences between the parties. Nevertheless, it does show the catholic intention at the beginning of the formulation of Lutheran confessions.

However, though Luther and the Augsburg Confession totally accepted the confessions of the ancient church, they placed them in a new perspective, in the perspective of what Luther called the gospel. Luther's original question had been: "How can I obtain a gracious God?" He was concerned with his own assurance of salvation. The answer was the gospel of the justification of sinners through grace alone. At issue in this answer was not primarily the content of one doctrinal statement, but rather the totality of the Christian faith, or, more precisely, a new "evangelical" view of all of it. The consequences of this new perspective can be illustrated either in terms of content, starting with the Reformation's material principle, or in terms of structure, starting with the formal principle. Neither of these principles is found in the Augsburg Confession, being the result of later systematization. However, both of them well express the Protestant perspective to which also the Augsburg Confession is indebted.

By the Reformation's material principle we mean the teaching of justification through grace alone and solely on the basis of faith. Starting at that point, Luther placed the trinitarian and christological confession of the ancient church in the perspective of the question of personal confidence of salvation. He was not concerned *per se* with the christological doctrine of two natures, but rather with the *"pro me"* of the Christ event. Thus dogma becomes *assertio,* a statement to which one holds unwaveringly, which one confesses and defends, and to which one clings invincibly and persistently. In this sense he criticized Erasmus in his *Concerning the Unfree Will: "Tolle assertiones, et Christianismum tulisti* (Do away with binding theological statements and you do away with Christianity.)" [10]

Although Luther himself did not play off personal trusting faith against the "objective" faith of the confessions, later Lutheranism was not always immune to this danger. Melanchthon's famous statement, *"Hoc est Christum cognoscere beneficia eius cognoscere, non quod isti docent, eius naturas, modos incarnationis contueri* [11] (To know Christ is to know his benefits; it is not, as they teach, to contemplate his natures and the manner of his incarnation)," was often understood as a warrant for making the doctrine of justification into an exegetical principle and so to deprive the confession of faith of its "objective" content, reducing its significance to an existential one. This attempt was undertaken by both liberal and existential theology. Rudolf Bultmann stated the problem in the form of an alternative: "Does he (Christ) help me because he is the Son of God, or is he the Son of God because he helps me?"[12] The Lutheran theologians who held fast to Luther's original intention have always sharply disagreed with such an abridgment.[13] They can appeal to the Augsburg Confession for support, which in its introduction describes itself as a confession "from article to article," and, in the conclusion of both its first and second parts, calls itself a "summary of doctrine." Nevertheless, the questions of the horizon of meaning and of the interpretation of the meaning of the ancient church symbols remains a serious ecumenical problem.

In addition to the problem of how to understand their content, there is the question of the formal authority of confessions. By the formal principle of the Reformation, we understand not only the teaching that "the Scripture alone" suffices to attest to the gospel of grace which alone justifies, but also the conviction that Scripture is, in respect to its central message and concern, clearly understandable and self-interpretive. The result of this teaching is that all the confessions, the ancient symbols as well as the Lutheran confessional writings, can claim to be valid and binding only because or insofar as they agree with Scripture. Scripture alone is judge, rule, and guide, and the other writings are witnesses to how the faith was understood and false teaching rejected at a particular time.[14] This understanding of Scripture does not take from the confessions their binding nature, but it precludes their having an infallible authority.

On the basis of their understanding of Scripture, the Reformers were, in fact, able to accept the entire confession of the ancient church. However, with the rise of historical-critical interpretation of the Bible beginning in the 18th century, this situation was radically changed. The controversy concerning the Apostles' Creed (1891-1892) revealed how critical the situation had become. Adolf von Harnack attempted to smooth things over: he showed respect for the Creed and counseled abstention from any and all polemics, but he reserved for himself the right to criticize it.[15] Though this did not become the official posture of the Lutheran Church, it has probably remained the de facto attitude of many Lutheran theologians, pastors, and laity. However, other Lutheran theologians recognize the indissoluble hermeneutical circle linking that preliminary understanding, guided by the confessions, which, at the very outset, permits one to see the Scriptures in a relevant way, and that interpretation of the Scripture which teaches a deeper and more comprehensive understanding of the confessions.[16] But even in this hermeneutically differentiated understanding, the binding nature of the ancient church confessions, or more exactly, the problem of authority, remains a grave ecumenical problem.[17]

Both the problem of how to understand the content of the ancient church symbols and the problem of their formally obligatory nature are issues which also agitate Catholic theology today. Many theologians of both churches are posing questions and arriving at answers which cut across the theologies of both churches. However, they approach these common problems from somewhat different suppositions. That is due to the fact that the Protestant view led to a new kind of confessional writings, of which the Augsburg Confession is the most important. The difference is discernible even on the level of language: Catholics normally speak of *professio* rather than *confessio*.[18] Behind this shift in terminology lies a change in substance which becomes clear when one considers the origin of these new confessions. They were formulated by theologians and princes of the empire, not by episcopal synods. Of course, as is said in the preface to the Augsburg Confession, they understood themselves as representatives of the pastors and preachers of their congregations, and they were expressing the overwhelming consensus of their churches (CA 1). Their original goal was, as is expressly stated in the Preface, to set in motion a process leading to a church council. They desired, as we can see, to remain within the old church, seeking even to have their Confession accepted by the universal church. Not until this had proved impossible (for many reasons) did a separate communion come into being in the crisis situation of those days, a communion institutionally expressed in confessional writings in the form of treatises. The changes in the office of bishop, especially, led to a new structuring of the ancient church's triad of Scripture, confession, and apostolic succession. Through the breaking of contact with the office of bishop, which leads back in historic succession to apostolic origins, there came into being a new type of confessional church, a church whose confessional writings possessed, in a certain sense, a greater importance than did those of the Catholic Church. Thus the Reformation, which originally had wanted to remain within the tradition of the ancient church's confessions, actually led, even in terms of its own understanding of confession, to something new.

Of course, this Protestant structure is not rigid, and is capable of various manifestations within history. Melanchthon and the Augsburg Confession were already placing the emphasis differently than did Luther himself. The Protestant Orthodoxy of the 16th and 17th centuries, furthermore, placed those accents differently than did the theology of the Enlightenment, liberal theology, or existential theology, which, in turn, differed from confessional Lutheranism of the 19th century and the 20th century theologians, who had come out of the "Luther Renaissance," and, in the church struggle under the Third Reich, had won a new understanding of the importance of a confession of faith (Barmen Declaration). In view of the explicit ecumenical and catholic intention which characterizes the Augsburg Confession, it is to be hoped that the original concern of Protestants can, within the ecumenical movement of our century, once more assume a form which can be recognized as an expression of Catholicism. But is the Roman Catholic position open to such a development?

1.4. The Traditional Catholic Understanding

The Catholic response to the challenge of the Reformation was necessarily more than a mere reestablishment of the ancient church's way of relating Scripture, creed, and apostolic succession within the sacramental *communio,* a relationship which had been but little thought through.

The reply to the challenge led to a new historical form of Catholicism, a form which now, with Vatican II, has come to an end.

At the very beginning, in its third session on February 4, 1546, the Council of Trent declared the Niceno-Constantinopolitan Creed to be the principle of church unity and the only, immovable foundation thereof.[19] Having basically taken its stand on the confessions of the ancient church, the Council turned, in the session of April 8, 1546, to the issues which had been raised. The point of departure was the question of the relation between Scripture and tradition, which, though it had hardly been expressly treated in the church Fathers or in scholasticism, had been made urgent by the Reformation.[20] The Council did not speak, as has long been wrongly interpreted, about two sources of doctrine. Rather, taking up the Reformation's question, it spoke of the gospel as the single source. However—and this is the cutting edge of its rebuttal against the Reformation—it spoke about *"evangelium in ecclesia."* [21] That means that for the Council of Trent, as it had been for the church Fathers, the church is the real location, vessel, and dwelling place of the gospel.

Concretely, the church finds the gospel in Scripture and in the tradition. Both, according to the Council, are to be revered with the same pious openness and respect. By tradition, however, the Council does not mean the human opinions rejected by the Reformers,[22] but exclusively the traditions which originated with Christ and the apostles, and which have been transmitted down to the present day. Thus the Council did not directly defend what the Reformers attacked. Nor did the Council say that the gospel is contained partly in Scripture and partly in the tradition; the relation between the content of both was not treated. Therefore, it is entirely possible, on the basis of the Council, to accept a fundamental and substantial completeness for Scripture, and to understand tradition as the Scriptural interpretation which lives in the church. The decisive point for the Council of Trent is not additions to the content of Scripture, but the interpretation of Scripture by the church, or, said in another manner, the indissoluble connection of the Scriptures with the church and with the sense of the Scriptures which both originated in the church and has continually been maintained by it.[23] Thus the ancient church's structure, which had been called into question by the Reformation, was to be held fast.

That which was characteristically new in post-Tridentine Catholicism in comparison to the old church consisted in the church's becoming increasingly and one-sidedly the clerical church, and ecclesiology was more and more becoming hierarchology.[24] Scripture and tradition were considered to be only the remote rule of faith *(regula fidei remota)*, while official church doctrine was called the proximate rule of faith *(regula fidei proxima)*. There developed an understanding of an infallible teaching office, unknown in that form in the ancient and medieval church. In the 18th century, the concept of dogma which has been definitive since that time was formed; i.e., a revealed truth solemnly defined as such by either the ordinary or the special teaching office of the church.[25] The apogee of this development was Vatican I (1869-1870), with its definition of the infallible teaching authority of the pope.[26] Popes have twice made use of this infallible teaching authority: at the elevation to the status of dogma of the Immaculate Conception of Mary, in 1854,[27] and, in 1950, at the promulgation of the dogma of Mary's bodily assumption into heaven.[28] Both dogmas have only an indirect basis in Scripture and in the ancient tradition. With both dogmas, therefore, there was a danger that the teaching authority was being separated from the witness of Scripture and of tradition. Characteristic is the statement attributed to Pope Pius IX: "I am tradition." The rule of faith seemed no longer to consist in the content of apostolic teaching, but rather in the formal criterion of authority founded on the apostles' authority, to which, under certain conditions, infallibility is guaranteed.

The danger inherent in the Catholic Church of the post-Tridentine and Vatican eras is basically the mirror-image and antithesis to the danger present in Luther's concentration on personal certainty of salvation. As in the first case everything is concentrated on an individual's subjective certainty, so in the second everything depends on the pope's personal decision. Admittedly, no such extreme papalism was enunciated by Vatican I, any more than Luther taught a subjective individualism in relation to salvation. Rather, the Council expressly stated that the pope, in his *ex cathedra* decisions, in which he speaks as universal shepherd and teacher, has at his disposal the infallibility which Christ has given to his church. In principle, therefore, the relationship of the pope's infallibility to that of the entire church was maintained. This infallibility, promised to the church and the pope together, does not, according to the Council, alter the "historical" nature of dogmas, that is, formulated as they are within the limitations of language and of their era's peculiar perspective, they are quite possibly amalgamated with error. Finally, infallibility is claimed only for the meaning of dogmas, not for the language in which they are clothed.[29]

These two points of view were not, it must be admitted, fully heard at Vatican I. But the fact that they continued to be expressed shows that even post-Tridentine and post-Vatican I Catholicism was not so closed that renewal could not come except by breaking with it. It contained, in fact, important elements which the Second Vatican Council and post-conciliar Catholic theology could take up and use in beginning to build, without loss of continuity, a new, ecumenically open, and historically realistic form of Catholicism. This post-conciliar Catholicism is, in relation to the questions which concern us here, characterized by a new awareness of the ancient church's basic structure, a structure which had become somewhat unbalanced in the Catholicism of the last centuries, as well as by a new ecumenical openness for Reformation impulses. This new style finds its clearest expression in the fact that Vatican II, though it took a decisive stand on the basis of received confessions and dogmas, did not itself declare any new dogma, preferring instead a pastoral style of proclamation and teaching. The question we now have to ask ourselves is this: What new form of church confession will result from this historical development, and what will be its consequences for a new evaluation of the basic Lutheran confessional writing?

2. Systematic-Theological Perspectives

2.1. Confession—Act and Content

The ancient credo-formulas do not say, "I believe that there is a God . . . that Jesus Christ is the Son of God . . . that the Holy Spirit is at work in the Church. . . ." Rather they say, "I believe in God . . . in Jesus Christ . . . in the Holy Spirit . . . ." [30] For faith is no mere assent to statements (dogmas) and facts (saving realities); faith is a direction, a movement in the direction of God and him alone. It is the projection of one's total being toward God. It signifies a total trust in God and a complete reliance on him, an amen to God, whatever the consequences might be. Faith is the unqualified yes of God as basis, destination, support, and content of life. Augustine stated the essence of faith in classic terms: "What, then, does it mean to believe in him? Through faith to be devoted to him, to love him by faith, by faith to turn to him and to be united with his members."[31] Therefore Vatican II said of faith that in it one delivers oneself over to God in total freedom when one subjects oneself totally, including both mind and will, to the God of revelation.[32] It is thereby reaffirmed that faith is a personal act involving the total human being, with intellect and will, something that has its basis, destination, and content in God alone.

Such faith is only possible as response to God's word, by means of which he himself addresses human beings and reveals himself to them. As faith looks ahead in hope to God, so it also looks back in remembrance *(anamnesis)* to God's words and actions in saving history. So faith is not empty wishful thinking, nor feeling devoid of content, nor pure dynamism which ends as pure silence. As response to God's word, faith has a concrete content. This content is not the subsequent objectification of a subjective belief, but the word of God's revelation which was first given once for all. The content which holds everything together is Jesus Christ, in whom God has spoken and acted with eschatological finality. Therefore faith according to the New Testament is always "faith in Jesus Christ," an entering and a being entered into the reality of Jesus Christ. The Christian faith is therefore an encompassing totality of act and content *(fides qua creditur* and *fides quae creditur),* and this totality must not be dissolved either objectively or subjectively.

Out of this interconnection of act and content follows the self-transcendence of every formula of faith and every confession. The act of faith, which does not take as its object a thing (doctrine, fact), but relates to God, transcends every formula and understands it as a likeness (analogy) of the God who is always greater. However great the similarity, it always contains within itself greater dissimilarity.[33] For this reason, Thomas Aquinas said of the act of faith that it does not relate to the statement but to the reality meant in the statement, that is, to God himself.[34] Following tradition, therefore, he defined an article of faith as *"perceptio divinae veritatis tendens in ipsam,"*[35] that is, an article of faith is a real appropriation of the truth of God, but one which necessarily tends to point beyond itself to truth. And so faith is essentially related to hope; it is the beginning and the anticipation of seeing God face to face.[36] Faith's hope-structure and hope-certainty correspond, in their basic intention, to Luther's certainty of salvation, and allow (better than was possible for the Council of Trent[37]) Luther's basic intention to be positively taken up and integrated into the totality of Catholic tradition.[38]

2.2. The Foundation of Confession in Scripture and Tradition

The "credo" is a personal act by which one joins in the credo of the church as the *congregatio fidelium.* The New Testament formula of faith was already an expression of the corporate, public, and binding faith which was formed in the church. In it we hear not the isolated "I" of a single Christian but the "we" of the ecclesial community of faith. Thus there is no such thing as a legitimate private Christianity. Believing is realized in and with the church. The confession of faith is therefore made in the name of the entire church united by faith. According to the original meaning of *symbol,* it is the sign by which Christians and Christian congregations recognize one another, and to that extent it is the bond which holds together all believers.[39] Faith is therefore within and with the church—but not a faith *in* the church! The ancient credal formulas are very precise at this point; they precisely differentiate between *"credere in Deum"* and *"credere ecclesiam."* The church is not God. Therefore though one can believe the church, one cannot believe in the church in the sense that one believes in God. The church is under God and subject to his word. It must be a hearing church before it becomes a teaching church, and its doctrine cannot be an end in itself, since its sole purpose is to lead people to God. The temptation for the church to make an idol of itself is indeed great. In that case, the obedience of faith becomes a faith of pure obedience. Rightly understood, the church is neither the basis nor the goal of faith. Rather, because it is a believing church, it is the witness, place, and home of faith.

The continually fresh hearing of the word of God which establishes the church is realized in hearing the testimony of Holy Scripture. In Scripture, in a Spirit-worked way (2 Peter 1:21), faith is transmitted to us once and for all (Jude 3). In it, therefore, God himself speaks through human beings in the same way that one person speaks to another.[40] The exposition of the Holy Scripture must therefore be like the soul of all the church's preaching, from which it continually needs to draw nourishment and strength.[41] "Not to know the Scripture is not to know Christ."[42] Because it is the Spirit-filled witness to the apostolic beginning of the church, Scripture is *norma normans non normata* for all the church's preaching, doctrine, and practice.

Just as it is true that Scripture is the norm for the faith of the church, so Scripture came into being in the church and for the church, and it was the church which gathered its books into the canon and transmitted them down to the present day. Only as that which is believed, witnessed to, and handed down by the church is Holy Scripture for us. It is therefore in every sense a book of the church, and cannot be theologically isolated from the church's transmitted faith. The gospel to which the Scriptures testify is surely not only something in history, but, as Christ promised, continually present through the Spirit in the faith of the church. That which is transmitted in faith is therefore not an additional, second source alongside Scripture, but is the living spiritual interpretation and reception of Scripture. "What then is tradition? The Christian sense of things, characteristically present in the church, and which is continued through Christian nurture, which cannot, however, be conceived of apart from its content; in fact, it has been so formed in and through this content that it could be called a disposition with content. The tradition is the living word which is perpetually present in the hearts of the faithful."[43] Based on the inner homogeneity of Scripture and tradition, it must be said that "the church does not gain from Scripture alone its certainty about all that which has been revealed."[44] The testimonies to that which has been handed down in the church (liturgy, councils, church Fathers, church teachers, pious practice, among others) need to be listened to each time, along with the Scriptures. In distinction to Scripture, however, they are only *norma normans normata* for the preaching, doctrine, and practice of the church. Understood in this way tradition does not, in principle, oppose the Lutheran thesis that Scripture interprets Scripture. Rather it takes up the concern of this thesis positively within the total structure of Catholic theology.[45]

2.3. Confession and Confessional Community

The question asked at the time remains the question for today: Where is this true church, the witness of the true gospel? The Catholic Church leaves no doubt about its conviction that the true church is not just a remembrance of the church of the first millenium, nor of the church of the first five centuries, nor of the New Testament, nor even of certain documents and strata in the New Testament which had not yet been influenced by early Catholicism. Nor is the true church only a matter of hope which must first be eschatologically realized. The true church is, as was promised by the Lord, something which is already present. It is not present "behind" or "over" the steeples of the various separated churches, it is rather present in the Catholic Church itself. That is the meaning of the famous *subsistit* in the church constitution of Vatican II: "This Church, which is constituted and ordered in this world as a community, is realized *(subsistit)* in the Catholic Church, which is guided by Peter's successor and by the bishops in partnership with him." [46] Of course, in this same passage the Council recognized that there are elements of the true church outside of the Roman Catholic Church. It spoke of churches and church communities outside its own borders. It firmly maintains, however, that the fullness of the means of salvation (not of salvation itself!) is to be found only in the Catholic Church.[47] By this statement, the Council held fast to the basic structure of the ancient church, according to which it is the concrete church, the church in communion with the apostolic ministry, which is a sign and witness to the truth of the gospel.

The concreteness of the church thus culminates, according to Catholic conviction, in the attachment of the church to the ministry that stands in apostolic succession, and in the attachment of the confession of faith to the authoritative teaching of this ecclesiastical authority. Of course one who holds this office is himself subject to the word of God; and because he is, he stands within the community of believers. That he nevertheless also stands over against it is something which is grounded in the nature of the gospel itself. For the church cannot speak the gospel to itself; the gospel is spoken to it with full authority. That the gospel is connected to ministry is not, therefore, an expression of an autocratic control of the gospel; rather the ministry expresses the indispensable "over-againstness" of the gospel to the church. The relationship of "in and over against" of teaching authority and church community is therefore essential for the church.[48] This pattern holds for all levels of the church's reality: that of the congregation, the diocese, and the universal church. Thus true proclamation of the gospel and the true church are only possible on all these levels in communion with churchly authority. At this point the Council of Trent's statement about *"evangelium in ecclesia"* has its most pointed application.

Because we have here come to the heart of the ecumenical problem, it is important to determine exactly what is meant by this expression. It is not an assertion that in the visible Catholic Church the fullness of the gospel is attested in an entirely perfect manner. The Council spoke simultaneously of the church's servant form, which also means that the church is a church of sinners. "She is at the same time holy and in need of purification, she is continually in the pathway of repentance and renewal."[49] To the servant form of the church belongs also the historically limited character of its statements of faith and confessions. This is expressly recognized in the most recent documents of the teaching office.[50] Accordingly, it is necessary to distinguish between the content or meaning of a confessional statement, which is to be held fast,[51] and the manner in which it is said, in respect to which the church is dependent on the expressive force of the language of a particular time. This does not imply a dogmatic relativism, in the sense that the confessions of faith would contain the truth only in an approximate, mutable, or only partially accurate sense. Rather, it belongs to the concreteness of the church "to hold fast to the truth in a particular form." [52] This historic givenness, of course, implies that this concrete form is continually in need of interpretation. To elevate a truth to the status of a confession means, therefore, to elevate it to what is enduringly worthy of reflection. The concrete church is thus, even with its concrete confession, a church that is under way. Even as a confessing church, it is the pilgrim people of God, who must witness to the once-and-for-all-delivered faith in a manner appropriate to the "signs of the time." [53]

This historical witness is entrusted to the whole church in the "in and over against" of the ministry and the congregation. Because of the enduring promise of the Spirit, the church as a whole cannot err when it testifies to its faith in general agreement and in community with the ecclesiastical ministry. [54] However true it is that every individual in the church possesses his or her own charisma, he or she is nonetheless to make use of it to build up church community (1 Corinthians 12). Consensus with the church as community of faith, and acceptance by it, are thus basic criteria for finding the truth in faith. [55]

This interconnection of confession and community of faith in the Catholic Church corresponds, in principle, to the basic intention of the Augsburg Confession, which was to find consensus with and acceptance by the Catholic Church. The Augsburg Confession too, says that the ministry was established in the church for the sake of the gospel (CA 5), and would even like to reestablish communion with the episcopal ministry of the Catholic Church (CA 28). This attempt failed for many reasons, some substantive and theological, others nontheological. That does not hinder us, however, from acknowledging that, from today's historical and theological perspective, the Augsburg Confession can be recognized as Catholic. Though this statement does not signify Catholic acceptance of the content of all statements in the Augsburg Confession, it does call for a thorough examination of its contents. [56]

3. Looking Ahead to a Future Ecumenical Form of Confession

We can state the result of what has thus far been said in this way: the original intention of the Augsburg Confession was to develop its "evangelical" understanding of the church within the communion of the Catholic Church. Especially in CA 7, the attempt was made to reach a kind of synthesis between the ancient church's idea of the church as *communio (congregatio) sanctorum* and the Lutheran understanding of the church, that starts with the gospel correctly proclaimed and the sacraments administered in accordance with the gospel.[57] This attempt at compromise failed at that time for a variety of reasons. What had begun as a document of unity became a document of separation, the foundation statement for a church communion separated from the Catholic Church. When today we discuss Catholic recognition of the Augsburg Confession, we are taking up its original intention again in the hope that in today's new ecumenical situation of churches moving closer to one another, the conditions might be better for agreement in those questions of content which were controverted then and still are so to some extent today.

Thus we have now entered what could be called a time of ecumenical confessional formation. It is characterized by a turning back to consider the basic structure of the ancient church, which is important also for drawing together ecumenically with the Orthodox churches, and by an openness to the "evangelical" impulses of the Reformation. For the Catholic Church, the urgency of this development arises out of its claim to catholicity. For this claim, as long as it meets qualified contradiction from a large part of Christendom, is not developed to its fullness. Therefore the Catholic Church is impelled to attempt to find a consensus with other church communions and to recognize and accept their legitimate concerns. The same is true in another sense for the churches who stand on the Augsburg Confession. They have not attained the universal consensus intended by the Augsburg Confession, and they must ask themselves whether the criticism of abuses in the second part of the Augsburg Confession still applies to the Catholic Church of today, or, put another way, whether the legitimate Reformation concerns expressed there could not also be attained today in communion with the Catholic Church. Second, the urgent need to form an ecumenical creed arises also from the present missionary situation, where Christians are able to witness credibly only in ecumenical community. Today the question, What is the church's official teaching? is being asked from differing suppositions in an entirely new way in both churches.[58] For this reason, a new ecumenical reading of their confessions has become the imperative of the hour for both churches.

The road to this ecumenical form of confession of faith emerging today consists in the attempt to transform, through mutual acceptance, the multiplicity of what have previously been mutually exclusive confessions into a new multiplicity in which one church can recognize its own faith in the confession of another, though it may find there a different form of expression arising from a different theology and a different history of piety. In addition it would have to be stated that past condemnations no longer apply today to the confessional stand of the other party. Such an ecumenical form of confession does not signify any fusion and leveling of positions, but clearly an accentuation of the position of each and a simultaneous recognition of the legitimacy of a variety of ways of expressing a concern which is mutually binding for all. Not, therefore, either the sole responsibility of one partner nor a pluralism of isolated, perhaps contradictory standpoints, but unity in multiplicity. Only such unity in multiplicity is capable of bringing to expression the entire fulness and richness of the gospel of Jesus Christ. The goal, therefore, is the unity of the church "in and from" many churches,[59] a conciliar community of churches. It should be clear to any clear-thinking person that such a mutual recognition between church organizations that have been separated for 450 years will be a long process of learning to know and understand one another, of reciprocal acceptance and solidifying cooperation.

The current discussion about a Catholic recognition of the Augsburg Confession is an important step along this way.[60] This discussion, however, necessarily leads beyond itself. The ultimate issue cannot be the recognition of a single confessional writing, but rather the recognition of the church community which appeals to this document and draws from it its self-understanding. Though the historical reconstruction of the original sense of this text is a considerable help in this direction, the decisive issue in respect to the church's recognition of the Augsburg Confession is the interpretation of it which is accepted and practiced in Lutheranism today. This recognition of a church community cannot be a one-way street. It must be a two-sided process. For this reason, a full Catholic recognition of the churches which appeal to the Augsburg Confession can be meaningful only when accompanied by a corresponding Lutheran recognition of the Catholic Church and of the authorities responsible for such a recognition.

The present discussion of a Catholic recognition of the Augsburg Confession is an important step along this way because it manifests the high degree of agreement already reached, and because it has moved beyond academic theology and is entering the consciousness of the churches. This result poses a question not only for the Catholic Church, but for both churches. For out of the presuppositions of both churches and in the light of this high degree of ecumenical commonality, renewed and deepened through the discussion of the Augsburg Confession, there are pressing implications for a higher degree of church community.

Notes

1. The investigation of NT confessions begins with A. Seeberg, *Der Katchismus der Urchristenheit* (1903; reprinted in Theol. Bücherei 26 [Munich: 1966]), continues with P. Feine, K. Holl, and H. Lietzmann. Important recent investigations include O. Cullmann, *Die ersten christlichen Glaubensbekenntnisse*, Theol. Stud. 15 (Zollikon-Zürich: 1949); V. H. Neufeld, *The Earliest Christian Confessions* (Leiden: 1963); H. Schlier, *"Die Anfänge des christologischen Dogmas"* in *Zur Frühgeschichte der Christologie*, B. Welte, ed., Quaest. disp. 51 (Freiburg-Basel-Wien: 1970).
2. There are important studies by F. Kattenbusch, H. Lietzmann, A. v. Harnack, J. de Ghellinck. The best recent presentation is in J. N. D. Kelly, *Early Christian Creeds* (London: 1960).
3. See J. H. Newman, *Ueber die Entwicklung der Glaubenslehre, Ausgew. Werke*, vol. 8 (Mainz: 1969).
4. *Adv. Haer.* 3, 24:1.
5. *De praescr.* 21.
6. DS 802.
7. *Summa theol.* II/II, 1, 8. 10.
8. See J. Koopmans, *Das altkirchliche Dogma in der Reformation*, Beitr. ev. Theol. 22 (Munich: 1955). On the present state of the question see W. Theurer, *Die trinitarische Basis des Oekumenischen Rates der Kirchen* (Bergen-Enkheim: 1967); H. J. Urban, *Bekenntnis, Dogma, kirchliches Lehramt: Die Lehrautorität der Kirche in heutiger evangelischer Theologie* (Wiesbaden: 1972). See also the chapter by K. Lehmann and H. G. Pöhlmann in this volume.
9. See also W. Maurer, *Historischer Kommentar zur Confessio Augustana*, vol. 2 (Gütersloh: 1979), esp. pp. 163-164, 191-192; G. Kretschmar, *"Die Bedeutung der Confessio Augustana als verbindliche Bekenntnisschrift der Evangelisch-Lutherischen Kirche"* in H. Fries and others, *Confessio Augustana:Hindernis oder Hilfe?* (Regensburg: 1979), pp. 31-77.
10. WA 18, 603.
11. Melanchthon, *"Loci communes von 1521,"* in *Ausgew. Werke* II/1 (Gütersloh: 1952), p. 7.
12. R. Bultmann, *"Das christologische Bekenntnis des Oekumenischen Rates"* in *Glauben und Verstehen*, vol. 2 (Tübingen: 1952), p. 252.
13. Esp. H. J. Iwand, *"Wider den Missbrauch des pro me als methodisches Prinzip in der Theologie"* in THL 79 (1954): 453-458; by the same author, *Rechtfertigung und Christusglaube*, Theol. Bücherei 24 (Munich: 1961); E. Schlink, *Theologie der lutherischen Bekenntnisschriften* (Munich: 1948), pp. 120-126.

14. BSLK 769.
15. See A. v. Harnack, *"In Sachen des Apostolikums,"* in *Reden und Aufsätze.* vol. 1 (Giessen: 1904), pp. 221-224.
16. For example, see E. Schlink, *loc. cit.,* pp. 23-55; W. Lohff, *"Bekenntnis-schriften IV"* in LThK ² 2 (1958), p. 152; G. Gloege, "Bekenntnis" in RGG³ 1 (1957), pp. 994-1000. However, p. 997: "A confession is valid only insofar as it is able to exercise the function of interpreting the Scriptures."
17. See G. Ebeling, *"Wort Gottes und kirchliche Lehre"* in *Wort Gottes und Tradition:Studien zu einer Hermeneutik der Konfessionen* (Göttingen: 1964), pp. 155-174, especially pp. 168-172.
18. See Y. Congar, "Confession," "Eglise," and "Communion" in *Irenikon* 23 (1950): 3-36. The connection between creed and sacramental Communio is very strongly stressed by Lutheran theologians like W. Maurer, *Bekenntnis und Sakrament* I (Berlin: 1939); W. Elert, *Abendmahl und Kirchengemeinschaft in der alten Kirche hauptsächlich des Ostens* (Berlin: 1954).
19. DS 1500.
20. On the interpretation of Trent, see E. Ortigues, *"Ecritures et traditions apostoliques au concile de Trente"* in RSR 36 (1949): 271-299; J. R. Geiselmann, *"Das Konzil von Trient über das Verhältnis der Heiligen Schrift und der nicht geschriebenen Traditionen,"* in *Die mündliche Uberlieferung.* Quaest. disp. 25 (Freiburg-Basel-Wien: 1965); Y. Congar, *Die Tradition und die Traditionen,* vol. I (Mainz: 1965), pp. 192-217.
21. DS 1501.
22. This misunderstanding is especially evident in the index of the official edition of the BSLK, which under the entry "Tradition" refers to the title, "human statutes."
23. DS 1507.
24. See W. Kasper, *Die Lehre von der Tradition in der Römischen Schule* (Freiburg-Basel-Wien: 1962), esp. pp. 40-47; Y. Congar, *loc. cit.* pp. 218-223; the same author, *"Bref historique des formes du 'magistère' et des ses relations avec les docteurs,"* in RSPhTh 60 (1970): 99-112.
25. See A. Deneffe, *"Dogma, Wort und Begriff,"* *Scholastik* 6 (1931): 381-400, 505-538; M. Elze, *"Der Begriff des Dogmas in der Alten Kirche,"* in ZThK 61 (1964): 421-438; W. Kasper, *Dogma unter dem Wort Gottes* (Mainz: 1965), pp. 28-38; K. Rahner-K. Lehmann, *"Kerygma und Dogma"* in *MySal* I (Einsiedeln-Zürich-Köln), pp. 639-660; G. Söll, *"Dogma und Dogmenentwicklung"* in *Handbuch d. Dogmengeschichte,* vol. I/5 (Freiburg-Basel-Wein: 1971).
26. DS 3074. It is not possible in this context to enter into the current, as yet unresolved inner-Catholic discusion of infallibility centering around H. Küng's *Unfehlbar? Eine Anfrage* (Zürich-Einsiedeln-Köln: 1970). In an ecumenical context it is preferable to limit oneself to interpretations which are more or less accepted within Catholic theology. See esp. G. Thils, *L'infallibilité pontificale: Sources-conditions-limites* (Gembloux: 1969). There are important beginnings for a solution of this still insufficiently discussed question in the results of Lutheran-Catholic dialogue in the U. S.A.: *Teaching Authority and Infallibility in the Church,* Common Statement (Minneapolis: Augsburg, 1980), pp. 11-38.

27. DS 2803-2804.
28. DS 3903-3904.
29. DS 3020.
30. Concerning what follows, see H. de Lubac, *Credo: Gestalt und Lebendigkeit unseres Glaubensbekenntnisses* (Einsiedeln: 1975).
31. See Thomas Aquinas, *Summa theol.* II, 2, 2.
32. *Dei verbum*, 5.
33. DS 806.
34. *Summa theol.* II/II, 1 and 2.
35. *Ibid.,* 1, 6.
36. *Ibid.,* 1 6 ad 1;1, 8; 4, 1 and other places.
37. See DS 1533-1534.
38. See St. Pfürtner, *"Luther und Thomas im Gespräch: Uber Heil zwischen Gewissheit und Gefährdung," Thomas im Gespräch* 5 (Heidelberg: 1961); O. H. Pesch, *Die Theologie der Rechtfertigung bei Martin Luther und Thomas von Aquin: Versuch eines systematischen Dialogs,* Walberberger Stud. 4 (Mainz: 1967).
39. On this see H. de Lubac, *op. cit.,* pp. 276-277.
40. *Dei verbum* 11-12.
41. *Ibid.,* 21; 24.
42. *Ibid.,* 25.
43. J. A. Möhler, *Symbolik,* J. R. Geiselmann, ed. (Darmstadt: 1958), p. 415.
44. *Dei verbum* 9.
45. See J. Ratzinger, "Tradition," in LThK² X (1965): 295.
46. *Lumen gentium* 8.
47. *Unitatis redintegratio* 3.
48. See *Evangelium-Kirche-Welt: Schlussbericht und Referate der römischkatholisch/evangelisch-lutherischen Studienkommission, "Das Evangelium und die Kirche,"* 1967-1971, H. Meyer, ed. (Frankfurt a M.: 1975), 21 (No. 50). A closer look at the question of ministry is found in the chapter by A. Dulles and G. Lindbeck in this volume, pp. 147ff.
49. *Lumen gentium* 8; see 15; *Gaudeum et spes* 43.
50. See John XXIII, *"Ansprache bei der Eröffnung des II Vatikanischen Konzils,"* in AAS 54 (1962): 792; Pastoralkonstitution *"Gaudium et spes,"* p. 62; Statement, *"Mysterium ecclesiae: Zur katholischen Lehre über die Kirche und ihre Verteidigung gegen einige Irrtümer von heute,"* K. Lehmann, ed., *Nachkonziliare Dokumentation* 43 (Trier: 1975), pp. 146-155 (Chap. 5).
51. DS 3020.
52. *Mysterium ecclesiae* 5.
53. *Gaudium et spes* 4; 11, and in other places.
54. *Lumen gentium* 12.
55. Concerning the fundamental meaning of acceptance, see Y. Congar, *"Die Rezeption als ekklesiologische Realität,"* in *Concilium* 8 (1972): 500-514; by the same author, *"La reception comme realite ecclesiologique,"* in RSPhTh 56 (1972): 369-403; A. Grillmeier, *"Konzil und Rezeption,"* in *Mit ihm und in ihm: Christologische Forschungen und Perspektiven* (Freiburg-Basel-Wien: 1975), pp. 303-334; concerning the ecumenical meaning of acceptance, see H. Mühlen, *Morgen wird Einheit seins: Das Kommende Konzil aller Christen: Ziel der getrennten Kirchen* (Paderborn: 1974).

The statement of Vatican I that papal *"ex cathedra"* decisions are *"ex sese, non autem ex consensu Ecclesiae"* inalterable does not contradict the principle of acceptance. For an interpretation, see H. Fries, *"Ex sese non autem ex consensu Ecclesiae"* in *Volk Gottes,* R. Bäumer and H. Dolch, eds. (Freiburg i. Br.: 1967), pp. 480-500.

56. See W. Lohff, *"Welche Folgen hätte eine Anerkennung der Confessio Augustana durch die katholische Kirche für die Evangelisch-Lutherische Kirche?"* in H. Fries et. al., *Confessio Augustana: Hindernis oder Hilfe?* (Regensburg: 1979), pp. 193-206.

57. See also W. Kasper, *Die Confessio Augustana in katholischer Sicht,* in LWB-Report 6/7 (1979): 88-93.

58. On the wider ecumenical context, see *Verbindliches Lehren der Kirche heute,* published by Deutscher Oekumenischer Studienausschuss (Supplement to *Oekumenischer Rundschau* 33) (Frankfurt a. M.: 1978).

59. See *Lumen gentium* 23.

60. See W. Kasper, *"Was bedeutet das Katholische Anerkennung der Confession Augustana?"* in H. Meyer, et. al., eds., *Katholische Anerkennung des Augsburgischen Bekenntnisses?* (Frankfurt a. M.: 1977), pp. 151-156.

3

God, Jesus Christ, and the Return of Christ

by Karl Lehmann and Horst Georg Pöhlmann

translated by Michael Rogness

1. The Structure of Article 1

The captions for each article of the CA were not in the original version but were added during the printing. However, they do mark the progression of thought: (1) God, (2) Original Sin, (3) The Son of God, (4) Justification.

The first article begins with the triune God, which is also the case with the CA's predecessors—the Athanasian Creed, the Schwabach Articles, and the Marburg Articles. What is surprising is that the article about Jesus Christ as God's Son does not follow immediately. This would have been suggested from the unity of the ancient church's doctrine of the Trinity and the closely related christology. But here the Second Article, about original sin, interrupts this progression. Article Four on justification appears as a synthesis of these preceding articles. This calls for careful interpretation.

1.1. The Placement of Article 2

In Luther's Great Confession of 1528 and in his Catechism of 1529 the treatment of the work of Christ precedes sin and the fall. Also in the Schwabach Articles (1529) christology is dealt with before the statements about sin (hamatiology). The same is true of the Marburg Articles. Why does the CA differ from these models and place original sin immediately following the Trinity, *before* christology?

The theological reason for this placement may well be the very starting point for Lutheran theology in terms of the history of salvation. Lutheran theology sees God's work not speculatively but dialectically, namely, the dialectic of law and gospel. This dialectic also permeates CA 2 and 3. Salvation is understood as the *answer* to the fall (original sin) and thus as an historical event. This understanding is similar to the New Testament, particularly when one considers the structure of the Epistle to the Romans. To put it briefly: "Without the knowledge of sin there is no salvation" (cf. Chapter 4 below, "Sin and Original Sin," pp. 94ff.) This is contrary to the supralapsarian understanding of salvation in later Calvinism and Karl Barth.

This dialectic of law and gospel corresponds to the ancient and catholic tradition.[1] The same is true of the threefold progress of salvation-history (generation, degeneration, regeneration), which can be recognized not only in the first three articles of the CA, but which determines the entire progression of the Confession as well.[2] The particular anthropological outlook of the Lutheran Reformation is also apparent in the placement of the article concerning sin before the paragraph on christology.

1.2. Purpose and Significance

The basic purpose of the CA—to maintain or restore the unity of the church (cf. the important Preface)—is nowhere so convincingly accomplished as in CA 1 and 3 (cf. Apol. 1,1; 3,1 [BC 100; 107]). The guiding motif of the CA, to present a "catholic confession,"[3] is most clear here, where the doctrinal decrees of the ancient church are preserved.

The church of the CA wishes to understand itself not as a new church, but as the renewed catholic church, an understanding which continues to this day. According to the paragraph concluding the first 21 articles, the purpose of the Confession is to show that its teachings agree with "the catholic church," yes, even with the "church of Rome," of which the supporters of the Augsburg Confession still considered themselves a part (cf. also Apol. 4,390 [BC 166]).

The continuity is carried out by accepting the ancient creeds, as well as citing many references from the ancient and medieval church. Some base this emphasis on continuity on nontheological factors. According to this view Luther and Melanchthon maintained the ancient doctrines of the Trinity and christology in the Confession for imperial-legal reasons, since they belonged to the unalterable legal foundation of the Holy Roman Empire of the German Nation on the basis of the Laws of Heresy of Theodosius (A.D. 380/381) and the Code of Justinian (A.D. 534). According to A. Ritschl this "proper stance . . . made it possible for the princes and authorities to tolerate, to protect, and even to make common cause with the reformers."[4] According to A. Harnack there is "no bridge" from the Reformation doctrine of justification to the dogma of the ancient church.[5] Actually a connection is not apparent at first glance. But appearances deceive. It is quite clear from the context of the Reformers' teaching of justification that they did not affirm the ancient church's dogma for official or legal reasons. As we shall see below, their reasons were *theological*. We are not dealing with a feeling of duty or a tactical maneuver on their part. The affirmation of this dogma comes from a deep and inner conviction (cf. the literature by W. Maurer, E. Schlink, and A. Peters in footnotes 9, 12, and 18). The extensive proof from the Scriptures indicates that it is assumed not superficially, but consciously. In the Reformation understanding, justification without the doctrine of the early church would be like writing checks with no money in the bank. For without that, Jesus would be only a man and not God, which means he could not redeem us human beings. Both the content and heading of the Reformation message is that human beings cannot save themselves. Only Jesus Christ can. This is why the CA and Apology rebuke heresy so sharply: whoever denies the ancient dogma stands "outside the church" according to the Apology.[6] Such persons are excluded from salvation because they have excluded themselves from salvation (cf. the Athanasian Creed, 1-2). With a sideward glance to Neo-Protestantism, H. Asmussen comments, "There is no legitimate understanding of the CA outside the limits of Article One. Whoever denies the Trinity . . . and confesses justification by faith is still outside the church." [7]

2. The Text of CA 1: The Threefold, One God

The text appears somewhat abstract, since the terminology of the classical doctrine of the Trinity and christology is used. The brief mention of the condemnation of heresy makes the transition to the central theological point of this First Article more difficult. Only through careful interpretation can it be articulated.

2.1. Occasion

There are two causes for the explicit acceptance of the Nicene Creed. On one side, the antitrinitarian Enthusiasts had surfaced compromising the Reformation. On the other side, J. Eck in his *404 Articles* had impugned antitrinitarian motives to Luther.[8] Eck had taken a statement out of context from Luther's writing against Latomus (1521), which sounded suspicious and which he used to count Luther among the heretics: "Even if my soul hated this word, *homoousios,* and I refused to use it, still I would not be a heretic." Of course Luther went on: "For who compels me to use the word, providing I hold to the fact defined by the council on the basis of Scripture."[9] In reference to the words of the ancient creeds, the CA "not only employs the exact words, but reformulates them in an interpretive fashion."[10] From the standpoint of the "word alone *(sola scriptura)"* principle, a simple repristination of tradition would be impossible. Tradition must be examined by the "norm" of the Scriptures (Formula of Concord, Epitome, 1, 7 [BC 465]). For this reason the scriptural basis of the doctrine of the Trinity was so important to the Reformers (cf. the Schwabach Articles). "Those parts of the tradition of the church, however, which prove to be based on Scripture also have authority, even though it is only a derived authority."[11]

Later Luther explicitly affirmed the Nicene concept of *homoousios,* because it contained "the meaning of Scripture . . . in a short and comprehensive word."[12] According to the inclusive scriptural principle of the Lutheran Reformation, the Scriptures are not subordinate to tradition, but tradition is valid insofar as it corresponds to and does not contradict the Scriptures.[13] It is not a matter of the Scripture alone being valid, but being primary, in contrast to "biblicism" with its exclusive scriptural principle. The reference of Article One to the Nicene Creed makes that clear.

2.2. The Soteriological Context of the Doctrine of the Trinity

In his Confession of 1528 as well as the Smalcald Articles Luther counted the Trinity among "the highest articles of the divine majesty." The article on the Trinity was placed consciously at the beginning of the CA, because "the doctrine of the Trinity is the basis of all statements of the Lutheran Confessions."[14] Furthermore, this is done for soteriological reasons. When the doctrine of God is dealt with first, and when the confession of an "eternal God" *("Deus aeternus")* and his three coeternal persons precedes all other confessional statements, that means: God is eternal, before human beings; before human beings do anything, God is at work; before human beings do anything, God is already eternally active within himself *("coaeternae")*. It is all grace. From eternity God encounters human beings through his limitless benevolence *("immensa bonitas")*, which he is within himself as the relation of love between Father and Son through the Holy Spirit. In the Large Catechism (1, 24-25 [BC 367-368]) the word *God* is derived from *good,* and God is described as the "eternal fountain which . . . pours forth all that is good."[15] The ever-present Trinity, which is spoken of in CA 1, guarantees that love is not simply an attribute of God; it is his very essence. He does not love as if he could do otherwise, but because he does not wish to do otherwise. He is irrevocably the loving one. He does not *have* love, like a human being, but he *is* love. His love knows no boundaries *("immensa")*. It is eternal, above all change, which characterizes human love. He is no egoistic solo-God, but rather a socio-God. Because he is that *within himself,* he is also that *for us.* The three-in-one Trinity is the basis for the ever-present Trinity.

But does not Luther put the greatest emphasis on the "economic" Trinity, as L. Grane claims? Grane correctly stresses that "the reference to the Trinity is not rejected as the expression for the inner essence of God, but is stressed in order to show that the inner essence of God is known to us only through his work in revelation."[16] The progression of the Confession's first three articles makes that clear. Furthermore, were it not for this progression of "God the Father, God the Son, God the Holy Spirit," Article Four on justification would ultimately be an unfounded illusion. First comes the fact that God himself is at work in redemption—God alone, not human beings—and from that comes the assurance of salvation for people and the gift of eternal life. The doctrine of the Trinity was no lifeless tradition for Luther, but rather "that which carried the presupposition of his theology."[17] R. Prenter believes that Luther restored the early church's doctrine of the Trinity to its original soteriological context, where Scholasticism in its synergistic teaching of salvation ascribed a role to human free will, "which in practice limited the comprehensiveness of the Son's working as well as that of the Holy Spirit."[18]

2.3. Limits and Objections

In view of the concern for continuity, the practical-soteriological and antispeculative thrust of the Lutheran concept of the Trinity is not made explicit in the Confession's First Article.[19] The same is true of the Third Article. The inclusion of Melanchthon's well-known statement from the Preface of the *Loci Communes* of 1521 would have caused new misunderstanding: "The mysteries of God's divinity are better adored than investigated *(mysteria divinitatis rectius adoraverimus quam vestigaverimus)*." Unfortunately the important conclusion of the First Article of the Marburg Articles was not included in the Confession, ". . . as in the Nicene Creed we read *and sing.*" One could have made clear with such statements that theology is doxology, not to be divided from the practice of faith. Even the language of the Confession here is academic rather than doxological. H. Asmussen's critical remark has some justification: "One cannot really *pray* any of the Confession's articles, including the first."[20] However this characteristic is shared by many other ecclesiastical pronouncements (cf. also the texts of the Council of Trent).

A. Peters brings forth another objection. He notes a shortcoming in the First Article in that "God's attributes are articulated more on the basis of ancient philosophy than on the Scriptures; he is 'eternal, without body, indivisible, omnipotent, omniscient and all-benevolent.' " Peters continues: "His holiness as well as his love for humanity is in the background. The biblical witness to the Father of Jesus Christ, who sent the Son and the Spirit into the world to save us, is concealed by the statement about the 'one divine essence' existing in three distinct persons."[21]

But this objection cannot be sustained when one considers how the important expressions concerning God's essence are precisely suited to the Trinity's soteriological purpose, as we have shown above. The specific characteristics of the Lutheran teachings of God which are not expressly mentioned in the Confession, are God's workings through anger and love *(deus absconditus, deus revelatus),* revealed through law and gospel. This is done because of the Confession's interest in continuity, particularly in the First Article. The same is true in the Third Article where some of the specific characteristics of Lutheran christology are missing, such as the *admirabile commercium,* for example. However, the concept of God's "essence" *(una essentia divina)* which A. Peters criticizes as being taken from Greek-Platonic thought, had been introduced early into theological language about God.[22] The concept of "one divine essence" does not intend to neutralize God into an impersonal and unhistorical "essence," but is rather—as we shall show later—a presupposition to express *essential* unity of Jesus with the Father, with which salvation stands and falls. "Essence" is that through which something is what it is—the "essence" of a thing (also called "substance," *substantia*).

2.4. "Three Persons": Antimodalism

The affirmation that in God there are "three persons *(tres personae)*" despite the "one essence *(una essentia)*" is meant to avoid the modalistic misunderstanding. The Father, Son, and Holy Spirit are not just different aspects or appearances of the one essence of God, but really different. It does not have to do with either a plurality of substance or attributes, but with a personal plurality *(pluralitas substantialis, pluralitas accidentalis, pluralitas personalis)*. In the church's tradition *persona* is not a "part" *(pars)* or a "quality" *(qualitas)* "in something else." A "person" is that "which consists of itself *(quod proprie subsistit)*." *Persona* is also not the same as today's concept of "person" or "personality" (which is *pluralitas substantialis*). In the *Loci* of 1559 Melanchthon defined *persona* in connection with church tradition (Boethius) as "indivisible, thinking, and unique substance *(substantia individua, intelligens et incommunicabilis),*" [23] that is, as an individual being with an intellectual capacity, an individual, intellectual existence. The three persons would therefore be three particular persons of the one being-substance of God, similar to—naturally any comparison is lame—three branches of a single tree. They are each the different and uninterchangeable means of encounter of the one God *(opera ad intra sunt divisa:* The activities of God within himself are exercised by the three individual persons—as expressed by the theology of the Middle Ages as well as the early Protestant Orthodoxy). "Single-being" and "other-being" are likewise both characteristics of the essence of love. (Where there are still two, there is no love; where there are no longer two, there is no love.) We are dealing here with history, not speculation, particularly when one observes that the three active divine characteristics—"power" *(potentia),* "wisdom" *(sapientia),* and "goodness" *(bonitas)*—correspond to the three persons in medieval theology. [24]

The emphasis on the tripersonality of God and the antimodalism of Article One in the Confession are determined by the situation. Among the "new Samosatenes" mentioned in the list of heresies the Confession has above all Johann Campanus in mind. It was he who in March,

1530, came to the court of the Saxon duke in Torgau, representing the doctrine that the Holy Spirit is no person and that Christ is not of the same essence as the Father.[25] "The denial of the divinity of the Son and the Spirit" meant for the Reformation "the surrender of the gospel itself" [26] (cf. 1.2 above). The rejection of the heresies of the "Arians, Eunomians, and Mohammedans" is likewise explained from soteriological concerns, which the Reformation joined to the dogma of the Trinity. Luther separated himself as sharply as possible from Arius and his christology,[27] through which the very center of faith would be betrayed. Luther's opinion is well known, that "Arius far outdid Judas." [28]

2.5. Emphasis on the Unity of God

Next to the antimodalistic note, as expressed in the definition of the concept of *persona,* there is a countervailing tendency in the First Article. On the whole the article accents the *unity* of God's being. This is made clear not only in the condemnation of the "Manichaeans, who assert that there are two gods," [29] but also in the repeated reference to God's unity *("de unitate essentiae divinae . . . quod sit una essentia divina . . . eiusdem essentiae").*[30] Above all, it is striking that the creation and preservation of the earth is ascribed not only to the Father, but to the *whole* deity: the *triune* God is "maker and preserver of all things visible and invisible." [31] In the Nicene Creed only the Father is described as "maker of heaven and earth and of all things visible and invisible." *Opera ad extra sunt indivisa:* "The works of God outside himself" take place with participation of all three persons, again as the theology of the Middle Ages and the early Protestant Orthodoxy said. The Nicene Creed is accepted as it is, but not just copied. From the Nicene Creed stems the theological basis for the creation of the "visible and the invisible," and from the Athanasian Creed comes the emphasis on the *unity* of the divine being (3, 6, 11-12, 14, 16, 18, 23, 25, 32-33, 34-35), as well as the conception of God as "eternal" *("aeternus,"* 10-11) and "unlimited" *("immensus,"* 9), plus the statement that the three persons are "equally eternal" *("coaeternae,"* 25).[32] This shows the extent to which the components of the classic trinitarian theology are assumed, but also how the basic structure and the decisive unfolding of the conception of the great trinitarian thinking stands behind the Confession as the grid behind the brief exposition—although not without new accents.

3. The Text of CA 3: The Son of God

The Third Article shows even more strongly how the traditional dogma of the ancient and medieval church is seen in the closest possible connection with the soteriological "work" of the "person" Jesus Christ. The construction of the article must be understood from the dynamic and varied word "that" (*ut;* 2, 3, 4, 6) in the text.

3.1. Occasion

Apart from the causes which led to the composition of the CA 1 (cf. above 2.1), the shape of CA 3 goes back above all to the controversy between Luther and Zwingli over the *communicatio idiomatum* and their understanding of the Lord's Supper. *Communicatio idiomatum* is the phrase which means that the characteristics of each of the natures of Jesus Christ—human and divine—can and must be stated through the hypostatic union of the one person of Jesus Christ.[33]

Evidence for this is the third of the Schwabach Articles, which sets the pattern for CA 3, which referred explicitly to this controversy and expressly opposed the ideas of Zwingli for betraying Nestorian features. The focal point was the so-called *alloeosis* ("exchange of properties"). According to this, the *communicatio idiomatum* is simply a figure of speech, intended only symbolically. *Alloeosis* means therefore that one speaks of the one nature using the concepts of the other. Christ suffered and died only according to the human nature, not the divine. In contrast to the "condescension theology" of Luther, Zwingli proceeded from a "transcendence theology" which was determined by the contrast between God and human beings. Consistent with that trend, he divided the two natures of Christ and distinguished the events in Jesus' life between one or the other nature.

Luther's christology, on the other hand, was determined by that of Cyril, with its accent on the unity of Jesus' person. The reformer saw both natures in the one person. Christ's action and suffering were ascribed to both natures. In Christ God himself suffered the death of the cross, not only the human nature. The statement from the Confession is surely meant for Zwingli: ". . . there are two natures, divine and human, inseparably conjoined *(inseperabiliter coniunctae)* in the unity of his person *(in unitate personae)* one Christ *(unus Christus)*."[34] It is "one" and "the same Christ" who was "born of the virgin Mary, truly *(vere)* suffered, was crucified, dead, and buried. . . ."[35] The repetition of the word *idem,* "the *same* Christ," in the continuing lines of the text underscores again the identity of Jesus Christ!

Later the Formula of Concord picks up this problem again (Solid Declaration 8, 39ff. [BC 598ff.]) and quotes among others the following statements of Luther's *Confession Concerning Christ's Supper* (1528):

Zwingli calls that an *alloe sis* when something is said about the deity of Christ which after all belongs to the humanity, or vice versa—for example, "Was it not necessary that the Christ should suffer these things and enter into his glory?" (Luke 24:26) Here Zwingli performs a sleight-of-hand trick and substitutes the human nature for Christ. Beware, beware, I say, of this *alloeosis,* for it is the devil's mask since it will finally construct a kind of Christ after whom I would not want to be called a Christian, that is, a Christ who is and does no more in his passion and death than any other ordinary saint. But if I believe that only the human nature suffered for me, then Christ would be a poor Saviour for me, in fact, he himself would need a Saviour . . . the deity surely cannot suffer and die. . . . That is true, but since the divinity and humanity are one person in Christ, the Scriptures ascribe to the deity, because of this personal union, all that happens to the humanity. . . . that is, this person who is God . . . is crucified according to the humanity.[36]

Apart from the clear similarity of the Confession's Article Three to the Apostles' Creed, it is also striking that the opening phrases are formulated very similarly to the *"Decretum pro Iacobitis"* of the Council of Florence (1442). Thus in spite of new emphases the acceptance of the christology of the early church includes to a certain extent the western-medieval theology.[37]

3.2. The Crucified God as the Center of Theology

Occasioned by this polemic against Zwingli's christology, the weight of CA 3 is on the affirmation of the "one *(unus)* Christ, true God and true man *(vere deus et homo),"*—that is, not only a man—who truly *(vere)* suffered, was truly crucified, and truly died.[38] The word "truly" *("vere")* really belongs to all the verbs. Then follows the soteriological purpose of CA 3: Jesus Christ, "true God," not only just "true man," died "that he might reconcile the Father to us and be a sacrifice *(ut reconciliaret nobis patrem et hostia esset)."* Even further, a sacrifice "not only for original guilt *(culpa originis)* but also for all actual sins *(actualia peccata)* of men." [39] The terms "true God and true man," literally "truly God" and "truly man" *(theos aläthos kai anthropos aläthos)* are taken from the Council of Chalcedon, likewise the formula of the "two natures" *(dyo physeis)* the divine and the human, which are indivisibly united in the "one person" *(hen prosopon, mai hypostasis)*. The "unity of person *(unitas personae)"* comes of course from the Athanasian Creed. These formulae were not disputed by Zwingli, but subverted.

The concept of "sacrifice" *("hostia")* is also used elsewhere in the confessional writings for the sacrificial death on the cross (cf. Apol. 24, 23 [BC 253]), since its double meaning in Latin alluded to the Eucharist—*"hostia"* and "host." The connection of christology and the Lord's Supper is visible not only in the controversy with Zwingli, but also in the discussion about the concept of the "sacrifice of the mass" in the Roman Catholic Church (cf. Apol. 24, 9-88 [BC 250-265] and the commentary to CA 10, 24 by E. Iserloh and V. Vajta, pp. 202ff. below).

According to CA 3, salvation stands or falls with the fact that Jesus Christ is not only true man, but also at the same time true God. Then, quoting Luther again according to Formula of Concord 8:

We Christians must know that unless God is in the balance and throws in weight as a counterbalance, we shall sink to the bottom with our scale. . . . If it is not true that God died for us, but only a man died, we are lost. But if God's death and God dead lie in the opposite scale, then his side goes down and we go upward like a light and empty pan.[40]

Thus the crucial decree made by the church at Nicaea concerning the union of essence and being between Jesus Christ and the Father assumes a central position in the Reformation.

CA 4 revolves around the axes of CA 1 and 3. "What does it profit you to confess that he is man, if you do not also believe that he is God?" asks Luther.[41] It is crucial that he *is* God, and not just God and man bound together. The Reformation also stands and falls here with the "it is" *("est")*, over against an implied "it signifies" *("significat")*, similar to the comparison of these terms in the discussion of the doctrine of the Lord's Supper. "The saving power of Jesus' death is contained right here in the diamond-hard reality of this *est."* [42] If God himself had not died on the cross, but only a martyr, then we would still be in our sins. In view of the reductionist christology of Neo-Protestantism and liberal theology one must say, if Jesus *is* not *himself* God, but only a man particularly and intensively united with God, or only the word of God, or only a man in whom God appears or reveals himself, then the salvation act of God in Christ would simply be deception. The saving act of Jesus Christ is thrown into question if his union with God is not a unity of being or essence *(est)*, but seen only as a unity of will, appearance, revelation, action, or word. When the Reformers in CA 3 speak about Christ as "truly God" *("vere deus")* and refer to his "divine nature" *("divina natura")*, they are not just assuming church tradition in a superficial way. Without Jesus' unity of *being* with the Father the justification of sinners would be an illusion.

One must consider whether the concept of "nature" can still be used today. In the time of the Reformation it was understood, but today the meaning is no longer so clear. Today "nature" has not only the sense of "essence" or "way of being," but also characterizes an area of reality subordinate to or even in contrast to "person," such as something which is universally accessible and capable of being objective, neutral, a disposition, a character, a fashion, or a concrete material thing. It is clear that the concept of "nature" with these kinds of meanings can hardly be applied to christology. Even the christology of the early church recognized a certain degree of flexibility in its language. The real sense of the "divine and human nature" seems best to be conveyed with the terms "true God" and "true man."

3.3. Christology and Justification

The purpose of Christ's act is, as already stated, reconciliation: ". . . that he might reconcile the Father to us and be a sacrifice. . . ." [43] It is not simply that *we* should be reconciled, but that the *Father* should be reconciled to us. Reconciliation is propitiation. God is not only subject, but also object of the reconciliation. The German text says, ". . . to propitiate God's wrath *(Gottes zorn versohnet)*." [44] The propitiatory sacrifice of Christ is in the center of the exposition of the Second Article of the Creed in the *Small Catechism,* as well as in CA 4: justification takes place—as it is twice stressed in CA 4—*"propter Christum,"* "on account of Christ." The *propter Christum* refers to the sacrifice of Jesus: "on account of Christ, who by his death made satisfaction for our sins *(propter Christum, qui sua morte pro nostris peccatis satisfecit)*." [45] This statement is the very middle and peak of CA 4, which in turn is the middle and peak of the CA. The Confession stands and falls with CA 4, but CA 4 stands and falls with CA 3, including its relation to CA 1. As a matter of fact, Christian theology stands and falls with justification. But justification stands and falls with Jesus Christ, for there is no reconciliation without propitiation. God's

forgiveness is not just an act of kindness, but truly a giving of himself
(condescendence). In the CA soteriology is not only the goal of christology, but christology is the foundation of soteriology. On this foundation soteriology stands and falls. Jesus Christ, who justifies *"sola
gratia sola fide"* ("by grace, by faith"), is the foundation word of the
Reformation.[46] Moreover, not only Jesus Christ in general, but Christ
as *vere deus* and *vere homo* ("truly God, truly man") and therefore as
propitiary sacrifice.

3.4. Salvation as Battle

With the statement that Jesus Christ is "a sacrifice not only for
original guilt but also for all the actual sins of men," [47] the first part
of this article ends, that part which marks the division between the
"state of humiliation" of Christ and his "state of exaltation." The
thrust of this sentence (as also in CA 24, 21-22) is against the notion
that Jesus Christ accomplished his sacrifice only for original sin, whereas the sacrifice of the Mass achieves the expiation for actual sins. Christ
is the single propitiary sacrifice for sins, and therefore the Reformation
understands the Lord's Supper not as a sacrificial offering but rather
as a thank-offering. The Apology (24, 9-88 [BC 250-265]) makes
this quite clear.[48]

The description of the "state of exaltation," as well as the "state
of humiliation," is closely related to the Apostles' Creed. The "state
of exaltation" begins in the CA with the descent to hell, as it does
in later Lutheran theology, in contrast to the Reformed tradition. The
descent to hell according to Luther is an act of war. Christ "strikes"
at the devil, "storms" hell and "seizes his own out of hell." [49] In CA
3 the death of Christ is explained, but the resurrection is simply mentioned without further explanation. It fades practically into the shadow
of the cross, a deficit not only in CA 3 and the Lutheran confessional
writings, but of western theology in general. However, CA 3 does go
further than the Apostles' Creed in adding that Christ will "forever
reign *(regnet)* and have dominion *(dominetur)* over all creatures
[compare the closing sentence of the Nicene Creed, Article Two!], and
sanctify those who believe in him by sending the Holy Spirit into their
hearts to rule, comfort, and quicken them and defend them against the
devil *(adversus diabolum)* and the power of sin *(vim peccati)*." [50] Salvation is understood here as an action of battle and under no circumstances as just a forensic-imputative act. According to L. Pinomaa,
"The motif of battle against the powers of corruption is the primary

emphasis in Luther's christology." [51] This emphasis comes to the fore
also in the exposition to the Second Article of the Creed in the Small
Catechism, and particularly the Large Catechism. In the same manner
the themes of Christ as victor *(Christus victor)* and salvation as an act
of battle are important elements of the theology of the Apology (Apol.
2, 46-50 and 4, 189-193 [BC 106 and 133]). Furthermore, cf. Section 5 below for a theological interpretation of the eschatological
statements, and cf. the comments of G. Müller and V. Pfnür on CA
4-6 for the pneumatological references, pp. 129ff.

3.5. Assumption Christology?

One often assumes an "assumption" christology in CA 3.[52] At the
outset it is stated that "the Word—that is, the Son of God—*took on*
man's nature *(assumpserit humanam naturam)."* The German text,
however, is somewhat different, stating simply that "God the Son became man." [53] The word "assumed" *("assumpserit")* does not occur in
the German text, and suggests that even in the Latin text one should
not read too much into it. It is apparently used merely to describe the
incarnation.[54] The assumption motif is also missing from the Schwabach
and Marburg Articles. W. Maurer writes that "the 'assumption motif' is
not really a part of Luther's own thought." [55] Nevertheless, an influence from the Athanasian Creed is reasonable, since its theology of unity
had an enduring influence on CA 1. There the assumption motif
emerges in the context of the theology of unity. Concerning Christ,
it states that he is "not two Christs but one Christ: one, that is to say,
not by changing the Godhead into flesh but by taking on the humanity
into God *(adsumptione humanitatis in Deo)."* [56] The context is the
"unity in one person *(unitas personae),"* [57] a concept which CA 3 takes
from the Athanasian Creed and which in both the Athanasian Creed
as well as the CA follows the idea of assumption. Both Luther—as
shown above—and Melanchthon stressed the unity of the person of
Christ. The best guarantee of maintaining the unity of the person of
Christ is through the christology of assumption.[58]

3.6. Basis and Limits of Theological Statements Concerning Mary

In contrast to the christological tradition of the Middle Ages, Mary
seems to play only a marginal role in CA 3. The basic motif of the CA
(cf. 2, 3 [BC 29]) and the Lutheran confessional writings (cf. Apol.
4, 2; 21; 44; FC, Epitome, 3, 10 [BC 107; 110; 113; 474]), namely the
honor of Christ and his exclusive function as mediator (cf. CA 21, 4;

Apol. 21, 14-31 [BC 229; 230-233]) appears to eliminate any kind
of Mariology. Nonetheless, the virgin Mary is mentioned twice in crucial statements: ". . . took on man's nature in the womb of the blessed
virgin Mary *(assumpserit humanam naturam in utero beatae Mariae
virginis)*" and "was born of the virgin Mary *(natus ex virgine Maria)*." [59] In CA 21, 1 (BC 46) and above all in the Apol. 21, 4-9 (BC
229-230) one can find the beginnings of an evangelical way of honoring the saints, a "threefold honor" *("triplex honos")*. This would
of course also apply to Mary, and one cannot dismiss this as simply a
minimal gesture. Luther writes in the Latin text of the Smalcald Articles about Christ, who was "out of Mary pure, holy and always (!)
virgin Mary *(ex Maria pura, sancta, semper virgine)*." [60] Similarly in
the Formula of Concord Mary is described as always virgin *(semper
virgo)*. Mary is called "the most blessed virgin," who

did not conceive a mere, ordinary human being, but a human being who
is truly the Son of the most high God. . . . [who] demonstrated his divine
majesty even in his mother's womb in that he was born of a virgin without
violating her virginity. Therefore she is truly the mother of God and yet
remained a virgin.[61]

Here Mariology is strictly christocentric, as it also is in the writings of
Luther. Luther's attitude toward Mary in his exposition of the Magnificat (1521) is revealing. It is strongly determined by his theology of
condescension: God, who looks not into the heavens, but below, looks
upon "the poor, disdained, plain maiden." Thus she praises neither her
own worthiness nor her unworthiness, but only "the favor of God."
With Mary it is clear that all is grace and that humanity lives from
grace alone. Precisely for this reason Mary has a special place,[62] and
is an "example of faith." [63] The intercession of Mary is not denied in
the confessional writings (cf. Apol. 21, 27 [BC 232]).

In today's theological situation this results in a strong basis of agreement with the renewed Roman Catholic consideration of Mary.[64] From
this basis we can approach anew the dogmas which still present difficulties, such as the "Immaculate Conception" (1854) and the "Bodily
Assumption into Heaven" (1950). G. Kretschmar and R. Laurentin
deal with the question of honoring the saints, below, pp. 262ff.

3.7. The Position of the Confutation

The Confutation to the CA accepted the First and Third Articles
of the CA in their entirety with no reservations.[65] It declared that

CA 1 in every aspect corresponds with the norm of faith and agrees with the Roman Church *("eorum confessio acceptanda est eo, quod per omnia ad normam fidei et cum Romana concordat ecclesia")*.[66] The agreement with the rejection of the heresies is specifically noted. The small differences in the "catalog of heresies" are virtually without significance; for example, in the Confutation the Muslims are not mentioned. The same is true for CA 3: there is nothing in the christological statements which might harm faith; the entire christological confession agrees with the Apostles' Creed and the true rule of faith *("in tertio articulo nihil est, quod offendat, cum tota confessio cum symbolo apostolorum et cum recta fidei regula conveniat")*.[67] The Apology needed therefore only to underscore the agreement on these two articles, whereby the binding character of the doctrine of faith from the ancient church is crucially reinforced because it is "firmly, surely, and irrefutably" based upon the Scriptures; "We steadfastly maintain that those who believe otherwise do not belong to the church of Christ but are idolaters and blasphemers." [68]

These factors are evidence that the two sides were united in these underlying principles of the Christian confession. One cannot overestimate this consensus when one considers the basic significance which CA 1 and CA 3 have for the rest of the CA. Here are the foundations for the "catholicity" of the CA. According to the opinion of both parties the separation does not extend into this basis.

4. The Contemporary Situation

This agreement described above is not at all self-evident. In view of the way the consensus has continued into subsequent history, it achieves a new significance which is not yet fully developed.[69]

The contribution of the period of Protestant Orthodoxy to the doctrine of the Trinity and to christology is on the whole more reproductive than productive. It consists partially at least in the not unimportant conceptual exposition and clarification of the thought of the traditional material in its relation to Scholastic-Aristotelian logic and ontology.[70] It should not be forgotten—as the modern research has emphasized[71]—that Orthodoxy formulated Lutheran theology with an original approach to metaphysical thought. In Neo-Protestantism the doctrine of the Trinity was in part simply given up or limited to an economical trinitarian view. With the concept of an immanent Trinity the unity of being between Jesus and the Father disappeared, and in its place emerged a unity of will,[72] a unity of revelation or a unity of word.[73] In the Enlightenment and in Neo-Protestantism Jesus was viewed in various ways merely as example or prototype of the human being. As a rule the notion of satisfaction was rejected. These characteristics of Neo-Protestant and liberal christology have had a strong effect in contemporary Protestant theology (cf. for example F. Gogarten, R. Bultmann, P. Tillich).

On the other side, the dogma of the ancient church was once again taken up in a largely positive way by evangelical theology after World War I, ever since the "dialectical" trend set in. This is similar to what happened earlier in the repristination and confessional theology of the 19th century. An explicit denial of the dogma of the early church is rare (cf. P. Tillich, D. Soelle). However, in spite of its formal and legal acceptance, it appears not to have been given the rank it deserves. Actually it often plays only a marginal role. Functional descriptions are commonplace which are not false, but in themselves are hardly sufficient. (These include such statements as, "Jesus belongs wholly on the side of God . . . God's ultimate revelation . . . God's Word.") Not infrequently the expressions about the identity of essence and divinity of Jesus Christ are abbreviated or simply supplanted. There are of course thoroughly understandable historical problems in the transmission of this dogma to the consciousness of our time. But this loss and obscuring must be openly addressed, particularly in connection with an interpretation of the CA.

Finally, we should look at three of the rather official trinitarian-Christological documents of our time.

The Barmen Declaration makes the exclusiveness of Jesus Christ prominent above all: "Jesus Christ . . . is the one Word of God which we hear, in whom we are to trust and obey in life and in death." Unfortunately the confessions of the ancient church are not expressly named, though they are assumed in the reference to the "confessions of the Reformation." [74]

The "Basis" of the Constitution of the World Council of Churches clearly refers to the dogma of the ancient church, in stating that the Council is "a fellowship of churches which confess Jesus Christ as God and Savior according to the Holy Scriptures and thus aspire to fulfill together that to which they are called, to the glory of God the Father, the Son and the Holy Spirit." [75]

The "Concord of Reformation Churches in Europe" (Leuenberg Concord) confesses the "common understanding of the gospel of Jesus

Christ . . . as the incarnate one, through whom God has bound himself to human beings." Furthermore, the Concord states that the condemnations made between Reformation groups in the 16th century in the area of christology should no longer stand as divisions between these churches.[76]

In this context one should recall that the Evangelical Church in Germany (EKD) and its members stand expressly "on the foundation of the confession of the ancient church" (cf. the Preamble to the Constitution of the EKD, July 13, 1948).

Naturally the same is true for the United Evangelical Lutheran Church in Germany (cf. the Constitution of Dec. 31, 1948) and also for the Evangelical Church of the Union (cf. the Order of Dec. 12, 1953, Article 4).

In the opinion of H. Asmussen, the Roman Catholic Church did not experience the drift away from the dogma of the ancient church which we find in Protestant theology since the Enlightenment.[77] One can surely agree with that, although there is no cause for triumph (cf. below, 6.1 and 6.3.1.). Of course, in Catholicism since Vatican II the acknowledgement of the christological confession of the early church is no longer simply self-evident. It is possible, for example, for H. Küng to express substantial reservations,[78] although one must of course not overlook the various clarifications from the teaching office of the church.[79] Even though there are no expressed denials of the ancient dogma, there are ambiguous and unclear formulations, particularly in the area of popular theology.

5. The Text of CA 17: The Return of Christ to Judgment

The Third Article with its christological focus sets the key for the whole Confession. This is true also for the eschatological dimensions of the Christian faith, which mention especially the kingship of Christ and his return. The unity of the person and work of Jesus Christ from the incarnation to his second coming should be emphasized. CA 17 picks up the conclusion of CA 3 and should therefore be dealt with here.

5.1. The Placement of CA 17

The statement about the coming of Jesus Christ in CA 17 forms the conclusion of the christologically accented pattern of CA 1-17, which is laid out in a trinitarian way and then progresses in a line corresponding to the history of salvation.[80] This displays an inner unity, but also a certain difference from the Apostles' and Nicene Creeds, both of which are oriented more strongly around the statements about the three persons. CA 3 integrates the basic statement about the Holy Spirit as gift and connects it with the sovereignty of the exalted Lord.[81] In contrast to Luther's Confession of 1528, there are no difficulties with concluding this section with the coming of Christ to judgment; this is due to the order of the CA which follows the sequence of salvation history. CA 17 brings together two articles of the classical confession of faith, namely, the second coming of Jesus Christ (end of Second Article) and the faith in the resurrection and eternal life (end of Third Article). Moreover, there is also an inner connection between CA 16 (civil affairs) and CA 17: the whole political life stands under the sign of the second coming of Jesus Christ.[82] From many points of view CA 17 has a theologically thoroughly reasonable and important position.[83]

5.2. Historical Background and Basic Theological Elements

The content of CA 17 was not at all controversial between the traditional Roman Catholics and the Reformers. There was no issue here; rather the teaching of the church should simply be confessed. Similarities can also be seen between this formulation and the Apostles' Creed and also the doctrinal declaration of the Fourth Lateran Council (1215),[84] which are already in the background of CA 3. A connection not only with the tradition of the early church but also that of the medieval church is again apparent. Thus it is not surprising that the Confutation agrees without reservation[85] and that the Apology acknowledges this agreement.[86]

CA 17 has a positive and a negative side. In its positive description of the doctrine, the basic elements are listed briefly: the return of Jesus Christ to judgment and the resurrection of all the dead, the granting of eternal life and joy to the believers and elect, and the condemnation of the godless and the devil to eternal punishment. The differences between the German text "our Lord Jesus Christ will return on the last day *(unser Herr Jesus Christus am jüngsten Tag Kummen wird)*" and the Latin text "at the consummation of the world Christ will appear *(Christus apparebit in comsummatione mundi)*" are not substantial. In contrast to the Apostles' Creed the CA stresses the eternal punishment of the godless and the devil. Due to some of the trends of that time going in the opposite direction, Luther's Confession of 1528 and the Schwabach Articles make a point of the eternal division between the believers and the godless.[87]

The second, negative part of the article deals with two opponents: the Anabaptists who had incorporated a teaching long before rejected, namely, the restoration of all things at the end of time (*apokatastasis,* in connection with Acts 3:21),[88] and groups of Jewish origin, which awaited an earthly "thousand-year" rule in this world preceding the resurrection of the dead.[89]

There was a reason for including this article in the CA as a precaution: the reformers wanted to protect themselves from being taken for one of these enthusiastic and apocalyptic sectarian groups.

The Anabaptists are condemned also here in sweeping terms with no reservation.[90] The apocalyptic spiritualism with its expectation of an earthly kingdom of God had given new life to the heritage of the various types of ancient Baptist movements following the suppression of the Peasants' Uprising.[91] The Anabaptist A. Bader, who came originally from Augsburg, was familiar with these expectations concerning the future of the Jews from Leipheim and Worms. He had announced Easter, 1530, as the start of the millennial reign. He had been executed in the spring of 1530, in Stuttgart, but in March of that year his confessions had been published in Augsburg. In this context one recalls also the work of M. Rinck, H. Hut, H. Denk, H. Leupold, J. Nespitzer, and others.[92] Finally, the emergence and effect of Thomas Müntzer also contributed to the Reformers' desire to prevent anyone from confusing them with these revolutionary–apocalyptic groups.[93]

5.3. Continuing Significance

There has not been a uniform interpretation of the meaning of the eschatological comments in CA 3 and 17, as well as in the other confessional writings. In the opinion of H. Asmussen, "In the whole of the Confession this article does not play an important role."[94] W. Maurer sees behind these articles (looking at them from Luther's own viewpoint) a "theology of the kingdom of God" never before articulated in this manner.[95] E. Schlink[96] and H. Fagerberg detect in these eschatological comments a hermeneutical key: eschatological concerns permeate and color all the other doctrinal themes.

The strong eschatological expectation of the period 1520-1530 can be noted in the text, and also in Luther's Confession of 1528.[97] However, it is not only subdued, but also sobered. Moreover, such comments are set in the framework of the traditional doctrine of the last things.

Perhaps on two points there is a new accent: (1) In CA 3 the heavenly Lord rules over all creatures until the judgment. The "interval" between the ascension of the Lord and his second coming is given a theologically positive quality. There are indications here of a theology of history. (2) One must pay close attention to the connection between CA 16 and 17. The order of these two articles is apparently consciously made, since in the Schwabach Articles it is the opposite. Worldly affairs are now so placed that the end of time and Christ's second coming are always on the horizon. "We are political beings, only as we know that this world will come to an end." [98]

These articles were not then, nor are now, controversial among the churches. They contain a basic claim and admonition for theology and piety, Christian life-style and the church's presentation of itself. The proclamation of the judgment has not infrequently been obscured in Christian churches by an almost subconscious faith in a world which is steadily progressing toward perfection. This obscuring also takes place by a secularization of eschatological tenets.[99] The connection of civil affairs and eschatology in the CA could contribute to an even more substantial restoration of lost ground.[100] This would be important, in order to establish more clearly the provisional character of politics in the face of totalitarian claims.[101] Finally, a renewed interest in eschatology makes it possible to hope that one may deal more irenically with the problem which the Confession omitted (in contrast to the Apology), namely, the Roman Catholic doctrine of purgatory.[102]

6. Challenging Questions

The consensus concerning CA 1 and 3 could make us complacent, since indeed there has been a consensus since 1530 to the present. In reality, however, it calls forth a series of questions.

6.1. Questions to both Lutherans and Roman Catholics

The Roman Catholic and Lutheran churches are united in acknowledging CA 1 and 3. The theological developments in our era and the actual christological discussions have made it clear that this unanimity is no insignificant matter. In 1975, for the 1650th Anniversary of the Council of Nicaea the Evangelical Church of Germany (EKD) and the German Roman Catholic Bishops' Conference published statements concerning the church's confession of Christ.[103] Unfortunately these received far too little attention. They cleared up much misunder-

standing on both sides and revealed a surprisingly broad convergence
of opinion.

At the same time, however, both statements made it apparent that
a great deal of intellectual effort is necessary for the effective interpretation of this confession of Christ. One has the impression that the
dogma of the ancient church is maintained formally and officially with
no reservations, but that it lives more in solemn preambles and repeated affirmations rather than in daily proclamation and instruction.
The same is true also for contemporary theology. Thus far theologians
have hesitated to engage in a strong, systematic, and renewed interpretation. Contemporary theologians have also tended to designate ancient
dogma with a "hellenistic" label[104] and have made too little use of
the rich new research into the history of dogma.[105] Instead they have
somewhat oversimplified and made it too easy for themselves by constantly and rather vaguely referring to the "failure of traditional forms
of thought" (cf. the "Leuenberg Concord" with its christological formulations). The early church, the medieval church, and the Reformation
church were conscious that its faith stood or fell with the great trinitarian and christological decisions. Both Protestants and Roman Catholics might well ask whether the same is true for them today.

In addition, there is a whole series of particular questions to both
Protestants and Catholics. The following is just one example: Does
the resurrection have the same importance in the CA and the western
tradition as it does in the New Testament? Is it not overshadowed by
the cross and sacrificial death of Jesus, even though in the New Testament it is fully as important as an act of salvation?

6.2. Questions from Roman Catholics to Lutherans

6.2.1.   The churches of the Reformation acknowledge the confessions of the ancient church. But since the CA is no longer "merely" a
witness to the catholicity of the evangelical faith—its original intent—
but has now become a document of church division, the question
arises how the Lutherans see themselves in view of this deep break with
the uninterrupted connection with the Apostles, a connection which
these ancient confessions are a part of.[106] Can the Protestant side continue to hold to the ancient dogma without also feeling a pull toward a
"communion" with the ancient church with its ecclesial basis and its
episcopal structure? How do the Reformation churches understand
their continuity with the ancient and medieval church? (cf. also this

problem in terms of CA 5, 14, and 28 as examined by A. Dulles and G. Lindbeck, pp. 147ff.).

6.2.2. The reception of the substance of the ancient confessions produces similarly structured questions. Does not the exclusive *sola scriptura* principle contradict the inclusive scriptural principle of the Lutheran Confessions, as it is expressed for example in the acknowledgement of the ancient dogma? Is there not here (as well as in the question of the canon, for example) an overlapping from the issue of the transmission of faith, which theologically has not been sufficiently worked out?

6.2.3. CA 1 and 3 are shaped deeply from the soteriological question. Is it not worthy of note that precisely with this basic orientation the relationship of the triune God and the Christ event to the church, to sanctification, to faith, to hope and love (with its fruits), and to the ecclesiastical office is missing? Are we not threatened with the danger of isolating the Christ *extra nos* and *pro nobis* at the expense of the Christ *in nobis?* Of course this does not refer to an existentializing or subjectivizing of the *pro nobis,* which has dominated chiefly since the end of the 18th century.[107]

6.3. Questions from Lutherans to Roman Catholics

6.3.1. The Roman Catholic Church and its theology has of course remained formally true to the ancient dogmas. Yet one can still ask whether this heritage is not infrequently understood as an obvious "possession" rather than a responsibility to realize its intellectual and spiritual content. Does not maintaining this heritage often take place at the expense of indispensable intellectual challenges? Finally, does one not occasionally receive the impression that theology and official ecclesiastical pronouncements have so often dimmed the soteriological and doxological background of the ancient confessions and have thus confirmed the disastrous interpretation that such pronouncements are directed toward a predominantly speculative interest? Has the Roman Catholic Church and its theology encountered the historical task with inner strength and intellectual vigor, positively and aggressively, and not only in an apologetic-defensive fashion, particularly in view of contemporary theological developments?

6.3.2. The Roman Catholic Church has recognized Jesus Christ as sole bringer of salvation—in ancient dogma, the subsequent Councils, and above all at Trent and in Vatican II. There is a tension between that view and any emphasis on human cooperation in the mediation of salvation and the various ways in which salvation might come. How can the unique place of Jesus Christ be made compatible with papal infallibility (1870) and the recent dogmas about Mary (1854, 1950), as well as the Catholic piety surrounding Mary and the many forms of venerating the saints?

6.3.3.   According to its own understanding of itself, the church of the Lutheran Reformation is a part of the catholic and even the Roman Catholic Church, as CA 1 and 3 show. The far-reaching common basis of the ancient confessions has never been questioned by either side. Why does the Roman Catholic Church not draw out the consequences of this fact and give greater regard to the "catholic" content of the evangelical confessions? Phrased very pointedly: Do the Roman Catholics acknowledge the Lutherans as "catholics"? Are they themselves really "catholic"?

7. Result: Common Heritage as Gift and Task

7.1.   The contents of CA 1, 3, and 17 come in large measure from the classic confessions of faith. Therefore the confession of a triune God and Jesus Christ, the Son of God, as Savior and Judge are not dogmatically controversial between the two churches. Because these articles form the weight-bearing foundation and inner outline of the entire Confession, this consensus—which has never been limited— simply cannot be valued highly enough.

7.2.   This is at the same time a confession of the faith of the ancient church. Since the tradition of ancient Christianity is not infrequently transmitted and received in the witnesses of the later, western church, further lines of connection and continuity with the Roman Church are apparent in the CA. Naturally serious questions also arise at this point (cf. above, 6.2 and 6.3).

7.3.   This common tradition does not consist in occasional items, but is apparent in the basic structures and often in the very unfolding of theological thought, such as, for example, in soteriology. The CA affirms this from inner conviction, not for any reasons of strategy or compulsion.

7.4.   Thus especially CA 1 and 3 are a solid foundation for the "catholicity" of the CA. The unanimity of the confession of the triune

God and Jesus as the Son of God is so central that one can speak of an unbroken center of the common Christian faith. In terms of the basic foundation of Christianity, the division among those parties assembled in Augsburg did not go as deep as these roots.

7.5.   There are therefore in the CA essential elements which need no recognition, for instance, from the Roman Catholic Church. They are already a reliable part of our common faith. Precisely for this reason, however, they are also a decisive challenge for us.

7.6.   History has shown that this confession of the triune God and of Jesus Christ as the Son, "being of one substance" with the Father, can be pushed off to the periphery theologically and practically in spite of its formal status and solemn declarations to the contrary. The acceptance of the ancient dogma by the CA was not simply a rote reproduction of the formulae. In many ways, however, new accents served as means to break the ancient confessions apart.

7.7.   On the other hand, an orthodoxy merely literally faithful could not adequately transmit the inner strength of these basic trinitarian and christological affirmations. Thus there is in our common heritage an ecumenical potential which has not yet been unfolded as much as it should be. Both Roman Catholics and Lutherans should take up the obligation within and among themselves to deal with these confessions, so that this potential might summon forth from the middle of our common faith a communion which has not yet been sufficiently revealed.

Notes

1. Additional comments can be found in H. G. Pöhlmann, *Rechtfertigung: Die geganwärtige kontroverstheologische Problematik der Rechtfertigungslehre zwischen der evangelisch-lutherischen und der römisch-katholischen Kirche* (Gütersloh: 1971), pp. 63-74. Concerning Luther's dialectic between law and gospel, cf. AE 27, 183ff. (WA 2, 466-467).
2. Cf. these concepts in F.H.R. Frank's book, *System der christlichen Wahrheit* (Erlangen: 1878-1880, 1894); trans. available under the title *System of Christian Certainty* (Edinburgh: T. and T. Clark, 1886).
3. K. Schmidt-Clausen, *Die Confessio Augustana als katholisches Grundbekenntnis der lutherischen Reformation: Vorträge auf den Michaeliskonferenzen der Kirchlichen Sammlung* (1978), p. 5.
4. *Die christliche Lehre von der Rechtfertigung und Versöhnung*, vol. 1 (Bonn: 1888-1889), p. 147.

5. *Lehrbuch der Dogmengeschichte,* vol. 3 (Darmstadt: 1964), p. 874; trans.: *History of Dogma,* vol. 7 (New York: Russell and Russell, 1958), p. 242.

6. Apol. 1, 2 (BSLK 145, German; CT 102, German [BC, 100]); cf. the rebuke in CA 1, 5-6 (BC 28).

7. *Warum noch lutherische Kirche? Ein Gespräch mit dem Augsburgischen Bekenntnis* (Stuttgart: 1949), p. 33.

8. Cf. L. Grane, *Die Confessio Augustana: Einführung in die Hauptgedanken der lutherischen Reformation* (Göttingen: 1970), p. 19; H. Fagerberg, *A New Look at the Lutheran Confessions (1529-1537)* (St. Louis: Concordia, 1972), p. 112. Historians agree that Luther did on occasion express himself in a careless and offhand manner on the christological dogma of the ancient church. Concerning Luther's christology, cf. D. Vorländer, *Deus incarnatus: Die Zweinaturenchristologie Luther bis 1521* (Witten: 1974); M. Lienhard, *Luther: Témoin de Jésus-Christ: Les étapes et les thèmes de la christologie du Réformateur,* in *Cogitatio fidei* (Paris: 1973), pp. 311ff.; R. Jansen, *Studien zu Luthers Trinitätslehre* (Bern-Frankfurt: 1976). These works include bibliographies.

9. AE 32, 244 (WA 8, 117-118).

10. W. Maurer, *Historischer Kommentar zur Confessio Augustana,* vol. 1: Einleitung und Ordnungsfragen; vol. 2: *Theologische Probleme* (Gütersloh: 1976-1978). To this point, cf. vol. 2, p. 11.

11. P. Althaus, *The Theology of Martin Luther* (Philadelphia: Fortress, 1966), p. 7.

12. *On the Councils and the Church* (1539), AE 41, 83 (WA 50, 572, 26-27).

13. Formula of Concord, Epitome, Comprehensive Summary, Rule, and Norm, 2 (BC 464-465).

14. E. Schlink, *Theology of the Lutheran Confessions* (Philadelphia: Muhlenberg, 1961), p. 62.

15. Large Catechism 1, 24-25 (BC 367-368).

16. L. Grane, *op cit.,* p. 21; cf. in the Large Catechism 2, 65 (BC 419).

17. *Ibid., p.* 22.

18. *Spiritus Creator: Studien zu Luthers Theologie* (Munich: 1954), p. 180. Whether this judgment can be substantiated is historically not yet clear. It hardly applies, for instance, to Thomas Aquinas, who preserves many salvation-history elements from the theology of the Greek fathers.

19. In the place of rational speculation (such as, "If God would have said . . .") it is the truth of Scripture which forms for Luther the foundation of the Trinity. Cf. for example, WA 34, 500.

20. *Op. cit.,* p. 35.

21. A. Peters, *"Geistliche Kernentscheidungen sowie theologische Mängel im Augsburgischen Bekenntnis,"* in *Die Confessio Augustana als Frage an die getrennten Kirchen. 11. Kirchberger Gespräch der Evangelischen Michaelsbruderschaft 13.-16. April 1978: Rundbrief der Evangelischen Michaelsbruderschaft. Sonderheft* (1978), pp. 33-55, to this point p. 42.

22. Augustine was primarily responsible for the introduction of the *essentia* concept in the doctrine about God. Cf. A. Adam, *Lehrbuch der Dogmengeschichte,* vol. 1 (Gütersloh: 1965), p. 279; the historical development until then, which reaches back into the Septuagint version of Exod. 3:14, is both varied and instructive. Cf. above all R. Braun, *"Deus*

christianorum." Recherches sur le vocabulaire doctrinal de Tertullien (Paris: 1972), pp. 167ff., 579-580; J. Moingt, *Théologie trinitiare de Tertullian* in *Théologie* 68-70, 75 (Paris: 1966-1969), above all pp. 368ff., 405, 414; Chr. Stead, *Divine Substance* (Oxford, 1977), pp. 28-29, 70-71, 77ff. The hesitation toward accepting this concept with the changes in thinking it brought about is a part of this early history.

23. *Melanchthons Werke.* R. Stupperich, ed., vol. II/1, *Loci Communes* of 1521; *Loci praecipui theologici* of 1559 (first part), H. Engellund, ed. (Gütersloh: 1952), p. 181 (or: CR 21, 613).

24. Cf. L. Grane, *op. cit.,* p. 18. Philo had already spoken of a similar triad: God as the Father of all things, wisdom as the mother of all things, and the logos as the soul of the world. (*De fuga,* pp. 109-110). Or he sees the divine wisdom as the mediating dynamic between the highest powers of the divinity—goodness and omnipotence (*De Cherubim,* pp. 27-28). Cf. to this A. Adam, *op. cit.,* p. 121.

25 L. Grane, *op. cit.,* p. 23. Cf. also H. W. Genischen, *Damnamus: Die Verwerfung der Irrlehre bei Luther und im Luthertum des. 16 Jahrhunderts* (Berlin: 1955), pp. 65ff.

26. Cf. L. Grane, *op. cit.,* p. 23.

27. AE 41, 80ff. (WA 50, 569ff.).

28. AE 41, 80 (WA 50, 569, 20).

29. CA 1, 5 (BC 28).

30. CA 1, 1-3 (BSLK 50; CT 102-103).

31. CA 1, 2 (BC 27). The Latin reads: *"creator et conservator omnium rerum, visibilium et invisibilium"* (BSLK 50; CT 102).

32. Cf. H. Fagerberg, *op. cit.,* p. 113. Cf. BC 19ff. for the text of the Athanasian Creed.

33. Cf. more specifically in LThK ², vol. 5, pp. 607-609 and RGG ³, vol. 1, pp. 1774-1775 and vol. 6, p. 1964.

34. CA 3, 2 (BC 29; cf. BSLK 54 or CT 44 for Latin). Cf. L. Grane, *op cit.,* p. 33. For Zwingli, cf. the newest work, G. W. Locher, *Die Zwinglische Reformation im Rahmen der europäischen Kirchengeschichte* (Göttingen: 1979), pp. 206ff., 315; for *"allöosis"* cf. pp. 207, 312, 314, 638.

35. CA 3, 2-6 (BC 29-30).

36. BC 589-599. Cf. AE 37, 209ff. (WA 26, 319ff.).

37. More details and further references can be found in V. Pfnür, *Einig in der Rechtfertigungslehre?, Veröffentlichungen des Instituts für Europäische Geschichte Mainz,* vol. 60 (Wiesbaden: 1970), p. 102 with footnotes 611 and 613, concerning CA 1 see p. 101, footnote 689.

38. CA 3, 2 (BC 29-30).

39. CA 3, 2-3 (BC 29-30).

40. Solid Declaration 8, 44 (BC 599). Cf. AE 41, 103 (WA 50, 590).

41. AE 34, 210 (WA 50, 269, 4-5).

42. P. Brunner, *Pro Ecclesia: Gesammelte Aufsätze zur dogmatischen Theologie,* vol. 2 (Berlin, 1966), p. 72.

43. CA 3, 3 (BC 30).

44. CA 3, 3, German (BSLK 54; CT 44; Cf. BC 30).

45. CA 4, 2 (BC 30; for the Latin see BSLK 56 or CT 44).

46. For a further reference that the Reformation understands Jesus Christ

himself rather than justification as the "principle article" of church and theology, cf. H. G. Pöhlmann, *op. cit.*, pp. 25-39.

47. CA 3, 3 (BC 30).

48. To this question, including the position over against the decisions of the Council of Trent, cf. below under the commentary to CA 10: "The Sacraments: Baptism and Lord's Supper," pp. 202ff.

49. WA 37, 63; on this matter cf. W. Mass, *Gott und die Hölle: Studien zum Descensus Christi* (Einsiedeln: 1979), pp. 273ff.

50. CA 3, 4-5 (BC 30; for the Latin see BSLK 54 or CT 44).

51. *Sieg des Glaubens: Grundlinien der Theologie Luthers* (Göttingen: 1964). p. 87 and cf. esp. pp. 82ff.

52. H. Fagerberg, *op. cit.*, pp. 117-118, F. Brunstäd, *Theologie der lutherischen Bekenntnisschriften* (Gütersloh: 1951), p. 36.

53. CA 3, 1 (BC 29; for the Latin and German see BSLK 54 or CT 44).

54. Cf. L. Grane, *op. cit., p.* 32.

55. W. Maurer, *op. cit.*, vol. 2, p. 30.

56. Athanasian Creed 32-33 (BC 20; for the Latin see BSLK 30 or CT 34).

57. Athanasian Creed 34 (BC 20; for the Latin see BSLK 30 or CT 34).

58. F. Brunstäd derives "assumption" christology from "logos" christology and places it over against the "two-nature" christology, cf. *op. cit.*, p. 36.

59. CA 3, 1-2 (BC 29-30), the German text mentions Mary only once: "born of the virgin Mary *(geborn aus der reinen Jungfrauen Maria)*"; for the Latin and German texts see BSLK 54 or CT 44.

60. Smalcald Articles 1, 4 (BSLK 414; CT 460 [BC 291-292]).

61. FC, Solid Declaration 8, 24 (BC 595).

62. W. Maurer, *op. cit.*, vol. 2, p. 157.

63. *Das Magnificat, verdeutscht und ausgelegt durch D. Martin Luther, Herder-bücherei 175* (Freiburg i. Br.: 1964), pp. 33-34, 58, 71.

64. To this new development, cf. above all A. Müller, *"Marias Stellung und Mitwirkung im Christusereignis,"* in J. Feiner and M. Löhrer, eds., *Mysterium salutis: Grundriss heilsgeschichtlicher Dogmatik* (Einsiedeln: 1969), vol. III/2, pp. 393-510; Pope Paul VI, *"Apostolisches Schreiben über die rechte Weise und Förderung der Marienverehrung* (Marialis Cultus)," in *Nachkonziliare Dokumentation* 54 (Trier: 1975); J. Ratzinger, *Die Tochter Zion: Betrachtungen über den Marienglauben der Kirche* (Einsiedeln: 1977); W. Beinert, ed., *Maria heute ehren: Eine theologisch-pastorale Handreichung* (Freiburg: 1977).

On the evangelical side cf. R. Schimmelpfennig, *Die Geschichte der Marienverehrung im deutschen Protestantismus* (Paderborn: 1952); W. Tappolet, ed., *Das Marienlob der Reformatoren* (Tübingen: 1962); R. Mumm, *Geboren aus der Jungfrau Maria: Zur Verehrung der Mutter des Herrn in der evangelischen Christenheit,* in *Internationale katholische Zeitschrift Communio* 7 (1978), pp. 55-69 (with many further references); M. Thurian, *Maria* (Kassel: 1967). A shortened and reworked version of this last work appeared in English under the title *Mary Mother of all Christians* (New York: Herder and Herder, 1964).

65. Immenkötter, pp. 78-79, 82-83.

66. Immenkötter, p. 79.

67. Immenkötter, p. 83.

68. Apol. 1, 2 (BC 100).
69. For the christology and doctrine of the Trinity of the Formula of Concord, which are not dealt with fully here, cf. J. Baur, *Einsicht und Glaube* (Göttingen: 1978), pp. 189-205, and also pp. 112ff. Cf. also J. Schöne, ed., *Bekenntnis zur Wahrheit: Aufsätze über die Konkordienformel* (Erlangen: 1978), pp. 49ff. (F. Jacob), and pp. 101ff. (U. Asendorf).
70. Cf. H. Schmid, *Die Dogmatik der evangelisch-lutherischen Kirche dargestellt und des Quellen belegt,* neu herausgegeben und durchgesehen von H. G. Pöhlmann (Gütersloh: 1979), pp. 96ff.
71. Particularly for the christology, cf. W. Sparn, *Wiederkehr der Mataphysik: Die ontologische Frage in der lutherischen Theologie des frühen 17. Jahrhunderts,* in *Calwer Theologische Monographien* 4 (Stuttgart: 1976), pp. 203ff.
72. Among others cf. E. Troeltsch, *Glaubenslehre* (München: 1925), p. 105.
73. Among others cf. A. Ritschl, *op. cit.,* p. 367; W. Hermann, *Ethik* (Tübingen: 1913), pp. 124-125; and H. Stephan, *Glaubenslehre* (Giessen: 1922), p. 193.
74. Cf. to this Chr. Barth, *Bekenntnis im Werden: Neue Quellen zur Entstehung der Barmer Erklärung* (Neukirchen: 1979).
75. W. Theuer, *Die trinitarische Basis des Oekumenischen Rates der Kirchen* (Frankfurt, 1967).
76. To this M. Lienhard, *Lutherisch-reformierte Kirchengemeinschaft heute,* in *"Oekumenische Perspektiven* 2 (Frankfurt: 1972), pp. 28-29, 73, 105ff. Also H. M. Müller, *Der Lehrbegriff der Leuenberger Konkordie und die Frage der Kirchengemeinschaft,* in *Kerygma und Dogma* 25 (1979), pp. 2-16.
77. *Op cit.,* p. 59.
78. Here we are concerned also about the identity of substance, preexistence, and the confessions of the ancient church. Cf. for example, H. Küng, *On Being a Christian* (Garden City, New York: Doubleday, 1976), pp. 443ff., 447-450, and others. To the preceding cf. W. Jens, ed., *Um nichts als die Wahrheit: Deutsche Bischofskonferenz contra Hans Küng* (München: 1978), and *Dokumentation der schriftlichen Vorgänge zwischen Professor Dr. Hans Küng und der Deutschen Bischofskonferenz,* ed. by the *Pressedienst des Sekretariates der Deutschen Bischofskonference, Dokumentation Nr. XXXVIII/77* of Nov. 17, 1977 (81 pages).
79. Cf. particularly *"Erklärung zu dem Buch, 'Christ sein' von Professor Dr. Hans Küng,"* of Nov. 17, 1977, in *Schriftenreihe "Die Deutschen Bischöfe,"* Heft 13 (Bonn: 1977). Meanwhile, in a "clarification" of Dec. 15, 1979, the Roman Congregation on Faith ascertained that Dr. Hans Küng deviated from the complete truth of the Catholic faith and therefore no longer could be considered a Catholic theologian nor teach as such. The christological opinions (above all the expressly mentioned "equality of essence" of Jesus with the Father) certainly are not the formal basis for the withdrawal of Küng's ecclesial teaching right, but they were enumerated among the consequences which were attached to his weakening of the gift of infallibility in the church. This fact shows that the teaching office insists on the complete recognition of the classical christological confessions. On the preceding cf. *"Dokumentation der Bemühungen der Glaubenskon-*

gregation des Apostolischen Stuhles und der Deutschen Bischofskonferenz um sachgerechte Klärung der umstrittenen Auffassungen von Professor Dr. Hans Küng," ed. by the *Pressedienst des Sekretariates der Deutschen Bischofskonferenz,* 64 pp., with a continuation of Dec. 31, 1967 (in total 67 items).

80. Cf. to this V. Pfnür, *op. cit.,* pp. 97ff. (further literature there).

81. Cf. the Commentary of G. Müller and V. Pfnür to CA 4-6, pp. 117ff.

82. L. Grane, *op. cit.,* p. 132; H. Asmussen, *op. cit.,* p. 211; W. Maurer, *op. cit.,* vol. 2, pp. 41ff.

83. In opposition is H. Bornkamm, *Augsburger Bekenntnis,* in RGG [3], vol. 1, p. 735, who treats CA 17 with CA 16 and 21 as "single problems" as opposed to the three "thematic circles" (CA 1-3; 4-6 and 18-20; 7-8 and 9-15).

84. Cf. DS 801: *"Venturus in fine saeculi, iudicaturus vivos et mortuos, et redditurus singulis secundum opera sua, tam reprobis quam electis: qui omnes cum suis propriis resurgent corporibus, quae nunc gestant, ut recipiant secundum opera sua, sive bona fuerint sive mala, illi cum diabolo poenam perpetuam, et isti cum Christo gloriam sempiternam."* Unfortunately we lack space here for a more exact comparison.

85. Immenkötter, pp. 116-117.

86. Apol. 17 (BC 224).

87. CA 17 (English in BC 38; German and Latin in BSLK 72 or CT 50). Cf. for the development of CA 3 and 17 especially W. Maurer, *op. cit.,* vol. 1, pp. 41, 66; vol. 2, p. 17; L. Grane, *op. cit.,* pp. 134-135; on the text itself see BSLK 72, note 1.

88. In one of the preliminary drafts of the CA (NA 16, cf. BSLK 72) the name of Origen was mentioned: "the followers of Origen." So-called "Origenism" was often rejected in the early church; cf. DS403-411, 433, see also W. Maurer, *op. cit.,* vol. 2, p. 66.

89. Cf. BSLK 72, note 3, and Immenkötter, p. 116, note 48 (literature).

90. Maurer, *op. cit.,* vol. 1, pp. 64-65; *Gensichen, ibid.;* pp. 65ff.

91. Cf. the report of the research by K. Deppermann, *Melchior Hoffmann: Soziale Unruhen und apokalyptische Visionen im Zeitalter der Reformation* (Göttingen: 1979), pp. 9ff. (lit.); R. van Dülmen, *Reformation als Revolution: Soziale Bewegung und religiöser Radikalismus in der deutschen Reformation* (München: 1977); F. Seibt, *Utopica: Modelle totaler Sozialplanung* (Düsseldorf: 1972), pp. 48ff., 134ff.

92. Cf. also H. -J. Goertz, ed., *Umstrittenes Täufertum 1525-1975: Neue Forschungen* (Göttingen: 1975); Th. Nipperdey, *Reformation, Revolution, Utopie* (Göttingen: 1975).

93. Cf. W. Ellinger, *Thomas Müntzer, Leben und Werk* (Göttingen: 1976).

94. *Op. cit.,* p. 120.

95. *Op. cit.,* vol. 2, pp. 35ff., 40ff.

96. *Op. cit.,* pp. 270ff.

97. *Op. cit.,* p. 297.

98. H. Asmussen, *op. cit.,* p. 211.

99. Cf. K. Löwith, *Weltgeschichte und Heilsgeschehen* (Stuttgart: 1967); U. Ruh, *Säkularisierung* (Freiburg i. Br.: 1980).

100. Cf. to this J. Ratzinger, *Eschatologie—Tod und ewiges Leben* (Regens-

burg: 1977); P. Brunner, *Eschata,* in *Bemühungen um die einigende Wahrheit* (Göttingen: 1977), pp. 269-291; also the *Schreiben der Kongregation für die Glaubenslehre zu einigen Fragen der Eschatologie,* in *Verlautbarungen des Apostolischen Stuhls 11* (Bonn: 1979).

101. Also K. Lehmann, *Nicht nur im Jenseits—die Weltperspektive christlicher Zunkunftserwartung,* in *Ich will euch Zukunft und Hoffnung geben 85: Deutscher Katholikentag in Freiburg i. Br.* (Paderborn: 1978), pp. 480-492.

102. This question cannot be discussed here. Such an investigation should take into account the most recent Roman Catholic discussion about purgatory in U. Ruh's *Perspektiven der Eschatologie,* in *Herder-Korrespondenz* 33 (1979), pp. 229-253 (literature).

103. Cf. the declaration of the Council of the Evangelical Church of Germany (EKD), *"Das Christusbekenntnis der Kirche: Ein Wort zum Nicäa-Gedenktag 325-1975,"* in *KNA—Katholische Nachrichten Agentur—Oekumenische Information,* no. 24 (June 11: 1975), pp. 5-7; *"Erklärung der Deutschen Bischofskonferenz zum Christusbekenntnis von Nizäa,"* in *Die Deutschen Bischöfe,* Heft 5 (Bonn: 1975), also in *Herder-Korrespondenz* 29 (1975), pp. 558-560.

104. Cf. A. Grillmeier, *Mit ihm und in ihm: Christologische Forschungen und Perspektiven* (Freiburg i. Br.), pp. 423ff., 489ff.

105. For a summary see A. Grillmeier's *Christ in the Christian Tradition. From the Apostolic Age of Chalcedon (451)* (New York: Sheed and Ward, 1965). Cf. also B. Welte, ed., *Zur Frühgeschichte der Christologie,* in *Quaestiones disputatae 51* (Freiburg i. Br.: 1970); B. Lonergan, *The Way to Nicea: The Dialectical Development of Trinitarian Theology* (London: 1976); K. Lehmann, *"Dogmenhermeneutik am Beispiel der klassischen Christologie,"* in B. Casper et al., *Jesus-Ort der Erfahrung Gottes* (Freiburg i. Br.: 1977), pp. 190-209 (lit.).

106. To this problem cf. K. G. Steck, *Lehre und Kirche bei Luther* (Munich, 1963); W. Höhne, *Luthers Anschauungen über die Kontinuität der Kirche* (Berlin: 1963); H. Beintker, *Die Bedeutung der Tradition bei Luther und im Luthertum,* in *Kairos 21* (1979), pp. 1-29; and especially H. Rüchert, *Vorträge und Aufsätze zur historischen Theologie* (Tübingen: 1972), pp. 12-18.

107. Cf. to this H. J. Iwand, *"Wider den Missbrauch des 'pro me' als methodisches Prinzip in der Theologie,"* in *Evangelische Theologie 14* (1954), pp. 120-125; H. Gollwitzer, *Die Existenz Gottes im Bekenntnis des Glaubens* (Munich: 1963), pp. 52ff., 178ff.; W. Krenck, *"Das reformatorische 'pro me' und die existentiale Interpretation heute,"* in W. Kreck, *Tradition und Verantwortung* (Neukirchen: 1974), pp. 145-168.

4

Sin and Original Sin

by Wilhelm Breuning and Bengt Hägglund

translated by James L. Schaaf

1. Toward an Understanding of Sin and Original Sin in the CA

1.1. The Context of the Doctrine of Sin

When the *Confessio Augustana* deals with the doctrine of sin in Article 2, directly after the doctrine of God in Article 1, this is an indication that no one can have a correct knowledge of God without a knowledge of sin, and that the doctrine of sin is the presupposition of the Christian doctrine of salvation. Those who see themselves as sinners honor God and open a possibility for salvation, but those who regard themselves as righteous fight against God and hinder his work. Without the knowledge of sin there is no salvation, no rescue from sin. In his explanation of Psalm 51 in 1532, Luther stated this at length and incorporated the theological knowledge of human beings in the doctrine of sin.[1]

The article on sin in the CA therefore also forms the relevant logical presupposition for Article 3 (Christ), since the benefits of Christ can only be truly understood and recognized as an effective help against sin. In the second part of Article 2 it is said that the Pelagians disparage the sufferings and merit of Christ, since they deny that original sin is really sin.

Like the doctrine of God, the doctrine of sin is also in the strict sense a confession; i.e., only in confessing before God can one acknowledge that one is a sinner and understand what that means. In other words, we are dealing with a knowledge that is theological. The article is thus not talking about sin as human experience, as actual sin; it does not treat the subject on the basis of an ethical judgment. Original sin is incomprehensible to reason and cannot be defined by an ethical value judgment.

In the above mentioned exposition of Psalm 51, which has a special significance in our context as a clear expression of Luther's method of teaching on this question, the confessional character of the doctrine of sin is strongly emphasized. The doctrine of sin is characterized as the special theological knowledge of man: "Therefore we are not dealing here with the philosophical knowledge of man, which defines man as a rational animal and so forth. Such things are for science to discuss, not for theology. So a lawyer speaks of man as an owner and master of property, and a physician speaks of man as healthy or sick. But a theologian discusses man as a sinner. In theology, this is the essence of man. The theologian is concerned that man become aware of this nature of his, corrupted by sins." [2]

1.2. Original Sin—Personal Sin

What is meant by "original sin"? Our article connects original sin with physical birth and conception. The German word *Erbsünde,* which corresponds to the Latin *peccatum originis,* is understood literally: sin is inherited not just from one's parents or from one's immediate ancestors, but precisely from Adam and Eve. Sin belongs to the common inheritance of the entire human race and is therefore implanted at birth in every person as a *habitus ingenitus.* [3]

Nevertheless, original sin is ascribed to each individual as guilt; it determines our existence as human, both as guilt which leads to condemnation by God and also as a concrete corruption of nature. "Inherited sin, as all the teachers unanimously write, is nothing else than a loss of our inherited righteousness, with which inherited sin we were punished in Paradise through Adam's first sin. And it is called inherited sin because we did not do it, but we inherit it from our parents and it is no less reckoned to us than if we had done it ourselves." [4]

Since original sin refers not to what a person does or does not do, but to the cause of sin present in our nature, it is referred to as "natural" or "personal" sin.

"Therefore our deficiency does not lie in our works but in our nature. Our person, nature, and entire existence are corrupted through Adam's fall. Therefore not a single good work can be in us until our nature and personal being are changed and renewed. The tree is not good; therefore the fruits are evil." [5]

Luther prefers the German expression *Erbsünde* (lit., "inherited sin") to the Latin *peccatum originis;*[6] but he can also give the latter expression a definite meaning: original sin is the source of all actual sins, *radix actualium.*[7]

1.3. Lack of Fear of God

This concept of original sin as a concrete corruption of human nature, which was common in the Reformation, forms the presupposition for the definition in CA 2: "All are full of evil lust and inclinations from their mother's wombs and are unable by nature to have true fear of God and true faith in God."

As the German version clearly shows, faith in God here is not thought of as a conscious attitude of an (adult) individual. The definition speaks of the inner presupposition of faith, about that which scholastic terminology called *actus primus,* in contrast to *actus secundus.*

In the Apology Melanchthon speaks about the *potentia,* the ability, to fear and love God. He explains this definition as follows: "This passage testifies that in those who are born according to the flesh we deny the existence not only of actual fear and trust in God but also of the possibility and gift to produce it." [8] This lack of fear of God, this inability to believe, affects the entire person—human nature. According to an expression of Luther's in his large *Galatians Commentary* of 1532, faith is the form, i.e., the essence, of the Christian soul;[9] similarly sin affects the entire person in his or her relation to God.

In the expression "without fear of God, without trust in God" we hear an echo of the old definition of *carentia originalis justitiae* ("lack of original justice"). Melanchthon explains in the Apology why he chose that expression. In opposition to the scholastic opinion that by nature we have the ability to love God above all else, he wants to show that we do not even have the ability to believe in God or to rightly fear him. He believes that this definition is implicit in the usual definition of original sin as *carentia originalis justitae.* Original righteousness consists primarily of having a true knowledge of God and true love and fear of God.

1.4. Concupiscence

The other aspect of original sin, concupiscence, is the one mentioned first in the German version: "all are full of evil lusts and inclinations from their mothers' wombs." This is connected to the old theological definition which had been common since Augustine. But Melanchthon interprets concupiscence differently than does scholasticism. He does not mean only an inclination to evil in the lower powers of the soul or an actual carnal desire, but a perpetual evil disposition which is in itself evil and which only begins to cease through a spiritual rebirth and through faith. Not merely carnal desires, but also the lack of fear of God, are the symptoms of concupiscence.

"We wanted to show that original sin also involves such faults as ignorance of God, contempt of God, lack of the fear of God and of trust in him, inability to love him. These are the chief flaws in human nature. . . ." [10]

As is the lack of fear of God, so concupiscence is also a characteristic of human nature itself, a *perpetua naturae inclinatio* ("continual inclination of nature"),[11] an inborn sickness. In the Apology Melanchthon uses the example of a child born of a slave mother. That child inherits its enslaved condition through no fault of its own. But original sin is not only this sort of condition or like a burden imposed from outside upon a person, but is like an illness which corrupts nature and is understood as personal evil, "since human nature is born full of corruption and faults." [12]

1.5. Totus homo

According to Melanchthon's own explanation in the Apology, the two definitions of original sin complement each other: "Evil lusts and inclinations" and the inability to have true faith in God. By defining it as concupiscence, he is saying that original sin is not merely a condition of nature, but a corruption of it; and by the definition *sine fiducia* ("without faith") he wants to prevent an interpretation of original sin as merely carnal desire.

Behind this lies Luther's view of man as *totus homo,* according to which human beings in their whole nature stand before God as sinners, a fact that we can hold fast only as we confess it. The notion that reason and will remain relatively unimpaired after the Fall, while sin as concupiscence involves chiefly the bodily passions, was no longer tenable as far as God's judgment on human beings is concerned. Luther interprets the passage in Psalm 51:8, *"In peccatis conceptus sum*

(In sin was I conceived)," to mean that we must confess that "whatever is reason and will in man is condemned and evil." [13]

1.6. Baptism and Sin

Through Baptism the guilt of original sin is forgiven. The verdict of condemnation is removed by the grace of God. On this everyone at Augsburg agreed. The point at issue was the question about sin after Baptism. Article 2 contains no explicit statement on this matter; but it was known in advance that Luther's opinion had been vehemently attacked by the Roman Catholic opponents. According to Luther, the concupiscence that remained after Baptism was really sin; it was not merely a "weakness" which was not sin in itself, and which only became sin when a person yielded to it and committed a definite actual sin.

Luther thought that Scripture spoke altogether differently about sin; "As yet I do not know whether sin ever refers in Scripture to those works which we call sin, for it seems almost always to refer to the radical ferment which bears fruit in evil deeds and words." [14] In the question about the status of sin after Baptism, Luther again and again referred to Augustine's statement, "All sin is forgiven in Baptism, not so that it no longer exists, but so that it is no longer imputed." [15]

Although sin is forgiven in Baptism so that it is no longer imputed as sin, yet sin remains as carnal desire, as the old person, the sinful body; not only as weakness or imperfection, but as real sin.

This question was dealt with several times in the debate with Roman Catholic theologians. In the bull *Exsurge Domine* of 1520, Pope Leo X had condemned Luther's second thesis at the Leipzig Debate: "To deny . . . that sin remains in the child after Baptism . . . is equivalent to crushing Paul and Christ under foot." [16]

That concupiscence remains after Baptism was clear to both sides. The difference lies in the interpretation placed on this fact and the anthropology which was presupposed.

For the Roman Catholic theologians at that time, concupiscence after Baptism was no longer sin. It could only be seen as a weakness, a residual inclination toward sin. Therefore it was interpreted with Augustine as a punishment, a burden which had been placed on the human race.

For Luther, on the contrary, the inner inclination toward evil is really sin. In fact it is just this root of all sins, present in everyone, which the Scripture primarily calls sin.

The terminology, of course, is not in itself the important thing. The matter deals with the judgment of one's self before God. Since sin remains, the *accusatio sui* is always the presupposition of justification, the other side of saying that God justifies us by pure grace. "Hence the definition of the just man in this life is the following: the just man is first one who accuses himself, so that Christian justice is self-accusation. As soon as self-accusation ceases, justice also recedes." [17]

1.7. Peccatum regnans et regnatum

There is an extensive argument for the thesis that original sin remains as real sin after Baptism, to be found in the dispute with the Louvain theologian Jacob Latomus, where this precise question was the main issue *(Against Latomus,* 1521).[18]

Building chiefly on Romans 6 and 7, this work emphasizes that even the one who is baptized and born again lives in sin (Rom. 6:6), and that one must continually battle against sin. So strongly is this sinfulness emphasized by Paul that he can say, "For I know that nothing good dwells within me, that is, in my flesh" (Rom. 7:18). A conclusion is that we cannot ascribe anything good to ourselves. Before God we are always sinners, and only by grace and through the forgiveness of sins do we receive ever anew the life of the Spirit. Although the regenerate person can work together with God and can be a tool for the working of the Spirit, it is not possible to contribute anything to one's own salvation or justification.

Romans 6 says that baptized persons should no longer obey sin; sin should no longer reign over them (v. 12). Christians should walk according to the Spirit, not according to the flesh (Rom. 8:4). Thus sin still remains after Baptism, but it no longer has the same ruling power as before. On this basis Luther distinguishes between *peccatum regnans* and *peccatum regnatum*. This distinction is not a new one invented by Luther, as Latomus claimed; Paul also speaks about sin's rule (Rom. 6:12).

The sense of this distinction is that the power of sin is restrained and fought against by the Spirit who works in and with faith. But when people give in and follow their evil inclinations, then sin reigns once again. The real point of controversy is whether controlled sin *(peccatum regnatum)* should really be termed sin. According to Luther it is not merely a weakness, punishment, or unfortunate condition, but a sinful inclination. Otherwise how could we say that we should not obey it or that an inclination to yield is sin? A condition of being without something, such as hunger or thirst, or a fate, such as death, is not something one can "obey" or avoid obeying.[19]

Therefore according to Luther's argument it is incorrect to say that after Baptism all that remains of original sin is a weakness or a punishment. Before and after regeneration, sin remains. It does not end until physical death. The difference is that sin should no longer reign, but through the working of the Spirit it is being changed from *Peccatum regnans* to *peccatum regnatum*. Not only the principles of Pauline anthropology, but also the daily experience of the saints, testify that the sinful inclination *(peccatum et concupiscentia)* remains after Baptism.

1.8. Malum internum et externum

Luther's concept of sin remaining after Baptism is only a consequence of the basic idea that sin in the biblical sense is not merely the acts to which this term is commonly applied, but that it is the inner roots of such acts, the *radicale fermentum*. The simple distinction based on Pauline anthropology which Luther developed in his writing against Latomus of 1521, and in other places, is as follows:

Scripture speaks in two ways about the evil that is connected with sin, as (1) a *malum internum*, i.e., the corruption of nature *(corruptio naturae)*, and (2) a *malum externum*, i.e., the wrath of God, death, and condemnation.

Over against sin, which is revealed by the law, the gospel proclaims the righteousness and grace of God.

Righteousness drives out the *malum internum*, and grace replaces the wrath of God, so that sin no longer leads to condemnation. *Iustitia* here does not mean imputed righteousness, but the healing righteousness which is given through faith and consists in the inner root *(intima radix)* being so changed that one can begin to love God and do what is good, a working of the Spirit through which the corruption of nature is gradually healed.[20]

1.9. Simul iustus et peccator

The purification from sin which begins through the working of the Holy Spirit does not change the fact that the person justified by grace remains a sinner, so that the Christian life remains until death a life in the forgiveness of sins. The formula often used by Luther of *simul iustus et peccator* does not mean only (1) that the remnants of sin are present with a Christian along with the beginning new life, but also (2) that the concupiscence that remains places its imprint on the entire person, so that in our judgment of ourselves before God we stand as sinners. Through the mercy of God, however, we are at the same time completely and totally received in grace and viewed as righteous.

In the first sense, one may speak about a partial aspect: Christians are partially sinners, in that remnants of sin are present in them, and partially righteous, in that good is worked in them.

In the second sense, the conclusion is different: before God *(coram Deo)*, persons in their totality are still sinners and cannot attribute to themselves anything good; they sin even in their good works. However, at the same time that they confess themselves to be sinners, they are justified in that their sins are forgiven for Christ's sake. Sin is no longer imputed to them. They are *"reputatione iustus."*[21]

It must be added that this understanding of a Christian presupposed a purely theological observation that must not be confused with any civil or ethical judgment of human actions.

This point of view is decisive for the concept of sin remaining after Baptism. One may say that the formula *simul iustus et peccator,* in the way Luther interpreted it, is the way the Lutheran Confession sums up the idea of sin remaining until death.

2. The Solidity of the Agreement at Augsburg

2.1. The Decisive Importance of the German Text of the CA

Catholic reaction to the CA's doctrine of sin creates conflicting impressions. Article 2 is the object of varied and strong criticism.[22] But where it came to discussion and negotiations at the Diet of Augsburg and again at religious colloquies a good decade later, indications of consensus emerged on the doctrine of original sin. This was true for the negotiations of the Committee of Fourteen during the Augsburg Diet. This was composed of seven representatives from each side and, on August 16, 1530, it discussed the article on original sin, among other things.[23] This was also true for the religious colloquy at Worms in 1541.[24] Expressly because this unity had been achieved, the Regensburg religious colloquy in 1541 refrained from further discussion of this subject.[25] On the other hand, the very extensive treatment in the Apology shows that the situation here is different than with the subject of God and Christ. The doctrine of original sin remains full of tension because of its relation to the other central themes of the Reformation.

But how should one objectively judge the agreement? Did it disintegrate because the unity only came about for political purposes in which the participants *wanted* to overlook the contradictions, or does it evidence a real unanimity on the issue?

We must look at the matter from several points of view. First there is the nearly unanimous witness that it was through the negotiations themselves that a consensus was achieved.[26] Thus is there a line of development to the recognition by the Committee of Fourteen which can make it understandable how such a change from the attacks of the Catholic side (as they still appear in the Confutation) could take place? Further, if the controversy over the doctrine of original sin continued in all its harshness after these attempts to reach a consensus, does that mean a change took place which rescinded the previously attained consensus and made it appear erroneous?

We must see what the substance of the issues in dispute was in order to find an answer about the intention and value of the statement of agreement.

As viewed by the Confutation—and later debates hardly differ—there are two criticisms of the doctrine of original sin in the CA which define the discussion. The first attack is made on the interpretation of the nature of original sin contained in the explanatory sentence: to be conceived in sin means that all are born "without fear of God, without trust *(fiducia)* in God." According to the views of the authors of the Confutation, "not fearing God, not believing in him" are actual sins. That is, they must be understood formally as the proper activity of each person affected. Consequently, according to this interpretation, what precisely is *not* expressed is the negative antecedent condition of the individual's own decision.

The second criticism deals with the question of the eradication of original sin in Baptism. It suspects that Baptism, according to the "new" doctrine, does not really remove sin. In reality both objections are more closely connected than might at first appear.

As to the *first* objection, one must return to the Latin text of the CA in order to understand it at all. For *both* objections the bare text of the CA in itself is not sufficient; one must include the chief points of the preceding discussions. As for the inclusion in the definition of original sin of lack of fear of God and trust, the German text, which has already been introduced and clarified in Part 1,[27] really excludes any way of understanding "without fear of God, without trust in God" as actual sin. It was previously mentioned in the explanation of this text that it deals with an *inability,* not with an act born out of unbelief. The German text is doubtless more clear than the Latin. It becomes obvious, as far as our chief question is concerned, that there is a firm and substantial basis for consensus in the development of the thought of the German text. Precisely the formulation which Melanchthon chose for the Apology and which was already utilized in the context above makes this most clear.

An additional important piece of information for interpreting the formula, "without fear of God, without trust in God," which points to the possibility of an agreement, is contained in the report of how Melanchthon connected this definition with the already mentioned definition of original sin as "lack of original righteousness." Melanchthon and his colleagues in the discussion of the Committee of Fourteen obviously were able to make plausible the substantial agreement between "lack of original righteousness" and "without fear of God, without trust in God." In any event, the report of Spalatin, the secretary for these discussions, referred to this: "Doctor Eck said about this: It is a new form of speaking. Otherwise they would already be agreed on this article. Only they have not used the same words." [28]

Even Luther himself could adopt the definition of original sin as "lack of original righteousness." [29]

The interpretation of the lack of "original righteousness" as the *inability* truly to fear God and faithfully to trust in God is suggested in the German text of the CA and is further developed on the basis of the German text in the Apology. It can therefore be understood as a basis for consensus. A new terminology!

Only new terminology? As for what is to be expressed, one might first say that the definition of original sin as inability to fear and trust God is more concrete. It reveals the point at which a human being is affected more directly than does the definition of original sin as loss of original righteousness. But it is precisely here that the consensus which was so clear threatens to collapse again. One must remember that the formula, "lack of original righteousness," seen against the background of the scholastic theological tradition, was understood by an important group of theologians at that time as part of a more comprehensive definition of original sin. They connected the lack of original and God-desired righteousness with the other aspect mentioned above, which had played a great role in the definition of original sin, that of "concupiscence." The CA also emphasizes this topic. The Latin version expressly employs this term at this point.

In order to comprehend the problem, it is useful to distinguish three factors here:

1. The initiation of the entire controversy in Luther's thesis about Baptism and original sin.

2. The more fundamental theological problem which here presents itself.

3. The background of the scholastic doctrinal tradition against which the actual controversy occurred.

2.2. The Effect of Baptism: Sin Mastered

Ad 1. Part 1 has already given us the information which allows us to see the actual course of development.[30] From there we can see that the question, "What remains in a child after Baptism?" always and consciously remains, at least for the Catholic side, the problem over which the spirits are to be divided. This also explains why this problem so dominated the Catholic argument with Augsburg, even though the direct, brief formulation of the doctrine of original sin in the CA says nothing directly about it. To show further how important this question was on the Catholic side, it is enough to note that the session of the Council of Trent which dealt with the doctrine of original sin began with this question.[31] Viewed existentially, of course, this question is not of the greatest importance, but it is seen as an important symptom of a serious difference.

Is there a development or a clarification that takes place in this circle which could make understandable the consensus reached at the Augsburg discussion? The Confutation sees a possibility of agreement when the representatives of the evangelical side "according to the opinion of St. Augustine, call original sin concupiscence, which in Baptism is taken away."[32] A memorandum by Eck calls concupiscence remaining after Baptism "vicious," speaks of it as a remaining sickness, and says that it "remained from sin and inclined to sin and can therefore be called sin," but also emphasizes that it is "neither really nor truly nor essentially sin when the will does not obey this vicious inclination so that it reigns in the mortal body."[33] Thus we see that Luther's distinction between "sin as master" and "sin mastered" is taken up positively by Eck. It provides an intelligible way of expressing the change that has

taken place through Baptism in the power of "sin," despite the remaining "vicious concupiscence."

The Apology takes up this theme extensively. Even though the recent
hardening of the fronts is evident here, one can clearly recognize the
basis for agreement which is offered by high scholasticism's doctrine
of original sin, and which Melanchthon is prepared to recognize even
immediately following the breakdown of the agreement. How extensive this basis of agreement was can be determined only in connection
with the third point.

2.3. The Sinner's "Own" Capacities

Ad 2. But first we must take a further step. Part 1 developed the
existential significance of the conception of sin.[34] We have seen that
the answer to the question of what remains after Baptism was important
as a symptom; but the existentially important matter in this dispute
is the question of the ability of human powers to attain salvation, and
here we have to do with the heart of the question of justification.[35]
To insist on the abiding weakness of the baptized person's own powers
was the consequence of the fundamental evaluation of the possibilities
for attaining one's own salvation.

Thus it has become clear that in understanding original sin as inability to fear and trust God one must speak differently of the situation
of the believing regenerate Christian. The faith that has been given to
such persons—and this is decisive in any way of speaking about abiding "sin"—has really overcome the inability; but the ability to do so
comes not from the sinners themselves, although the faith and trust
which is a gift is their own and innermost attitude. Just what this means,
the Apology is already able to state clearly, as we can see from the general tenor of Article 2. It makes a sharp distinction between actual sin,
original sin, and remaining concupiscence: "For we say that in all the
children of Adam there is an evil inclination and desire, and that no
one is able to make for himself a heart which can know or trust God,
fear him from the heart. . . . Therefore when we speak of inborn evil
desire, we do not mean merely the act, evil work or fruits, but the
internal evil inclination which never ends as long as we are not reborn
through the Spirit and faith." In fact the new ability not to let sin
rule over one depends always on the working principle given by God
—the Spirit, faith, grace. But must that mean that deep inside, so
to speak, one still remains a sinner? Or is it supposed to make clear
how serious a matter it is that, as far as one's own power is concerned,

one can fall back into the dominion of sin at any time, and that happens not by chance, but "from the heart"? In these difficult questions one must, as much as possible, attend to what is actually meant, and—because of the nature of the matter, not because of weakness in thinking—in every case what is needed is certainly an *interpretatio benigna,* an interpretation that seeks understanding, if a consensus is to be arrived at. What is needed is also a way of speaking that does not seek exaggeration and excessive subtleties.

Recent Catholic investigations of the phase of Reformation theology to which the CA belongs—a phase of thoughtful search for links with the genuine valid contents of the tradition of faith, and for which the courteous manner of a Melanchthon had an important positive significance—have acknowledged the Reformation attempts to return to a common basis for a consensus.[36] Even while Melanchthon is defending his own position (as can be seen in the Apology) and attacking scholastic theories, he understands himself to be in agreement on original sin not only with Augustine, but also with Thomas and Bonaventure. In the end it is not what is said in the CA and the Apology that the Catholic theologians attack; they agree with the substance of what is said there. The attacks which meanwhile were also renewed on the Catholic side, on the matter of original sin, as on other points as well, are based on differences stemming from the beginning of the 1520s.[37]

The brief statements of the CA cannot convey to us the contents of the discussion and agreement of 1530. The reports of the negotiations can do this better, and the Apology with its relatively compact theology can do it best. It clearly reveals to us the conception of things which the evangelical side was combatting. It rejects most sharply the teaching "that man can obey the commandments of God by his own powers."[38] "They do not know what they are talking about when they teach that by one's own powers one is able to love God above all things."[39] Melanchthon knows that it is "modern theologians" with which he has to deal.[40] The older ones, even the scholastics, he knows are on his side. He firmly reminds us that these modern theologians trivialize concupiscence. He chiefly opposes the idea that the strings of concupiscence—seen from the viewpoint of nature—are indifferent.[41]

The scholastic opponents who are the target here are those who claim that solely by one's own natural powers one is in a position to love God above all else and completely fulfill the material demands of his commandments.[42] This points in the direction of an anthropology and doctrine of grace that is shaped by nominalism. Recent investigations

have been able to show more precisely that it was Gabriel Biel's commentary on the *Sentences* on which both Luther and Melanchthon
focused.[43] The following comment from his commentary on the *Sentences* may give us a representative view of Biel's empty concept of
grace which *de facto* makes it impossible to conceive a content of grace
relevant for a human being. Here it is said that in the present order
of salvation no one can love God in the manner necessary for salvation
without grace; but this divine arrangement must in the final analysis
appear as something quite arbitrary: "Since the law commands that the
act which falls under the commandment take place in grace, which is
a supernatural *habitus,* one who stands outside grace consequently even
though able to love God above all else out of purely natural powers,
does not fulfill the commandment of the one who gives it, if not in
grace." [44]

In view of such a text we can perhaps understand that the strong
emphasis of the Reformers on human weakness and sinfulness is only
one side of the coin. The reverse side shows that a living experience
of what grace really is requires one to look into the abyss, i.e., to see
what one really is and "can do" without grace. When one reads these
words of CA 2 together with the additional explanation provided by
CA 18 and Article 2 of the Apology, one must note that the doctrine of
original sin has reached a concentration which draws together many
points of view, yet which strikes right at the heart: What is one before
God? Precisely in view of grace, where is one to recognize one's truth?
How can one experience the fact that his ability to believe and love
lies in God? The CA had found a basis for agreement, even though it
had not worked out all the previously disputed issues. This one can
conclude from the intention and tone of the Apology, to say nothing
of the not trivial agreement which, according to the accounts of the
discussions, had been reached on CA 18.

By way of transition to the next point of view, we must still show
that in the effort at mediation lay a possibility of deepening and focus-
ing the doctrine of original sin, a possibility not sufficiently exploited
then or to the present day. It dealt with the inner connection between
the usual understanding of concupiscence as evil inclination and what
the Apology continually referred to as one's inability, apart from Christ's
justifying grace, to believe in God, to fear him, and to trust him. The
Catholic participants in the debate, as we have already seen, continually stumbled over translating what the scholastic tradition called
lack of original righteousness as "without fear of God, without trust

in God." They let themselves be convinced that essentially the same thing was meant as lack of original righteousness and thus they were able to accept the new terminology. But did they also perceive that the new manner of speaking offered a deepened understanding of the doctrine of concupiscence? This would open up the possibility of making fruitful use of the positive side of Augustine, and thus of course using him selectively. For one may find in his writings suggestions that the evil inclination is located not in sensuality, but in the disrupted relationship of the entire person to God. In scholastic terminology, however, the concept of "concupiscence" had lost much of this deeper meaning. It was explained almost axiomatically and at least with too little reflection in dualistic terms as rebellion of the "lower" powers in human nature. Here too we see Augustine's influence, but the influence must be judged an unfortunate one. It seems to us that a great accomplishment of the remarkably consistent explanation of this point in the Apology lies in the fact that the evil of concupiscence is based precisely on the inability to love God and believe in him. The virulence of evil in every sphere of human activity—and about this virulence there was no controversy—was consequently derived from the basic human inability to conduct oneself rightly before God. It was surely a defect of the scholastic theory about concupiscence that it did not focus, at least not convincingly enough, on how a human being is afflicted by the loss of grace.[45]

Even if the importance of this theological effort could not at that time be sufficiently appreciated, still that theology in its inner consistency, along with an old traditional formula of the scholastic doctrine of original sin, provided the basis and even the vocabulary for expressing the agreement reached. We refer to the Thomistic doctrine of original sin, according to which the lack of original righteousness is related to concupiscence in the same way as the forming, defining element is related to an underlying "matter." With this we come to the third and final factor.

2.4. The Formula of Agreement

Ad. 3. The scholastic doctrine of original sin did contain significant presuppositions and elements for a doctrine of original sin about which the theologians agreed, but they possessed no unified theory about it. Beyond the elements on which they agreed, there were strong differences which made the dispute with the evangelical theologians even more difficult. The Council of Trent is very instructive on this point.

It did not want to deal with the opinions of different schools and could not at first say where it agreed against the errors, which again were still too unnuanced and extreme statements of Lutheran anthropology of the early 1520s. Thus the Council of Trent in its canons on original sin did not rely on any one of the scholastic definitions.[46] The one which corresponds to the CA, which we have noted above was Thomistic, was used in preliminary drafts, but was finally replaced with a more open definition. It is even more noteworthy that the Apology is open to this scholastic formula. The reports of the negotiations show that it did in fact carry the agreement.[47] Its origin in scholasticism, its meaning, and its importance must be indicated briefly. As has already been pointed out in Part 1, the Lutheran interpretation of original sin is close to the scholastic definition of *"carentia originalis iustitiae,"* which goes back to Anselm of Canterbury.[48] In order to understand the development, one must realize that in the 13th century there were two contrasting "definitions" of original sin.[49] The first identified it with what ever since Augustine had been called concupiscence—although Augustine vacillated, sometimes identifying concupiscence as the total relationship of human beings to God, and sometimes conceiving it as rebellion of sensuality. In early scholasticism "concupiscence" was taken over in a crude, one-dimensional way and in a dualistic context.[50] The second definition goes back to Anselm of Canterbury and is theologically much more exacting and more deeply thought through. While it does not stand outside the great Augustinian theological tradition, it offers a completely independent and at first unnoticed starting point for the doctrine of original sin: original sin is constituted as sin because human beings do not possess (since Adam lost it) the original righteousness which according to God's will they should have. As reflection on this doctrine proceeded at the beginning of high scholasticism, Anselm's formula was adopted, and the early scholastic interpretation of original sin as concupiscence was attached. This view, which was brought into prominence by the master of the Sentences, Peter Lombard, quickly ran into serious difficulties. Interestingly, the same problem arose which, relative to Luther, also proved to be the stumbling block. If original sin in its essence *is* concupiscence, what then does Baptism accomplish? The answer that original sin is reduced in intensity was felt rather as an embarrassment. The other alternative may be traced farther back in the tradition and would be eagerly seized on by the Lutheran side in the discussions during the Reformation:[51] concupiscence indeed remains but its guilt is removed.

Binding and loosing may certainly not be understood as ordained in an arbitrary and purely external way. In fact, the Aristotelian model, according to which the lack of original righteousness is the formal, and concupiscence is the material principle of original sin, brings a considerable advance. This model was first used by Alexander of Hales and was differently elaborated by Bonaventure and Thomas, and not without reason does the Apology cite these last two. This model is used in the attempt to bring the entire disorder within human beings into connection with the history of humanity's sin, which had its origin in he disruption of the life-granting communion of persons with God. Concupiscence is the *effect* of humanity's loss of the openness and loving readiness to respond to God which is necessary for its life. The expressions of human life remain disassociated without this righteousness that unifies human beings in a relationship with God. Loss of original righteousness and concupiscence are related (in Aristotelian terminology) as form and matter.

The advantages of this model are obvious. A dualistic interpretation of concupiscence can thus be overcome. The threat of sin affects one's heart, one's relationship to God. From this we can understand what Baptism accomplishes. The new relationship which God graciously grants accomplishes the real historical turn in human life. It remains clear, however, that this remission of sin can and should have a further history until it permeates all the expressions of life. That which is overcome by God's grace in a continually growing way is not *merely* a creaturely weakness for which one cannot really be reproached. What is fought against is the entire real history of sin in this world, from which especially one who is justified—no one knows this better—has not escaped by his or her own powers. In other words, though the Reformation theologians can hardly be suspected of wanting to build on Aristotle, the matter-form model of Bonaventure[52] and Thomas, could hardly be put aside, even if they tried, when the reformers had to give expression to their own deepest intentions, and when it was possible in this way. It is precisely the correspondence of loss of original righteousness with the inability to believe and love—and the latter is certainly the very heart of the Reformation's concept of original sin—which offered a solid foundation for the well-known word of Augustine. One could now say, in a meaningful logic of faith, that guilt-afflictedness in its essence has been overcome through Baptism. Melanchthon's cautious concession in this direction, which is revealed in the Apology, should not be interpreted as an estrangement from and weakening of what was originally another intention, but as a mature realization of his basic concern.[53]

Yet a consensus can never be stronger than the weakest link of the chain of considerations. However, in what follows we are not exactly speaking about a disagreement which might once again draw a dividing line between Catholic and evangelical theologians. The situation at Augsburg offers a common basis for dialog in which both partners might be able to speak directly to one another. If we speak of the weak links in the chain of argument, this applies not only to the two partners in their relationship to each other, but in a sense to each separately. For example, we see at Trent that an intra-Catholic struggle also took place. Two points especially seemed to need clarification. Melanchthon's accusation may be unfriendly, but he is right when he charges that the scholastics had not thought enough about "original righteousness." [54] In fact it was not possible then or later to give a clear definition of "natural powers" that was acceptable to all. Behind this lack of clarity lay questions of substance. If the CA's position could be accepted in the dialog at that time even though there was no discussion of what "nature" meant, such unsettled questions should not destroy the consensus.[55] Even Trent did not collapse over theological disagreements. But that the situation is threatened by "instability" cannot be denied. Both the CA and Trent have shown how one can live and come to agreement in spite of very deep theoretical differences.

A second source of instability is the understanding of concupiscence, the general subject of debate. Even in the Catholic camp, as Trent shows, people were far from having such unanimity that they could not fall into sharp controversies.[56] Could it be that they did not succeed in completely carrying through the impulse of high scholasticism or Melanchthon's more concrete impulse toward a *theo*logical concentration of the understanding of sin? Considering the past history of the concept, that is hardly surprising.[57] A brief consideration of the doctrine of concupiscence of the Tridentine decree on original sin will show that it unmistakably teaches the actual forgiveness of original sin in its character as guilt. But the council fathers were unable to come to agreement on a more precise definition of the phenomenon of concupiscence. It is rather the concrete historical description of the justified baptized person that allows us to see that we are genuinely bound to Christ, that the Christian life is marked by concupiscence, that the human situation arises from sin and inclines toward it. Thus it is made credible that salvation is founded on grace, grace that is ultimately a reality in concrete human history.[58] That the evangelical side so strongly emphasized the historical power of sin can be understood as arising out of its opposition to the nominalistic *de facto* abstraction of grace. On the other hand, though the Catholic theologians object that the evangelical theologians do not give enough attention to the historical reality of grace, the discussion of 1530 shows a clear attempt on the evangelical side not to reject this objection apologetically, but to include it in a positive way in the doctrine of original sin. To the Catholic theologian what appears fruitful in this synthesis is the coming together of the theory of original sin which sees its essence as lack (lack of original righteousness) with the "virulent" element of original sin. Another service that is here offered is that this virulence is not based on a rebellion of a lower sensuality, but rather the conception of the historical power of sin converges with the theory of lack, so that the negative concept of lack of righteousness is at the same time comprehended as the cause of the human inability to believe in God and to love him completely.

3. Prospect and Result

There is hardly any point of doctrine in Reformation theology that is more disputed in the later tradition, chiefly since the Enlightenment, than the radical doctrine of sin confessed in Article 2 of the CA. But in contemporary Catholic theology too there is no lack of attempts to give a new interpretation to the doctrine of original sin and inherited sin.

The present-day presuppositions for explaining and understanding this doctrine are completely different from what they were then. Indeed, the many attempts to reinterpret the doctrine of original sin show how difficult it is to make the agreements and issues of that time accessible to contemporary understanding. Nevertheless, the subsequently almost forgotten fact that the theologians at Augsburg reached an apparently solid agreement seems significant as a basis for our work today and in the future; to give its rightful place to the deeper dimension of the anthropology of the classical Christian tradition.

The theological work of that time has something to say directly to the contemporary question of what is to be said about the inner effect of the history of sin on each of us, antecedent to our own personal decision. We will not simply repeat what the 16th century has already done, but we must not fall short of the theological depth which was evidenced in the Augsburg consensus and the efforts that lay behind it. For the contemporary question of ecumenical unity it is important to see Augsburg neither as an extremely dangerous tightrope act, nor as a minimal consensus reached against one's will, but rather as a hermeneutically substantial bridge from which it has been possible, in the shallows of sometimes one-sided and mistakenly formulated discussions, to sink foundations which rest on firm bedrock. For the present resumption of the conversation, one may formulate this question: Are not the intentions of Augsburg a reliable hermeneutical principle?

Notes

1. AE 12, 344-345 (WA 40, 376); cf. AE 12, 356-357 (WA 40, 393). The following presentation of the doctrine of sin of the CA presupposes that the brief formulations of the text of the Confession have as their presupposition and context Luther's explanations of the matter, especially those written around that time. The explanations given in the Apology do not appear to contradict this view. Among others, these writings are important: *Enarratio Psalmi LI* (1532), the *Commentary on Galatians* of 1531 (1530), *Against Latomus* (1521), and several of the disputations.
2. AE 12, 310-311 (WA 40, 327).
3. WA 39, 95.
4. WA 17, 282.
5. AE 52, 151 (WA 10, 508).
6. WA 39, 305.
7. WA 39, 121.
8. Apol. 2, 3 (BC 101).
9. AE 26, 430 (WA 40, 649).
10. Apol. 2, 14 (BC 102).
11. Apol. 2, 3 (CT 104; BC 101).
12. Apol. 2, 6 (BC 101; CT 106; *"quod natura hominum corrupta et vitiosa nascatur"*).
13. AE 12, 357 (WA 40, 393).
14. AE 32, 224 (WA 8, 104: *"Haud scio, an peccatum in scripturis unquam accipiatur pro operibus, quae nos peccata vocamus. Videtur enim ferme radicale illud fermentum sic vocare, quod fructificat mala opera et verba."*).
15. Augustine, *De nupt. et concup.* 1, 25 (MSL 44, 430); AE 32, 209 (WA 8, 93): *"Peccatum in baptismo remittitur, non ut non sit, sed ut non imputetur.";* cf. Apol. 2, 36 (BC 105).
16. AE 31, 317 (WA 2, 169); cf. CR 27, 88 and Apol. 2, 35 (BC 104-105).
17. WA 2, 420; *"Proinde definitio iusti in hac vita est haec: Iustus primo accusator est sui, ideo iustitia Christiana est accusatio sui; quam cito perit accusatio sui, statim recedit quoque iustitia."*
18. AE 32, 220-221 (WA 8, 101).

19. AE 32, 213-214 (WA 8, 96).

20. AE 32, 224ff. (WA 8, 104-105).

21. *"Verum vos scitis nos esse quidem iustos, puros, sanctos, esse etiam pecca-*
    tores, iniustos et damnatos, sed diverso respectu: sumus etiam iusti, quod
    ad reputationem seu misericordiam Dei in Christo promissam, hoc est
    propter Christum, in quem credimus . . . . sed secundum formam aut
    substantiam, seu secundum nos, sumus peccatores iniusti et damnati, quia
    certe nihil est in tota natura hominis, quod opponi possit iudicio Dei"
    (WA 39, 492); cf. 563-564. *III. Disp. gegen die Antinomer*, 1538). On this
    theme see, among others, Otto Hermann Pesch, *Die Theologie der Recht-*
    fertigung bei Martin Luther und Thomas von Aquin (Mainz: 1967), pp.
    109-122; Gustav Ljunggren, *Synd och skuld i Luthers teologi* (Stockholm:
    1927), pp. 252-346; Wilfred Joest, *"Paulus und das Lutherische simul*
    justus et peccator," Kerygma und Dogma 1 (1955): 269-320; Kjell Ove
    Nilsson, *Simul* (Lund: 1966), pp. 310-329; and Karl-Heinz zur Mühlen,
    Nos extra nos, Beiträge zur historischen Theologie 46 (Tübingen: 1972),
    pp. 140-146.

22. Cf. the survey which V. Pfnür makes possible: *Einig in der Rechtfer-*
    tigungslehre: Die Rechtfertigungslehre der Confessio Augustana (1530) und
    die Stellungnahme der katholischen Kontroverstheologie zwischen 1530 und
    1535, Veröffentl. des Instituts für europ. Geschichte Mainz, vol. 60,
    Abt. Abendl. Religionsgeschichte, hrsg. v. J. Lortz (Wiesbaden: 1970). He
    deals fully with CA 2.

23. Cf. Pfnür's proofs, pp. 253-256. This is not the place to discuss the pros
    and cons of the concept of "inherited sin." But permit the observation
    that the discussion which is necessary today about the meaning and limits
    esp. of the concept of inheritance (the Latin phrase *"peccatum originale"*
    is less likely to be misunderstood) ought not lead us to view the traditional
    doctrine only historically. In fact it deals with matters which are equally
    relevant today.

24. CR 4, 32.

25. Cf. Eck's note which Pfnür cites from the *Apologie . . . adversus mucores*
    et columnias Buceri, super actis Comitiorum Ratisponae (Cologne: 1532),
    cited in note 269, p. 255.

26. Pfnür introduces evidence from G. Brück, Spalatin, Cochlaeus, and Vehus,
    and esp. makes intelligible Eck's development to an agreement, pp. 253-
    256.

27. Cf. above pp. 95ff.

28. *Urkundenbuch zu der Geschichte des Reichstages zu Augsburg im Jahre*
    1530, K. E. Förstemann, ed. (Halle: 1835), 2:223-224; cf. Pfnür, p. 253.

29. Cf. the text referred to in note 4.

30. Cf. above, pp. 98ff.

31. Cf. H. Jedin, *A History of the Council of Trent,* vol. 2 (Edinburgh:
    Thomas Nelson and Sons, 1961), p. 134; cf. also pp. 143-144.

32. *Confutatio:* CR 27, 88-89 (or Immenkötter 82-83).

33. *Quellen und Forschungen aus italienischen Archiven und Bibliotheken*
    (Rome: 1958), 38:225, translation quoted from Pfnür, p. 254.

34. Cf. above, pp. 94ff.

35. Cf. above, pp. 96ff.

36. Pfnür, pp. 110-39, also pp. 64-77.
37. Cf. Pfnür, pp. 117, 138.
38. Apol. 2, 46 (BC 106).
39. Apol. 2, 25 (BSLK 152; CT 110, German); cf. also Apol. 13, where this line of thought appears even more clearly.
40. Apol. 2, 32 (BC 104).
41. Apol. 2, 42-45 (BC 105-106).
42. Cf. Apol, 2, 7 (BC 101).
43. P. Vignaux, *"Luther lecteur de Gabriel Biel," Eglise et théologie* 22 (1959):33-52; L. Grane, *Contra Gabrielem: Luthers Auseinandersetzung mit Gabriel Biel in der Disputation contra Scholasticam Theologiam 1517* (Aarhus: 1962); H. A. Oberman, *The Harvest of Medieval Theology* (Cambridge: Harvard University Press, 1963); H. J. McSorley, *Luther: Right or Wrong?* (New York: Newman Press, 1968); Pfnür, pp. 68-77.
44. Biel, Coll. 1. III d. 27 q a. 3 dub. 2 prop. 5 lit. R.
45. Cf. Apol. 2,14 (BC 102); 2, 25 (BC 103); 2, 28-29 (BC 104); 2, 34 (BC 104).
46. Cf. Jedin, pp. 150-151.
47. "That there is original sin is agreed, but what original sin is, is interpreted in a Lutheran way. But they agree with us that original sin is a lack of original righteousness, that the sensual inclination that grows out of original sin remains *(quoad materiale, sed tolli in baptismo quoad formale)."* CR 3, 1055 .
48. Cf. above pp. 97ff.
49. For the following see O. Lottin, *Psychologie et Morale aux 12e et 13e siecle,* vols. 2,1 and 4,1; *Problemes de Morale* (Louvain-Gembloux: 1948 and 1954); W. Breuning, *Fall und Erhebung des Menschen nach Ulrich von Strassburg, Trierer Theol. Stud.,* 10 (1959), pp. 136-157.
50. A peculiar note is contained in the doctrine of original sin of Hugh of St. Victor, which the Apology to its credit quotes approvingly. He did have a dualistic understanding of concupiscence, but recognized an element of original sin that affected the spirit: a blindness toward God. Cf. Apol. 2,29 (BC 104).
51. The statement of Augustine referred to in Part I forms the heart of this thought. Cf. above, p. 98.
52. Here Bonaventure is esp. interesting. He does use the matter-form scheme in this context, but with restraint. Yet the facts he adduces belong clearly to the subject under debate. Bonaventure especially emphasizes the dynamic effect of sin, which Trent later incorporated into the doctrine of concupiscence: concupiscence comes from sin and leads to sin. Cf. DS 1515.
53. Although Melanchthon did not use the Thomistic formula as such, the substance of it is contained in the text, and he continually referred to it in the context of speaking about the guilt that remains by using the expression of *"materiale" peccati originalis,* although with the slight reservation of *"ut isti vocant."* In the concluding part he also uses the phrase *"formale" peccati originalis,* though with the comment that the scholastic theologians are not able to give the proper content to the term. Apol. 2, 51 (BSLK 157; CT 119).
54. Apol. 2, 15 (BC 102).

55. "Natural" means "without grace" in a kind of pragmatic but legitimate sense, but this pragmatic sense also includes "in the real order of salvation, in which human beings themselves are sinners." Though Catholic theologians will be aware of a more exacting definition, they can go along with the pragmatic meaning in a context defined by the question above.
56. Cf. Jedin, *op. cit.,* pp. 143-152.
57. In this context one can certainly agree with Pfnür's judgment which rejects Rischar's thesis that there was finally no agreement on the concupiscence question. But one must also see that the concept of concupiscence produces instability because of the tension that is inherent in it. Thus it is not so surprising that the conflict broke out more on this front after the attempts at unity. K. Rischar, *Johann Eck auf dem Reichstag zu Augsburg 1530* (Münster: 1968).
58. Cf. esp. the evaluation of Melanchthon's contribution in Pfnür's careful study, pp. 110-139.

5

Justification-Faith-Works

by Gerhard Müller and Vinzenz Pfnür

translated by James L. Schaaf

1. The Doctrine of Justification as
Articulus stantis et cadentis ecclesiae

"The first and chief article is this, that Jesus Christ, our God and Lord, 'was put to death for our trespasses and raised again for our justification' (Rom. 4:25). . . . .Inasmuch as this must be believed and cannot be obtained or apprehended by any work, law, or merit, it is clear and certain that such faith alone justifies us. . . . Nothing in this article can be given up or compromised, even if heaven and earth and things temporal should be destroyed. For as St. Peter says, 'There is no other name under heaven given among men by which we must be saved' (Acts 4:12)." [1] With these words in the Smalcald Articles Martin Luther asserted the significance of the event of justification. Accordingly, in all Lutheran churches in which the Book of Concord enjoys confessional status, this statement of the Wittenberg reformer is valid, for the Smalcald Articles have become part of this collection of confessions. It is well said that it is not a formalistic doctrine of justification which is here put forward as a confession, "but the crucified and risen *Christ*. . . . The emphasis lies upon Jesus Christ and his saving act, not on justification." [2] Yet it would be wrong not to connect the act of the Son of God as closely as possible with justification. For it is Luther's conviction that human salvation is possible only through the forgiveness of sin wrought by Jesus Christ and the righteousness before Good which results. This is precisely what is meant by justification, namely *iustificatio impii,* justification of those who cannot find the way to God by themselves. For Luther, justification is based on Jesus Christ alone and is possible only through him. This understanding of salvation implies an anthropology which gives God glory for the sake of the work of the Son of God alone. Hence it is indeed the correct understanding of justification which determines whether the church is really the church.[3] This is why it is not incorrect to speak of this doctrine as the *articulus stantis et cadentis ecclesiae;*[4] but it must be observed that this is not just one part of a theological system, but the center of the entire Christian teaching and life. Here is the fundamental decision which has consequences for the understanding of both God and human beings.

Therefore it is not only understandable, but also consistent, that Luther demands just one thing from the church: the right proclamation of the justification of those far from God. He was even prepared—even after 1530—to recognize the pope, if only Rome would accept this *conditio sine qua non.*[5] Holy Scripture must of course be the norm of the church, but this does not in principle rule out a priority of the Roman bishop before the other members of the church.[6] But is not this emphasis on one doctrine the mark of heresy, where a single special teaching is given inordinate importance? We must answer this question negatively: for with the *articulus stantis et cadentis ecclesiae* we are not dealing with one theological doctrine out of many, but with the basic aspect of theology and religion on which all the various doctrines depend. More important is another objection. It is well-known that the question about salvation was Luther's very personal question which troubled him for years. Can or should such an individual problem be so elevated, so absolutized even, that a protest movement develops within the church? The very fact that the question of a single man was echoed by so many of his contemporaries is evidence that he was articulating a current and obviously widespread problem. At the beginning of the 16th century people were not just longing for salvation, but they were also unsure of salvation, so much so that turning away from human activity and concentrating on God's attitude toward us was perceived as unburdening and freeing. The only thing which can explain such a heated debate over the question of justification is this presupposition, a presupposition which no longer exists today, something which we must keep in mind during our discussions. During the years around 1530, however, considerable debate took place on all sides about the cause and certainty of salvation, so that even when apparently completely different questions were discussed—such as the presence of Christ in the Lord's Supper or the capacities and limits of the human will—this question was discussed too and stood unspoken in the background.

The CA deals expressly with the question of justification. Since this document has become a confession of many Protestant churches, we must inquire as precisely as possible how it explains justification. Our interpretation must be historically oriented and should not project our own reservations into the 16th-century text. Rather we must inquire how justification is understood and interpreted in the CA on the basis of the work of Philip Melanchthon, the actual writer, and also with reference to Martin Luther, the leading theologian of Electoral Saxony. It will be helpful to make clear against whom they were polemicizing and from whom they wished to dissociate themselves. The earliest commentary on the CA is Melanchthon's Apology. In view of the great amount of literature which the lengthy Article 4 of the Apology has called forth,[7] only what appears absolutely necessary for directly understanding the CA's doctrine of justification will be taken from this article. Anything more would go beyond a commentary on this confession of 1530. It is more important for us to comprehend the fundamental directions and intentions of the CA. For this reason a few clarifications of terms might be helpful. We refrain from a systematic approach, since this would not meet the confessional character of the document of Augsburg, but we will not avoid clear assertions, since the confession itself uses them and does not want to communicate indifferent phrases.

2. Toward an Interpretation of the Doctrine of Justification

2.1. How Justification Fits into the Structure and Arrangement of the CA

Articles 1-21 form the first part of the CA and deal with the chief articles of faith. Articles 1-17 present a summary of the history of salvation, extending from the Trinity to eschatology, with a christological emphasis. Articles 18-21 form a sort of appendix. Article 20, dealing with "Faith and Good Works," is especially important for our purposes. It is crucial that what is said about justification in Article 4 is connected with what is said about Jesus Christ in the preceding article. The basis for what is to be said about justification is laid there, and one can understand Articles 4-17 as an explication of what is confessed in Article 3. What Article 5 says about the Holy Spirit follows the statement in Article 4 that justification *propter Christum per fidem* ("for Christ's sake, through faith"), and what the next article says about the fruits of faith, is connected with Article 5. The articles that follow deal with ecclesiology and sacraments, church usages, civil government, and finally the return of Christ.

Luther in his Confession of 1528 had divided the essentials of a doctrine of justification into two appendices to the Apostles' Creed.[8] But what Luther had referred to the glorified Lord and to the work of the Spirit in the church, Melanchthon then combined into one article and attached it to what was said about Jesus Christ. In the preliminary draft of the CA known as Na this problem was solved by making "the entire event of justification the work of the Spirit whom Christ sends into our hearts" (W. Maurer). The assertions in Na 5 are determined by what precedes, and thus are attached to the work of the Spirit, as we also see in the biblical quotation in Na 5: "As Paul says in Galatians 3:14, we receive the promise of the Spirit through faith." In the CA Melanchthon changed this arrangement by reversing Na 4 and Na 5 and replacing Na 5 by CA 4. In this way the new article is directed toward CA 3 and is christologically based. However, we must notice that the work of the Spirit is included in CA 3. While sanctification might normally be understood as the work of the Spirit, here it is associated with the work of the Son.

This concentration of christology gives rise to the question about the relationship of sanctification and reconciliation. This is answered in Article 4. Reconciliation is called (following Paul) "justification through faith." Thus it is faith that brings about justification, a faith that lives by looking at Christ, "who by his death made satisfaction for our sins" (CA 4, 2), and which is worked by he Spirit. The article on justification has its foundation in the act and work of Christ, in Christ's sacrifice of reconciliation, and it introduces the working of the Spirit who is given through office, word, and sacrament in the church (Article 5). Article 4 is therefore based on Article 3, but at the same time is closely connected with Article 5. Because of its location, Article 4 becomes the very heart and connecting link of the Confession. Wilhelm Maurer has therefore called Article 4 the "chief article" of the CA and "the *articulus stantis et cadentis ecclesiae.*" [9] This is true not just for the first part of the Augsburg Confession, but also for the second, which deals with "abuses" within the church. Here too are statements about justification,[10] and it is the interpretation of Article 4 that provides a norm for determining what are abuses in the church.[11]

The position of Article 4 is also christologically determined. In no way can we conclude that Article 4 is antiecclesiastical, antihierarchical, or anti-Roman, on the grounds that it is not until Article 6 that "good works" are spoken of, and the church not until Articles 7 and 8. Precisely because it is dependent on Article 3, Article 4 is directed toward the lordship of the exalted Christ, toward the kingdom of grace that is realized in the church through the Spirit's working. Just as Article 4 is more precisely defined by Article 5, so is Article 5 by Articles 7-14; Articles 7, 8, and 14 pick up on the term *"ministerium"* (office), while Articles 9-13 further develop the phrase "gospel and sacrament." Thus we see the ecclesiological reference of Article 4. There is a saying in the pre-1530 evangelical catechetical tradition that justification and forgiveness of sins are found only in the church.[12] This holds as well for the CA.

2.2. The Position Which Is Rejected by the Augsburg Confession

CA 4 makes not only positive statements, but also negative ones. For example, it rejects a justification *"propriis viribus, meritis aut operibus* (by our merits, works, or satisfactions)."* Reservations against Ulrich Zwingli[13] and the Catholic side are indicated here. Yet it does not condemn the Catholic position wholesale—the Augsburg Confession regards itself as a confession of and witness to the one, catholic church—but it attacks assertions and tendencies which had been represented within the western church. This is why Articles 20, 3-4, and 25, 5-6, also distinguish between the doctrines of contemporary opponents and those of earlier theologians.[14] The opponents intended are not the Catholic apologetic theologians, but the *"recentiores,"* [15] viz., the recent scholastics, chiefly Gabriel Biel, whom the Apology mentions by name four times. He and those who share his views are accused of representing the opinion that God's law can be fulfilled through loving God and one's neighbor by one's own powers without grace.[16] The Augsburg Confession does not believe that this tendency has been entirely overcome in 1530;[17] but because of the Reformation proclamation, such Pelagian and semi-Pelagian statements[18] are no longer being so rashly advanced.

The opponents' position becomes quite clear in Apology 4. At the beginning of the exposition, where Melanchthon is explaining the bases of the opposing doctrine,[19] we read: They "have invented this dream that human reason without the Holy Spirit is able to love God above all else." [20] Apology 2 puts it this way: "They even attribute to human nature unimpaired power to love God above all things and to obey his commandments 'according to the substance of the act *(quoad substantiam actuum).'* " [21] Apology 18, 10 speaks of "those who dream that men can obey the law of God without the Holy Spirit and that the Holy Spirit is given to them out of regard for the merit of this obedience." [22] It is therefore not a "realistic" theology which the opponents hold; they have neither recognized God's law nor understood the seriousness of sin, but they have "dreamed." Melanchthon accuses the representatives of the other side of believing "that good works done without grace and those done in grace are of one and the same sort, that grace only adds the aspect of merit to them. They attribute so much to human powers that they think that human beings do not need the Holy Spirit. In fact, they even doubt whether grace works anything at all in the justified." [23] So that the opponents do not completely ignore Christ's name, they teach that Christ earned for us a *habitus,* or the initial grace, "which they understand as a disposition inclining us to love God more easily." But thereby nothing decisive is accomplished. For "the act of the will before any *habitus* is present, and the act of the will after the *habitus* is there, are of one and the same sort." Besides this, they teach, "that this same *habitus* must be earned through our preparatory work, and that through the work of the law we earn an increase in such a good intention and eternal life." The consequences are considerable: in this way "the people hide Christ and bury him anew; that we cannot recognize him as mediator." [24] Even the forgiveness of sin, according to these theologians, can be obtained by human beings through reason and love. "In this way the scholastics teach men to merit the forgiveness of sins by doing what is within them *(faciendo quod in se est),* that is, if reason in its sorrow over its sin elicits an act of love to God *(hoc est, si ratio dolens de peccato eliciat actum dilectionis Dei)."* If a person acts this way, God will necessarily give him grace, by "the necessity of unchanging order, not of compulsion *(necessitate non coactionis, sed immutabilitatis)."* [25] Thus the opponents are accused of having a false understanding of God, of burying Christ who is no longer necessary for salvation and redemption, and of totally misunderstanding human nature.

The polemics against this position, which the Apology attributes to the scholastics,[26] go back to the beginning of the Reformation movement. In his lectures on Romans in 1515-16 Luther already condemned the view that without the grace of God and solely by human powers a person could love God above all else and fulfill the works of the law "according to the substance of the act, even if not according to the intentions of Him who gave the commandments *(secundum substantiam facti, Sed non ad Intentionem precipientis)*." [27] He condemns the use of the word *formatum,* because it implies the view that the soul before and after the infusion of the *habitus* of love is one and the same.[28] The professor of Wittenberg rejects the axiom that "God infallibly pours his grace into him who does what is within his power *(facienti, quod in se est, infallibiliter Deus infundit gratiam),*" since it makes us believe that grace depends on our good pleasure.[29] Even in the later period Luther and Melanchthon had this scholastic position in mind. Precisely which scholastic theology they referred to was made clear in Luther's *Disputatio contra scholasticam theologiam* of 1517,[30] and in his marginal notes on Gabriel Biel.[31] It is the late scholastic semi-Pelagianism which he believed he found in some of the nominalist theologians and which he held responsible for the abuses in theology and the church.

The rejection of justification "by our own merits, works, or satisfactions *(propriis viribus, meritis aut operibus)*" in CA 4 is directed against this theology, which the young Luther was familiar with and which left his quest for salvation unanswered. Luther believed that for Biel and his friends it was no longer the redemption wrought by Jesus Christ that was decisive, but the satisfaction which human beings were able to accomplish. In place of the doctrine of faith (this was Melanchthon's criticism in Apology 12, 116-117), "the dangerous error of *satisfactiones*" entered, by which "our opponents" claim that "satisfaction is such a work that it placates the divine wrath and displeasure." [32] The claim that righteousness, grace, and salvation are obtained *ex opere operato* through external works is also met with sharp and frequent criticism.[33] However, Melanchthon, Luther, and the other reformers did not advance a completely new doctrine of justification— quite the contrary. They felt their interpretation corresponded to that of the teachers of the true church. Their opposition was addressed to those theologians who had exchanged theology for philosophy. Their influence in the church must be rooted out. The reformers believed that this could be accomplished by a return to the true teaching. What did they understand this to be?

2.3. The Positive Exposition of Justification

To *"iustificare coram Deo propriis viribus, meritis aut operibus,"* CA 4 opposes the justification which takes place, *"gratis," "propter Christum per fidem"* ("by grace for Christ's sake through faith"). In this we must already pay attention to the *"coram Deo"* ("before God"). It expresses the place where justification occurs. To stand before God means, according to the biblical tradition, to stand before the righteous judge. But Christians also stand before God when they stand before Jesus Christ, the crucified and risen one, who died for us and was raised to new life. Whoever stands before God stands "unconditionally" before him. Here judgment is pronounced, but grace can also be in effect. For " 'in standing before God' forgiveness of guilt and new life in the Spirit are conveyed for Christ's sake. Thus Article 4's introductory formula of *'coram Deo'* includes all the major motifs that are contained in Articles 4 through 6." [34] This we must develop.

2.3.1. *Justification by Grace.* Justification takes place *"gratis,"* "by grace," "freely, purely, gratuitously, without merit." All of these words express the same intention: it is God *alone* who forgives sins and creates salvation, although the "alone" is not expressly used. It appears only in Article 6, 3 in a quotation from Ambrosiaster. Melanchton probably wanted to avoid giving offense, especially since Luther had added "alone" to his translation of Rom. 3:28. This was in keeping with the meaning, but still it was an addition to the biblical text. [35] He explains in the Apology, however, that the word *"gratis"* used in CA 4 has the same exclusive character. Thus any reliance on our own merit is excluded, but not word and sacrament or the fact that love should follow. [36] The short word *"gratis"* is a witness *"that* grace is grace." [37]

2.3.2. *Justification for Christ's Sake.* Moreover, justification takes place *"propter Christum,"* "for Christ's sake." Thus his merit and not our own is decisive. Christ is described in this context with the terminology of sacrifice: he is *hostia; oblatio et satisfactio* take place. The Son of God is the only true propitiation; as the means of atonement he is the only savior, mediator, and advocate. That is, *"propter Chris-*

tum" (which is interchangeable with *per Christum*) thus relates to his death as well as to his sitting at the right hand of God. It means the entire work of the Son, on earth as well as in heaven. By it "all of our meritorious works lose their value." [38] This thesis is thus excluding a position, and the position against which it is directed is the same one as before.

On this point the Reformation stands in the tradition of Anselm's *Cur Deus homo?* But where Anselm tried to explain it logically, the reformers, chiefly Luther, thought concretely in terms of the history of salvation and not abstractly. What was important for Luther was what the mystics had called the "joyous exchange" between Christ and the Christian; that is, the exchange of my sins (which Christ takes upon himself) for his sinlessness (which he grants me). Luther spoke this way not only in the period around 1520, but later as well. Christians do not only become righteous for Christ's sake, but through God's Son become themselves children of God. This takes place through faith, which accomplishes the union with Christ and the joyous exchange.[39] *"Propter Christum per fidem"*—What does this mean?

2.3.3. *Justification Through Faith.* The concept of faith is used in different ways in the Bible (e.g., faith of demons; beginning of faith; believing, but not confessing—John 12:42). CA 4 draws on Rom. 3:28 and Gal. 3:14 and understands faith as the opposite of righteousness of the law.[40] This faith has to do with the righteousness of faith, with salvation and reconciliation, with justification and sanctification. Faith and God's grace, the promised mercy, go together: "And so at every mention of mercy we must remember that this requires faith, which accepts the promised mercy." [41] Through faith we seize the grace of God, we receive the righteousness. Through faith the promise becomes a reality for me and in me. Faith is the realization that, for Christ's sake, I have attained the righteousness promised through Christ.

If we compare the Reformation way of speaking about "justification through faith" with the scholastic "justification through the grace created in man" (*gratia creata*), we can see that both have the same intention. The Reformation formula of "justification through faith" (*iustificatio per fidem*) is equivalent to the scholastic formula of "justification through the grace that makes one acceptable to God" (*iustificatio per gratiam gratum facientem*). This is confirmed by the unifying formula pertaining to Articles 4-6 of the CA, adopted by both sides in the Committee of Fourteen in August, 1530, "that forgiveness of sins takes place formally and properly through the grace which makes us acceptable to God and through faith, and through word and sacraments as through means (*quod remissio peccatorum sit per gratiam gratum facientem et fidem formaliter et per verbum et sacramenta instrumentaliter*)." [42] That the intention is to equate grace (*gratia*) and faith (*fides*) is confirmed by the preliminary draft of the Confutation, the *Responsio Catholica,* and the Apology. The Catholic theologians noted about Article 13 of the CA: "But the preachers always reminded us of nothing else but faith, whenever they were supposed to speak about grace." [43] As Article 4, 116 of the Apology shows, Melanchthon also could identify *fides* and *gratia gratum faciens* (grace that makes us acceptable to God): "And since this faith alone receives the forgiveness of sins, renders us acceptable to God, and brings the Holy Spirit, it should be called 'grace that makes us acceptable to God' (*gratia gratum faciens*) rather than love, which is the effect resulting from it." [44]

When Melanchthon nevertheless refrains from using the formula "justification through grace (*iustificatio per gratiam*)," the reason is to be found in his belief that the concept of "grace" has been "perverted" by the scholastics who have equated it with the *"habitus,* through which we love God." This "points to us, and not to God's grace," Melanchthon argued in the Committee of Fourteen in 1530.[45] In the Apology Melanchthon attacks his theological opponents: "From ancient writers they have taken certain sayings, decrees as it were, and these they quote in a twisted way, boasting in the schools that good works please God because of grace and therefore we must place our confidence in God's grace. Here they interpret grace as a disposition (*habitus*) by which we love God, as though the ancients meant to say that we should put confidence in our love. . . ." [46] In the background here is, first, the late scholastic identification of *gratia gratum faciens* with *caritas* (love) and, second, Biel's interpretation which holds that the *habitus* only makes it easier for one to do what one is already able to accomplish with one's purely natural powers (cf. Apol. 4, 17). Contrary to this interpretation, Melanchthon and Luther understand *gratia* first of all as God's *favor.*

For this reason the formula *"iustificatio per gratiam"* (justification through grace) has become unusable. It contains the danger of understanding justification as justification on the basis of our love, and also as justification through God's "favor" it says too little. For God's favor applies to all, but not all are justified—only those who believe. Thus Melanchthon opposes *iustificatio per legem* (justification through law) and *iustificatio per promissionem et fidem* (justification through the promise and faith). The use of *per fidem* is intended to express the subjective side, the coming of grace to me and in me. This is why the German version of the agreement of the Committee of Fourteen says: "Explanation of the fourth, fifth, and sixth articles: we confess that the forgiveness of sins takes place through grace by which we have a gracious God, and this takes place in us through faith, and by God's word and sacrament as through means." [47]

What the Augsburg Confession intended to say about the connection between justification and faith should now be sufficiently clear. The work of Jesus Christ is indeed the necessary presupposition that makes salvation possible. But this work becomes relevant for me only when I accept it in faith.[48] Therefore we can say: "The doctrine of justification is the doctrine of faith. Faith and justification are not two entities related to each other, but two sides of the same thing."[49] Faith does not imitate Christ; it directs itself toward him. For "we were not justified by the faith with which Christ believed, but by the faith with which we believe in Christ." [50] This faith frees us from human judgments, for the one who is justified knows that he is free through God alone. But justifying faith remains challenged, because alongside it sinful desires still exist. However, because it is aware of the forgiveness of sins by Christ, it remains in lively action and does not degenerate into an idle quality.[51] Justification *per fidem* proves itself to be another instance of divine action. He who created the world from nothing also works creatively in the event of justification. From the natural person of sin emerges the new person who is born again in faith and is one with Christ, i.e., with God.[52]

2.3.4. *Acceptance into Grace and Forgiveness of Sins.* "The *'in gratiam recipi'* restates the substance of the doctrine of justification in an exemplary way." [53] Believers know that they have been accepted into God's grace which alone is valid for them. No longer is there a place for counting or not counting human efforts, but simply the gift of the Father who forgives guilt and repays evil with love. Human reason just cannot understand this: "That we are justified freely before Christ by believing that we are accepted by the Father into grace for Christ's sake—of this reason has not the slightest idea." [54] But the conscience of the *believer* is comforted. When we were previously summoned to perform good works and thus to depend on ourselves, "many . . . discovered that they did not obtain peace by such means. It was therefore necessary to preach this doctrine about faith in Christ and diligently to apply it in order that it may be known that the grace of God is appropriated without merits, through faith alone" (cf. CA 20, 15-22). This comfort is the most important result which the Reformation proclamation accomplished.

Alongside the "reception into grace," the Latin text of CA 4 places the forgiveness of sins *"propter Christum."* In a brief passage this basis is spoken of twice: for Christ's sake believers are justified, and for Christ's sake their sins are forgiven. Thus reception into grace, justification, and forgiveness of sins are seen as closely bound together: all three expressions express what is new in the human relationship to God that Jesus Christ has made possible. In the German text the close connection of forgiveness of sins and righteousness before God appears right at the beginning of Article 4: "It is also taught among us that we cannot obtain forgiveness of sin and righteousness before God by our own merits. . . ." Righteousness before God, justification, is where the forgiveness of sins results. Martin Luther spoke especially often about this great good. For "as a result of forgiveness Christ is lord over sin, death, and the devil; he should and will raise this article above everything in heaven and on earth."[55] With God, grace and forgiveness of sins are directly connected. He proves that he is gracious in forgiving sins; and this does not remain a formal judgment, but it creates new life and new obedience (CA 6).

2.3.5. *Reckoning Faith as Righteousness.* The concluding sentence of CA 4 refers again to the indispensibility of faith. It does not merely say that the righteousness of Christ is reckoned to us, but that faith is reckoned as righteousness; or, as the German text puts it, "For God will regard and reckon this faith as righteousness." This reckoning is based on the relationship to God which is characterized by the promise of grace and by faith. This also means that this relationship to God exists only so long as faith is present and is not extinguished by mortal sin and lack of diligence in love. Melanchthon says this clearly in Apology 4, 48: "Those who are accounted righteous before God do not live in mortal sin." [56] It is considered impossible to combine serious sins and conscious disobedience toward God with faith and justification: "Therefore, such a faith does not remain in those who obey their lusts. . . ." [57] *"Iustum reputari"* has an end for the one who loses faith through mortal sin. Only faith which relies on God in all temptations is reckoned as righteousness.

Only faith counts as righteousness; i.e., neither love arising from one's own powers nor works. Faith lives by the promise of God. Believers know they are accepted by God and that their relationship with God is created *"gratis propter Christum."* The relationship with God is not constituted by the works which proceed from the new being, nor is it improved by them. It is granted by God to those who are accepted through faith into grace and whose sins have been and will be forgiven for Christ's sake.[58]

2.3.6. *The Holy Spirit and Faith.* It is not only the Father and the Son who are involved with justification, but the third person of the Trinity as well. This is clear from CA 5, where it is asked how it is possible to obtain the faith upon which rescue and salvation depend. In contrast to those who hold that the inner word, the immediate illumination from God, is decisive, the CA identifies the proclamation of the gospel and the administration of the sacraments as necessary. For the Holy Spirit uses these as "means" through which to work faith as he wills. Those who despise and scorn the word and sacraments deprive themselves of access to faith.

But what is the word, the gospel?[59] CA 5 answers that the gospel teaches that "it is not on account of our own merits but on account of Christ that God justifies those who believe that they are received into favor for Christ's sake." Thus the gospel is nothing else but the message of justification. In the church's proclamation the central element can and must be solely the reference to salvation which goes back solely to the Son of God. God is gracious to us, as the German text says, not for our sake, but for the sake of Christ's merit.

Here we come again to the message of justification as the *articulus stantis et cadentis ecclesiae.* Anabaptists and others who trust in their "own preparations, thoughts, and works" are condemned. What is demanded is churchly preaching and churchly rites which the Holy Spirit will use to awaken this all-decisive faith.

2.3.7. *Good Works—The New Obedience.* Good works, which come forth as fruits of faith, are not unimportant for Christians. It was a serious misunderstanding at the time of the Reformation period to interpret the evangelical polemics against the view that good works were the cause of justification as a rejection of all good works. This is why CA 6 emphasizes that faith must produce "good fruits" and that it is necessary "because it is God's will" to do the good works he has commanded. But then we are immediately reminded that "we do not rely on such good works to merit justification before God." Obviously this creates a different misunderstanding: good works make me acceptable to God; therefore, Christ's work takes a backseat to my own works. This is rejected with a reference to Jesus' statement that we are still unprofitable servants when we do all that is commanded us. Thus it is again repeated—an indication of how important this statement is—that "we receive forgiveness of sins and righteousness through faith in Christ."

Though good works are not the basis for justification, they are essential in the life of the justified. They are to be done to "do God's will and glorify him." [60] They are also necessary "so that faith may be exercised, grow, and increase." [61] Indeed, "because of faith they are nevertheless holy and divine works, sacrifices, and the reign of Christ, whereby he shows his rule before the world." [62] It follows that the life of a person who claims to be a Christian, but who does not do good works, is not a testimony to Christ's lordship; for this is present only where one acts according to God's commandment. Works do not earn blessedness, but the degree of glory is related to good works.[63] The consequences of Christian action go beyond this earthly life. Just as justification is made possible through Jesus Christ and is imputed to each Christian through faith, so does the new obedience have its place: it proves itself to be the *new* obedience when it is performed by those who gratefully recognize that the saving act of Jesus Christ belongs to them.

2.4. *Clarification of Terms.* How one understands *iustificari* is crucial. One should not interpret this term within the context provided by the Osiandrian Controversy, where the question was whether justification took place solely *in foro coeli* or whether it had affective results in the believer. Although a forensic doctrine of justification is attributed to the old Melanchthon, it is correct to say that "the Augustana did not intend a mere forensic doctrine of justification." [64] Rather there are three conceptual areas which may be connected with the verb *iustificari*.

2.4.1. *Iustificari=iustum effici.* In the Apology the process of justification is described as a *iustum effici*, a "being-made-righteous." This takes place when a sinner is made righteous *(ex iniusto iustum effici)* and obtains the forgiveness of sins (cf. Apol. 4, 72: *hoc est, accipiat remissionem peccatorum).*[65] This process is labeled *"renasci"* and *"regenerari."* [66] But what is "regeneration?" According to CA 2, regeneration takes place "through Baptism and the Holy Spirit," by which the condemnation wrought by original sin comes to an end. The Apology calls regeneration the work of the Holy Spirit, and it also speaks about a person who is born again through faith.[67] Regeneration is accomplished when a Christian receives the Holy Spirit. The reason why one may also speak about faith here is that the Apology connects the coming of the Holy Spirit directly with faith: "So through faith the Holy Spirit comes into our heart, which renews our heart."[68] The renewal consists in this, that "the divine wisdom and righteousness, which is of God, is formed in us; we thereby know God and God's light is reflected in us." [69] Justification, through which sins are forgiven and the unrighteous becomes righteous, establishes a new being, is a new birth.[70] In summary we may say: "In the personal relation of the Holy Spirit and faith a new relationship to God is established. We are born anew as righteous. We are the image of God, 'participants in his divine nature,' for through Christ we attain righteousness, holiness, and truth, and in faith's knowledge of God, God is reflected, and thus 'God is continually in the soul.' To be made righteous and to be born again, therefore, means to stand in living fellowship with God." [71]

2.4.2. *Iustificari=sanctificari.* Although the Formula of Concord limits the term "sanctification" *("sanctificatio")* to moral renewal through virtue and good works and thus contrasts it to justification,[72] it is not yet interpreted in this way in Luther's Large Catechism, the Augsburg Confession, and the Apology. In CA 3 the work of the glorified Lord is described as the sanctification of believers through the Holy Spirit. In the Apology *iustificare* and *sanctificare* are identified,[73] and in the Large Catechism Luther says: "Therefore to sanctify is nothing else than to bring us to the Lord Christ to receive this blessing, which we could not obtain by ourselves." [74] Here *iustificare* and *sanctificare* are identified. It is always the same reality that is being spoken of, which can neither be limited to the realm of experience nor equated with a formal divine judgment. Rather, justification takes place "in receiving through faith the Holy Spirit, who brings us to Christ, who reveals Christ in our heart." Now no longer do Satan and sin reign—"ruling sin becomes ruled sin"—but Christ the Lord.[75]

2.4.3. *Iustificari=iustum reputari.* In Apology 4, 252, Melanchthon says that being regarded as righteous depends on a judicial decision.[76] God's office of judge is therefore exercised in the event of justification. What is judged? Does this deal with a new aspect of the CA's doctrine of justification—with perhaps wide-reaching consequences—or are the concepts *iustum effici* and *iustum reputari* (or *pronuntiari*) used "almost synonymously" by Melanchthon? [77]

Apology 4, 78 identifies the forgiveness of past sins with justification and regeneration: ". . . making an unrighteous man righteous or effecting his regeneration." [78] Beyond this, the justified person continually needs the forgiveness of sins, for "in our present weakness there is always sin that could be imputed to us." [79] In his *Annotations on Romans* of 1530 Melanchthon says that justification means that sins are not imputed.[80] He thus repeats that justification does not refer to our own works, but to God's grace which does not impute sins. Not imputing sins means, therefore, that God does not stop with a onetime forgiveness, but that he ever anew imputes to believers what is still lacking in fulfilling the law.[81]

If, as Edmund Schlink says, both concepts—*iustum effici* and *iustum reputari*—are necessary to characterize the Reformation doctrine of justification, then we must finally ask how the two are related to each other.[82] We have to recognize that we must distinguish between the initial being-made-righteous and the continuation of justification, "which is conceived of as a continuing *actus*." [83] "While *'iustum effici'* relates primarily to *'iniustus iustificandus,' 'iustum reputari,'* on the other hand, relates to *'pius iustificandus.'* " [84] Here we must notice that *iustum effici* refers to a sacramental regeneration effected by God's word which takes place in us in and through faith. In no way does *iustum effici* create a natural condition of unlimited duration; that would deeply contradict the Reformation's *simul iustus et peccator.* While the *"iustum effici"* occurs *"per fidem,"* the *"iustum reputari"* happens *"propter fidem."* [85] Through faith the sinner is *made* righteous, as the joyous exchange takes place between him and Jesus Christ; for faith's sake the justified, who is also a sinner, is *considered* righteous and the *remissio peccatorum,* which remains under gospel and sacraments, is pronounced anew. Also according to Luther, the fellowship with Christ given in faith is requisite for the *"reputatio,"* the regarding as righteous: "Here it is to be noted that these three things are joined together: faith, Christ, and acceptance or imputation. Faith takes hold of Christ and has him present, enclosing Him as the ring encloses the gem. And God accounts as righteous whoever is found having this faith in the Christ who is grasped in the heart." [86] Making righteous, sanctifying, and declaring righteous are different but closely connected aspects of the event of justification, in which, according to the Augsburg Confession and the Apology, the active part is always on the side of the Triune God.

3. Toward Understanding the Catholic-Lutheran Controversy Over the Doctrine of Justification at the Time of the Reformation

To understand the theological controversy over the doctrine of justification correctly, we must remember that it is imbedded in the many-layered and quite diverse motives and factors of the conflict which led to the formation of different positions, groups, and confessions. The danger of death and persecution for the Lutheran side cannot be overlooked in attempting to understand the background. The understanding of most of the Catholic opponents of Luther was affected by reports and personal experiences of disturbances and excesses, which grew out of a widespread anticlerical sentiment and accompanied the spread of the Reformation in the first half of the 1520s. This was expressly formulated by Johannes Mensing: "To tell the truth, this is why we are unwilling to trust them when they say something that otherwise we might be willing to tolerate and which could be given a favorable interpretation, the way we interpret many words of the blessed teachers. . . . These pious teachers do not frighten us, for we know they are above suspicion. But because you have brought forth innumerable errors, unrest, and false doctrine, we do not believe you, even when you sometimes also speak a true word." [87] In addition, there is the fact that the theological dispute itself primarily focuses on the extreme positions of the opposite side. If we ignore this, we might postulate the existence of divisions and separate confessional positions, when we are really dealing with discussions of various theological schools. Thus in the question about justification it is not primarily the area of the so-called double justification which is the subject of the theological dispute. This is somewhat clear in the Apology: "Although a few teachers have written that, after the forgiveness of sins, we obtain grace not through faith but through our own works, they have nevertheless not held that the forgiveness of sins occurs for the sake of our works and not for Christ's sake" (Apol. 20, 3).

The position opposed by the CA has already been described (see above, 2.2). In what follows, individual examples will illustrate the Reformation position which was rejected by the Catholic side.

One cannot overestimate the importance for the traditional Catholic view of the Reformation and of the Lutheran position of the catalogs of heresies drawn chiefly from statements by the Reformers of the first half of the 1520s, principally by Johannes Cochlaeus, Johannes Eck,

Johannes Faber, and Alphonsus de Castro.[88] According to this view, the focal point of the Lutheran doctrine and the "source and origin of almost all other heresies" is Luther's doctrine "that faith alone is sufficient for the salvation of everyone." [89] The Reformation way of speaking about faith alone justifying was interpreted as teaching that the sacraments accomplish nothing, that good works are superfluous, and that nothing can endanger faith.[90] This view was supported by quotations of exaggerated Reformation statements taken out of context, and often obtained second- or thirdhand.

The Council of Trent in canon 19 of the decree on justification, for example, condemned those who say "that nothing besides faith is commanded in the Gospel, that other things are indifferent, neither commanded nor forbidden, but free; or that the ten commandments in no way pertain to Christians." [91] Behind this canon are three statements of Luther which the council fathers had only as isolated excerpts.[92] In its context Luther's statement that "the Ten Commandments do not pertain to us," but to the Jews, had a different intention. It was directed against the enthusiasts who wanted to follow the letter of the Old Testament, and Luther limited its meaning by adding, "unless he [Moses] agrees with both the New Testament and the natural law." [93] As an isolated statement this sentence should be rejected, and it conveys a picture of the Lutheran doctrine of justification which contradicts the statements of the Lutheran Confessions on the meaning for Christians of the Ten Commandments and good works.

In the decree on the sacraments the Council of Trent condemned the statement, "that the baptized cannot, even if they wish, lose grace, however much they may sin, unless they are unwilling to believe" (Denzinger, 1619). Behind this stands a statement of Luther in 1520, frequently quoted by the Catholic theologians in the controversy, in which the significance of faith is emphasized in an unreserved and excessive way.[94] This condemnation does not apply to the Lutheran confession, however. In the Smalcald Articles, for example, Luther condemns the fanatics who cry out, "Do what you will, it matters not as long as you believe, for faith blots out all sins." [95] The CA condemns those who "deny that those who have once been justified can lose the Holy Spirit" (CA 12, 7).

In the background of canon 6 of the decree on justification are statements by Luther and Melanchthon from 1520-22 about God's working of evil, so that the betrayal of Judas is no less his work than is the conversion of Paul.[96] These statements were subsequently modified by

Luther and corrected by the CA and Melanchthon. Martin Chemnitz correctly commented on this condemnation of the Council of Trent: "I am not ignorant about what is being argued by some about the will and working of God in the evil acts of human beings. But what the position of our churches is Article 14 of our Confession clearly shows." [97]

The Reformers' statement that faith in the divine promise alone is sufficient to obtain grace is understood by the Council of Trent as disputing the working of the sacraments *ex opere operato* (cf. Denzinger, 1608). When the Apology attacks a justification *ex opere operato* ("without a good disposition in the recipient"),[98] it misses the point of why the Catholic doctrine of the sacraments describes their efficacy with the expression *ex opere operato*. Yet it expressly opposes the "dangerous opinion" of its opponents that the word *sola* excludes gospel and sacraments in the sense "that thereby the Word and sacraments are futile" (Apol. 4, 73).[99]

The Reformers' rejection of a justification by one's own power and *ex opere operato* no more applies to the theological position of the Council of Trent than does the Catholic rejection of an antisacramental and libertinistic interpretation of a justification through faith alone apply to the theological position of the Lutheran confession. With these clarifications not all the issues of substance in the doctrine of justification have been completely discussed, as both the intra-Lutheran and intra-Catholic arguments on this subject show, but the central polemic which divided the confessions has lost its object. This is confirmed by the fact that in Augsburg in 1530, as well as in Worms and Regensburg in 1541, a substantial agreement on the doctrine of justification was achieved. The principal reason that this did not last was that neither side could accept the trustworthiness of the other: so significant was the image of the other as stranger and as enemy in that situation of rigid separation.[100]

4. Further Development of the Evangelical Doctrine of Justification in the 16th Century

Though the Council of Trent's statements on justification were indeed noticed by Protestantism,[101] they had no immediate results. But the discussion among the Evangelicals themselves again and again turned to this doctrine. Even while Luther was still active in Wittenberg, Johann Agricola had aroused a great deal of unrest with his claim that human penitence is not caused by the law, but by the gospel. Luther had demanded that law and gospel be distinguished and now it seemed to him that the gospel was being misunderstood as law and that the law was being annulled. Such an antinomianism would remove the comforting power of the gospel, he believed, for it would now be assigned the task of also revealing sin. This would endanger the foundation of the message of justification. Agricola felt that he had been misunderstood and was unable to avoid breaking with Luther. On the basis of these early disputes one could say "that Antinomianism can always be a possible danger for the development of Reformation theology." [102]

With Agricola the question was about the relationship of law and gospel in the conversion of sinners. With the so-called Antinomians of the 1550s the question was then whether the law was of importance for the converted. Their answer was, No! For Christians fulfill God's will on the basis of the Holy Spirit living in them; they are directed not by the law, but by love. The law has nothing to do with the life of the justified. Melanchthon's teaching that the law also directs the regenerate was sharply rejected.[103]

Even more serious was the controversy which developed from Andreas Osiander's preaching in Königsberg after 1549. Osiander, who had gone to Prussia because of the Interim, rejected a concept of imputation according to which God declared a *sinner* righteous. He believed that this contradicted the divine nature of God, who could have nothing to do with sin. The death of Christ on the cross is only the redemption and thus just the presupposition for justification, the latter taking place through the indwelling of the divine nature of Jesus Christ in Christians. Thus a doctrine of effective justification was being taught, but it was connected with a doctrine of God which had completely new accents. Though Osiander claimed to be in agreement with Luther,[104] it is not surprising that his attack on imputation, coupled with his argument against the validity of Luther's *"simul iustus et peccator,"* stirred up keen excitement and indignation.

Not only Melanchthon and his disciples, but also opponents of theirs like Nikolaus von Amsdorf or Matthias Flacius, were unanimous in their rejection of this doctrine. Only Johannes Brenz and the Württembergers sought to mediate. They thought that it had not been proved that Osiander had really rejected the *iustitia imputativa*. Some things were attributed to him which he had never taught. But his opponents declared that justification and redemption could not be separated from one another; they must be recognized as identical. Justification contained not only the forgiveness of sins, but also regeneration, which therefore may not be traced back to a special indwelling of the divine nature of Jesus Christ. The righteousness *extra nos* which is attributed to us, and which must not be confused with a righteousness infused into us, remains decisive.[105] The controversies were fought with great vehemence, a sign of how little people were unanimous about this central Reformation doctrine.

The question about the quality of God's action gave rise to sharp debate. So too did the question of human participation in the event of justification. Melanchthon identified three causes of conversion: God's word, the Holy Spirit, and the human will which assents to God's word and does not resist it. Some of his students emphasized more strongly than he that the reason for the conversion of one person and the rejection of God by others must lie in individuals themselves. Amsdorf and Flacius vehemently objected to this, since it underestimated the seriousness of sin which opposed God, and would limit God's power by human freedom of choice.[106] Thus the center of the Reformation message was disputed: the synergists emphasized human cooperation while their opponents emphasized God's sovereign activity in conversion as the act through which justification begins.

So that nothing might remain undisputed—from the presuppositions of justification and its beginning to its results—good works once again had to become a subject for debate. The Leipzig Interim in 1548 had already "put emphasis on the necessity of Christian virtues for salvation and on the reward of good works." [107] When this was criticized by Amsdorf, it was defended by one of those attacked, Georg Major, after whom this controversy is named. Major declared that good works are necessary for salvation, and then later said more precisely that they are necessary not to obtain salvation, but to retain it. Then Amsdorf, appealing to Luther, declared that works are harmful to salvation. Luther had indeed said that works could be injurious, but he had not declared that as an absolute, but always said that they are injurious when one presumes to rely on them for salvation. Melanchthon kept rather distant from all these controversies. In the Majoristic Controversy he took the side that the formula, good works are necessary *for salvation,* should be avoided because it could be misunderstood: they are required instead because the Christian is obligated to obey God.[108]

All of these disputed questions remained without a satisfactory answer, although what was being debated was what made the church the church. Hence the representatives of the efforts at unification in German

Protestantism, the framers of the Formula of Concord of 1577, had to take a stand on this. This they did by speaking of free will, the righteousness of faith, good works, law and gospel, and the importance of the law for believers under the heading of "The Third Function of the Law" (Art. 2-6). It is understandable that solutions were sought in the Formula of Concord which could be accepted by as many people as possible, which of course did not contribute to clarity. There were considerable distortions of rejected doctrines,[109] which shows that these theological problems would really have had to have been approached with great precision if they were to be recognized or indeed solved.

Of free will, it says that human nature is incapable of spiritual things and blind over against God. Indeed, one always inclines toward evil and is spiritually dead. One is awakened to life not by one's own power, but by God alone, who through preaching calls his creatures to himself and opens their hearts through the Holy Spirit. Accordingly everything depends on God's grace; there is no real human cooperation in conversion. Though we possess free will (about which CA 18 also spoke), it is of no use in the spiritual realm, where dependence on God is asserted. We are not able to make a beginning which God would then seize and bring to completion. Rather everything relative to salvation depends on God (Formula of Concord, Article 2).

Osiander's teaching that Jesus Christ is our righteousness according to his divine nature is rejected. The entire Son of God as true God and true man (and not just his divine nature) accomplishes our righteousness by pure grace in that God reckons to us the righteousness of his Son. Not the indwelling of God in man, but faith that recognizes the gracious God and trusts in him is decisive, since God regards us as righteous on the basis of this faith. The distinction between redemption and justification which Osiander had advanced is also rejected. Justification is at the same time a declaration of the forgiveness of sins and regeneration as a new human being. This also means that faith must be understood as active in love (Article 3). Thus they tried here to connect imputation and regeneration without completely answering Osiander, who had incorrectly been accused of a tendency toward works righteousness.

In the following article good works are called the "natural" result of faith. As a good tree produces good fruit, so do good works follow true faith. But the opinion is sharply rejected that good works can produce justification and salvation; if that were true, Jesus Christ would not have had to suffer and die for the sake of justification. But all are obligated to obey God and do good works. This is especially true for the regenerate who owe God voluntary obedience. Christians may not cease doing good or intentionally persevere in sin, but are to do good works for the love of their Redeemer and righteousness and not out of fear of God's punishment. If the regenerate remain imperfect, for Christ's sake their lack will not be reckoned to them. Where they do good works they are a testimony to the working of the Holy Spirit (Article 4). Georg Major's exaggerated formulation of the necessity of good works for salvation is therefore rejected and at the same time the requirement of good works in the Christian life is emphasized.

In "Law and Gospel" (Article 5) it is said that the two must be carefully distinguished. The law punishes everything which is against God's will. Everything which punishes sin, therefore, belongs to the preaching of the law. But the gospel proclaims God's grace. This differentiation is relativized, nevertheless, by explaining, in accordance with the biblical usage of the word, that the term *gospel* may also include Jesus' entire teaching. In this case the gospel may be the preaching of repentance as well as of the forgiveness of sins. It depends on what usage of the word is intended. If gospel in the narrow sense is used *(proprie dicta),* then there is no preaching of the law. The authors of the Formula of Concord remind us that Jesus' proper work is the promise of grace, a reference that they have appropriated from Luther. Therefore it is clear that law and gospel must be distinguished; what is continually in question is "whether this distinction will be perceived in a theologically adequate way or not." [110]

Of the "third use of the law," finally, it is said that those who are converted are indeed free from the *curse* of the law, but do not live without the law. Rather they should exercise themselves in it "day and night" (Article 6). Thus antinomianism is rejected. Even believers need to have the law preached, for despite their regeneration they are still burdened by sin. The difference in the way the penitent and impenitent keep the law lies in this, that the former willingly keep the law while the latter do it reluctantly and by coercion. It is disputed whether the Formula of Concord teaches a sort of *tertius usus legis* by which the regenerate receive direction for their life from the law.[111] There are two reasons for the hesitation here by the authors of the Formula. One is the fact that the matter was in dispute in the Lutheran tradition: Luther, in contrast to Melanchthon, did not speak of the third use of the law. The other is the fact that the entire question of the Christian life was connected with it, and this was being answered in different ways in the second half of the 16th century.

In summary we must say that the achievement of the authors of the Formula of Concord was respectable.[112] Yet it is in the nature of compromises—on which the writing of this document depended—that they do not always speak as clearly as one might wish. It is well-known that the attempt to pursue a middle way which could be followed by as many as possible was not a complete success. But it was precisely in dealing with justification that the Formula of Concord worked with great intensity to achieve the right understanding, a sign of how important the *articulus stantis et cadentis ecclesiae* was for the life of the Lutheran church in Germany in the second half of the 16th century.

5. The Message of Justification and Christian Proclamation Today

Theological development in the evangelical world did not cease with the Augsburg Confession, and in the Roman Catholic Church the decree on justification of the Council of Trent did not remain the final word on the subject. The various disputes about Augustinianism should especially be cited here as developments which brought further clarifications. In Protestantism the Variata of the Augsburg Confession in 1540 already brought new emphases.[113] Others grew out of the doctrinal controversies within Lutheranism after Luther's death. But it was above all the Enlightenment that destroyed many of the self-evident presuppositions which were starting points in the Reformation era: concentrating on one's own salvation, faith in a direct intervention of God, or the knowledge of the gravity of sin. This is why almost all evangelical theologians of the age of the Enlightenment developed and propounded a new doctrine of justification which had hardly anything in common with the Augsburg Confession.[114] The result of this was that to the present day in the evangelical church "neither the classical formulation of the doctrine of justification nor more recent interpretations have been able to achieve anything even approaching a comparable consensus." [115] As contemporary society comes up against limits, it once again becomes possible to ask about the meaning of life and freedom from compulsion, and to these questions the proclamation of justification may be able to give aid and answer.

Thus the classical confessional boundaries and exclusions are largely relativized, if not completely left behind. Our glance at history shows now that the theologies of the Reformers and of the Catholics were not as far apart as both sides thought. The Roman Catholic controversialists were not representatives of a semi-Pelagian nominalism, and the Reformers wanted to be anything but founders of a new church or inventors of a new doctrine. Different emphases still remained in August, 1530, with the agreement on the doctrine of justification. Those who know how much importance different emphases can have for theologians will not be surprised that the attempts at understanding forced by state pressure were soon followed again by polemics. It is especially puzzling that it was *not* possible to draw from this basic theological agreement the same consequences relative to the so-called "abuses." For "it would be a misunderstanding of CA 7 if ecclesiastical regulations and practices would be seen as irrelevant and their carrying out a matter of indifference. It is instead characteristic of the CA that the life forms of the church must be subjected to the gospel of justification as the central theological criterion. If this examination of questions of order cannot lead to solutions which can be tolerated by both sides, the consensus reached in the first part is threatened. That was the case in 1530." [116]

This does not change the fact that such a broad consensus was present in the Reformation era concerning the understanding of justification that it would surely be difficult today for the theologians of a *single* church to reach a similar unanimity. But if it is clear that "a doctrine recognized as false cannot again become an expression of the truth of God's Word," we must search anew for positive statements about justification made in the tradition of the church. In this process the place value of such statements may remain different for Catholicism and Lutheranism.[117] By the nature of its structure the Roman Catholic Church can more easily absorb and integrate a statement intended to be absolute than can the relatively small Lutheran Church. Also the message of justification in Catholicism has thus far not held the central position that it does in traditional Protestantism. There it can be said: "The freedom granted in justifying faith, freedom from the demands of the church and freedom of an individual from the demand for securing his 'perseverence in faith' cannot be annulled, but remains valid." It remains here a reference to the help for understanding the Scriptures, which the doctrine of justification provides: "The Reformation hermeneutic aids the preaching of the church toward a normative interpretation of the Scriptures, for it develops the gospel of redemption in Christ as the center of the Scriptures." [118]

Just as a discussion of justification can proceed profitably on the basis of the efforts of the Reformation era, as had already been shown, it must not be limited to each side's 16th-century documents. Both churches have moved forward and neither will find the other where it stood several centuries ago. In Protestantism one will do well to examine anew the statements of the Reformation age on the basis of the Holy Scriptures as *norma normans,* a starting point that accords with that of Catholicism and which can bring new viewpoints into the discussion. This is already evident in the "Report of the Evangelical Lutheran-Roman Catholic Study Commission" on "The Gospel and the Church," where it says: "Both Lutherans and Catholics are convinced that the gospel establishes Christian freedom. This freedom is described in the New Testament as freedom from sin, as freedom from the power of the law, as freedom from death, and as freedom for service to God and one's neighbor. Since Christian freedom is nevertheless connected with the testimony of the gospel, it requires an institutional form for its mediation. The church must therefore understand and realize itself as an institution of freedom. Structures which endanger this freedom cannot be legitimate in the church of Christ." [119]

Notes

1. BC 292.
2. H. G. Pöhlmann, *Rechtfertigung: Die gegenwärtige kontroverstheologische Problematik der Rechtfertigungslehre zwischen der evangelisch-lutherischen und der römisch-katholischen Kirche* (Gütersloh: 1971), pp. 25-26.
3. Cf. G. Gassmann, *"Die Rechtfertigungslehre in der Perspektive der Confessio Augustana und des lutherisch-katholischen Gesprächs heute,"* *Luther: Zeitschrift der Luther-Gesellschaft* 50 (1979): 52-54.
4. F. Loofs, *"Der articulus stantis et cadentis ecclesiae,"* ThStKr 90 (1917): 323-420.
5. Cf. J. Lortz, *"Martin Luther: Grundzüge seiner geistigen Struktur,"* *Reformata Reformanda: Festgabe für H. Jedin,* vol. 1 (Münster/Westf.: 1965), p. 245.
6. Cf. G. Müller, *"Martin Luther und das Papsttum,"* *Das Papsttum in der Diskussion,* G. Denzler, ed. (Regensburg: 1974), pp. 90-92.
7. Cf. the list in V. Pfnür, *Einig in der Rechtfertigungslehre? Die Rechtfertigungslehre der Confessio Augustana (1530) und die Stellungnahme der katholischen Kontroverstheologen zwischen 1530 und 1535* (Wiesbaden: 1970), p. 155, note 95.
8. Cf. AE 37, 360-372 (WA 26, 499-509).
9. *Historischer Kommentar zur Confessio Augustana,* vol. 2 (Gütersloh: 1978), p. 68.

10. Cf. *ibid.*, p. 74.
11. Cf. Gassmann, p. 53.
12. Cf. Pfnür, p. 107, note 645; cf. also CA 28, 8-9 (BC 82).
13. Cf. W. Köhler, *Das Marburger Religionsgespräch 1529* (Leipzig: 1929), pp. 8, 53.
14. Cf. BC 41 and 62; AE 34, 12 (WA 30², 275); AE 21, 284 (WA 32, 535).
15. Cf. Apol. 21, 41 (BC 235); Apol., first draft, 24 (BSLK 352, 47).
16. Cf. Pfnür, pp. 39-88.
17. Cf. CA 20, 4 (BC 41).
18. Cf. G. Müller, *Die Rechtfertigungslehre: Geschichte und Probleme* (Gütersloh: 1977), pp. 19ff and 31ff.
19. Cf. Apol. 4, 4 (BC 107-108).
20. Apol. 4, 9 (BSLK 160; CT 122; German).
21. BC 101-102; cf. also the *Editio princeps* of the Augsburg Confession of 1531 in the formula of condemnation of CA 18 (BC 40, note 5; see also BC 224-225).
22. BC 226.
23. K. E. Förstemann, *Urkundenbuch zu der Geschichte des Reichstags zu Augsburg im Jahre 1530,* vol. 2 (1835; reprint ed., Osnabrück: 1966), p. 488; cf. *ibid.,* 534-535.
24. Apol. 4, 17-18 (BSLK 162-163; CT 124; German).
25. Apol. 4, 9-11 (BC 108); in Luther's and Melanchthon's writings of the period directly after 1533 the opposing position is similarly characterized, cf. Pfnür, pp. 65-66.
26. Cf. also Apol. 4, 9 (BC 160).
27. AE 25, 261; Cf. AE 25, 266, 344, and 348 (WA 56, 274; 279; 355; and 359).
28. AE 25, 325 (WA 56, 337).
29. AE 25, 497 (WA 56, 503); in his first lectures on the Psalms in 1513-15 Luther still approved this axiom, cf. AE 11, 396 (WA 4, 262).
30. Cf. Pfnür, pp. 67-84.
31. Cf. H. Degering in *Festgabe der Kommission zur Herausgabe der Werke Martin Luthers 10 Nov. 1933;* H. Volz in ZKG 81 (1970): 207-219.
32. BSLK 276, CT 286 (German); with the formula *fieri eam ad placandam divinam offensam* the Apology refers to the definition of *satisfactio* by Duns Scotus and Gabriel Biel (cf. Pfnür, pp. 40-41); cf. Apol. 12, 68 (BC 192).
33. Cf. BC 125, 135, and 150, as well as Förstemann, 2,499; see Pfnür, pp. 39-64.
34. Maurer, pp. 77-78; with the concept of *coram Deo* that of *iustitia Dei seu spiritualis* is closely associated (CA 18, 2); cf. also H. Fagerberg, *Die Theologie der lutherischen Bekenntnisschriften von 1529 bis 1537* (Göttingen: 1965), pp. 150-155.
35. Cf. Apol. 4, 73-74 (BC 117).
36. Cf. *ibid.;* Melanchthon expresses himself similarly in his Commentary on Romans of 1532; cf. Maurer, p. 79.
37. Maurer, p. 80.
38. *Op. cit.,* p. 91.
39. Cf. *op. cit.,* pp. 95-100.

40. Cf. also BC 113-114, and Pfnür, pp. 150-154.
41. Apol. 4, 55 (BC 114).
42. H. Immenkötter, *Um die Einheit im Glauben: Die Unionsverhandlungen des Augsburger Reichstags im August und September 1530* (Münster: 1973), p. 39, note 53; Pfnür, p. 152, note 83.
43. J. Ficker, *Die Konfutation des Augsburgischen Bekenntnisses: Ihre erste Gestalt und ihre Geschichte* (Leipzig: 1891), pp. 48, 22ff.
44. BC 123.
45. Förstemann 2,226 (Spalatin's protocol). Melanchthon reported to Luther on August 22, 1530 about the negotiations concerning the doctrine of justification in the Committee of Fourteen. He related that John Eck had not rejected the substance of the formula *sola fide* (through grace alone), but that he would not accept it for the sake of the inexperienced. "Then I forced him to admit that righteousness is properly ascribed by us to faith. Then he wanted us to write *quod iustificemur per graciam et fidem*. I had nothing against this, but *ille stultus non intelligit vocabulum 'graciae'*" (WA Br 5, 555; also *Melanchthons Werke in Auswahl, vol. 7/2*, H. Volz, ed. [Gütersloh: 1975], p. 266; *ibid*, p. 294).
46. Apol. 4, 380-381 (BC 165).
47. Förstemann 2,231.
48. "The contemporary interpretation of the article cannot too strongly emphasize the connection between *per fidem* and *propter fidem*" (Maurer 2, 102).
49. *Op cit.*, p. 101.
50. *Op. cit.*, p. 105.
51. Cf. *op. cit.*, pp. 107-110.
52. Cf. P. Althaus, *The Theology of Martin Luther* (Philadelphia: Fortress Press, 1966), pp. 120-121.
53. Maurer 2,79.
54. CR 15,452, 450, 483; quoted in Maurer 2,81.
55. Maurer 2,87.
56. BC 114; cf. Pfnür, pp. 182-193.
57. Apol. 4, 144 (BC 127); cf. also Melanchthon's *Loci* of 1535: "*Sed est aliud quoddam genus actionum, quae sunt eiusmodi, ut qui eas admittunt, excidant gratia Dei, hoc est desinant reputari iusti et damnentur nisi resipiscant. Hae actiones vocantur peccata mortalia*" (CR 21, 448).
58. Cf. Pfnür, pp. 193-197.
59. Both expressions are used *promiscue*, but here mean the same.
60. CA 20, 27 (BC 45).
61. Apol. 4, 189 (BSLK 197; CT 174; German).
62. *Ibid.*
63. Cf. BC 133-134 and 160-161.
64. Maurer 2,85.
65. Cf. BC 117 (CT 140) and BC 142-143; cf. also Pfnür, pp. 157ff.
66. Cf. BC 117, 123, and 155-156 (CT 140, 154, and 206).
67. Cf. BC 111-112, 124-125, 143-144, and 155-156.
68. Apol. 4, 46 (BSLK 169; CT 132; German).
69. Apol. 2, 20-21 (BSLK 151; CT 109-110; German).

70. "Justification through grace is more than a doctrine which one hears and internalizes. It is a new birth; the evil man, born of God, becomes good and acts well toward his neighbor" (Maurer 2,83).

71. Pfnür, pp. 164-165.

72. Cf. BC 546.

73. Cf. Apol. 3 (BC 107; CT 118); cf. BSLK 598 (German) with the notes to lines 8-16 (CT 622; BC 385).

74. BC 415-416; cf. also AE 51, 169 (WA 30¹, 94): "The Holy Spirit sanctifies me through his word and the sacraments, which are in the church, and will sanctify us wholly on the last day."

75. Cf. Pfnür, p. 166.

76. Cf. BC 143.

77. Cf. M. Greschat, *Melanchthon neben Luther* (Witten: 1965), p. 127.

78. BC 117.

79. Apol. 4, 168 (BC 130).

80. Cf. Pfnür, p. 171.

81. Cf. Apol. 4, 177 (BC 131).

82. E. Schlink, *Theology of the Lutheran Confessions* (Philadelphia: Muhlenberg Press, 1961), p. 95.

83. J. Kunze, *Die Rechtfertigungslehre in der Apologie* (Gütersloh: 1906), p. 179; quoted in Pfnür, p. 178.

84. According to F. Loofs, K. Thieme, E. F. Fischer, O. Ritschl, and H. Fagerberg, *iustum reputari* of the Apology presupposes *iustum effici*. Cf. the discussion of this dependent relationship in Pfnür, pp. 178-181.

85. A distinction that goes back to E. F. Fischer; cf. Pfnür, p. 180.

86. AE 26, 132 (WA 40 ¹, 233); cf. Pfnür, p. 181.

87. Johannes Mensing, *Antapologie:* Erst teyl (n.p., n.d. [Frankfurt/Oder: 1533]), Fo. VIIIr-XIIIIr.

88. Cf. Pfnür, pp. 226-227, note 54.

89. Andreas de Vega, *Opusculum de iustificatione, gratia et meritis,* 1546, in *De iustificatione* (Cologne: 1572), 2,721; cf. Pfnür, *"Zur Verurteilung der reformatorischen Rechtfertigungslehre auf dem Konzil von Trient." Annuarium historiae conciliorum* 8 (1976):410.

90. Cf. Domingo de Soto, *De Natura et gratia II* (Paris, 1549), 5:112r.

91. DS 1569.

92. Cf. V. Pfnür, *"Zur Verurteilung,"* p. 422.

93. *Ibid.,* p. 417; Pfnür, *"Katholisch-lutherische Verständigung über das Augsburger Bekenntnis,"* Oekumenisches Forum: Grazer Hefte für konkrete Oekumene 2 (1979): 73-74; AE 35, 165 (WA 16, 373f); this isolated sentence was repeated by the Catholic polemical theologians of the following period, cf. Carolus Scribanius, s.j., *Orthodoxae fidei controversa 1. I* (Antwerp: 1609), p. 116.

94. Pfnür, p. 186, note 305; Pfnür, *"Zur Verurteilung,"* p. 411, note 33, and p. 418, note 50.

95. BC 310.

96. Cf. Pfnür, *"Zur Verurteilung,"* pp. 425-426.

97. Martin Chemnitz, *Examination of the Council of Trent,* vol. 1 (St. Louis: Concordia Publishing House, 1971), p. 419.

98. See above, note 33.

146   *Gerhard Müller and Vinzenz Pfnür*

99. Cf. Gemeinsame römisch-katholische/evangelisch-lutherische Kommission, *Das Herrnmahl* (Paderborn and Frankfurt-am-Main: 1978), pp. 93-100.
100. Cf. Pfnür, pp. 385-399; Pfnür, *"Die Einigung in der Rechtfertigungslehre bei den Religionsverhandlungen auf dem Reichstag zu Augsburg 1530,"* in *Confessio Augustana und Confutatio,* E. Iserloh and B. Hallenslaben, eds. (Münster: 1980); Pfnür, *"Einigung bei den Religionsgesprächen von Worms und Regensburg 1540/41 eine Täuschung?"* in *Die Religionsgespräche der Reformationszeit,* G. Müller, ed. (Gütersloh: 1980).
101. Cf. e.g., J. Calvin, *Acta Synodi Tridentinae: Cum Antidoto* (1547), in CR 35, 441-486, and Chemnitz, *Examination of the Council of Trent,* pp. 457-544, concerning the doctrine of justification of the council.
102. Joachim Rogge, "J. Agricola," *Theologische Realenzyklopädie,* vol. 2 (Berlin: 1978), p. 117.
103. Cf. P. Tschackert, *Die Entstehung der lutherischen und der reformierten Kirchenlehre* (Göttingen: 1910), pp. 483-487.
104. M. Stupperich, *Osiander in Preussen* (Berlin: 1973), pp. 130ff.
105. Cf. Stupperich, *"Lehrentscheidung und theologische Schematisierung: Die Sonderrolle Württembergs im Osiandrischen Streit und ihre Konsequenzen für die Formulierung des dritten Artikels der Solida Declaratio,"* *Widerspruch, Dialog und Einigung: Studien zur Konkordienformel der Lutherischen Reformation,* ed. by W. Lohff and L. W. Spitz (Stuttgart: 1977), pp. 171-195.
106. Cf. Tschackert, pp. 521-522.
107. *Ibid.,* p. 514.
108. Cf. *ibid.,* pp. 514-517.
109. Stupperich, *"Lehrentscheidung,"* pp. 184-190, gives evidence of this for Osiander's position.
110. Lutz Mohaupt, *"Gesetz und Evangelium nach Art. V der Konkordienformel,"* *Widerspruch,* W. Lohff, ed., p. 219.
111. Cf. Hans Philipp Meyer, *"Normen christlichen Handelns? Zum Problem des tertius usus legis,"* *Widerspruch,* W. Lohff, ed., p. 227.
112. Cf. Gerhard Müller, *"Um die Einheit des deutschen Luthertums: Die Konkordienformel von 1577,"* *Jahrbuch des Martin-Luther-Bundes* 24 (1977): 16-36.
113. Cf. B. Lohse, *"Augsburger Bekenntnis,"* *Theologische Realenzyklopädie,* vol. 4 (Berlin: 1979), pp. 625-627.
114. Cf. Müller, *Die Rechtfertigungslehre,* pp. 83ff.
115. *Rechtfertigung im neuzeitlichen Lebenszusammenhang: Studien zur Neuinterpretation der Rechtfertigungslehre,* W. Lohff and C. Walther, eds. (Gütersloh: 1974), p. 7.
116. *"Einheit und Erneuerung der Kirche: Wirkungen des Augsburgischen Bekenntnisses heute,"* *Lutherische Monatshefte* 18 (1979):434.
117. Cf. Müller, *op. cit.,* pp. 113-116.
118. *"Einheit und Erneuerung,"* pp. 433-434.
119. *Um Amt und Herrenmahl: Dokumente zum evangelisch/römisch-katholischen Gespräch,* G. Gassmann, M. Lienhard, H. Meyer, and H.-V. Herntrich, eds. (Frankfurt/Main: 1974), pp. 33-34 (cited from the so-called Malta Report).

6

Bishops and the Ministry of the Gospel

by Avery Dulles and George A. Lindbeck

The texts of the Augsburg Confession on ministry[1] can be examined in two different sequences. One may begin either with the theological foundations outlined in Part I, or with specific controversial issues such as are dealt with in Part II. The second order is rarely followed, but it has much to recommend it.

One advantage is that it corresponds to the order in which the CA was composed. Article 28 on "The Power of Bishops" or "Ecclesiastical Power"[2] was among the first to be drafted, and is much the longest in the entire Confession. The 21 articles testifying to the common faith in Part I, and the first six articles on abuses in Part II were in large measure developed subsequently as a rationale or justification for the Reformers' attitude toward episcopal authority. It makes sense, therefore, to begin with CA 28 in the study of the CA as a whole, as Wilhelm Maurer had done in his two-volume *Historischer Kommentar zur Confessio Augustana*.[3] In reference to the doctrine of the ministry, this is perhaps the only procedure. Only by considering the practical concerns of the Reformers at Augsburg can one understand both what they said and left unsaid in the more strictly theological first part. We shall

148   *Avery Dulles and George A. Lindbeck*

therefore deal in the first section of this commentary with the bishops' power as treated in Article 28, and then turn to the theological foundations of the Reformers' teaching on ministry as presented in Part I of the CA. A third and final section will examine controversies about the ministry which were, and in some cases remain, important, but which were not explicitly discussed in the CA.

1. Episcopal Authority

There were both practical and theological reasons for the importance of the issue of episcopal authority at Augsburg. The abolition of that authority in the areas where the Reformation was victorious created major legal and organizational difficulties for both state and church. The bishops' temporal rights and privileges, and not only their ecclesiastical ones, were part of the fabric of medieval society. Tampering with them was politically more threatening than any of the other changes introduced by the Reformers which are defended in Part II of the CA. There were many on the Roman Catholic side who sympathized in varying degrees with Communion in two kinds (CA 22), marriage of priests (CA 23), and reform of the mass (CA 24), of penance (CA 25), of fasting (CA 26), and even of monasticism (CA 27), but who were nevertheless troubled by the irregular way in which these changes had been introduced in defiance of the bishops' prerogatives. This lack of due process undermined the juridical foundations of western Christendom and gravely hampered its ability to present a unified front against Anabaptist anarchy from within and the Turkish menace from without. So compelling were these secular considerations that, when conjoined with pressure from the emperor, even basically antiepiscopal Protestants such as Philip of Hesse and the citizens of Nürnberg were willing to consent to some restoration of the bishops' power. Melanchthon believed in addition, with at least the partial concurrence of Luther, that ecclesiastical good order demanded it. Some kind of oversight was needed, and it was better that this be exercised by bishops than by princes.[4] Further, the Reformers had not yet taken the crucial step of ordaining their own ministers. They were still in the situation where, without bishops, there could be no new pastors. They thus had compelling practical reasons for seeking the restoration of episcopal authority.

On the more specifically theological side, the claim of the Reformers to agree with the ancient catholic tradition favored episcopacy. On most points the Reformers could appeal with some plausibility to the first four centuries against medieval developments, but not for non-episcopal church government. They recognized that episcopacy seemed to have roots even in the New Testament, and were well aware that it had been the uninterrupted and universal form of polity from the immediate postbiblical period to their own day. Its antiquity was equal or superior to that of creed, canon, and the basic liturgical and sacramental patterns which the Reformers continued to accept. Thus rejection of bishops would gravely imperil their claim to catholicity.

The CA therefore simply assumes that episcopacy should be retained. No alternative was conceivable, especially not as a proposal to the Imperial Diet. It was not even necessary to articulate this commitment to episcopacy in the text of the CA, although this was done elsewhere, not least in the Apology: "we have given frequent testimony in the assembly to our deep desire to maintain the church polity and various ranks of the ecclesiastical hierarchy. . . . Thus the cruelty of the bishops is the reason for the abolition of canonical government in some places, despite our earnest desire to keep it." [5] No reasons for this preference other than the practical needs of unity and order were advanced by Melanchthon or the other Reformation theologians (including Luther) during this period. Whether this absence of an affirmation of the superiority in principle of an episcopally structured ministry weakens the claim to catholicity is a question which will be discussed later.

The question, therefore, was not whether episcopacy in general was the best way of governing the church, but rather, given bishops, what should be their powers. Here the CA sounded so traditional that the Confutation declares "that to the most reverend bishops and priests, and to the entire clergy, all ecclesiastical power is freely conceded that belongs to them by law and custom." [6] This legitimate power is of three kinds.

The first and indispensable power which is "by divine right" or "according to the Gospel" (Latin) is "to preach the Gospel, forgive sins, judge doctrine and condemn doctrine that is contrary to the Gospel, and exclude from the Christian community the ungodly whose wicked conduct is manifest."[7] There have been disputes among Lutherans as to whether these powers are simply kerygmatic (that is, a function of proclamation through word and sacrament),[8] or whether they also involve the juridical right and duty to condemn false teaching and excommunicate the openly wicked. In view of how these words were no doubt understood in their original setting, as well as the distinction

Melanchthon adopts in Apology 28,13 between the power of order and that of jurisdiction, and what Luther says in the Smalcald Articles 3,9 about the "lesser" or "truly Christian" excommunication (i.e., one without civil penalties), there can be no doubt that jurisdiction also was intended. "A bishop has the power of order, namely, the ministry of word and sacraments. He also has the power of jurisdiction, namely, the authority to excommunicate those who are guilty of public offenses or to absolve them if they are converted and ask for absolution." [9] Both these powers, to repeat, belong to bishops by "divine right."

A second form of authority which belongs to the church and may be exercised by church leaders, but is not specifically said to be theirs by divine right, is that of making regulations "so that everything in the churches is done in good order." [10] The CA cites St. Paul's injunctions regarding women covering their heads (1 Cor. 11:5) and preachers not speaking all at once (1 Cor. 14:30) as examples,[11] but the most notable instance is that of Sabbath observance: "because it was necessary to appoint a certain day so that the people might know when they ought to assemble, the Christian church appointed Sunday for this purpose." [12] Such disciplinary measures are optional: they could have been different without contradicting God's Word or will. Yet their contingent character does not deprive them of force. "It is proper for the Christian assembly to keep such ordinances for the sake of love and peace, to be obedient to the bishops and parish ministers in such matters, and to observe the regulations in such a way that one does not give offense to another and so that there may be no disorder or unbecoming conduct in the church." [13] With the differences to be noted below, this second form of episcopal authority might be said to correspond to the traditional Catholic *potestas legislativa* from which comes "merely ecclesiastical law *(lex mere ecclesiastica)."*

Thirdly, the secular rights, privileges, and power with which the bishops have been endowed may be legitimately retained (although with a restriction which we shall note in the next paragraph). They can, in the medieval terminology employed by the CA, wield the temporal sword, that is, use coercive legal means in discharging their civil responsibilities.[14] Clearly, there was substance to the Reformers' claim that "It is not our intention that the bishops give up their power to govern," nor to "restore peace and unity at the expense of their honor and dignity." [15] All the politically crucial features of the medieval ecclesiastical establishment were acceptable to the CA.

This politically conservative willingness to restore episcopal authority incensed some of the Protestant rulers and cities who had profited from the bishops' loss of privileges. Although Luther also favored the restoration of episcopal jurisdiction in evangelical territories (cf., his *"Vermahnung an die Geistlichen"* of May 5, 1530),[16] he was difficult to attack, and Melanchthon bore the brunt of the accusations. At least in part because of his stand on episcopacy, it was said, for example, that "none at the diet in Augsburg did more harm to the gospel than Melanchthon." [17]

Yet the emphasis in the text of the CA is not on the restoration of episcopal jurisdiction, but on the ways the bishops had exceeded the limits of their legitimate authority, not simply by personal faults which charity requires us to tolerate, but by teachings and ordinances contrary to the gospel and the Word of God. Here acquiescence is impossible. God must be obeyed rather than human beings,[18] even if this leads to the dissolution of canonically ordered ministry. It is the bishops, not the Reformers, who are to blame if episcopacy perishes and Christendom is divided.[19] In short, "Churches are therefore bound by divine law to be obedient to the bishops according to the text, 'He who hears you hears me.' However, when bishops teach or ordain anything contrary to the Gospel, churches have a command of God which forbids obedience: 'Beware of false prophets.' " [20] With this rule, furthermore, both canon law and church Fathers such as Augustine were in agreement.[21]

The first of the three types of abuse of ecclesiastical authority which CA 28 distinguishes is that of confusing the power of the gospel with that of the temporal sword. The bishops failed to maintain the necessary distinction between the two regiments, the two coordinate instrumentalities, through which God rules in the church and world respectively. They "should not invade" the function of civil government, "should not set up and depose kings, should not annul temporal laws or undermine obedience to government, should not make or prescribe to the temporal power laws concerning worldly matters." [22] This is not to deny, as was earlier mentioned, that bishops may have civic responsibilities, for example, in matrimonial cases or the collection of tithes,[23] but if so, this is only to be delegation from and in subordination to the secular authorities.[24] Their use of temporal authority (i.e., "the sword") is simply as agents of the state, not as ministers of the gospel, and it can be used only in the temporal realm, not on behalf of the church or to maintain specifically ecclesiastical discipline.

According to the CA, the importance of this distinction between the two swords or regiments cannot be overestimated, for the very truth and nature of the gospel are at stake. The gospel is "for the sake of comforting consciences" [25]—that is, justification by faith—but this is denied when bishops use temporal means to rule outside it.[26]

At certain points within the CA, the distinction between the two regiments is made to seem absolute. The ministry of the church, exercised through preaching and sacraments, deals only with justification through faith and with eternal life, not at all with the ordering of human society, while civil government, on its side, is concerned only with protecting "bodies and goods from manifest harm." [27] The power of the church "interferes with civil government as little as the art of singing interferes with civil government." [28]

While this problem of the two regiments or two kingdoms is treated at greater length elsewhere in this volume, it does need to be observed here that both Catholics and Lutherans can now agree that the abuses of episcopal power against which the distinction was directed were genuine, but that both parties also now generally have difficulties with the manner and sharpness with which the distinction was drawn. Indeed, the Reformers themselves were not in favor of any absolute disjunction. Luther, for example, in his discussion of the second table of the law in the Large Catechism[29] or in his "Sermon on the Estate of Marriage" [30] makes it clear that the church also has God-given responsibilities for the definition and maintainence of rights and duties in the secular sphere.

The second and third abuses attacked by CA 28 can exist without the first, although they are, needless to say, intensified by the wrongful use of the temporal sword. The second abuse is to teach that obedience to church regulations merits grace or is necessary for salvation, and that their omission is sinful.[31] Canon law in optional matters such as Sunday observance can be disregarded by individuals in those instances where no offense is given. To hold otherwise is once again to deny justification by faith and to suppress the Christian liberty which flows from faith. Catholics hold that the obligation to obey canon law is stronger than this seems to imply, and that it is not contrary to Christian freedom or justification by faith. This may be a point where the question of justification requires further discussion between Catholics and Lutherans. On the other hand, however, it should also be observed that the Reformers did not think the following of church practices on such matters as attendance at Sunday services was simply a matter of personal whim or preference. For them, as the catechisms in particular make clear, the regular use of the public means of grace was a matter of great importance both for the individual and the community.

The third abuse is to impose practices which are contrary to the gospel or Word of God, and therefore cannot be adhered to without sin or the troubling of consciences. Communion in one kind and clerical celibacy are Melanchthon's favorite examples.[32] He does not argue, however, that these customs are necessarily or unconditionally wrong in all circumstances: "Perhaps there were acceptable reasons for these ordinances when they were introduced, but they are not adapted to later times." [33] His contention rather is that "new"[34]—i.e., postbiblical— regulations cannot be made universally binding; and that therefore those who disobey or abolish such church laws out of the honest conviction that they are detrimental (and therefore "against conscience" and "sinful" to observe) ought not be treated, as the bishops were doing to the Reformers, as heretics or schismatics. To do this is to divide the church over nonessentials. It is equivalent (as we shall see when we turn to Part I) to denying that justification by faith is alone essential, and that therefore its communication through right preaching and sacraments suffices for the unity of the church (CA 7).

In terms of Catholic tradition, there can be no *dogmatic* objection to giving the chalice to the laity and permitting priests to marry. The *Confutatio,* in answer to the CA, defended the reservation of the chalice to the clergy and the mandatory celibacy of priests as practices imposed for good reason and concordant with the Scriptures. Without ruling out the propriety of arguing for a change in the existing western discipline on these two matters, the Roman theologians held that the current discipline should be obeyed as a legitimate decision of competent authority.

Nor will the Catholic student of the CA have difficulty in accepting what is positively affirmed about episcopal jurisdiction, namely, that it extends to the excommunication and reconciliation of grave public sinners. Further, the principle that episcopal jurisdiction does not extend to permitting or commanding anything contrary to the gospel gives rise to no objections. The controversial points concern rather the applications of this latter principle. The CA, for example, holds that episcopal authority has no power or jurisdiction by divine right to decide legal cases concerning matrimony;[35] that bishops or pastors have no authority "to introduce ceremonies in the church and make laws concerning foods, holy days, grades or orders of ministers, etc.";[36] and that they may

not bind anyone under sin to recite the canonical hours.[37] Without denying that the then-prevailing regulations in these matters often needed
to be changed, still it seems that the doctrine of the CA reflects a more
restricted view of the scope of episcopal government in the areas of
worship and discipline than has been recognized in Roman Catholicism,
which acknowledges the power of bishops to issue commands and enact
laws that are binding on a conscience. We must now turn to a consideration of the theological principles invoked by the Reformers in defense
of their restrictions of episcopal authority.

2. Theological Foundation of the Office of Ministry

It will be recalled that the first 21 articles of the CA were drafted
after the seven articles which deal with abuses. In view of this order,
the doctrinal principles formulated in the first part should not be treated,
as is sometimes done, as premises from which a complete theology of
ministry can be derived. They should rather be regarded as the basis or
rationale both for the reforms and for the adherence to catholic structures proposed by the Confession. We shall therefore ask whether the
doctrinal principles provide (1) adequate warrants for the reforms, and
are (2) consistent with or (3) sufficient for the claims to catholicity.
In reply, we shall suggest that the first and second questions can be
answered affirmatively, but not the third. The doctrinal principles need
to be supplemented by other considerations if what are ordinarily
thought of as catholic answers are to be given to the problems regarding ministry examined in the previous section and left open by the CA.

As noted in the discussion of CA 28, the doctrinal bases for the
reforms of ministerial authority are found chiefly in the articles on
justification (CA 4) and the unity of the church (CA 7). As these articles are discussed at length in other chapters of this commentary, we
can for our present purposes simply summarize their significance for
reformation. They require opposition to everything in the practice and
teaching of the church which hinders the communication, through the
"external word" (CA 5) of gospel preaching and sacraments, of that
Spirit-effected and justifying faith in God's promises in Jesus Christ
from which flow the works of love (CA 6, 20). The adequacy of this
rule as a warrant for the reforms proposed by the CA has rarely, if
ever, been challenged.

Indeed the rule has often been thought of as more than adequate.
Justification by faith alone and the sufficiency of agreement "concern-

ing the teaching of the gospel and the administration of the sacraments"
for "the true unity of the church" [38] have often been taken as demand-
ing a more radical break with the catholic tradition than the CA proposes. In reference to ministry, for example, it has been argued that it
is only the functions or activities of witnessing and of sacramental celebration which are essential to the church, but not an ordained ministry.
The official public ministries which have developed in the course of history are sometimes regarded as simply human and pragmatic devices
designed to insure that everything, as St. Paul puts it, "be done de-
cently and in order" (1 Cor. 14:40).[39] Thus the logic of the Reformation position might seem to imply that when the Confessions speak
of "ministry" (*ministerium, Amt,* etc.) they refer to that office which
is "the common property of all Christians," to a "ministerial office"
which is part of the universal priesthood and in virtue of which every
believer proclaims and witnesses to the gospel in a variety of ways.[40]

Such arguments are perhaps plausible if one takes CA 4 and 7 as
premises or as constitutive of a doctrine of ministry, but not if they
are rationales for reform, that is, regulative or corrective principles. In
the CA, they clearly function as the latter. Justification by faith is not
the basis of, for example, trinitarian, christological, or sacramental affirmations, but rather serves as a norm for how to understand and use
these doctrines. The same applies to the doctrine of ministry. Read in
their historical context, there is no doubt that for those who presented
and heard the *Confessio Augustana,* "ministry" and equivalent terms
(wherever they occur, including CA 5) immediately brought to mind a
public office involving particular rights and duties to be exercised only
or chiefly by the limited number of individuals who are formally in-
ducted into it. This is made explicit in CA 14, *de ordino ecclesiastico:*
"Our churches teach that nobody should preach publicly in the church or
administer the sacraments unless he is regularly called." [41] This *rite
vocatus* involves ordination as Melanchthon makes clear in Apol. 14,1
in reply to a question raised on this point by *Confutatio.*[42]

It is thus the official ministry of regularly called and ordained persons which is referred to in the crucial Article 5, *de ministerio ecclesiastico.* The stress falls, however, on what ministers do, on their functions, not on their ordination. It is in this sense that the Lutheran position is opposed to "clericalism." The ministry is described in terms of
"teaching the Gospel and administering the sacraments" (Latin) or, as
in the German, the office, the *Predigtamt,* is put in apposition to, and
thus inseparably linked with, "the Gospel and the sacraments." [43] Of-

fice and function cannot properly exist without each other. A ministry without preaching and sacramental celebration is not the full public ministry of the church, and conversely, nonministerial preaching and sacramental celebration are not what they should be.

An explanation for this linkage of office and function is suggested by the last part of the article: "Our churches condemn the Anabaptists and others who think that the Holy Spirit comes to men without the external Word, through their own preparations and works." [44]

It may seem strange to choose the article on ministry to anathematize the Enthusiasts for their neglect of the *verbum externum,* the objective means of grace. Cannot one have those means of grace without an ordained clergy? The unexpressed premise, however, is that the ministerial office is necessary to preaching and sacraments. The word of God communicated orally and sacramentally does not retain its true life-giving character as God's word, not ours, unless it is offered by ministers who stand over against the congregation, whose authority comes from God rather than human beings, who represent, as Melanchthon puts it in the Apology, not themselves, but "the person of Christ" *(Christi personam).*[45] This objectivity of the ministerial office is strengthened by the CA's acceptance of the anti-Donatist decision of the early church: "Both the sacraments and the Word are effectual by the institution and commandment of Christ even if they are administered by evil men." [46]

The inseparability of office and function explains, in turn, the declaration that "God instituted the preaching office *(Predigtamt).*" [47] The office is needed for preaching and sacraments, and these actions in turn, are needed for justifying faith: "In order that we may obtain this faith, the ministry of teaching the Gospel and administering the sacraments was instituted. For through the Word and the sacraments, as through instruments, the Holy Spirit is given, and the Holy Spirit produces faith where and when it pleases God in those who hear the Gospel." [48] It is therefore because of its indispensable instrumental or serving role that the ministry is *de iure divino* and necessary to the church. This, it should be noted, does not contradict the *satis est* of CA 7, but it does imply that the ministerial office is so interwoven with "the teaching of the Gospel and the administration of the sacraments" that the agreement on the latter, which is sufficient for true unity, also requires some kind of agreement on the former.

It seems clear from this survey of the CA's doctrinal affirmations about ministry that they are not inconsistent with the earlier catholic tradition taken as a whole. For both, there is a special ordained ministry which is *de iure divino,* whose authority is derived from God rather than the congregation (even though the congregation may select persons to fill the office and exercise that authority), and the efficacy of whose ministrations is not dependent on the moral or spiritual qualities of the ministers. The theological reasoning in support of these shared doctrines is in part different. The connection between function and office is much closer in the CA than it had become in the Middle Ages, and thus the understanding of ministry as a whole is, as is often said, "functional" rather than juridical or ontological. Yet as long as the theological principles enunciated in articles 4, 5, and 7 are understood as corrective of the historic ministerial structures rather than as providing foundations for new ones, they do not seem to be opposed to the catholic tradition. Before we conclude to the catholicity of the CA, however, we must look at some of the controversies which were important then and later, but which it does not discuss.

3. Points of Controversy

The gaps in the doctrine of ministry in the CA may in part result from its focus on the canonical issue of ecclesiastical authority. Whatever the reason, however, it is silent on many of the ministerial questions most hotly debated both in the 16th century and later times. There is nothing in it, as we have already noted, about whether episcopacy is in principle superior to other ways of structuring ministry. Also absent are discussions of papacy, the distinction between the special ministry and the general priesthood of all believers, the sacramental nature of ordination, and the priestly character (i.e., *character indelebilis*). What we now need to ask is whether the CA is open to, even if it does not affirm, traditional catholic positions on these problems, or if it perhaps implicitly excludes them.

There are many ways of trying to fill the gaps, but for our purposes, four different methods can be distinguished. (1) Probably the most common is to interpret the CA in the light of later developments. Lutherans, like the adherents of other traditions, try to justify what has happened in their churches by reference to earlier authoritative documents. Given the break with Rome and the forced establishment of new and discontinuous church orders, they have read approval of these later developments into the silences of the CA. Its failure to speak of the details of ecclesiastical polity and of ministerial order is taken as proof that these are adiaphora, matters of theological indifference. All practically expedient ways of organizing the church, whether congregational, consistorial, or episcopal, are equally valid, as long as the gospel and the sacraments are present. (2) and (3) Two other ways of trying to fill the silence are more fruitful, yet also seem incapable of producing agreed results. First, one may attribute to the CA what the Reformers say on ministry in other writings. Second, one may try to infer systematically from the Reformers' major principles what they should say in the CA. The difficulty with the first procedure, as we are all aware, is that Luther in particular was notoriously varied in his utterances on this as on other topics. He did not, perhaps, contradict himself, but he said such different things in different contexts that it is often difficult to discern the inner consistencies. Depending on which statements and which periods in his life one emphasizes, one can develop either protestantizing or catholicizing interpretations of his view of the ministry and of church order. It is doubtful that a consensus can be achieved on what the "real Luther" thought on these matters by a historical study of his writings.

Not only the complexity of the material, but also the inevitable intrusion of systematic considerations make unlikely the attainment of agreement on the CA's doctrine of ministry by this method. We inescapably ask what view of the ministry is consistent with the Reformers' fundamental principles, and once we do this, we are embarked on the systematic method of trying to fill the gaps in the CA's teachings. Although systematic reflection is legitimate and necessary, it is, if anything, less capable than historical research of reaching agreed conclusions. There is no objective way, for example, of adjudicating between the more catholic and the less catholic reconstructions of Luther's thought represented by, for example, Regin Prenter and Gerhard Ebeling, and yet each has different implications for the theology of the ministry. If we are to fill the CA's silences, we must make use of systematic as well as historical investigations of the thinking of the Reformers, but neither separately nor in conjunction will they lead us to agreement.

The only alternative which comes to mind is to make an obvious move which, nevertheless, has been widely ignored. It may be that only in the recent discussion of the so-called "recognition" of the CA has this fourth methodological possibility begun to be taken with full seriousness. It consists, quite simply, in making hermeneutically primary the text itself rather than collateral historical or systematic investigations.

What counts above all are the expressed intentions of the confessors as manifest in the document. The emphasis here is exactly where it was for the original audience, viz., on truth claims or propositions, on what was proposed for acceptance or rejection.

The major claim of the CA, as we have been repeatedly reminded in recent times, is to catholicity: "there is nothing here that departs from the Scriptures or the catholic church or the church of Rome." [49] If one takes the stated purpose of the text seriously, this claim should be the controlling norm for interpreting every article, and for filling every gap. The interpreter is not at the mercy of competing historical and systematic opinions, but rather possesses a principle of selection in this hermeneutically normative claim to catholicity. The Reformation as represented at Augsburg wanted to retain the catholic substance of the ministry, and this intention is fundamental in determining what the CA would have said on those aspects of the ministry on which it is silent. It would have been, to put it simply, as catholic as possible.

A comment on the CA's silence on the papacy is first in order. The possibility of recognizing the primacy of the pope *de iure humano* insofar as he grants freedom to the preaching of the gospel (together with a condemnation of him as Antichrist if he does not) [50] was proposed in an earlier draft, the so-called Torgauer Articles, prepared by Wittenberg theologians, probably on March 15-16, 1530, and perhaps reworked by Melanchthon on March 27. [51] This section was, however, later omitted, perhaps under political pressure, as was also a strong condemnation of the sacramentarian (i.e., antirealistic) eucharistic view, in order to make the final version acceptable to Protestants who were more uncompromisingly antipapist and less sacramentally realistic than the Wittenberg theologians. [52] It may be, therefore, that Luther was unfair when, on July 21, frustrated by the failure of the Augsburg negotiations, he criticized Melanchthon for his "pussyfooting" *(Leisetreten)* in failing to attack the papacy in the CA. Perhaps he did not take account of the possibility that the purpose of the omission was, not to curry favor with the papists, but to maintain a united front with Protestant antipapists. [53] In any case, the silence of the CA on this issue means that it is compatible either with Luther's total rejection of the papacy in the Smalcald Articles (1537), or with the more open position of Melanchthon in the Appendix to the Smalcald Articles, and which is also represented by some contemporary Lutherans. [54]

In reference to episcopacy, the CA, as has already been noted, is also silent. It simply assumes the existence of bishops, and calls for the restoration of their jurisdiction on the condition that they allow for what it regards as freedom for the gospel. This, however, leaves unanswered two closely related questions which have subsequently been much discussed. First, is the episcopal—as distinct from the presbyterial or priestly—office of human or divine origin? Is it, to use the conceptuality of the 16th century, *de iure humano* or *de iure divino?* Second, how essential to the church is the historic apostolic succession in the ministerial office?

Melanchthon takes up the second question in the Apology. He there follows Jerome and much of the medieval tradition by holding that the distinction between bishop and presbyter is *de iure humano:* the "various ranks of the ecclesiastical hierarchy . . . were created by human authority." [55] This opinion was consistently maintained by the Reformers, and is also presented at length in the *Treatise on the Primacy and Power of the Pope* which was officially adopted in 1537 as a supplement to the CA.[56] According to this view, all pastors were at the beginning bishops, and the differentiation of ranks, such as that between bishops and priests, is of human origin.[57]

The second question, however, is not thereby answered. It is quite possible to agree, as did Jerome and those who followed his interpretation in the Middle Ages, that the distinction between bishop and presbyter is not essential or *de iure divino,* and yet hold to the necessity of the visible succession in the apostolic office. The Reformers, with their stress on maintaining as much continuity as possible, generally thought in these terms. In the *Tractatus,* for example, Melanchthon argues that pastors may ordain pastors when the bishops fail, but he nowhere suggests that even this ordination by pastors is dispensable.[58] "Since the distinction between bishop and pastor is not by divine right, it is manifest that ordination administered by a pastor in his own church is valid by divine right." [59] "Wherefore, when the bishops are heretics or refuse to administer ordination, the churches are by divine right compelled to ordain pastors and ministers for themselves." [60] In later discussions, however, the two questions—that of episcopacy as a distinct rank, and that of the historic succession in the ministerial office—have often been equated. It has been assumed, not only by Catholics, but also by many Lutherans, that the loss of the episcopacy in Reformation churches was equivalent to the loss of the historic succession. This has favored a tendency among Lutherans to conclude that continuity in ministerial structures, however desirable for practical reasons, is not theologically indispensable or *de iure divino.*[61] It is, they believe, an adiaphoron, a matter of indifference. The church can be just as much the church without it.

On this point, it must be emphasized, the CA is simply silent. It does not raise the question of whether the historic succession belongs— as Anglicans might phrase it—to the *esse,* the *plene esse,* or the *bene esse* of the church. Thus it has been possible for adherents of the CA to subscribe to a wide range of positions on the theological importance or lack of importance of visible continuity in the ministerial office in general or the episcopacy in particular.

Another question on which the CA is silent is whether lay people can perhaps perform all the functions of an ordained minister at least in times of emergency. To put the issue in the form in which it is sometimes discussed, may not an isolated congregation without a pastor select one of its own members to perform all the duties of the pastor, including the celebration of the Eucharist?

Such actions have not traditionally been allowed by Catholics, and they appear also to be excluded by the contemporary teaching of the Roman Catholic Church: "Only a priest is able to act in the person of Christ in presiding over and effecting the sacrificial banquet wherein the people of God are associated with Christ's offering." [62]

There are also some Lutherans who believe that lay celebrations are excluded when CA 28, 5-6 links the ministry to the commissioning of the apostles by Christ: "the power of the keys . . . is a power and command of God to preach the Gospel, to forgive and retain sins, and to administer and distribute the sacraments. For Christ sent out the apostles with this command, 'As the Father has sent me, even so I send you. . . .' " [63] They can appeal in support of this position to Luther's reluctance to approve lay eucharistic celebration,[64] and to the absence of any authorization for such actions, not only from the CA, but from the Symbolic Books in general. Lay exercise of special ministerial functions is mentioned only in reference to absolution: "So in an emergency even a layman absolves and becomes the minister and pastor of another." [65] The priesthood of all believers is never mentioned as either a basis or a restriction of the ministerial office.

The CA, therefore, says nothing to approve emergency lay celebrations, but it also does not exclude them. The question is thus left open. What is clearly assumed by the CA, however, is that the historic succession, whether episcopal or presbyterial, is the normal way of inducting ministers into their office.

Another question which is left open is that of the sacramental nature of ordination, but this time there is no doubt what Melanchthon would have said if he had dealt with this topic in the CA. It was omitted presumably in order to avoid dealing with the intricate yet (from the Reformers' viewpoint) secondary issue of the number of the sacraments, but the Confutation objected to the failure to enumerate all seven sacraments (Part I, Art. 13), thus inducing Melanchthon to reply in the Apology.[66]

"If ordination *(ordo)* is interpreted in relation to the ministry of the Word, we have no objection to calling ordination a sacrament," because "it has God's command and glorious promises." [67] The rite of laying on of hands can also be termed a sacrament in view of the fact that "the church has the command to appoint ministers; to this we must subscribe wholeheartedly, for we know that God approves this ministry and is present in it." [68] To be sure, the ministry and ordination should not be placed on the same level as the "three sacraments of salvation," "Baptism, the Lord's Supper, and absolution." Sacraments in the strict sense are (a) rites "which have the command of God," (b) "to which the promise of grace has been added," and in which (c) the grace conferred is that of the "New Testament," i.e., "salvation" or "the forgiveness of sins." [69] In the case of the ministry the last condition is lacking. Grace is given the minister, in the words of Luther, "not for himself nor for his person but for the office." [70] It is, therefore, only in a broader or secondary sense that the ministry is sacramental.

On the other hand, there are many passages in Luther, especially from the early Reformation period, which seem wholly opposed to a sacramental understanding of the ministry and of ordination; but these are always directed against the rite as it had come to be practiced, not against the "apostolic rite" of the laying on of hands.[71] Further, it is clear that Luther held that induction into the ministry involves a blessing[72] and a gift of grace from the Holy Spirit to the minister for the exercise of the office which is so thoroughly "objective" that heretical ordinations are valid and this gift of the Spirit works judgment on the unfaithful officeholder.[73] His frequent attacks on the notion that ordination confers grace refer to the grace of personal justification and sanctification, not to the grace of an office. A failure to note this distinction has led even some recent investigators to suppose that Luther did not recognize an *Amtscharisma;*[74] but when one does recognize it, and notes the importance of the laying on of hands for Luther, there is no doubt that he persistently, if not always consistently, thought of the ministry as sacramental.[75] Further, contrary to the view of some Lutherans, he clearly held that ordination as an act or rite distinct from *vocatio* or *electio* is not an *adiaphoron*, but is an essential condition for entrance into the ministry.[76] A similar position was taken in the case of John Freder by a Pomeranian Synod in 1556 with the concurrence of Melanchthon and the Wittenberg faculty. Thus despite certain early Reformation utterances and the silence of the CA, it is necessary to say that the Reformers had a sacramental understanding of ministry and ordination, although they did not regard it as a sacrament in the full sense.[77]

This, to be sure, is not in full agreement with the Catholic position. In view of the decrees of the Council of Florence (*DS* 1310, 1326) and Trent (*DS* 1601, 1771, and 1773), the designation of ordination as a sacrament may be regarded as mandatory in Roman Catholic usage. Yet the Catholic theological tradition leaves room for distinctions between "major" and "minor" sacraments, between those instituted for the sanctification of the recipient and those instituted for the sanctification of others, etc. The contemporary ecumenical problem between Lutherans and Catholics, therefore, is not so much whether ordination is to be labelled a sacrament as whether it is of such a nature that it fits within the concept of sacrament as Roman Catholics have traditionally defined it. The preceding analysis gives grounds for thinking that this question can be answered in the affirmative.

This brings us to a fifth point of dispute on which the CA is silent, that of the permanence of ordination or, in medieval terminology, the priestly *character indelebilis*. The Council of Florence (*DS* 1313), followed in this by Trent (*DS* 1609), taught that the sacrament of order imprints a character on the soul, i.e., a kind of indelible spiritual sign, but this was denied by the Reformers.

Before further discussing the indelible character, it should be noted that reordination of ministers who have apostatized or been laicized was not an issue at the time of the Reformation, and neither the CA nor the later confessional writings discuss the matter. For these reasons there are no clear-cut reports of reordination in 16th-century Lutheranism, and it has continued to be either rare or entirely lacking (although there have been numerous instances of Lutherans reordaining ministers from non-Lutheran churches). In practice, Lutherans have acted as if they believed that at least their own ordinations had the operational equivalent of the *character indelebilis*. The commissioning to the *ministerium verbi* is in principle lifelong, and so it remains in effect even when a person fails to perform the functions to which he or she has been called and ordained.

Now it is true that Luther, in the early period, did say that a man who has once been made a priest can become a layman again, since "there is no true, basic difference between laymen and priests . . . except for the sake of office and work." [78] Given his own practice,[79] however, this must be understood as a polemic against an ontologically conceived indelible character, not as a denial of the irrevocability of the commission and the associated blessing.[80] There is thus reason to believe that the Reformers were open to the affirmation of an "indelible ministerial character" as long as this was understood not in metaphysical-individualistic categories, but in functional-ecclesial terms related to the *ministerium verbi*.[81] In harmony with this, the International Lutheran-Roman Catholic Study Commission on the Gospel and the Church concludes that "Lutherans have the equivalent of the Catholic doctrine of the priestly character in so far as they do not repeat ordination," [82] and with this the CA, given its interest in claiming catholicity, would presumably have agreed if it dealt with the issue.

4. Contemporary Discussion

Of all the omissions we have reviewed, perhaps the most serious from a contemporary Roman Catholic perspective is the absence of a clear affirmation of the abiding importance of the historic apostolic succession. The CA wished to maintain the traditional polity, but why? Were the reasons purely prudential, pragmatic, and temporary? Because this question is not discussed, there is nothing in the CA which explicitly opposes the view which later became common among Lutherans that the divine institution of the pastoral office is entirely vertical, not at all horizontal. Many claim that God's continuously operative command to preach the gospel and celebrate the sacraments is the sole theological basis for the ministry, and therefore nothing of theological significance is lost when the succession is interrupted. The Reformers' desire at Augsburg to reestablish the episcopacy is dismissed by such Lutherans as of no abiding theological importance. They admit that reestablishment was in that particular time and place the only politically feasible way of restoring the peace and unity of the church, but then argue on the basis of their belief in the theological equality of the episcopal and nonepiscopal polities that the better way in most circumstances to restore the unity of the church is for each side to recognize the full legitimacy of the other and to strive each in its own way to be faithful servants of the Word. Such a position was not conceivable at the time of the CA, but for this reason it was also not formally excluded. This failure to exclude a purely adiaphoristic view of episcopal polity is probably the point at which the CA is, as we have already said, most obviously insufficient from the point of view of traditions which stress the historic succession.

The CA, however, does not affirm an adiaphoristic view. It is also open to the contrary position that the apostolic succession in office is in principle positively desirable and, other things being equal, is preferable to alternatives. Episcopacy can be a powerful symbol, an efficacious sign, of the unity of the church in space and time, and thereby strengthen the witness to the universality of the redemption in Christ. Such considerations, although formulated in contemporary rather than 16th-century terms, are in full harmony with the functional emphasis of the CA and the Lutheran Reformation. They do not grant any inalienable or divinely guaranteed indefectibility to the historic episcopacy, such as the Reformers deny, but they do recognize that it has a special potential for becoming a sign of great evangelical importance when it acts in obedience to the Word.[83] The CA, it seems clear, is open to this view that the reestablishment of episcopacy is desirable, not only in the peculiar circumstances of the 16th century, but as a visible mark of the unity of the church down through the centuries and throughout the world.

Further, there is no need from a contemporary perspective to assume, as did both the Reformers and the Catholics in the 16th century, that episcopacy must be thought of as either entirely of divine institution or as entirely human. In the light of our increased historical awareness, no neat and permanent line can be drawn between *ius divinum* and *ius humanum*. The Israelite monarchy, for example, is depicted in 1 Samuel 8 as being the product both of divine institution and historical development. In the light of doubts about the direct dominical institution of Baptism and the Lord's Supper, perhaps something similar (though not with the implication of temporariness) must be said about even these two sacraments. The same principle applies even more forcefully to the ministerial structures of the church. Structures which are essential either to the being or well-being of the church's mission (and in this sense *de iure divino*) may vary considerably in different circumstances.[84] Once this is admitted, it is no longer necessary, despite what many Lutherans have thought, to suppose that the resistance to bishops authorized by the CA implies that the historic episcopal structure of the church is of purely human origin. It may have developed under providential guidance and may, in its normal and proper functioning, be a God-willed means for helping to preserve the church in the apostolic faith. Such a view, although developed subsequently to the CA, does provide a basis for the positive attitude the latter adopts toward the restoration of episcopal jurisdiction once abuses are removed, and is therefore more consistent with its fundamental tenor than is the adiaphoristic alternative.

It is convenient at this point to utilize the formulations of a German theologian in summarizing the CA's teaching on ministry from a contemporary Lutheran perspective.

1. There is a single ministerial office instituted by God and therefore *de iure divino* and, in the full sense, essentially necessary to the church (cf. CA 5).

2. A series of functions belong *de iure divino,* to this office, some of which (especially the proclamation of the gospel and administration of the sacraments) are exercised by the pastor or priest (i.e., the leader of the individual congregation), while others—often designated in our day by the concept of episcope—can be effectively carried out only by officeholders at a higher level. These latter exercise church and, more especially, teaching discipline, and in cooperation with the congregations call and ordain new pastors or priests.

3. The obvious way to exercise the functions of episcope is by means of the institutional structure which has in fact developed for this purpose, *viz.,* the historical succession of bishops in office. This structure should be maintained when possible for the sake of the preservation of the unity of the church. Yet when, for the sake of the gospel, it cannot be maintained, the church's being is not thereby lost.

4. The CA is open to the following further interpretation suggested, after centuries of development, in view of the variety of contemporary church situations: although the differentiation of the ministry into presbyterial and episcopal offices in an historical structure arising from "human authority" (according to Apol. 14, 2), yet the guidance of God's Spirit can be seen in its development. Thus the historic episcopate is, on the one hand, a human order, but it is also at the same time more than that. This position corresponds to the more flexible understanding of *ius divinum* sketched above.

5. Even if the decision of the Reformers to deny obedience to the bishops of their time for the sake of the gospel was unavoidable, damage was yet done to the ecclesial reality of the church by this breach in its continuity and structural unity.

6. Although we [as Lutherans] affirm that this breach did not deprive the churches (cf., no. 3. *supra*), yet the resultant ecclesial deficiency (a deficiency in the church's unity) constitutes for both sides an abiding challenge to seriously consider the importance of the historic episcopate for the unity of our churches.[85]

Official Catholic teaching, both at Trent and Vatican II, has not directly contradicted these principles, but also has not affirmed them. It simply assumes that episcopacy (in fact if not in name) has always existed in the church, that it is essential to the church, and that its indefectibility is divinely guaranteed. Whether a more flexible approach to *ius divinum* and a clearer recognition of historical changes may lead to the idea of an episcopate which has "developed under providential guidance" and which is, without being divinely guaranteed, a "powerful symbol" of the unity of the church—all this remains a theme for ecumenical discussions such as are now taking place between Lutherans and Roman Catholics.

In conclusion, then, the positive affirmations of the CA on ministry and episcopacy appear to be in harmony with those of the catholic tradition. Further, it seems that what a contemporary Roman Catholic might regard as insufficiencies can be supplied by principles which, while not affirmed by the CA, are compatible with it. Whether contemporary Lutherans and Roman Catholics can reach agreement on these principles is a matter still to be ascertained.

Notes

1. Unless otherwise indicated, "ministry" in this chapter will refer to what is variously called the official, public, special, or ordained ministry of the church, and what in the CA is termed at times the *ministerium verbi* or *evangelii,* or *Predigtamt.*
2. BC 81ff. (German and Latin titles, respectively).
3. Gütersloh: Gerd Mohn, 1976 and 1978. The first volume in particular is largely devoted to documenting the priority of Article 28. This volume also provides the fullest available treatment of the historical background of the CA. The following paragraphs are indebted to it.
4. For the last three sentences, cf. Vinzenz Pfnür, *Einig in der Rechtfertigungslehre* (Wiesbaden: Franz Steiner, 1970), pp. 20-27.
5. Apol. 14, 1-2 (BC 214).
6. Immenkötter, p. 197.
7. CA 28, 21, German except as noted in text (BC 84).
8. A. Kimme describes and argues against such a kerygmatic view in *"Die ökumenische Bedeutung der Augsburgischen Konfession,"* in *Die Aktuali-*

tät des Bekenntnisses (Hamburg: Lutherisches Verlagshaus, 1971), pp. 38ff. It should be noted that the reduction of the CA's view of ministerial powers to proclamation is possible only if one starts with an *a priori* interpretation of CA 5 and imposes this on later texts. This procedure becomes questionable, however, if one remembers, as we are doing, that CA 28 was drafted earlier and independently of CA 5.

9. Apol. 28, 13 (BC 283).

10. CA 28, 53, German (BC 90).

11. CA 28, 54 (BC 90).

12. CA 28, 60, German (BC 91).

13. CA 28, 55, German (BC 90).

14. CA 28, 19 and 29 (BC 83 and 85, respectively).

15. CA 28, 77, Latin, and CA 28, 71, German, respectively (BC 94 and 93, respectively).

16. WA 30, 340-344.

17. A statement of the Nürnberg delegate, Baumgartner, in a letter of Sept. 15, 1630. CR II, 372.

18. CA 28, 75 (BC 94).

19. CA 28, 76-77 (BC 94).

20. CA 28, 22-23, Latin (BC 84).

21. CA 28, 27-28 (BC 85).

22. CA 28, 13, German (BC 83).

23. CA 28, 29 (BC 85).

24. CA 28, 19 (BC 83-84).

25. CA 28, 4 (BC 81).

26. One of the major objections of the Confutation to CA 28 was against the CA's position on the separation of powers. It argues that clerical immunities and the bishops' right "of ruling and forcibly correcting in order to direct subjects to the goal of eternal life" pertain to the spiritual power and are *de iure divino (Confutatio* 2, 7; Immenkötter 197). In Apol. 28, 2 (BC 281) Melanchthon replies that "we do not criticize" clerical immunities as "gifts" of princes, but of course denies that they belong to the *ius divinum.*

27. CA 28, 11, Latin (BC 82).

28. CA 28, 10, Latin (BC 82).

29. BC 379-411.

30. AE 44, 7ff. (WA 2, 167ff.).

31. CA 28, 36 and 56 (BC 86 and 90).

32. CA 28, 69-70 (BC 93). The oath required by the Catholic bishops not to preach the evangelical doctrine of justification is also mentioned in this context, but this was from the Reformation perspective so unconditionally "against the gospel" that it belongs in a different category.

33. CA 28, 73, Latin (BC 93).

34. CA 28, 72 (BC 93).

35. CA 28, 29 (BC 85).

36. CA 28, 30, Latin (BC 85).

37. CA 28, 41 (BC 87).

38. CA 7, 2, Latin (BC 32).

39. This *locus classicus* for "transferal *(Ubertragung)*" theories is cited only

once in the Confessions (Apol. 15, 20), and then in reference to "rites and seasons," not the institution of the ministry.

40. Rudolph Sohm, *Kirchenrecht*, vol. 2 (Leipzig: 1923), pp. 140ff. This position is critically discussed by Edmund Schlink, *Theology of the Lutheran Confessions* (Philadelphia: Muhlenberg, 1961), pp. 244-246.

41. CA 14, Latin (BC 36).

42. See also Arthur Carl Piepkorn, "The Sacred Ministry and Holy Ordination in the Symbolical Books of the Lutheran Church," in *Lutherans and Catholics in Dialogue IV: Eucharist and Ministry* (Minneapolis: Augsburg, 1979), pp. 101-119, esp. p. 114, notes 22-23. Luther's positive view of the importance of ordination in the period after the CA is apparent in "The Private Mass and the Consecration of Priests" (1533; AE 38, 147-214; WA 38, 195-256). Cf. W. Stein's analysis in *Das Kirchliche Amt bei Luther* (Wiesbaden: 1974), pp. 177-201.

43. CA 5, 1, Latin and German respectively (BC 31).

44. CA 5, 4, Latin (BC 31). In apparently denying that the Holy Spirit can be given without the external preaching of the gospel, the early Lutheran doctrine may be thought, at least from a modern Catholic view, to exaggerate the necessity of the church's ministry (cf. *Lumen gentium* 16 and *Gaudium et spes* 22; English translation in W. Abbott, ed., *The Documents of Vatican II* [New York: Herder and Herder, 1966], pp. 34-35 and 220ff., respectively). It should be remembered, however, that the dispute of the Reformers with the Anabaptists was not over the salvation of non-Christians, of those who "through no fault of their own do not know the gospel of Christ or his church" (*Lumen gentium* 16) but rather concerned the place of word and sacraments within the community of explicit Christian faith which is the church. On this point, on the indispensability of the external means of grace within the church, the Reformers were thoroughly catholic.

45. Apol. 7, 28 (BC 173).

46. CA 8, 2, Latin (BC 33).

47. CA 5, 1, German (BSLK 58; CT 44).

48. CA 5, 1-2, Latin (BC 31).

49. CA, Conclusion to Part I, 1, Latin (BC 47).

50. The condemnation, but not the possibility of a conditional recognition, is echoed in Apol. 15, 18 (BC 217), but the conditional recognition is also later expressed in the Lutheran confessional writings in Melanchthon's Appendix to the Smalcald Articles of 1537.

51. See Maurer, *op. cit.,* vol. 1, pp. 11-12, 29-32.

52. See Maurer, *op. cit.,* vol. 1, p. 31.

53. *Ibid.,* p. 41.

54. As is well known, the First Vatican Council in 1870 taught that it is by divine institution that blessed Peter has perpetual successors in the primacy over the universal church (DS 3058). This doctrine was reaffirmed by Vatican II in 1964 (*Lumen gentium* 18, trans. Abbott, *op. cit.,* pp. 37-38). The question whether Lutherans in rejecting the claim of the papacy to exist by divine right are denying what Catholics affirm when they teach this depends on what precisely is understood by the terms "divine right" and "papacy." Notable convergences on the papacy have been reached by

Lutherans and Catholics in the Malta Report, and in *Papal Primacy and the Universal Church* (Minneapolis: Augsburg, 1974).

55. Apol. 14, 1 (BC 214).

56. See esp. Treatise, 61-67 (BC 330-331).

57. The Council of Trent in its Decree on the Sacrament of Order, can. 6-7 (DS 1776-77), states that there is a divinely instituted hierarchy in the Catholic Church; that the heirarchy *de facto* comprises bishops, presbyters, and ministers; and that bishops are superior to presbyters. It does not, however, state that the distinction of grades is a dogmatic distinction based on revelation or that the distinction must forever exist in the church. Vatican II, in *Lumen gentium* 28, made a very circumspect statement: "Christ . . . has, through His apostles, made their successors, the bishops, partakers of His consecration and His mission. These in their turn have legitimately handed on to different individuals in the Church various degrees of participation in this ministry. Thus the divinely established ecclesiastical ministry is exercised on different levels by those who from antiquity have been called bishops, priests, and deacons" (Abbott, *op. cit.,* pp. 52-53). The distinction of grade between bishops and presbyters is not here attributed to Christ himself but rather, at least by implication, to the bishops of the early church. The Council did not attempt to resolve the questions whether the distinction, once made, is a matter of divine law and whether it is irreversible. See Bernard Dupuy, "Is There a Dogmatic Distinction Between the Function of Priests and the Function of Bishops?" in H. Küng, ed., *Apostolic Succession: Rethinking a Barrier to Unity,* Concilium, vol. 34 (New York: Paulist, 1968), pp. 74-86.

58. From a Roman Catholic point of view the concept of presbyterial succession is not free from difficulty. For according to Catholic doctrine, presbyters do not have the fullness of the sacrament of orders—a fact that remains true even if it be conceded (with the Reformers) that the distinction between bishops and presbyters is of human institution. In the Catholic tradition the conferring of orders is reserved, at least normally, to bishops (cf. Trent's seventh canon on the sacrament of orders, DS 1777; also Vatican II in *Lumen gentium* 21, in Abbott, *op. cit.,* pp. 40-42). As Joseph Lécuyer remarks, the formulation of Vatican II in the latter text is very prudent. "It is not explicitly stated that only bishops, without any possible exception, can consecrate another bishop"—and Lécuyer suggests that in his view the Council has been excessively prudent. See J. Lécuyer, *L'Episcopat comme Sacrement"* in G. Barauna, ed., *L'Eglise de Vatican II,* vol. 3 (Paris: Cerf, 1966), p. 760. Rahner rightly observes that the Constitution on the Church in this passage "does not intend to touch on the question of whether a simple priest may in certain circumstances and under certain conditions validly ordain a simple priest," K. Rahner, in H. Vorgrimler, ed., *Commentary on the Documents of Vatican II,* vol. 1 (New York: Herder and Herder, 1967), pp. 194-195. Thus Vatican II neither excludes nor supports the open attitude toward the possible validity of Lutheran orders adopted by the Catholic participants in the U.S. Lutheran/Roman Catholic Dialogue (*Lutherans and Catholics in Dialogue IV: Eucharist and Ministry, op. cit.,* esp. pp. 31-32). For an introduction to the history and theology of ordinations by simple priests, see P. Fransen, "Orders and

Ordination," in *Encyclopedia of Theology: The Concise Sacramentum Mundi*, vol. 4 (New York: Seabury), pp. 1122-1147.

59. Treatise, 65 (BC 331).

60. Treatise, 72 (BC 332).

61. It is by no means self-evident, however, that what exists by divine right must also be indispensable. According to standard Roman Catholic moral teaching, an affirmative divine precept, such as the precept to receive sacramental Baptism and to enter the church, admits of excusing causes. Thus even if the church can exist without the historic succession, this does not logically imply that succession is merely *de iure humano*. It could still be obligatory rather than a matter of indifference.

62. The quotation is from the Document on the Ministerial Priesthood issued by the Second General Assembly of the Synod of Bishops. *AAS* 63 (1971): 906, trans. from *Catholic Mind* 70, no. 1261 (March, 1972): 40; cf. *Lumen gentium* 28, in Abbott, *op. cit.*, pp. 52ff.

63. CA 28, 5-6, German (BC 81-82). Jürgen Roloff, "The Question of the Church's Ministry in Our Generation," *Lutheran World* 11 (1964): 402, has pointed out the centrality of this passage for the high-church Lutheran interpretations of the Confessions.

64. Luther comes closest to authorizing such celebrations by those who have not been canonically ordained (but who have been called and appointed by fellow Christians) in his early "Concerning the Ministry" (1523; AE 40, 7-44) which was directed to the problems of the Bohemian Utraquists (Hussites). Here, in contrast to his later statements, he seems to derive the special from the general ministry, for the ones so chosen "even before such election . . . have been born and called into such a ministry through Baptism" (AE 40, 37; WA 12, 191, 36-37). This traditional interpretation is represented, *inter alia*, by Jaroslav Pelikan, *Spirit versus Structure* (New York: Harper and Row, 1968), pp. 32-49. W. Stein, however, disagrees in his analysis of this same treatise, *op. cit.*, pp. 144-168 and p. 176, Ap. 178. For a summary of Luther's varying views and practice in these matters, see Brian A. Gerrish, "Luther on Priesthood and Ministry," *Church History* 34 (1965): 404-422, and more fully, in Peter Manns, *"Amt und Eucharistie in der Theologie Martin Luthers,"* in Peter Bläser, ed., *Amt und Eucharistie* (Paderborn: Bonifacius, 1974), pp. 68-173.

65. Treatise, 67 (BC 331).

66. The following material on the sacramentality of ministerial orders and the *character indelebilis* is largely reproduced from G. Lindbeck, "The Lutheran Doctrine of the Ministry: Catholic and Reformed," *Theological Studies* 30 (1969): 588-612.

67. Apol. 13, 11-12 (BC 212).

68. Apol. 13, 12 (BC 212).

69. Apol. 13, 3-4 and 14 (BC 211 and 213).

70. WA 28, 468: *"nicht fur sich selbs noch fur seine Person, Sondern fur das Ampt."*

71. See H. Lieberg, *Amt und Ordination bei Luther und Melanchthon* (Göttingen, 1962), pp. 229ff.

72. *Ibid.*, pp. 214ff.

73. *Ibid.*, pp. 223ff.

74. E.g., W. Brunotte, *Das geistliche Amt bei Luther* (Berlin: 1959), pp. 188ff.
75. P. Manns, *op. cit.,* pp. 131-133, note 128.
76. WA Br 5, 659 and WA Br 6, 43.
77. Lieberg, *op. cit.,* pp. 360-371.
78. AE 44, 129 (WA 6, 408, 26-28).
79. The widespread opinion that Luther at one time approved reordination for those reentering the ministerial office or taking up a new charge has been shown to be an inference for which definite evidence is lacking. Lieberg, *op. cit.,* p. 227, note 315.
80. Lieberg, *op. cit.,* pp. 227-228, and J. Heubach, *Die Ordination zum Amt der Kirche* (Berlin: 1956), pp. 80-81. Heubach even speaks of a "benedictional indelibility" *(Benediktionsindelebilität)* in Luther, *ibid.,* pp. 112-118.
81. Roman Catholics now often interpret the *character indelebilis* in these latter terms. See, e.g., Joseph Ratzinger, *"Das geistliche Amt und die Einheit der Kirche,"* in J. C. Hampe, ed., *Die Autortät der Freiheit,* vol. 2 (Munich: 1967), pp. 417-433. Eliseo Ruffini, "Character as a Concrete Manifestation of the Sacrament in Relation to the Church," *Concilium,* vol. 38 (New York, 1968), pp. 101-114; E. Schillebeeckx, *The Mission of the Church* (New York: Seabury, 1973), pp. 221-228.
82. Malta Report, p. 60.
83. One thoroughly confessional Lutheran who has developed an argument of this kind is Edmund Schlink, *The Coming Christ and the Coming Church* (Philadelphia: Fortress, 1968), pp. 186-223.
84. For a further consideration of these problems see A. Dulles, *"Ius Divinum* as an Ecumenical Problem," *Theological Studies* 38 (1977), pp. 681-708; and G. Lindbeck, "Papacy and *Ius divinum:* A Lutheran View," in *Papal Primacy and the Universal Church, op. cit.,* pp. 193-207.
85. Harding Meyer, *"Das Bischofsamt nach CA 28,"* in E. Iserloh and B. Hallensleben, eds., *Confessio Augustana und Confutatio* (Münster: 1980).

7

The Concept of the Church in the Augsburg Confession

by Harding Meyer and Heinz Schütte

translated by James L. Schaaf

The explicit statements of the Augsburg Confession about the church, found chiefly in Articles 7 and 8, received relatively little attention at the Diet of Augsburg in 1530 and hardly engendered a controversy. At least this is the conclusion we reach when we hear what the Confutation said and look at the discussions that took place in the committees and special negotiations. The only objection (aside from the reference to preserving rites that are universally practiced) that the Confutation raises appears at first glance to have only the value of a footnote which took care of itself in the transition from Article 7 to Article 8 of the CA and proved to be superfluous. In the only two-day-long negotiations about the doctrinal articles of the CA of the Committee of Fourteen (August 16 and 17, 1530) it could hardly have been otherwise. There are, in fact, a number of witnesses which expressly report on the unanimity in ecclesiological questions.

However, we must observe a peculiar fact: The question about the church is taken up in a surprisingly thorough way in Melanchthon's Apology. Along with justification and penitence it suddenly becomes one of the most thoroughly treated points among the 21 doctrinal articles, and aspects are addressed which one does not suspect exist at first glance at the Confutation's brief treatment.[1]

Therefore, in looking at Melanchthon's Apology one perceives a steadily increasing significance of the ecclesiological problem, which had certainly begun to move into the center of the dispute ever since 1517. The later religious colloquies of the Reformation period provide proof of this,[2] and it appears that the contemporary situation is similar, for on the original point of contention, the doctrine of justification, "a far-reaching consensus has been reached." [3]

1. Article 7 of the CA—the Unity of the Church

In dealing with the question of the CA's understanding of the church one will naturally have to begin with Article 7, although that is really not the only place in the CA where ecclesiological statements are made. Here at least is the point where they are concentrated, and from here the connecting lines lead to other parts of the CA.

In this article it says: "It is also taught among us that one holy Christian church will be and remain forever (*perpetuo mansura*). This is the assembly of all believers (*congregatio sanctorum*) among whom the Gospel is preached in its purity (*pure docetur*) and the holy sacraments are administered according to the Gospel (*recte administrantur*). For it is sufficient (*satis est*) for the true unity of the Christian church that the Gospel be preached in conformity with a pure understanding of it and that the sacraments be administered in accordance with the divine Word. It is not necessary (*nec necesse est*) for the true unity of the Christian church that ceremonies, instituted by men, should be observed uniformly in all places. It is as St. Paul says in Eph. 4:4,5, 'There is one body and one Spirit, just as you were called to the one hope that belongs to your call, one Lord, one faith, one baptism.' " [4]

This text has impressive unity and precision. The beginning is the confession of the continuity; the conclusion, the (Pauline) confession of the unity of the church. In the center are the statements about the true unity of the church. They are derived from the preceding sentence about the nature of the church and lead to a statement about what is not necessary for the true unity of the church.

The dominant thought is as elementary as it is simple: What is necessary for the unity of the church coincides with what makes the church the church; and, vice versa, what makes the church the church coincides with what is necessary for the unity of the church. What is equally necessary for the existence as well as the unity of the church is the gospel which is promised and communicated to human beings under the form of the preached word and the administered sacraments. In this gospel Christ is present and unites human beings with himself and with one another into one body.

To be sure, in all of this it is decisive that the gospel be preached in its pure and genuine form and the sacraments be administered in accordance with this gospel. Where this proclamation and administration of the sacraments according to the gospel occurs, there is the church. And where agreement on this subject exists among Christians and churches, there is unity of the church and decisive prerequisites for church fellowship are fulfilled.

In such a radical concentration of the ecclesiological (and also ecumenical) problem upon the question of the right proclamation of the gospel in sermon and sacraments, and not so much in an exhaustive and all-inclusive description of the nature of the church, lies the proper and specific Reformation concern of this article. This is brought out in a twofold way. First, it is emphasized that unanimity in proclamation of the word and administration of the sacraments is "enough" for true unity *("satis est"); * and this is immediately developed by saying that a uniformity in rites and ceremonies instituted by man is "not necessary" *("nec necesse est").*

2. Confession of Continuity, Catholicity, and Apostolicity of the Church

2.1. Continuity

The first statement of Article 7 of the CA expresses a fundamental conviction of the Reformation: the church of Jesus Christ has never ceased to exist and "will be and remain forever." The Reformers' theological striving and the origin of Reformation congregations is enclosed by this confession of the church's continuity and is very precisely qualified by it: What is going on is not a break with the previous church and an establishment of a new church; what is happening is precisely a striving for a right way of remaining in the "one holy Christian church."

This must be seen against the background of the certainty of faith shared also by the Reformers that God preserves the church in his truth. "They have to confess that the holy Christian church must be holy and a bulwark of the truth, without error or falsehood, because the church cannot err *(quia ecclesia non potest errare)*. . . . for the church ought not and cannot teach lies and error. . . . For God's mouth is the mouth of the church, and vice versa. God cannot lie, nor can the church." [5]

The CA as a whole—in its Preface and its Conclusion as well as in each individual article—is profoundly dominated by this thought of the church's continuity and the will to preserve this continuity and very emphatically expresses it. This is also true of Luther's thought.[6] It is "dangerous and frightening to listen to or believe anything contrary to the unanimous witness, faith, and teaching of the entire holy Christian church, which has been preserved unanimously in all the world from the beginning for more than fifteen hundred years," is the way a 1532 message from Luther to Duke Albrecht of Prussia puts it.[7] One of his later writings was dedicated entirely to proving that the Reformation congregations have not, as has been claimed, fallen away from the ancient church and founded a "new church," but "have remained faithful to the true ancient church." [8] Luther's struggle for the renewal of the church is therefore also a struggle for the continuity of the church which, according to his conviction, will be preserved in its renewal. The reason why Luther never dared to use the term *reformatio* with reference to the movement started by him is probably because this concept would have been "incompatible" with his view of continuity.[9] *"Summa summarum:* Beware of new doctrines and *retinete vetus."* [10]

This confession of the continuity of the church, as Article 7 of the CA expresses it, is appreciated by the *Confutation:* "Yet here they are properly praised for saying that the church will remain forever." [11]

2.2. Catholicity

The first sentence of Article 7 of the CA is also a confession of the catholicity of the church, building (most clearly in the German version) on the text of the Apostles' Creed: "One holy Christian church." The difference is chiefly a linguistic one, in that the Latin "catholica" of the Apostles' Creed is rendered here, as it is elsewhere, as "Christian" without any sort of polemic intention.[12] That this is in fact a purely linguistic question is made clear by the Apology. It emphasizes that Article 7 of the Augsburg Confession deals with "the catholic or universal church which is assembled from all nations under the sun."[13] At the same time this gives an interpretation of the term "catholic": The church to which the *"perpetuo mansura"* applies is the *universal*

Christendom, the—as the German version says—"assembly of *all* believers." [14]

With this confession of the catholicity of the church, Article 7 of the
CA brings a fundamental ecclesiological thought of Luther to expression, just as it did with the confession of the church's continuity.[15]
In his Confession of 1528 Luther had said that he believed "that there
is one holy Christian Church on earth, i.e. the community or number or
assembly of all Christians in all the world. . . ." [16] The Schwabach and
then the Torgau Articles pick this up[17] and lead into the Augsburg
Confession. Therefore the CA expresses no "independent" concept of
the church which limits the church to individual local congregations and
would be in danger of losing sight of the catholicity of the church.
In local churches the universal church is concrete. As surely as the gospel
is proclaimed in the respective local communities of believers, so does
Article 7 of the CA look beyond the largeness or smallness of the local
assemblies to the entire Christendom on earth.[18] It is only for this entire
Christendom on earth that the *perpetuo mansura* can be claimed.

This idea of the church's catholicity is, so the Apology emphasizes
in looking at the struggle of the Reformation—its dangers and its
temptations—"extremely necessary" and "completely comforting." [19]
The Apology picks up what was already in Luther's Confession and
was emphasized in the Schwabach and Torgau Articles, but was present
only implicitly in the CA.[20] The understanding of the church's catholicity in the sense of its universal commission and the universal spread
of the church doubtless stands in the foreground of the CA. But the
other important dimension of catholicity out of which the CA grew,
which is of foremost importance for Catholic sensitivity, is also present
and not at all strange in the thinking from which the CA developed—
the church's catholicity in the sense that the fullness of revelation is
entrusted to it. Just as little as the Reformation wished to introduce
"novelties" and thus question the continuity of the church, did it wish
to absolutize partial aspects of the faith and thus abandon the fullness
of revelation. Even if its real pathos lay in purifying the faith, the
church's proclamation, and the life of the church from distorted "additions" and in restoring the "pure teaching of the gospel," the Reformation was concerned simultaneously with "the entire holy Christian
faith" and "the entire Christian church." [21] It claimed, in fact, "that
many most high and necessary articles of Christian doctrine, without
which the Christian church, together with the entire Christian teaching
and name would be forgotten and disappear, had been brought again

to light by us." [22] Only as the church of the "pure Gospel" is the church "the pillar of truth," is it built on the foundation which is Christ,[23] and is it Christ's "body, the fulness of him who fills all in all" (Eph. 1:22-23).[24]

The Catholic understanding that, as a service for the unity of the universal church, the office of Peter—entrusted to the bishop of Rome —also belongs to the church's catholicity, opens a complex of questions which, as is well-known, is not directly addressed in the CA, and was in all likelihood even consciously excluded. As necessary as the exploration of this complex of questions may be for a Catholic-Lutheran understanding, to explore it here would lead us far beyond the contents of the CA. Moreover, because of inner Catholic developments, chiefly those formulated in the doctrinal declarations of Vatican I, the question of the papal office is confronted today in a considerably different form than in 1530. Since Vatican II the perspectives have changed again. The recently begun ecumenical dialogs on the papal office and the service of Peter[25] are now helping to present the question of the pope differently than was done at the time of the Reformation and during the Reformation's confession-making process, with its mostly very negative attitude toward the papal office. This is why the CA does not provide a starting point for the discussion of this complex of questions.[26]

2.3. Apostolicity

There cannot be the slightest doubt that, according to Lutheran understanding and the intention of the CA, "apostolicity" belongs to the church's essential attributes. This continuing steadfastly in the apostles' doctrine (Acts 2:42) and being "built upon the foundation of the apostles" (Eph. 2:20) is what constitutes the church. The CA's confession of the church's continuity includes this fundamentally. The statement "guard against new doctrine and retain the old" becomes for Luther immediately "guard against those who teach something other than what the apostles have taught!" [27] Here a basic consensus exists which goes far beyond Catholics and Lutherans: "The church is apostolic as long as it rests on this foundation (i.e., the apostles) and remains in the apostolic faith." [28]

Yet it is questionable whether the text of the CA and especially the statements of Articles 7 and 8 form a particularly suitable starting point to support and develop this existing consensus. Aside from the fact that Article 7 of the CA, despite all its cohesiveness and precision, does not intend to present a complete doctrine of the church, we must note that the CA's statements about the church are related to the Apostles' Creed, where the attribute "apostolic" does not appear. This is also true in the ecclesiological statements of Luther's Confession and in the Schwabach and Torgau Articles. Thus neither in the CA's preliminary forms, in the CA itself, nor in the later Lutheran confessions does "apostolicity" of the church become an express subject for discussion.[29]

Nevertheless, there are two points in the context of the CA's ecclesiological statements on the basis of which we can take up and develop the confession of the church's apostolicity. *First* is the question concerning the office of the ministry, which, as will be shown, is addressed implicitly in Article 7 and explicitly in Articles 5, 14, and 28. Thus it is necessary to investigate how far the Augsburg Confession understands this necessary office as an "apostolic" office, especially in the sense of the historic succession of office guaranteed by episcopal ordination *(successio apostolica),* which the Catholic side regarded as unabandonable, or at least how far it is open to such an understanding. This important complex of questions, however, is reserved for another chapter in this book. Therefore we can here give only a hint and thus leave the treatment of the church's understanding of the question of the episcopal office open.[30] The *second* point, according to Reformation thinking, where the idea of apostolicity is revealed with special emphasis, even though the CA does not elaborate it, is the concept of "gospel," which appears three times in the German version of Article 7 of the CA. We have already shown that according to Article 7 and in the sense of Reformation theology, "gospel"—proclaimed in sermon and sacraments— makes the church the church and that the dominating and characteristic when Article 7 emphasizes that the gospel must be preached "purely" concern of Article 7 is to relate all ecclesiological questions to the proclamation of the gospel, indeed to concentrate them and place them under the primacy of the gospel.

The content of this gospel is defined in Article 5 (with reference to Article 4) as the message of justification for Christ's sake through faith, and in Article 7 (with reference to Article 5) formally as "preaching," i.e., as oral proclamation and as administration of the sacraments. Thus it is always implicit in Reformation thinking that this goal is by definition the gospel founded *on the apostles* and attested to as normative for all future Christian and churchly proclamation. Therefore when Article 7 emphasizes that the gospel must be preached "purely" and the sacraments must be administered "rightly," i.e., "according to the gospel," this is a reference to that apostolic testimony of the gospel and an indication of the necessary essential "apostolicity" of the church. "The church is apostolic as the assembly of believers among whom the same gospel is preached which Jesus Christ once commissioned the apostles to proclaim." [31]

3. The Key Ecclesiological Concept of "Congregatio sanctorum"

Although the confession of the church's continuity and catholicity earned the Confutation's praise, the designation given in Article 7 of the CA of the church as *"congregatio sanctorum"* ("assembly of all believers") caused reservations and criticism. The writers of the Confutation feared that here evil people and sinners were excluded from the church and consequently a church is envisioned that in the history of the church was known as the "ideal of a Novatian church." They confronted this view with those New Testament passages that spoke of the church in its concrete form, in its temporal reality, as consisting always of good and evil people, believers and unbelievers (chaff and wheat; foolish and wise virgins; evil and good fish) which would finally achieve its complete purity at the last day.[32]

That is the one serious attack that was made in Augsburg against the Reformers' understanding of the church which was articulated in Article 7 of the CA. And this criticism, as was said, appears to take care of itself in the continuing elaboration of the CA. For the following Article 8 ("What is the Church?") is directed against precisely this understanding or misunderstanding of the church that the opponents at Augsburg attributed to the concept of *"congregatio sanctorum."* Article 8 says: "Although the Christian church, properly speaking, is nothing else than the assembly of all believers and saints *(congregatio et vere credentium)*, yet . . . in this life many false Christians, hypocrites, and even open sinners remain among the godly. . . ." [33] The Donatist error is rejected *expressis verbis.*

Therefore Melanchthon can say in his Apology: "The eighth article exonerates us sufficiently. We confess and say too that the hypocrites and evil men also may be members of the church in external fellowship of the name and offices, and that one may rightly receive the sacraments from an evil man." [34]

The question is: Are the critical questions about Article 7 of the CA raised by the Confutation in fact answered by this? In Augsburg it appeared that they had been. The electoral chancellor Brück wrote:

"In the seventh article they agree. In the eighth article on the church we confess that there will be many evil people and sinners in the church in this life." [35] And from the Catholic side Eck conceded: "In saying that the church is an assembly of believers they have come to terms with the explanation of the tiny word *sanctorum*. When they confess that good and evil men are in the church, we are agreed." [36]

In fact it was clear at the Diet that in the labeling of the church as *"congregatio sanctorum"* there existed a deep commonality which was to be retained. Although the word *"sanctorum"* may at first glance have engendered the above-mentioned reservations of the writers of the Confutation, it became clear—as Melanchthon showed in the Apology[37] —that here the *"communio sanctorum"* of the Apostles' Creed was once again picked up. The replacement of *"communio sanctorum"* with *"congregatio sanctorum"* or *"congregatio vere credentium"* is no grave and suspicious innovation, as a glance at the Middle Ages shows, especially at Thomas Aquinas, for there the description of the church as *"congregatio fidelium"* is frequently found. In Thomas' *In Symbolum Apostolorum Expositio* there is a definition of *"Sanctam Ecclesiam Catholicam"* that is reminiscent of Articles 7 and 8 of the CA: ". . . Ecclesia est idem quod congregatio. Unde Ecclesia sancta idem est quod congregatio fidelium."* [38] With the term *"congregatio sanctorum"* the CA used a term which is completely in accord with the tradition of the church.

We know now that the term *"communio sanctorum,"* which corresponds to *"congregatio sanctorum,"* had from olden times both a neuter and a personal meaning; it deals with communion or participation in the *"sancta,"* especially the sacraments, and at the same time with communion among "sanctified" people.[39] There can be no doubt that Luther himself,[40] as well as the CA, especially emphasized the personal aspect. Nevertheless, it is completely clear that the church is not merely an association of like-minded people based on their faith, their personal holiness, or their common confession. The relative clause in the statement of Article 7 of the CA is, as the Lutheran side has emphasized again and again, an essential relative clause, without which the essence of the church cannot properly be described: The church "is the assembly of all believers among whom the Gospel is preached in its purity and the holy sacraments are administered according to the Gospel *(in qua evangelium pure docetur et recte administrantur sacramenta)."* That means the church is a community of people which is created and preserved through the Lord present in word and sacrament.[41] The "vertical" dimension of participation *(communio)* in the gifts of salvation is, as Luther put it, God's work and strength *(opus et virtus dei),*" [42] as *"nova creatura dei,"* it is thus preserved. The description of the church, like an ellipse, has two foci. The church is a fellowship of people, the people of God, *populus fidelium,* and it is—by virtue of the gospel mediated in preaching and the administration of the sacraments—the creation of God, "the body of Christ," [43] "the bride of Christ." [44] All of this does not in fact create a point of contention between the Reformers and the Catholics. The foundation of the ecclesiology of the ancient church is not abandoned. Here both sides stood in the same tradition. We need only think of Vatican II's Constitution on the Church in which the first two chapters describe this double dimension of the church: the church as "mystery" and church as "the people of God."

But there is still an unresolved and extremely important remnant. In order to see it we can begin anew with the Confutation's fear that Article 7 of the CA meant a church of sinless people. Interestingly, the Confutation did not mention the Donatists as the deterring example —it does that in Article 8—but rather Hus. It fears that in Article 7's understanding of the church Hus' error is arising again. And this error of Hus, condemned at Constance, which itself went back to Wycliff and displayed lines of continuity with the spiritual Franciscans, is that the church in the final analysis is an invisible fellowship of those who are predestined, the mystical spiritual body of Christ, whose head is Christ alone.[45]

The subject of concern on the part of the Confutation extends farther than it appears at first glance at the Augsburg negotiations. It is the concern about a "spiritualized" understanding of the church that ignores and minimizes the visible, constituted, institutionalized form of the church and a concern that is understandable in view of the clearly spiritualizing tendencies of the young Luther.[46]

Melanchthon's Apology clearly reflects this comprehensive problem, as do the Confutation and the negotiations at Augsburg, i.e., the problem of visibility and hiddenness of the church, of the relationship of the church as *"societas fidei et spiritus sancti in cordibus"* with the church as *"societas externarum rerum et ritum."*

Melanchthon allows no doubt to remain that the Reformation will have nothing to do with a spiritualized understanding of the church. Against the accusation that the evangelical side is talking "about a dreamed-up church *(civitas platonica)* which is nowhere to be found," he replies that they are dealing with a church which "truly is and remains on earth," and that has "external marks" *(notae, externa signa)* by which it can be recognized, "the office of the ministry or the gospel and the sacraments." [47] But at the same time, building on Article 8 of the CA, he emphasizes the distinction between *"ecclesia proprie dicta"* and *"ecclesia large dicta,"* [48] and says that "the church here [i.e., during its earthly pilgrimage] is hidden among the great crowd and multitude of godless people." [49]

Even this concept of church and membership in the church in a "real" and in an only "external" sense, and the talk of "visibility" or "hiddenness" of the church,[50] which later in the Reformation became more prominent and displaced or reinterpreted the (questionable) way of speaking about the church as "visible" or "invisible," more commonly used at the beginning, is now in our opinion no essential point of dissent.[51]

The understanding of the church as evidencing a certain "double layered-ness" is from the very beginning a characteristic of the concept of the church. It appears already in the New Testament comparisons (good and bad fish, wheat and chaff, wise and foolish virgins) and surfaces again and again, especially in Augustine's terminology of the church as *"domini corpus verum atque permixtum,"* or *"permixta ecclesia,"* and his distinction between *"communio sacramentorum"* and *"societas sanctorum,"* [52] or between belonging to the church *"corpore"* or *"corde,"* which was then adopted by Vatican II.[53] Thomas too distinguished a twofold connection between human beings and Christ, the head of the church, and consequently a twofold form of belonging to the church as *corpus mysticum:* first the real belonging *(actu),* which is given in the view of God *(per fruitionem patriae),* through love *(per caritatem),* and through faith *(per fidem);* then the merely potential belonging *(in potentia)* which all other human beings possess.[54] It is an important concern of Reformation ecclesiology that this differentiation does not become a dichotomy. If certain statements of the Apology should nevertheless point in this direction, that should be criticized on the basis of the total context of the Lutheran confessions and of Reformation theology, chiefly on the basis of the doctrine of justification *(justifcatio impii; simul justus et peccator).*[55]

Yet we can hardly overlook the fact that differences became evident between the Reformation and the established church's understanding of the nature and extent of the church's visibility and institutionalization. The Reformation side emphatically maintained and claimed the visibility of the church, and supported this by referring to the two external marks of word and sacrament. But beyond these external marks and that which they in themselves imply—especially the office of the ministry given by God to the church, with its different functions[56]—the visibility and institutionalization of the church did not enter the description of the church's *essence.*

Melanchthon's Apology sees these differences very clearly and emphasizes them surprisingly strongly when it places the Reformation statements about the church over against what it calls a "new Roman definition of the church," one that is characterized chiefly by institutional elements like monarchy, pope, and bishops.[57] The element of external institutionalization is by no means lacking in the Reformation understanding of the church, but this element has a less important extent and a different weight than word and sacrament.[58]

4. The *"satis est"* and the Question of the Church's Ordained Office

The question of why this is so leads to the concept which more than any other has attracted attention to itself in both inner-Lutheran and also ecumenical discussions about the CA's understanding of the church and church unity. It is the expression *"satis est* (it is sufficient)."

Although what Article 7, together with Article 8, says positively about the church provides no serious problems for mutual understanding, things are obviously very different if we concern ourselves with what this article does not say, or rather appears to exclude from the description of the church by the famous *"satis est"* and includes in the *"nec necesse est* (it is not necessary)."

In Augsburg the Catholic side saw no serious problem here, at least as far as the particular formulation was concerned. But in fact a decisive point of divergence can here be found in the judgment of many Catholics as well as Protestants. According to the frequently uttered Catholic interpretation, the *"satis est"* or the *"nec necesse est"* signaled a serious defect in Reformation ecclesiology, insofar as it excludes or is indifferent to aspects which are constitutive of the nature of the church, for example those aspects which are described in the Constitution on the Church of Vatican II (*Lumen gentium,* Chapter 3) under the heading of the "hierarchical structure" of the church.

How are we to move beyond this? Catholic and Lutheran interpretaion agrees that we have to understand the *"satis est"* on the basis of the following negative sentence. This sentence says what things are "not necessary" for the true unity of the church (and in the context of Reformation thinking this always means for the very existence of the church): "It is not necessary that human traditions or rites and ceremonies, instituted by men, should be alike everywhere." This is the text of the Latin version of the CA's Article 7.

However, before we now ask in detail just what things are excluded, or, to be more precise, are given a lesser importance by the *"satis est"* or the *"nec necesse est,"* it is necessary to give an account of what the word *"necesse est"* means, for here, as in most of the other places where we find it in the Lutheran Confessions, it has a very specific meaning. It does not mean generally "being necessary," but it talks about that which is "necessary" in an ultimate sense, namely, "necessary for salvation" or "necessary for justification *(necessarius ad salutem; necessarius ad justificationem)."*

Thus with one stroke it becomes visible—even terminologically—how the Reformation conception of the justification of man *sola gratia, sola fide* is also determinative for ecclesiology and leaves its imprint upon it.

In the *"satis est"* or the *"nec necesse est,"* there is no iconoclastic pathos. It is also not—at least not primarily—an expression of ecumenical openness and freedom over against the varieties of existing church orders, forms of piety, procedures of organizing worship services, and ecclesiastical customs and usages. It is also not primarily a pastoral expression in the sense that it does not want to burden "poor working people" with too severe regulations about fasting and too many holidays.[59]

The primary sense of the *"satis est"* or the *"nec necesse est"* is rather that only those things that mediate salvation, justification *sola gratia, sola fide,* are permitted to be signs and constitutive elements of the church.

In the final analysis the human ecclesiastical traditions, rites, and ceremonies in CA 7 are considered as something not necessary for the church and its unity because they feared that the attempt to retain ecclesiastical ordinances and ceremonies contained the danger of reintroducing the idea of works and they wanted *a limine* to exclude this. Thus for the CA in the doctrine of the church the doctrine of justification, the center of the Reformation movement, is at stake. This article must be maintained and asserted even in ecclesiology.

This becomes clear in CA 28, where, among other things, the question under consideration concerns the theological significance of humanly-ordered ecclesiastical constitutions, regulations, and ceremonies. There it says: "Inasmuch as such regulations as have been instituted as necessary *(necessarius)* to propitiate God and merit grace are contrary to the Gospel, it is not at all proper for the bishops to require such services of God. It is necessary to preserve the teaching of Christian liberty in Christendom, namely, that bondage to the law is not necessary for justification *(non sit necessaria . . . ad justificationem)*, as St. Paul writes in Gal. 5:1. . . . For the chief article of the Gospel must be maintained, namely, that we obtain the grace of God through faith in Christ without our merits; we do not merit it by services of God instituted by men." [60] In short: not only not necessary for the sake of unity, but first and foremost not necessary for salvation, for justification; not only for ecumenical freedom, but first and foremost for Christian freedom, i.e., freedom from the coercion of the law and of self-justification—this is the scopus and the basic motif of the *"nec necesse est"* expression in CA 7.

The Apology makes this connection between ecclesiology and the doctrine of justification, which is recognizable in CA 7, completely clear. It admits in Article 7 that "it also pleases us that the universal ceremonies be maintained uniformly for the sake of unity and good order. So in our churches we observe mass, the Lord's day, and the other important feast days. And we cherish all the good useful human ordinances. . . ." Yet it then says: "But here the question is not whether human ordinances are to be kept for the sake of external discipline or for the sake of peace. It is a completely different question, namely, whether the observance of such human ordinances is an act of worship by which one propitiates God and that without them no one may be righteous before God. That is the chief question." [61]

We can pointedly say, but without any exaggeration: the statement of CA 7 with its *"satis est"* or *"nec necesse est"* is primarily not a statement about the unity of the church, but about salvation; it is primarily not an ecclesiological, but rather a soteriological statement.

After this clarification regarding the meaning of the *"satis est"* or the *"nec necesse est"* it is possible to see better just *what* is excluded by these words or put aside in their significance in regard to the church and its unity. What are these "ceremonies instituted by men," these *"traditiones humanae seu ritus aut ceremoniae ab hominibus institutae"?*

CA 7 does not develop this in detail. But it becomes clear from the broader context of the CA, perhaps from Article 15 (church usages) and primarily from the discussions and negotiations during the Diet of Augsburg itself. Here two things become apparent:

First: In the category of ceremonies and rites instituted by human beings fall first and foremost pious practices as, for example, regulations about foods, fasts, abstinence, holding of church festivals, celebrations and their dates, regulations about clothing, use of images in the church and in worship, times of prayer, pilgrimages, processions, hymns, ringing of bells, regulations about pericopes or lessons, regulations about church law, and questions of external order which serve discipline and the proper common life. They deal largely with church customs, usages, and regulations which have originated in history and are conditioned by time and situations. They may have their legitimacy and their value, but they do not form the essence of the church and therefore are necessary neither for the existence nor for the unity of the church. One will hardly argue about their classification as "not necessary things," if one accepts the sense of the definition of "necessary" given above. There is also no reason to view the *"satis est"* or the *"nec necesse est"* as the "heart of the problem." Furthermore the Confutation reacted generally positively to Article 7 as well as to Article 15 and only demanded that a distinction be made between "special" rites and ceremonies, i.e., ones strongly determined by place or region, on the one hand, and "universal rites" and ceremonies, on the other hand, which are valid in all Christendom and presumably stem from the apostles. With the former variety is necessary and changes are possible, but not with the latter.[62] Moreover, it appears that they had achieved agreement in individual questions at the negotiations at Augsburg.[63]

But more important than this first point is the *second*. It goes directly to the "heart of the problem." An overview of what Article 7 of the CA sees as ecclesiologically secondary items makes one thing clear in the entire Lutheran *corpus doctrinae*—nowhere is the office of the ministry included among the items that are not necessary or among the traditions, rites, and ceremonies instituted by human beings. Quite the contrary! CA 5 says very clearly that the office of the ministry, the *"ministerium docendi evangelii et porrigendi sacramenta"*—in contrast to the "ceremonies instituted by men"—is "instituted by God" and thus exists *iure divino*. The office of the ministry, as Article 5 expresses it, is necessary for salvation, insofar as it is a prerequisite for obtaining the *"fides justficans."* The Schwabach Articles (Article 7) had already spoken this way of the office of the ministry: "There is no other means or method, neither way nor path, to obtain faith. . . ." [64] And CA 28 says: "These gifts [viz., eternal righteousness, the Holy Spirit, and eternal life] cannot be obtained except through the office of preaching and of administering the holy sacraments. . . ." [65] And this office is not simply the universal priesthood, but the special ecclesiastical office of those who are "regularly called" (*rite vocati*, CA 14) and ordained with prayer and the laying on of hands.[66] "When they offer the Word of Christ or the sacraments, they do so in Christ's place and stead (*Christi vice et loco*)"; they "represent . . . the person of Christ (*repraesentant Christi personam*)" [67] and thus stand in the congregation and with the congregation under Christ and yet at the same time with Christ's word and sacrament they stand "over against" the congregation.

Thus, according to the CA, the office of the ministry belongs to what determines the essence of the church. The reason that CA 7 does not mention this expressly is that this ecclesiastical office is in fact implicit in the preaching of the gospel and the administration of the sacraments. For it is always only as the *proclaimed* gospel and the *offered* sacraments that the gospel and the sacraments are the *signa* that create the church, or the *notae ecclesiae.* Characteristic of this is the way the Reformation not infrequently equates ministry and word or ministry and gospel, something that can be understood only in the sense just mentioned. For example, the Apology speaks about "ministry or gospel" [68] and the Schwabach Articles say that God instituted the "office of the ministry or the oral word, namely, the gospel." [69]

The fact that the CA does not especially need to name the office of the ministry as constitutive of the essence of the church since it is implied in the preaching of the gospel and the administration of the sacraments is indicative of a specifically Lutheran or Reformation nuance in the understanding of the church and the ministry. They want to connect the office of the ministry as closely as possible with word and sacrament in order to avoid the danger of an independent existence of the office and to preserve the subordination of the ministry to the two primary *signa* or *notae ecclesiae* and thus maintain the sovereignty of the gospel over the church. Insofar as a special accent in the Lutheran or Reformation understanding of the church in fact exists here, this in no way needs to become a Catholic-Lutheran point of contention. For also in Catholic theology the office of the ministry as an essential element of the church is not considered to be on the same level as word and sacrament.[70]

5. Teaching and Governing Authority in the Church

According to CA 7 the church stands and falls with the "pure" preaching of the gospel and the "right" administration of the sacraments according to the gospel. From this immediately follows the demand "not to receive or hear false teaching." [71]

But how is one to guard this necessary purity and correctness of the proclamation of the gospel in preaching and sacraments in the life of the church and how should one decide between true and false proclamation and doctrine?

This question was indeed not a theme of the CA; but it does not remain completely unraised and unanswered in the total context of the CA.

One thing is immediately apparent; the judgment about and the concern for the pure gospel in the church is not left to individuals and to the subjectivity of their faith. And a further item becomes clear too—the question about the pure gospel in the church is not answered by means of a mere reference to the canon of Holy Scripture. Rather it is true that the judgment about and the concern for the true and false proclamation of the gospel is the prerogative of the church and belongs to its life. In the Augsburg Confession's judgment the church therefore does not just have the power of the keys, i.e., the authority "to forgive and retain sins," [72] something that was undisputed by Catholics and Lutherans. As the bearer of such keys the church is an authority over teaching and proclamation which cannot be taken away by either the autonomy of an individual believer's conscience or the loyalty to Holy Scripture. The CA is just as far removed from a subjective approach as it is from an isolated scriptural principle. In other words, obligation of conscience and obligation to the Scriptures in no way exclude the authority of the church.

It is not so much isolated statements in the CA, but primarily the CA as a whole—in its existence, its self-understanding, and its method of argumentation—which expresses this ecclesiological situation which is further elaborated at a later point in the Lutheran confession-making process.[73] At least such an exclusive *sola scriptura* is supported by the CA neither in principle nor in practice. This is especially evident where it argues about existing differences with the Roman Catholic Church or the problems of abolishing "abuses" (CA 22-28). The reference to the Holy Scriptures (or the "command of God," "God's word," or sometimes also the "gospel") plays a very decisive role there; nevertheless the argumentation is never "biblicistic," but always goes hand in hand with references to the tradition of the church, the church Fathers, the laws of the church, the history of the church, etc. This corresponds to the twofold reference in the preceding articles on doctrine (CA 1-21) —to the biblical witness as well as to the confession and antiheretical decisions of the universal church.

The elaborations contained in the CA follow the principle expressly and frequently stated that it intends to represent only what is not contrary "to the Holy Scriptures and . . . the universal Christian church." [74] A tendency in favor of arguing from Scripture is apparent but this is natural in the situation and does not—at least at present— pose a point of contention between Catholics and Lutherans.

Real authority is attributed to the church in respect to the truth of Christian doctrine and proclamation in the Augsburg Confession as such. For it cannot be overlooked that the CA intended not only to describe what was then being preached, taught, performed, and instructed in the Reformation congregations. [75] From the beginning it had the character of a binding normative "confession," in that those who presented it openly pledged themselves and obligated themselves to it. The *"magnus consensus"* of the Reformation churches and congregations, which the Augsburg Confession claims to be, describes both what *is and what should be preached* and taught in these churches and congregations. "The legal validity [viz., of the CA] was . . . only the external seal of the internal claim to be from the very beginning a norm of doctrine and a 'confession' at the same time." [76]

This concept of *"consensus"* which is characteristic of the entire Augsburg Confession occurs again, as is well-known, in the ecclesiological Article 7 (. . . *consentire de doctrina evangelii et de administratione sacramentorum* . . .). Here it should not be burdened with everything which can be said about the confession of the church as an expression of *"consensus ecclesiae"* and as norm of ecclesiastical doctrine and proclamation. The confession of the church would then suddenly appear alongside preaching of the gospel, administration of the sacraments, and the office of the ministry as a constitutive element of the church, as has sometimes been held among Lutherans. But the fact that *"consensus"* appears or is implied in Article 7 of the CA must be understood in the sense that the concern for a binding theological consensus *of the church,* oriented toward proclamation and teaching, is considered as task and as privilege, as obligation and as authority, and that it belongs to its life.

With regard to the Augsburg Confession an important fundamental agreement here becomes evident between the Roman Catholic and the Lutheran concept of the church. One has not always and everywhere been sufficiently aware of it.

Here a further series of questions will still open up, and differences will appear in the process of answering them. Yet these differences should not obscure or devalue the common basic conviction that on both sides authority is ascribed to the church as such, not only the authority of the power of the keys, but also authority and the office of guardian in regard to the truth of Christian doctrine and proclamation.[77]

The questions which follow are addressed primarily to two points: first, the question about how and by whom this authority is exercised in the church, and second, the question about the nature and extent of this authority. Both questions are discussed in Article 28 of the CA ("The Power of Bishops"; "Ecclesiastical Power") and are discussed in this book where that article is the special object of investigation. Here at least a few chief topics will be mentioned.

On the question of how and by whom teaching authority is exercised in the church, the CA expresses itself *expressis verbis* in only one place. It is the reference to the office of bishop in Article 28: To "the office of the bishop" belong, "according to divine right"—along with the preaching of the gospel and the office of the keys—the responsibility to "judge doctrine and condemn doctrine that is contrary to the Gospel." [78] There can be no doubt that the Lutheran Reformation saw here a specific task of the bishop and wanted to have this task of the bishop's office preserved in some form in the church.[79]

But this reference to the exercise of ecclesiastical teaching authority by the bishops is not the CA's only answer. The *church's confession* is a way in which the church exercises its teaching authority. The CA itself—in its existence and its self-understanding—demonstrates this fact, also the later intensive process of confession-making of the 16th century. In the face of existing or newly-occurring doctrinal controversies it shows precisely how important this form of exercising ecclesiastical teaching authority is for the Reformation churches. But since this confession of the church understands itself and comes into existence as the *"magnus consensus"* of congregations or local churches, the exercising of teaching authority in the church had generally a *conciliar-synodical* element which was further developed and shaped in the course of the history of the Reformation churches.

The three aspects of the exercise of ecclesiastical teaching authority—the episcopal, the confessional, and the conciliar-synodical aspects—are also basically familiar in the ancient church and the Roman Catholic Church. Even when the question about the relative weight of these various elements or aspects brings certain Catholic-Lutheran differences to light, there is still a broad commonality between the Roman Catholic view and the Lutheran view manifested in the Augsburg Confession.

Whether ecclesiastical teaching authority is located in an ecclesiastical office, in an ecclesiastical confession, in a conciliar-synodical institution, or in a cooperation of these three elements, it is certainly clear that ecclesiastical authority is not absolute but has limits, something which is also acknowledged on the Catholic side.[80] On this point the CA speaks with great emphasis, as we have seen above.

It is fundamentally true that the church in its teaching and preaching remains bound to what is revealed in Christ. The pope—and the church in general—has no power to "establish articles of faith," as the Apology and also many other places in the Lutheran Confessions say.[81] In view of the faith necessary for salvation, the church may add nothing to what is given by revelation.

But what does that mean *in concreto?* What are the available criteria which mark these limits? As we have already shown, the tradition of the church and—in even stronger measure—the canon of Holy Scripture and thus the testimony of the apostles contained in the Scriptures, play an important role.[82] But these strongly formal criteria, as important as they are, remain themselves, along with all ecclesiastical authority, subordinate to an ultimate material criterion—the "gospel."

A more thorough examination of the 32 places in which the term "gospel" is used in the CA[83] is surely needed than is possible in this context. But even a brief overview will show that while the term "gospel" is indeed not always used in an exactly identical sense,[84] yet it is reserved with a surprisingly high degree of consistency as a label for the message of justification. The term refers either directly to the message of justification *sola gratia, sola fide* (more frequently called "the doctrine of faith"),[85] or it stands in a context unmistakably closely related to this content.

Here in this "gospel," according to the CA, all ecclesiastical authority, especially the teaching authority, finds its real "touchstone" and its final limit. Wherever ecclesiastical authority teaches or orders something that obscures or contradicts this gospel, it forfeits its authority and must be opposed. This is shown in the CA chiefly in the context of Article 28, which deals with the *"potestas ecclesiastica,"* and characteristically the term "gospel" appears a total of 15 times as a criterion and limit of this ecclesiastical power and authority, thus almost as frequently as in all the other articles of the CA together. This concept of gospel as a limitation of ecclesiastical teaching authority is sometimes combined with the term "Christian liberty"[86] or, especially, "conscience."[87] They, too, may define the limits of ecclesiastical authority. Of course this does not mean a modern subjectivism. Rather, both terms are most closely coupled with the content of the concept of gospel. The "Christian liberty" which is to be preserved consists in this, "that bondage to the law is not necessary for justification,"[88] and that the "conscience" may not be "bound" and "burdened" by means of ecclesiastical regulations and orders which, although good and useful,[89] are claimed to be necessary for salvation and for obtaining grace, although they are not and cannot be that, without thereby to "coercing [human beings] to sin."[90]

6. Results

6.1.   The CA's understanding of the church presented above—interpreted in the context of the Lutheran Confessions—evidences *fundamental agreements* with that of the ancient church and the Roman Catholic Church, which was of course also the express intent and conviction of the Augsburg Confession.

6.2.   The ecclesiological statements of the CA are in great degree determined *by the perspective of the doctrine of justification.* This results in specific accents and differences which one should not hastily regard as separating churches, especially since they were not judged so in Augsburg in 1530.

6.3.   *The following objections* often raised by the Roman Catholic side pertain to incorrect interpretations, which occasionally were made, *but not to the understanding of the church grounded in the CA.* These objections are:

● The article on justification leads to an incomplete concept of the church which regards many things, essential according to the Catholic view, only as *"usus."*

● The church is conceived of as invisible *(invisibilis).*

● To the church, according to the CA, belong only true believers, but not sinners.

● There is only the priesthood of all believers, while a special order of service to which definite persons are ordained is not constitutive for the church.

● The *"satis est"* in Article 7 of the CA means a fundamental indifference to church structures.

● On the basis of the *"sola scriptura"* principle a binding ecclesiastical decision on questions of doctrine is not possible and all ecclesiastical statements of faith are totally subject to revision at any time.

6.4.   There still exist *open questions and unresolved problems*. Some things are not treated in the CA; among them are some aspects of the episcopal structure of the church, the obligatory nature of conciliar statements, and the papal office. Against the background of this fundamental commonality in the understanding of the church we see in these problems tasks that we should try to resolve together. In the official Catholic-Lutheran dialog, important convergences have already been achieved.[91] This fact justifies the hope that solutions may also be found to the questions still open.

Notes

1. Did the Confutation's critique of CA 7, despite its inexactness and imprecision, hit a vital point? H. Immenkötter is perhaps correct when he writes: "In the sense of the CA, Eck's implied accusation was unjustified, as CA 8 shows . . . , and yet Eck did hit an important controversy about the reformers' concept of the church which had not come out at Augsburg." *Um die Einheit im Glauben—Die Unionsverhandlungen des Augsburger Reichstages im August und September 1530* (2nd ed.; Münster: 1974), p. 40.

2. Thus, for example, the "Regensburg religious colloquy" of 1541, the last of the great religious colloquies between the Roman Catholic Church and the Lutheran churches before the resumption of the dialog in our day, collapsed primarily on ecclesiological questions after it was believed an agreement had been reached on the interpretation of justification. Cf. H. Jedin, *A History of the Council of Trent,* vol. 1 (New York: Thomas Nelson and Sons, 1957), pp. 381-385; see also the "Regensburg Book" with its two ecclesiological articles: Art. 6 *(De ecclesia, et illius signis ac autoritate)* and Art. 9 *(De auctoritate Ecclesiae in discernanda et interpretanda scriptura),* CR 4:201ff. and 208ff.

3. "In the interpretation of justification today a thoroughgoing consensus is showing itself," says the final document of the Evangelical Lutheran-Roman Catholic study commission, *"Das Evangelium und die Kirche"* (= *Malta Bericht),* 1972, no. 26. But what really causes trouble, so we hear time and again, are questions about the understanding of the church and closely connected are questions about the ministerial office, its self-understanding, its exercise, and its validity. One speaks about the remaining differences in

view of the "ecclesiological consequences and implications" of the interpretation of justification.

4. CA 7 (BC 32).

5. AE 41, 215-216 (WA 51, 515-516). "For the Church is ruled by the Spirit of God and the saints are led by the Spirit of God (Rom. 8). And Christ remains with his Church even to the end of the world; and the Church of God is the pillar and ground of the truth. These things, I say, we know; for the creed that we all hold affirms, 'I believe in the holy catholic Church'; so that it is impossible for the Church to err, even in the smallest article" (AE 33, 85; WA 18, 649-650).

6. Cf. especially the conclusion of the first part of the CA (BC 47-48) and the conclusion, 5 (BC 95). Cf. on this the studies of W. Höhne, *Luthers Anschauungen über die Kontinuität der Kirche,"* (1963), and W. Maurer, *"Luthers Anschauungen über die Kontinuität der Kirche,"* in *Kirche, Mystic, Heiligung und das Natürliche bei Luther,* I. Asheim, ed. (Göttingen: 1967), pp. 95ff.

7. WA 30, 552.

8. AE 41, 194 (WA 51, 478-479).

9. W. Höhne, *op. cit.,* pp. 162-163.

10. WA 20, 647.

11. Immenkötter, 96.

12. In Luther's 1528 "Confession" (AE 37, 367; WA 26, 506), or in his two Catechisms (1529; BSLK 511 and 653; cf. BC 345 and 415), the attribute *"catholica"* is always rendered as *"christlich"* ("Christian"). The one-sided use of the term "catholic" in the sense of "Roman Catholic" and the problems associated with that term especially in German-speaking areas did not yet exist at the time of the Reformation. It is, as is well known, of much more recent date.

13. Apol. 7, 9 (BSLK 235, German; CT 228, German).

14. E. Schlink says in view of CA 7 and Apol. 7: "Since the catholicity of the one church has its reality in the rule of the one Christ, *catholica* is rendered in the Lutheran Confessions simply Christian. . . . The catholicity of the church is the catholicity of its commission with which the Lord sends his people to all nations, and the catholicity of its Lord, who is present and active wherever the Gospel is preached according to his commission and the sacraments are administered." *Theology of the Lutheran Confessions* (Philadelphia: Muhlenberg Press, 1961), p. 208.

15. Cf. on this what W. Maurer says about the "universality" of the church in his commentary on CA 7 and 8, *Historischer Kommentar zur Confessio Augustana,* vol. 2 (Gütersloh, 1978), pp. 163ff.

16. AE 37, 367 (WA 26, 506).

17. Schwabach Articles, Art. 12 (WA 30, 81); Torgau Articles, see K. E. Förstemann, *Urkundenbuch zu der Geschichte des Reichstags zu Augsburg im Jahre 1530,* vol. 1 (1833; reprint ed. Osnabrück, 1966) p. 70.

18. E. Schlink, *op. cit.,* pp. 202-203; cf. A. Kimme, who gives his interpretation of CA 7 and 8 the title "The Church Universal," in *Theology of the Augsburg Confession* (1968), pp. 48ff.

19. Apol. 7, 9-10 (BSLK 235-236, German; CT, 228, German).

20. Cf. AE 37, 367 (WA 26, 506); Schwabach Articles, Art. 12, *op. cit.;*

Torgau Articles, *op. cit.* In fact this usage of the idea of catholicity has a slightly polemical note. For the confessional statement about the catholicity of the church gives the Reformers the assurance that the "one holy Christian church" is not bound to "a place and time" and to "a person" (Schwabach Articles, Art. 12, *op. cit.;* cf. Torgau Articles, *op. cit.*) and therefore exists "not only among the Roman church." One may criticize this polemically-tinged usage of the idea of catholicity, but it also shows how important and fundamental the confession of the catholicity of the church is for the Reformation and the CA.

21. Apol., Preface, 16 (BSLK 144, German; CT 102, German).
22. Apol., Preface, 17 (BSLK 144, German; CT 102, German).
23. Apol. 7, 20-22 (BC 171-172).
24. Apol. 7, 5 (BC 169).
25. Cf. on this *Des kirchenleitende Amt: Oekumenische Dokumentation,* vol. 5, G. Gassmann and H. Meyer, eds. (Frankfurt: 1979).
26. Cf. the brief references to the papal office in the following article by A. Dulles and G. Lindbeck in the context of their development of the episcopal office.
27. WA 20, 647 and 748.
28. Report of the Evangelical Lutheran-Roman Catholic study commission, *"Das Evangelium und die Kirche"* (= *Malta-Bericht*), 1972, no. 52. According to common Catholic and Lutheran conviction the real sense of the doctrine of "apostolic succession" lies here: "It is the basic intention of the doctrine of apostolic succession that the church in all historical change of its proclamation and its structures at all times be directed back to its apostolic origin." *Ibid.,* no. 57.
29. The place where one most quickly refers to "apostolic" in the Lutheran Confessions is in the question about the sources and norms of ecclesiastical doctrine and proclamation. This question, as we know, is not treated thematically in the CA. This first occurs later in the Lutheran Confessions, chiefly in the Formula of Concord of 1577 (BC 464ff.), where in the beginning it is said about the "rule and norm" of the church's teaching that "the prophetic and apostolic writings of the Old and New Testament are the only rule and norm. . . ."
30. Here the matter may rest with the reference in the *Malta-Bericht,* no. 57: "Within the apostolicity of the entire church succession is to be seen in a special sense—the succession of the unbroken chain of continuity in office. In the early church primarily in connection with the refutation of errors it was a sign of the inviolate transmission of the gospel and a sign of the unity in faith. . . . The significance of such a special succession may be admitted by the Lutheran side, if the succession of doctrine is recognized as preeminent and if the unbroken chain of continuity in office must not be regarded *ipso facto* as a sure guarantee of the continuity of the right proclamation of the gospel."
31. E. Schlink, *op. cit.,* p. 204.
32. Immenkötter 94-95.
33. CA 8, 1 (BC 33).
34. Apol. 7, 3 (BSLK 234, German; CT 226, German).
35. Förstemann, *op. cit.,* vol. 2, p. 231.

36. CR 3:1055; Spalatin also writes in his report about the negotiations of the Committee of Fourteen in Augsburg (August 16-19, 1530): "About the Christian churches and evil priests. Doctor Eck says he hopes there will be no argument about this article. For the church is certainly beautiful, but at the same time black, as *de virginibus and de piscibus*. Held officially to the comparison that the word that stood was not *sanctorum,* but *sanctam*. Doctor Eck also said that he maintained that we were basically not different *"in fundamento,"* Förstemann, *op. cit.,* vol. 2, p. 227. Cf. *"Gutachten Johann Ecks über die Confessio Augustana,"* in *Quellen und Forschungen aus italienischen Archiven und Bibliotheken,* G. Müller, ed., vol. 38 (Tübingen: 1958), p. 227.

37. Apol. 7, 1ff. (BC 168-169).

38. *In Symbolum Apostolorum Expositio,* Art. 9; Cf. Thomas Aquinas, *IV Sent.,* d.20 g. la. 4 sol. 1; *De veritate,* q. 29 a. 4 obj. 4; *C. Gent.,* IV, 78; *S. Th.* I q. 117 a 2 obj. 1. Also Y. M. Congar, *"Die Weseneigenschaften der Kirche,"* *Mysterium Salutis,* vol. IV/1 (Einsiedeln: 1972) pp. 375-376.

39. On this, chiefly F. Kattenbusch, *Das apostolische Symbol* (1900; 2nd ed. Darmstadt: 1962), pp. 927ff. *(Sanctorum Communionem),* esp. p. 938; cf. also E. Wolf, *"Sanctorum communio,"* in *Peregrinatio,* vol. 1 (Munich: 1954), pp. 279 ff., esp. pp. 285-286.

40. For example, in the Large Catechism at the exposition of the Third Article of the Creed, 47-53 (BC 416-417).

41. Luther's well-known statement about the church in the Smalcald Articles says: "Thank God, a seven-year-old child knows what the church is, namely, holy believers and sheep who hear the voice of their Shepherd." (3, 12; [BC 319]); cf. also Luther's similarly well-known word in his writing to Ambrosius Catharinus (1521): *"Tota vita et substantia Ecclesiae est in verbo dei,"* WA 7, 721.

42. AE 11, 13 (WA 3, 532).

43. Apol. 7, 5 (BC 169).

44. Apol. 7, 10 (BSLK 236, German; CT 228, German).

45. DS 1201ff.

46. John Eck could already observe this tendency in Luther during the Leipzig Debate (1519). Luther there made himself the defender of the concept of the church represented by Wycliff and Hus—the church as *"praedestinatorum universitas."* WA 2, 287; Cf. W. Elert, *The Structure of Lutheranism,* vol. 1 (St. Louis: Concordia Publishing House, 1962), pp. 258-259.

47. Apol. 7,20-22 (BSLK 238, German; CT 232, German). On the basis of this observation one should not conclude that "office of the ministry" or "gospel" are alternatives. We shall speak later about ministry belonging to the essential characteristics of the church.

48. Apol. 7,29 and 10 (BSLK 241 and 236, Latin; CT 236 and 228, Latin).

49. Apol. 7,20 (BSLK 238, German; CT 232, German).

50. One should also think of the extensive descriptions of the *"notae ecclesiae"* by the mature Luther, where he calls them "public signs" by which one may "externally recognize" the church. AE 41, 148ff. (WA 50, 628ff.) and AE 41, 193ff. (WA 51, 477ff.).

51. J. Hamer, O.P., *"Les pécheurs dans l'Eglise: Etude sur l'écclesiologie de Melanchthon dans la Confession d'Augsbourg et l'Apologie."* In *Reformation: Schicksal und Auftrag: Festgabe für Joseph Lortz,* vol. 1 (Baden-Baden: 1958) pp. 193ff. is certainly of a different opinion. He sees a concept of the church presented especially in the Apology—less in the CA itself—that understands the church only from the personal holiness of its members, so that sinners and evil people cannot in any way belong to it (pp. 203 and 206). H. Bornkamm, *"Die Kirche in der Confessio Augustana,"* in *Das Jahrhundert der Reformation* (Göttingen: 1961), p. 136, correctly sees exactly the opposite portrayed in Apol. 7: "Beyond the text of Art. 7 of the Augustana, evil people are now considered members of the church." E. Schlink, *Theology of the Lutheran Confessions, op. cit.,* p. 221 notes in looking at the CA and the Apology that the church properly speaking "can be found only in the church in the larger sense," and that one can recognize the church only by the outward signs in which the hypocrites also participate. Whether it is *"ecclesia proprie dicta"* or *"ecclesia late dicta,"* it is in either case still the church. *Ibid.,* p. 222.

52. According to R. Seeberg, *Lehrbuch der Dogmengeschichte,* vol. 2 (4th ed., Darmstadt: 1953), pp. 465-466, with notes; *ibid.,* p. 470.

53. *Lumen gentium* 14; see also the statement in *Lumen Gentium* 6, about the *"vita Ecclesiae abscondita";* (for an English translation see W. Abbott, ed., *The Documents of Vatican II* (New York: Herder and Herder, 1966), pp. 32-33 and 18ff., respectively); cf. also K. Rahner, *"Sündige Kirche nach den Dekreten des Zweiten Vatikanischen Konzils,"* in *Schriften zur Theologie* 6 (1965): 321, note 1.

54. Unbelievers *(infideles)* belong to the church only as a possibility *(etsi actu non sint de ecclesia, sunt tamen de ecclesia in potentia; S. Th.,* III, 8,3 ad 1; a formula which is strongly reminiscent of the Apology's formulation of the distinction between *"ecclesia proprie dicta"* and *"ecclesia late dicta"!).* Even the (believing, baptized) mortal sinners, according to Thomas, belong to the church not actually, but only potentially. One could call them "dead members" *(membrum mortificatum,* ibid., ad 2); a similar statement is in III Sent. d. 13, q. 2 a 2 sol. II. It is interesting that Suarez still defines the church as *"congregatio fidelium hominum in Christo credentium."* For him the constitutive element for church membership is therefore faith, cf. also L. Hoffmann, *"Die Zugehörigkeit zur Kirche nach der Lehre des Franz Suarez,"* in *Trierer theologische Zeitschrift* 67 (1958): 146-161.

55. E. Iserloh also, similar to J. Hamer, still sees a problem here. He believes that in his Apology Melanchthon "did not succeed in clearing away the objection of the Confutation." Rather, "the basic question of whether the holiness of the body of Christ can be united with the fact that there are always *'mali'* and *'impii'* in the church is finally answered negatively by Melanchthon." However Iserloh points simultaneously to the discrepancy arising within the Reformation, that the anthropological *"simul iustus et peccator"* is abandoned ecclesiologically. Iserloh is convinced "that the positions are not as different as it appears," that here we are dealing rather with an inadequate "theological formulation" of a proper

"intention to make a statement"; nevertheless it is clear to him that Lutheran theology does not hold the idea of a church without sinners and never wanted to hold it. E. Iserloh, *"Die Confessio Augustana als Anfrage an Lutheraner und Katholiken im 16. Jahrhundert und heute,"* in: *Catholica* 33 (1979): 42.

56. See below, pp. 187ff.; CA 28,21; cf. the chapter by A. Dulles and G. Lindbeck in this volume, pp. 147ff.

57. Apol. 7,23 (BSLK 239f., German; CT 234-235, German; cf. BC 172-173).

58. This distinction must also be emphasized according to Catholic interpretation—"the ministry *attests,* word and sacrament *established* the church and its unity." H. Schütte, *Protestantismus* (2nd ed., Essen: 1967) p. 445; cf. J. Ratzinger, *"Das geistliche Amt und die Einheit der Kirche,"* in *Catholica* 17 (1963): 178.

59. Cf. H. Immenkötter, *Um die Einheit im Glauben, op. cit.,* p. 49.

60. CA 28, 50-52 (BC 89).

61. Apol. 7, 33-34 (BSLK 242-243, German; CT 238, German).

62. Immenkötter, pp. 96-97.

63. Cf. H. Immenkötter, *Um die Einheit im Glauben, op. cit.,* pp. 100-101. Yet another clarification is needed about what has been said in the preceding about what the CA says about ceremonies, rites, etc.: May not something be considered "not necessary" by the Lutheran side, which, according to Catholic interpretation, belongs to the essentials? Seen "soteriologically" it is true that we are redeemed through Jesus Christ, that the saving act of God in Christ is mediated to us through word and sacrament. This is proclaimed or given in the liturgy. "Ecclesiologically" we cannot do without the liturgy in the service of the saving act of God in Christ. In the liturgy God's new and eternal covenant with us is actualized, God deals with us through Christ in the Holy Spirit; consequently our answer is possible and required "through Christ and with him and in him," cf. E. Lengeling, *Die Konstitution des Zweiten Vatikanischen Konzils über die heilige Liturgie* (2nd ed., Münster: 1965), p. 27. The concern that the idea of works might enter in with the liturgy is unjustified. It is not that we propitiate God in the liturgy; CA 28,35 [BC 86] and also CA 28,5 [BC 81] correctly reject the idea that we obtain grace or are justified through ecclesiastical statutes. If the accusation of Apol. 7,33-34 [BC 174-175] is directed against the liturgy, it misses the mark. On the other hand, it is understandable that with the proper understanding of liturgy the discussion cannot be only about regulations which are to be kept "for the sake of love and tranquility" (CA 28, 55; BC 90). As the reform of the liturgy after Vatican II has shown, liturgical regulations are capable of being changed; but when they are established one cannot do away with them as if they were not obligatory. That such a liturgy can "be observed without sin" (CA 15, 1; BC 36) is clear; it does not oppose the gospel or justification. But then, also according to CA 15, this applies: *"Servanda est!"* Its acceptance is not a matter of choice.

64. WA 30, 88.

65. CA 28,9 (BC 82).

66. Apol. 13, 12 (BC 212).

67. Apol. 7,28 (BC 173). Cf. *Malta-Bericht*, no. 50.
68. Apol. 7,22 (BSLK 238, German; CT, 232, German).
69. WA 30, 88.
70. Certainly, it is completely possible in the realm of Reformation/Lutheran theology to cite the office of the ministry specifically as one of the marks of the church. This happens, for example, in Luther's *On the Councils and the Church* (AE 41, 153ff; WA 50, 632ff.) and in *Against Hanswurst* (AE 41, 195-196; WA 51, 481). Interesting in this context is also the attitude of the estates adhering to the Augsburg Confession toward the disputed articles of the "Regensburg Book," which were written by Melanchthon and then presented to the emperor (May 31, 1541). There it says in the article *"De unitate Ecclesiae et ordine ministrorum Evangelii":* *"Consistit igitur unitas Ecclesiae in hac consociatione sub uno capite per idem Evangelium et idem ministerium, cui debetur obedientia, iuxta illud; Qui vos audit, me audit, ut retineantur unitas fidei, similis usus Sacramentorum, et disciplina mandata in Evangelio,"* CR 4,368. A thorough discussion of the question about the office of the ministry and its form is contained in another contribution to this volume (A. Dulles and G. Lindbeck).
71. Apol. 7,48 (BSLK 246, German; CT 242, German).
72. CA 28,5 (BC 81); cf. CA 25,4 (BC 62), CA 28, 2ff. and 21 (BC 81ff.); see on this the subsequent article by H. Fagerberg and H. Jorissen.
73. Cf. especially the first article of the Formula of Concord of 1577, "The Summary Formulation, Basis, Rule, and Norm," in the Solid Declaration (BC 503ff.) as well as, especially, in the Epitome (BC 464ff.).
74. Conclusion of the First Part, 1 (BC 47); Introduction to the "Articles about Matters in Dispute" (22-28), 1 (BC 48-49); Conclusion, 5 (BC 95).
75. Preface, 8 (BC 25).
76. G. Kretschmar, *"Die Bedeutung der Confessio Augustana als verbindliche Bekenntnisschrift der evangelisch-lutherischen Kirche,"* in *Confessio Augustana: Hilfe order Hindernis?* (Regensburg: 1979), p. 38; cf. pp. 32ff.
77. Cf. the work of H. J. Urban, *Bekenntnis, Dogma, Kirchliches Lehramt* (Weisbaden: 1972).
78. CA 28, 21 (BC 84); cf. Torgau Articles, Förstemann, *op. cit.,* p. 79: "It is the chief part of ecclesiastical jurisdiction to reprove erroneous doctrines; for this is commanded in the Scriptures and the canons."
79. This intention is well proved and documented in studies of the history of the Reformation. Cf., for example, B. P. Brunner, *"Vom Amt des Bischofs,"* in *Schriften des Theologischen Konvents Augsburgischen Bekenntnisses,* vol. 9 (Berlin: 1955); H. Meyer, *"Behindern Amtsbegriff und Kirchenverständnis in der Confessio Augustana ihre Anerkennung durch die katholische Kirche?"* in *Confessio Augustana:-Hilfe oder Hindernis?* (Regensburg: 1979), pp. 160ff., with a further bibliography.
80. In the "Dogmatic Constitution on Divine Revelation" (no. 10) of Vatican II it says: "This teaching office is not above the Word of God, but serves it, teaching only what has been handed on, listening to it devoutly, guarding it scrupulously, and explaining it faithfully by divine commission and with the help of the Holy Spirit; it draws from this one deposit of

faith everything which it presents for belief as divinely revealed." (W. Abbott, *op. cit.*, p. 118).

81. Apol. 7,23 (BC 172); Treatise on the Power and Primacy of the Pope, 39-40 (BC 327), et. al.
82. See above, pp. 178ff.; cf. also CA 28,28: "One should not obey . . . [bishops] if they err or if they teach or command something contrary to the divine Holy Scriptures" (BC 85).
83. It is found (in the German text) in the CA once each in CA, 12, 16, and 20; twice in CA 15; three times each in CA 5, 7, 26, and 27; and 15 times in CA 28.
84. It is often connected with the term "God's command" or "God's word" and can sometimes also designate the Scriptures or the Gospels.
85. For example, CA 15 (BC 36-37); CA 20, 10-11 (BC 42); CA 26,20 (BC 67).
86. CA 28,51f. (BC 89-90).
87. For example, CA 28,42 (BC 88); CA 28,49 (BC 89); CA 28, 53 (BC 90); CA 28,77 (BC 94).
88. CA 28, 51 (BC 89).
89. Apol. 7, 34 (BC 175).
90. CA 28,77 (BC 94).
91. Cf. on this, among others, the sections on *"Die geschichtliche Entwicklung der kirchlichen Strukturen"* and *"Das Verständnis der apostolischen Sukzession"* in the *Malta-Bericht,* 1972, nos. 55-58; the soon-to-appear document of the joint Roman Catholic-Evangelical Lutheran commission on *"Das geistliche Amt in der Kirche unter besonderer Berücksichtigung des ordinierten Bischofsamt."* In addition, *"Die Frage des päpstlichen Primats,"* *Malta-Bericht, nos.* 66 and 67; *"Lutherisch-katholischer Dialog in den USA, Amt und universale Kirche,"* in *Papsttum und Petrusdienst,* ed. by H. Stirnimann and L. Vischer (Frankfurt, 1975), pp. 91-140; "Lutheran-Roman Catholic Dialogue, Teaching Authority and Infallibility in the Church," *Theological Studies* 39 (March, 1979): 113-166.

8

The Sacraments:
Baptism and the Lord's Supper

by Erwin Iserloh and Vilmos Vajta

translated by Darold H. Beekmann

1. The Sacraments in the Triune God's Economy of Salvation

In order to offer an appropriate interpretation, the connection between all the statements about the sacraments throughout the entire Augsburg Confession (CA) must be considered. These statements are not found exclusively in those articles under the obvious headings, which, in fact, were not added until the CA was published.

Following its unequivocal witness to the early church's doctrine of the Trinity (Article One), the CA addresses the subject of fallen humanity and, already at this point, indicates that no one can be saved from that fateful condition who is not born again through Baptism and the Holy Spirit (CA 2). The two central articles of the CA (three and four) explain how this salvation has come about through the incarnate Son of God and how the Holy Spirit can make alive and can justify persons "for Christ's sake, through faith." It is the office of the Spirit[1] to save human beings through faith in the Son of God, sacrificed for us (CA 5), to justify human beings before God, to guard human beings from sin and the devil (CA 3,5) and to incorporate human beings into the divine life of grace (CA 4,2). Thus the sacraments are incorporated into the Triune God's economy of salvation. Through the Holy Spirit, the word and sacraments are called into service, in order that the church as "the assembly of saints and true believers" will be and remain forever *(perpetuo mansura sit,* CA 7 and 8).

As a result, therefore, the sacraments are rightly interpreted only if they are viewed as part of the whole structure of the Triune God's economy of salvation, his saving work in Christ through faith given by the Holy Spirit. This does not mean, however, that in light of justification by faith, the CA holds it necessary first to reflect on the transmitted teachings about the sacraments and out of that to draw various logical consequences. It works quite the opposite: the justifying activity of God is so unfolded that the sacraments are already essentially drawn in and are in no sense viewed as an appendage. The juxtaposition of proclamation of the word and administration of the sacraments is to be understood in a similar way. In both instances, the Holy Spirit exercises his office *(Amt—ministerum)* and effects the salvation of human beings according to the merciful will of the Triune God.

2. What Is a Sacrament?

It is surprising that in the CA one does not find an article dealing with *De sacramentis*.[2] After the discussion of Baptism (9) and the Lord's Supper (CA 10), confession (CA 11) and repentance (CA 12), there does, indeed, follow an article on the use of the sacraments (CA 13); but this does not express all that is to be said about the nature of the sacrament.

At this point it is helpful to refer back to Article Five, which indeed is entitled "The Office of the Ministry *(De ministerio ecclesiastico),"* but which actually discusses the activity of the Holy Spirit in word and sacraments. According to Article Five, word and sacraments are the means *(instrumenta)* through which the Holy Spirit is given. Through this means, the Spirit in turn effects faith, which holds fast to the fact that we "become righteous before God by grace, for Christ's sake" (CA 4). The issue is justifying faith, bound to word and sacrament as external means. In this way the CA not only rejects the Enthusiasts' *(Schwärmer)* tendency to depreciate grace hidden "in externals" but also the belief that one can acquire grace through one's own preparation and works. The work of the sacraments, carried out through God's Spirit, cannot be replaced by human works. Grace is placed under the power of the Holy Spirit alone, who works "when and where it pleases God *(ubi et quando visum est Deo)."* The sacraments bear Christ's promise that they are to be the tools of his saving activity. He has bound himself to external signs, which does not mean that his saving activity is limited to these signs, but it is not left to the wishes of human beings whether or not to make use of these signs.

The sacraments are "signs and testimonies" of the divine will to save (CA 13). God has not only demonstrated his saving will toward human beings through the surrender of Christ on the cross, but through Christ has instituted the sacraments and left them as a mandate for the church *(ordinatio et mandatum Christi),* in order to make Christ's saving work contemporary and concretely accessible to human beings. Thereby the CA adopts a pair of concepts which became decisive for the definition of the sacraments especially in Luther's Large Catechism.[3] These two concepts not only provide the basis for the certainty of faith but, at the same time, also refute Donatistic tendencies. For it is made clear that the efficacy *(efficacitas)* of the sacraments is based neither on the faith of the officiant nor on the faith of the recipient.

God remains faithful, even when confronted with the unfaithfulness of his people. The sacraments are signs of his saving work, independent of the worthiness of those who administer them; and, from the perspective of the recipient, faith does not constitute the sacrament; rather, faith receives it. Faith is the condition for the fruitful working of the sacrament. That is what is meant by the Catholic doctrine of *opus operatum,* which in its intention was not contested by Luther or the CA. At this point, Lutheran theology can acknowledge a legitimate concern of Catholic theology.[4] At the same time, Lutheran theology must continue to stress clearly, with no less emphasis, that God's action in the sacraments effects *salvation* where these means of the Holy Spirit are received and used *in faith.* The offer of salvation and the presence of salvation according to God's merciful will in Christ are taken seriously only in this perspective.[5]

On one occasion Luther pointed out that the sacramental gift is in no way diminished by the stress on faith; it works *"suum opus* (its own work)" in the faithful, nonetheless, *"in incredulo operatur alienum opus* (in the unbeliever it accomplishes an alien work)."[6] In other words, if it is said that the sacraments effect grace *sola fide,* then we are dealing with the saving use, with the subjective appropriation of the salvation that has been offered.[7]

According to CA 13, the saving will of God is attached to the "signs and testimonies *(signa et testimonia)*." These are given "for the purpose of awakening and strengthening" the faith of the recipient. Here the connection of faith with the sacraments is given even stronger expression. The dual concept of "word and sign" is common in Luther's theology of the sacraments.[8] With this concept, however, an essential role is attributed to the "sign." In a sense, this has to do with the peculiar value of the sign which, together with *(simul)* the word, offers the promised work of the sacrament and holds it before one's eyes *(per sacramenta exhibentur et ostenduntur)*. In this sense, with reference to Augustine, the Apology speaks of the sign *(signum)* as "the visible Word *(verbum visible)*" (Apol. 13, 5 [BC 212]) and underscores the working together of word *(verbum)* and rite *(ritus)*. The sacramental sign presents visibly what the word makes audible. Appropriate to our human nature, the sacraments employ two inseparable "languages." In this manner, the gift of the Holy Spirit becomes communicable.[9]

Here "sign" is not intended to mean only the elements (water, bread, wine). Signs are the elements bound up with the word and incorporated into a liturgical action.[10] This does not signify a weakening of the sign, but instead its qualification within God's economy of salvation. Such a concept of the sign appeared already in Luther's early writings on the sacraments. In fact, "the significance" of the sacrament —as Luther developed it already in his sermon on the sacraments from 1519—is not simply identical with "the word," rather, at the same time, it is rooted in the sign itself. In Baptism, "sign" is the baptized's sinking under and rising up out of the water while the Holy Trinity is being invoked. What this signifies is the death of the old person and the rising of the new in the sacramental union with the death and resurrection of Christ.[11] In the Lord's Supper also, "sign" is the body and blood of Christ presented for eating and drinking for the forgiveness of sins. The sign embodies within itself something ontological. It corresponds to the saving action of God, which does not take place through a word of amnesty but rather through the surrender of Christ on the cross. Precisely this offering of the body and blood has sign character, both in the historical as well as in the sacramental event.[12]

Against this background, the placing of "sign and testimony" side by side takes on a special meaning. Even if the concept *testimonium* is given the primary meaning of verbal testimony, this is not its only meaning. In the biblical sense, the *testimonia Dei* are also the historical acts of God. These acts bear testimony to God's faithfulness and to his gracious leading of his people. This must also be noted with regard to the concept of *promissio* in Article 13. The faith that is associated with the sacraments, according to the text of the CA, is that "which believes the promises that are offered and made visible through the sacraments *(quae credat promissionibus, quae per sacramenta exhibentur et ostenduntur)*." Consequently, here *promissio* is not intended to mean merely *verbum audibile,* but rather the sacramental sign which is associated with this *verbum.* Toward this sacramental reality faith is oriented and in this respect can be designated as *fides sacramenti.* For faith relates to an object, in this case, to the sacraments as signs and word, and uses them as the promises through which God's saving will toward humankind is fulfilled.[13] Only against this background can the sacraments also be "signs by which people might be identified outwardly as Christians" (CA 13), which they are, however, only secondarily. They are fully comprehended as sacraments only there where the divine redemptive activity is acknowledged in them through word, sign, and faith.

The Confutation to the CA accepted and approved the understanding of the sacraments as sign and testimony of the divine will expressed in CA 13. However, the Confutation insisted on an explicit yes to the seven sacraments.

The CA, in Articles 9-12, deals only with three sacraments: Baptism (Article 9), the Lord's Supper (Article 10), and penitence (Articles 11 and 12). In the structure of the CA, these articles on the sacraments represent the explication of Article 7 (on the church). In that article, the church is defined as "the assembly of all believers among whom the Gospel is preached in its purity and the holy sacraments are administered according to the Gospel." The teaching on the sacraments is concluded with Article 13, which deals with the reception of the sacraments.[14] The Apology (13,3-5 [BC 211]) explicitly characterizes Baptism, the Lord's Supper, and penitence as sacraments in the proper *(proprie)* and true *(vere)* sense. Constitutive for the strict concept of sacrament employed here is: (a) divine institution *(mandatum Dei)* and (b) the promise, i.e., the efficacious promise of grace *(promissio gratiae)*. Accordingly, the Apology defines as sacraments in the true sense those external signs and rites *(ritus)* which have the command of God and to which the promise *(promissio)* of grace has been added. On the contrary, rites which are merely instituted by humans and, therefore, do not contain any promise of grace are not sacraments in the true sense, namely: confirmation and extreme unction. They were not established by God but rather by the Fathers, and even the church has never viewed them as necessary for salvation (Apol. 13,6 [BC 212]). If marriage is to be considered a sacrament, one must also number other secular callings among the sacraments (Apol. 13,14-15 [BC 213]). For that matter, there are still other things which have God's *mandatum* that could be viewed as sacraments. Yet "no intelligent person will quibble about the number of sacraments or the terminology (sacrament), so long as those things are kept which have God's command and promises" (Apol. 13,17 [BC 213]). With regard to ordination (the office of ministry), the Apology recognizes the possibility of allowing ordination to be considered a sacrament if ordo is understood as *ministerium verbi et sacramentorum* (Apol. 13,7-13 [BC 212-213]); for "the church has (God's) command to appoint ministers . . ." (Aprol. 13, 12 [BC 212]).

Luther's attitude toward penitence as a sacrament wavered. In the Babylonian Captivity of the Church (1521), he excluded penitence from the list of sacraments in the true sense because it lacks a divinely instituted external sign.[15] So, in fact, as the Lutheran Church developed, is held to the view that there are only two sacraments: Baptism and the Lord's Supper. And it is with these two sacraments that we shall deal in the following pages.

3. The Saving Presence in the Sacraments

3.1. Baptism

The sacraments are the place where the salvation given in Jesus Christ is made present. As it relates to Baptism, the CA addresses this aspect of making present or contemporary in a very brief and concise manner: "The grace of God is offered through Baptism"; and the baptized "are received into his grace" (Article 9). The Confutation approves this article and, thereby, confirms that there is no controversy with regard to Baptism.[16]

It is noteworthy, however, that in the CA, Baptism is understood as a sacrament of justification. For the words "received into God's grace" refer back to Article 4, where this expression is used to describe justification by faith *propter Christum*. According to this, God's saving action through the death and resurrection of Christ is effective as God's offer of grace through Baptism. In Baptism, through the water connected with the word, the baptized are drawn into the Christ event as their salvation. Consequently, in Luther's Small Catechism two scripture texts dealing with the presence of salvation are quoted in addition to Christ's command to baptize.[17] First we find Titus 3:5-8, which establishes Baptism as "the washing of regeneration and renewal in the Holy Spirit," i.e., water Baptism is a "gracious water of life" through the Spirit of Christ. Then Romans 6:4 is quoted with reference to the ongoing fulfillment of the baptismal event insofar as we die daily to sin through sorrow and repentance and arise cleansed and justified to a new life for God (compare CA 2,2). It is significant that sorrow and repentance are included in this baptismal action, viz., life in the Holy Spirit is a constant returning to baptismal grace, even as it is also a moving forward on the pilgrimage toward the day of resurrection. In this way, spiritual growth, the sanctification of human beings, is connected with Baptism. This centrality of Baptism as the locus of the saving presence also explains the CA's criticism of the practice of viewing monastic vows as equal with Baptism and the monastic life next to Baptism as a *via perfectionis*.[18] Through the doctrine of justification by faith, Baptism is decidedly lifted up as the fundamental sacrament of the daily life of a Christian.

3.2. The Lord's Supper

The new life in Christ, which is given sacramentally through Baptism as a onetime event, is preserved and maintained by Christ himself until the day of judgment through the holy sacrament of his body and blood which were sacrificed on the cross.[19] In CA 10 this saving presence is unmistakably acknowledged: "It is taught among us that the true body and blood of Christ are really present in the Supper of our Lord under the form of bread and wine and are there distributed and received. The contrary doctrine is therefore rejected." According to the Latin version of this article, "the body and blood of Christ are truly present and are distributed to those who eat in the Supper of the Lord *(vere adsint et distribuantur vescentibus in coena Domini)*." The Confutation finds nothing objectionable about this article: "Because they confess that in the Eucharist, after the consecration lawfully made, the Body and Blood of Christ are substantially and truly present." [20] In addition, however, it should be noted that under either form Christ is totally present. Also, the transformation of the substance of the bread into the body of Christ should be acknowledged. Consequently, those who formulated the Confutation appear to have understood that the

CA contained the teaching about transubstantiation, even if they did not explicitly state this. The formulation "under the form" in the German version is a form of expression that comes out of the doctrine of transubstantiation.

In the negotiations that followed the reading of the Confutation, those who represented the Roman Church were satisfied with the Lutherans' readiness to emphatically stress the real presence through the insertion of the words *"vere et realiter,"* in German, *"wesentlich"* ("substantially") and, thereby, to distance themselves even more clearly from Zwingli and the South German cities.[21]

The Apology complied with this even more than was required when it speaks of *"vere et substantialiter."* It states, "They (the authors of the Confutation) approve the tenth article (of the CA), where we confess our belief that in the Lord's Supper the body and blood of Christ are *truly and substantially (vere et substantialiter)* present and are truly offered with *(cum)* those things that are seen, the bread and the wine, to those who receive the sacrament" (Apol. 10, 1 [BC 179]).

The Apology does not hesitate, along with the Greek liturgical tradition, to speak of a transformation.[22] This reference is significant. For Greek theology, following the patristic tradition, uses a variety of terms with which to designate the transformation into the body and blood of Christ which results from the sacramental use of bread and wine.[23] The fact that something actually happens with the bread and wine when it is consecrated through Christ's words of institution and through the eucharistic prayer is not open for discussion in Lutheran theology. But the doctrine of transubstantiation is not the only way to express this saving presence theologically. The terminology may vary, yet the fact still can be confessed together. When Melanchthon gave expression to this reality through the verb *mutare,* he joined Luther in his own practice of frequently using this term with reference to the consecration of bread and wine.[24] The fact that this term is used by the authors of the Confutation themselves offers the Lutheran partners a possibility—without employing the concept of transubstantiation—of coming closer to a mutual understanding without concealing the terminological diversity.[25]

Protestant research has also come to see that in the formulation of the CA, Melanchthon had the canons of the Fourth Lateran Council in mind and took them into consideration.[26] W. Maurer has pointed out evidence of the usage of decrees from the Council in Articles 1 and 19 as well as in the entire CA, and has determined that "in his German text, Melanchthon very nearly approached the classical formulations which the Fourth Lateran Council of 1215 found in the Innocentianum." [27]

The concern that "the specific Reformation position is not explicitly put into words in the Latin and even less so in the German version of Article 10" [28] has led to an attempt to stress even more emphatically the difference between the German and the Latin versions of Article 10 and to give programmatic significance to this difference. Due to the fact that only the Latin text contains the term *"vescentibus,"* B. Möller concludes, along with W. Maurer,[29] that there is a principal divergence insofar as "in the German version the terms used to describe the body and blood of Christ ('present,' 'distributed,' 'received') are placed beside each other so that the presence of the gifts and benefits of the Lord's Supper also appear to be assured *extra usus;* while in the Latin version, the presence of the body and blood is limited, through the term *'vescentibus,'* to *usus.* . . . In the Latin text, despite all of its indefiniteness, the *'extra usus'* is nevertheless excluded." [30] Here differences have come to receive greater emphasis from the perspective of a later point of controversy. For to whom then are the elements to be "distributed" and by whom are they to be "received"? The answer, "by those who participate in the meal, who eat," is so self-evident that it need not be stated; in fact, it could also be added without changing the content of the article. But what is the distinction beween "really present . . . and are there distributed and received" (by those who eat) and *"vere adsint et distribuantur vescentibus"?* Had Melanchthon been aware of a distinction here, he would have formulated Article 10 of the Apology differently.[31]

Here also a consideration of the Orthodox liturgical tradition can be of assistance. The concern of Roman as well as certain Lutheran theologians to determine the moment and the duration of the presence is foreign to eastern liturgical thought. In this respect, the involvement of the Orthodox tradition in the ecumenical movement has had a liberating effect and has in recent times enriched ecumenical discussion.[32] If in the CA—as in the whole of Lutheran theology—the saving presence is viewed as being closely connected with Holy Communion, is it not to be understood as though this presence of Christ were to be considered only for the moment of the eating and drinking? "Present" and "distributed" must not be separated.[33] The Apology approaches the Orthodox tradition—although certainly only in a groping manner—when it relates the entire worship service *(totus cultus, ritus, cere-*

monia) to the question of the saving presence, and in just this manner attempts to preserve the *mysterium sacramenti* as part of the sacramental saving presence (Apol. 24:88,93 [BC 265, 267]). For this reason, Melanchthon spoke of "the power of the mystical benediction" (Apol. 10:3-4 [BC 179-180]) whereby, according to the witness of the apostle Paul, we participate in the body of Christ through the sacramental bread. He defended "the doctrine received in the whole church—that in the Lord's Supper the body and blood of Christ are truly and substantially present and are truly offered with those things that are seen *(vere et substantialiter adsint . . . et vere exhibeantur cum his rebus, quae videntur, pane et vino)."* [34]

4. The Sacraments as Offering

4.1. Baptism

According to Article 9, Baptism contains a double movement: on the one hand, in this sacrament the grace of God is offered *(quodque per baptismum offeratur gratia Dei);* on the other hand, the baptized are committed to God *(oblati Deo)* and thereby are received into God's grace. The Latin word *offere* is used for both of these movements. It is thereby indicated that with God's offer of salvation through Baptism, the trust and confidence of the baptized are connected with the name of the triune God. The promise of salvation is recognized in faith when people are brought for Baptism. This offering of the congregation, which occurs through its prayer, is included as a part of God's own action. "All of our gifts to God can be offered only in connection with his gift, his grace to us." [35] God's action and our action are not separated into two different occurrences. The latter is dependent on God's activity and included in it so that God himself carries out his activity in the congregation as it acts in faith.

The thought which is expressed here is not spelled out more specifically in the CA, but it can easily be demonstrated in Luther's theology. For in *The Babylonian Captivity of the Church* he speaks of the "praying and believing church" which through its offering in prayer stands with the baptized *aliena fide.* Through the invocation of God as the one who acts through his name in Baptism, the baptized are offered to God so that they may take part in the promised salvation.[36] This offering of the congregation of believers is its "cooperation" in the divine grace. The act of carrying the baptized forth, according to Luther's *Treatise on Baptism,* represents the diligent prayer "for aid and grace through Baptism that he may become a child of God." [37] The prayer of supplication, which qualifies the offering as an act of faith by the congregation *(aliena fides)* does not, however, take the place of the faith of the baptized; rather, it requests it as a gift and activity of the Holy Spirit. The *fides ecclesiae* suffices as a commitment of a person to God, who himself, however, gives faith to each person and thereby allows them to take part in the divine life and everlasting salvation. God himself retains control over the gift of the Holy Spirit. Yet he promises it to those who are received into his baptismal covenant. For this reason, a congregation can in firm trust also baptize children and commit them to God's grace which he has offered. In this sense, one can speak of an offering of the sacrament of Baptism within the framework of justification by faith.

4.2. The Lord's Supper

This understanding of *"offere"* as "offering" could have provided the possibility of relaxing the bitter controversy over the question of the Eucharist as sacrifice. Luther's apprehension of 1520 "that there is at the present more idolatry in Christendom through the Mass than ever occurred among the Jews" [38] reached its culmination with regard to the Eucharist as sacrifice in the Smalcald Articles in the shocking conclusion that "accordingly we are and remain eternally divided and opposed the one to the other." [39] In this regard, one is obliged to ask which type of Mass and which theology of eucharistic sacrifice is meant and whether this judgment was perhaps only justified with respect to the teaching and practice of the Mass during a particular period of time. In Article 24, the CA deals with the Eucharist in terms of "abuses." Consequently, this does not offer a primarily positive description of the Lord's Supper as Mass, that is, as liturgical celebration. At the outset, the accusation that the Mass was being abolished is refuted: "Actually, the Mass is retained among us and is celebrated with the greatest reverence" (24:1 [BC 56]. The Lutherans had simply added German hymns to those in Latin in order to instruct the people concerning the sacrament and the proper reception of it and convey to them the necessary knowledge of Christ. It is not mentioned that the canon of the Mass and other passages talking of sacrifice had been eliminated. In this connection, mention is simply made of the communion of the congregation: "The people are also admonished concerning the value and (proper) use of the sacrament and the great consolation it offers to anxious consciences, that they may learn to believe in God and ask for and expect whatever is good from God. Such worship pleases God, and such use of the sacrament nourishes devotion to God. Accordingly it does not appear that the Mass is observed with more devotion among our adversaries than among us" (24:7-9).

At this point, Catholic theology is inclined to raise the question whether, according to this view, Christ has come to be viewed only as the host of the Lord's Supper and no longer as the head of the congregation, which through him, with him, and in him, comes before the Father. The movement of the congregation to God appears to be lost, for there no longer seems to be a place for the aspect of the "offering" of the congregation. This question still needs further clarification.

According to the CA, evangelical congregations celebrate communion Mass only on Sundays and on festival days or when the sacrament is otherwise desired (24:34). They abolished as an evil misuse the Mass without a congregation and, thereby, the multiplicity of private Masses. It is the Mass for a fee that led to the abuse that the Mass came to be celebrated for "monetary considerations." Private Masses have "infinitely" increased "the abominable error" that Christ had by his passion made satisfaction for original sin and had instituted the Mass in which an oblation should be made for daily sins, mortal and venial" (24:21). Thus the Mass came to be viewed as a work, which by its mere performance would take away the sins of the living and the dead. The speculation that a Mass which was read for many would be of less merit for the individual than if it were offered for one person alone, finally produced that "infinite proliferation of Masses." [40] For according to this presupposition, the increase in the number of Masses also signified an increase in the atoning power of the Mass, the so-called fruits of the eucharistic sacrifice.

On the contrary, the CA emphasizes that Christ's sacrifice on the cross is an event that occurred once and for all time, that he has made complete satisfaction for the atonement of all sins (Heb. 10:10, 14), and that we are justified before God through faith in Christ and not through our works. If simply through the performance of the Mass *(ex opere operato)* the sins of the living and the dead are taken away, then one achieves justification through the work of the Mass and not through faith. This interpretation of *"ex opere operato,"* as though the Mass had a saving effect irrespective of faith and devotion *(fides et devotio)* of the living and the dead, for whom it is offered, is reiterated in the Apology more than 30 times.

According to the CA, the Mass is not a sacrifice for our sins—that happened on the cross; rather, it should awaken our faith and comfort our terrified consciences, in that it promises grace and the forgiveness of sins. In accordance with Christ's command: "Do this in remembrance of me" (Luke 22:19), his saving acts are remembered. This remembering, however, is not a mere recollection of that which is historically past; for Jews and the godless are also capable of doing this. Through the remembrance we become fully conscious, we come to feel, that the saving acts are truly bestowed on us *(sentire, quod vere exhibeantur nobis)*. The CA thereby makes a strong endeavor to understand remembrance as something more than an act of making contemporary in a psychological sense. Catholic theology, however, misses the more precise deployment of the concept, that in the Lord's Supper, as an act of remembrance of the death of Christ, the one-time sacrifice of the cross is sacramentally—that is, under the signs of the bread and wine—truly made present.

The Confutation raises strong objection against the insinuation that the daily Masses had their origin in the teaching that Christ through his suffering and death on the cross had made satisfaction only for original sin and had instituted the Mass as satisfaction for actual sins. That was never asserted by "true Christians," indeed, it has persistently been denied by them.[41] According to true doctrine, the forgiveness of sins is not the business of the Mass; for this penance is available as a specific saving means. The Mass removes the penalties that result from sin, completes satisfaction, increases grace, and gives the hope of divine consolation and aid.[42] To assert that Christ is not sacrificed in the Holy Mass is to fall into the Arian heresy[43] which Augustine had rejected. The pure offering predicted by Malachi (1:10-11) can be none other than the "sacrifice of the altar of the most pure Eucharist." [44] The Confutation collects an extensive list of church Fathers in support of the view that, since the time of the early church, the Mass has been viewed as a sacrifice. According to the Confutation, the "once for all" of Heb. 10:10 does not argue against the sacrificial character of the Mass; for this passage is speaking of the bloody sacrifice of the lamb slain on the altar of the cross from which all sacraments, including the sacrifice of the Mass, receive their power and efficacy. "Then he, Christ, was offered . . . on the cross . . . with the shedding of his blood . . . in a visible form capable of suffering; today he is offered in the Mass veiled in mysteries, incapable of suffering, just as in the Old Testament he was sacrificed typically and under a figure." [45] The Confutation finds further verification of the sacrificial character of the Mass in the word *Missa,* the Hebrew word *misbeach,* and the Greek word *thysiastirion,* and in addition to that, in the expression *facite,* with which Christ gave the charge to celebrate the Eucharist, and which in many places in the Old Testament means "to sacrifice." [46]

The Confutation did not attempt to deny that the Mass is a memorial of Christ's passion and of God's benefits. However, for the Confutation that is not sufficient, for the paschal lamb already constituted such a memorial (Exod. 12:1-14). In the Mass, the church offers to God the Father, in remembrance of the sacrifice on the cross and veiled in mystery, the most hallowed sacrament of the altar.[47]

Certainly, the princes and congregations are not to be faulted for retaining one common Mass, provided they do this according to the regulation of the gospel and the traditions of the church. The participation in the sacraments of all who are present is also to be welcomed. "Would that all were so disposed as to be prepared to partake of this bread worthily every day. But if they regard one Mass as advantageous, how much more advantageous would be a number of Masses." [48]

After considering all these factors, the Confutation concludes this article by insisting that the new forms of celebrating the Mass must be abolished and use of the primitive form of the Mass resumed according to the practice of all Christendom.[49]

What is important with regard to the controversy is to determine out of the argumentation of the Confutation that Christians, in a posture of faith and devotion, should participate in the Mass, the goal of which is the remembrance of the suffering of Christ. The Confutation makes an effort to demonstrate that the nonbloody, sacramental sacrifice, veiled in mystery, does not stand in contradiction to the "once and for all time" character of the bloody, historically visible, sacrifice on the cross. The Mass is a remembrance of the suffering of Christ. However, that is not sufficient as a basis for the sacrificial character of the Mass, because both sides in the debate, influenced by the nominalistic thought of that day, understood "remembrance" as "to recollect," as a making present in consciousness, and not as an actual bringing into the present. So for the authors of the Confutation, to view the Mass as memorial was not to view it as a sacrifice. In addition, there must be a real occurrence, the offering of the body and blood of Christ. However, such a sacrifice, according to the Reformation understanding, contradicts the "once and for all time" character and full satisfaction character of the sacrifice of the cross.

The CA and the Confutation are of one mind regarding the view that the Mass grants participation in Christ's sacrifice, that in accordance with his promise in the Lord's Supper as well as in Baptism Christ offers the grace of God. He "sacrifices himself" on the altar for eating and drinking so that we can believe in his offer of salvation and in him receive salvation in its fullness. What was disputed was whether in the Mass we, as a congregation with Christ as the head, offer to the Father the onetime propitiatory sacrifice for the sin of the world. According to the Reformation view, the sacrifice of praise and thanksgiving, which the congregation in the celebration of the Lord's Supper offered through Christ in the Holy Spirit, was its only access to the Father opened up through Christ's sacrifice on the cross.[50] The question Catholic theologians posed in return continued to be whether the movement by which the congregation through, with, and in Christ comes before the Father is here fully seen. Does not the church in the Mass offer the onetime propitiatory sacrifice in sacramental form? Does not the offering of his truly present body and blood become part of the remembrance of the suffering of Christ? These questions were, at that time and in the centuries that followed, answered in the negative from the side of the Reformation, because the "once and for all time" character of sacrifice seemed not sufficiently safeguarded by the identification of the sacrifice of the cross with the sacrifice of the Mass as its memorial and representation.

In its answer to the objections raised in the Confutation, the Apology (24, 16 [BC 252]) seeks to provide clarification by adopting from medieval theology the questionable distinction between sacrament (*sacramentum*) and sacrifice (*sacrificium*) and between propitiatory sacrifice (*sacrificium propitiatorium*) and sacrifice of praise (*sacrificium eucharisticum*). The sacrament is an offer of grace from God to us. Baptism, for example, is not a work which we offer to God but a work of God whereby God, through his servants, baptizes us and gives us the forgiveness of sins according to his promise. "By way of contrast, a sacrifice is a ceremony or act which we render to God to honor him" (24, 18). In this way, a careful distinction is made between two types of sacrifice, which are not to be confused in the discussion: the propitiatory sacrifice, which is solely Christ's death, and the eucharistic sacrifice, which is offered by the congregation of the reconciled out of gratitude for the forgiveness of sins and other blessings received. The propitiatory sacrifice consists solely of the death of Christ (24, 22-24); all other sacrifices are sacrifices of praise and thanksgiving. As such, the

Apology lists the proclamation of the gospel, faith, prayer, thanksgiving, confession of faith, and the afflictions of the saints, "yes, all the good works of the saints" (24, 25). These sacrifices are not satisfactions for our misdeeds, nor are they transferable to others so that they might serve *ex opere operato* for their forgiveness of sins and reconciliaton. For "those who bring them are already reconciled" (24, 25). These are the sacrifices of the new covenant according to 1 Peter 2:5 and Rom. 12:1. They are spiritual sacrifices because they occur through the operation of the Holy Spirit in us. At the same time, according to Heb. 13:15 they are offered "through Christ," that is, our eucharistic sacrifice occurs through him in faith (24, 26). In the Apology sacrifice *(sacrificium)* is defined as "an act which we render to God to honor Him" (24, 18). Thereby, precisely this work of faith, which Christ accomplishes in people through his Holy Spirit, is retained *("motus spiritus sancti in nobis,"* and *"per ipsum"* [24, 26]).

This interpretation also gives prominence to the "eucharistic sacrifice" within the entire Mass and places it in close connection with the whole Mass, while at the same time denoting the entire spiritual life of faith as a "daily sacrifice *(iuge sacrificium)"* (24:35). The priesthood in the New Testament is the ministry of the Spirit (2 Cor. 3:6) which offers to us the gospel and the sacraments in such a way that we are brought under the power and effect of the Holy Spirit *(mortificatio et vivificatio)* (24:59).

In the eyes of a Catholic theologian it is difficult to establish in the Apology, because of its separation of sacrament from sacrifice and sacrifice of thanks from propitiatory sacrifice, a sacramental representation of the one and only propitiatory sacrifice of Christ in the "eucharist," the church's sacrifice of thanks. Although the Apology attempts to connect the "daily" sacrifice *(iuge sacrificium)* with the whole Mass—"provided this means the whole Mass, the ceremony and also the proclamation of the Gospel, faith, prayer, thanksgiving"—it nevertheless appears that this represents at the same time a narrowing of the proclamation of the Lord's death (1 Cor. 11:26) to preaching ("instituted because of them" [Apol. 24, 35; BC 256]). The church's sacrifices of praise and thanksgiving, the "good works of the saints" (24, 25), are then not perceived in relation to the Christ who is present in the sacrament, who as the *"principalis offerens"* makes us part of his sacrifice, and whose work the Mass is above all.[51]

However, if the *sacrificium* is by definition a work which we render to God and not the work of Christ, the mediator, which has been bestowed upon us, then we must come to a definite rejection of the doctrine of *opus operatum,* particularly when this is understood as an automatic application of the atoning power of the sacrifice.

In Apol. 24 ("The Mass") the formula *ex opere operato* is explicitly attacked more than thirty times. In so doing, the doctrine of *opus operatum* is not understood in the sense that the sacrament is valid regardless of the dignity of those who administer it (which as a matter of fact is also taught in CA 8), rather, the exclusive concern is the effect of the sacrament in the recipient. In the Apology the expression *"ex opere operato"* is stereotypically explained by such additions as *"sine bono motu accipientis"* (4, 63 [BC 115]), and *"sine bono motu cordis, hoc est, sine fide"* (24, 13, 18, 23 [BC 251-253]); cf. 7, 21 and 12, 12 [BC 172 and 184]. With regard to the Lord's Supper it states that it "does not grant grace *ex opere operato.*" The view of the opponents is expressed as though the Mass could obtain *ex opere operato* forgiveness of sins and release from guilt and punishment for the priest and for others to whom it is applied (24, 9 [BC 250]), so that finally the sacrifice of the Mass becomes a work "that justifies *ex opere operato* or that merits forgiveness of sins when applied to others" (24, 35 [BC 256]; cf. also 24, 63, 96 [BC 260, 267]). Against this, it is emphasized that "the forgiveness of guilt can be obtained only by faith. Therefore the Mass is not a satisfaction but a promise and a sacrament requiring faith" (24, 90 [BC 266]).

The "crowd of scholastics" against which the Apology polemicizes cannot be the Catholic opponents of the 1520s or the theologians at the Diet of Augsburg, i.e., the authors of the Confutation, because they did not represent such views. At best, it could have had reference to the Nominalists of the outgoing Middle Ages, who represented "Scotist teachings about the sacraments as seen through the spectacles of Gabriel Biel."[52]

This misunderstanding of the opposing position has seriously hampered dialog in this theological controversy. No agreement was reached on the question of *opus operatum* because those representing the Reformation point of view were too little prepared to distinguish between the sacraments as an efficacious cause, on the one hand, and the necessary disposition of the recipient requisite to a fruitful consequence, on the other hand. When the Council of Trent emphasized, with regard to the "Canones de sacramentis" (Canon 8), that "anyone who says that grace is not transmitted *ex opere operato* by the sacraments of the new covenant themselves, but rather that mere faith in the divine promise is sufficient for the attainment of grace, shall be excluded," [53] or in Canon 6 condemns anyone who denies that the sacraments impart grace to those who erect no barriers *(obex)* against them,[54] then it is thereby placing emphasis on the sacraments as God's work, which have power in themselves, independent of the worthiness of the person. It remains uncontested that the sacrament attains its goal—the justification, i.e., the pardoning of the person—only if the person is receptive to it, in other words, sets up no obstacles against it. The grievous sin, in the first instance, unbelief, represents such a barrier *(obex)*. The sacraments do not function mechanically; rather, they function in conformity with the believing devotion *(fides et devotio)* of the recipient. It was from this point of view that the Council of Trent prohibited the series of Masses to which had been attributed in many instances guaranteed efficacy during the late Middle Ages.[55]

Insofar as the doctrine of *opus operatum* attempts to represent the sacraments as actions of Christ and in the *opus operantis* requires faith as requisite to a fruitful effect in the recipient, it does not stand in contradiction to the intention of the Reformation; rather, it actually represents its concerns. For indeed, Luther and Melanchthon did not want to deny the objective character of the means of grace. In Article 4 the Apology explicitly defends itself against the accusation that the *"sola fide"* is directed against the sacraments: ". . . . Therefore we want to show first that faith alone makes a righteous man. . . . We exclude the claim of merit, not the Word or the sacraments, as our opponents slanderously claim. We said earlier that faith is conceived by the Word, and we give the highest praise to the ministry of the Word." [56] With its polemic against the *"ex opere operato"* the Apology took a stand against something which, indeed, the Catholic theologians did not advocate but which the Reformers, nevertheless, perceived on the basis of the practice of the private Masses and of popular theology. What is expressed by the phrase *ex opere operato,* as it relates to the efficacy of the sacraments, is also Lutheran doctrine with regard to the matter at hand: "God's offer of grace does not stand or fall with human faith or unbelief. The effectiveness of the sacraments does not depend on the worthiness of the minister." [57] However, already before 1530 the Roman Catholic theologians involved in the controversy[58] spoke of an evident misunderstanding of the doctrine of *"opus operatum"* by the Reformers.[59] The authors of the Confutation protested that a doctrine was being ascribed to them which they themselves opposed. In view of the fact that Melanchthon did not allow himself to be persuaded of this and in the Apology on an even more massive scale attributed to the Catholic side positions which had long since been rectified, the theologians who represented the Catholics in the controversy in their argument against the Apology defended themselves vigorously against Melanchthon's insinuations, describing them as malicious and ridiculous, and reproaching him for fighting with ghosts.[60]

Granted that the theology of the late Middle Ages and also the theology of some contemporaries of the Reformers denied this, nevertheless, in the canon of the Roman Mass it is expressed that the "fruits" of the Mass will be imparted only to those who in faith are open to this. In the *"Momento vivorum"* the reference is to those whose faith and devotion God knows—*"quorum tibi fides cognita est et nota devotio"*—and, in the remembrance of the dead, these are designated as such persons "who have gone before us marked with the seal of faith *(cum signo fidei)* and who now rest in peace." In both instances it is a matter concerning those who have been justified, who in faith have been open to the saving action of God. Thus it is not a matter of justification and the forgiveness of sins; rather, it is a matter of the strengthening and realization of the communion with Christ and of cleansing and release from the punishment for sins. It has to do with forgiveness of sins only in an indirect sense, only insofar as grace brings about repentance and love is increased. Exactly because the Mass is not a new sacrifice but is rather the act of making the sacrifice of the cross present and contemporary, it is, according to the Council of Trent, as such a propitiatory sacrifice.[61]

We dare not draw our concept of the propitiatory sacrifice from the realm of the history of religion or from the practice of non-Christians. The Letter to the Hebrews does not speak of the propitiatory sacrifice insofar as God atones, but insofar as the person is cleansed and thereby is made fit for communion with God (Heb. 9:13-14). It is not a matter of making God feel gracious, but through his gracious action toward us he makes us worthy for communion with him, he reconciles us to himself. "The mass produces no new grace-giving and saving will of God. . . . (rather) it is simply a way in which God's saving will, already always definitively present, visibly meets man and lays hold of him here and now in the concrete circumstances of history." [62]

"In the Eucharistic sacrifice and through it, man turns to God, offers him in the mystery of the church Christ's sacrifice on the cross as his own oblation. God therefore turns to him with the whole love He bears to man because of Christ's act of atonement. Man receives the effect of this reconciling, forgiving and helping love of God in the finite measure of his inner readiness and openness." [63]

5. The Church as Sacramental Community

The church is constituted as a community in which people are born again through Baptism in the Holy Spirit and participate in salvation. They form the one body. Through the Lord's Supper the exalted Lord prepares and maintains communion with his people in their battle against sin and the devil. Consequently, the sacraments provide the basis for and maintain the ecclesial communion as the one body of Christ.

It is within this context that we must deal with questions concerning the practice of Communion under one kind and the practice of the so-called private Masses, which are both contested in the CA.

5.1. Communion Under Both Kinds

This question is dealt with in CA 22 under the section dealing with abuses. Along with the marriage of priests (CA 23) and the private Mass (CA 24), the chalice for the laity was the primary object of the negotiations in Augsburg. It appears that it was briefly considered possible that the Lutherans might be reconciled if the Catholics gave in at this point. The papal legate, Lorenzo Campeggio, himself did not seem to exclude the possibility of a compromise.[64] CA 22 reads: "Among us both kinds are given to laymen in the sacrament. The reason is that there is a clear command and order of Christ, 'Drink of it, all of you' (Matt. 26:27). Concerning the chalice Christ here commands with clear words that all should drink of it. . . . This usage continued in the church for a long time, as can be demonstrated from history and from writings of the Fathers. . . . It is evident that such a custom [to use but one kind], introduced contrary to God's command and also contrary to the ancient canons, is unjust. Accordingly, it is not proper to burden the consciences of those who desire to observe the sacrament according to Christ's institution or to compel them to act contrary to the arrangement of our Lord Christ. Because the division of the sacrament is contrary to the institution of Christ, the customary carrying about of the sacrament in processions is also omitted by us." [65] The last sentence of this article was first incorporated into the text at a later stage in the formulation of the CA, most likely in order to justify the position of the Protestant princes, who had refused to take part in the Corpus Christi procession at the opening of the Imperial Diet on June 16, 1530. It is noteworthy that against processing with the sacrament it is not argued that the presence is limited to the *"in usu,"* or that the body of Christ is not present for the purpose of adoration; rather, reference is made to the fact that the one kind should not be isolated from the other, which certainly was the case in the procession with the bread alone.

As did the Catholic theologians involved in earlier controversies, the Confutation makes reference to the custom of the primitive church in defense of Communion under one kind. They see evidence of this custom in Acts 2:42; 20:7; and in Luke 24:30, where only the breaking of bread is mentioned. The "drink of it, all of you" in Matt. 26:27 was addressed to the apostles, and therefore is intended only for priests. Also, on the basis of the custom of bringing the sacrament to the sick only under one kind, it is concluded that one kind was held to be sufficient. In addition, out of penitential canons from various synods which allow only lay Communion for guilty priests, it seemed to follow that Communion under one kind was the custom in many places in the early church. The Confutation cannot dispute that Communion under both kinds was originally the general practice. This practice came to be discontinued because of the danger of spilling and the difficulty in preserving the wine. It was possible to forego the second kind because the entire Christ was present under each kind and Christians received no less under one kind than under both. Only as heretics began to teach that both kinds were necessary for salvation did the church forbid what had previously been a matter of choice.[66] Although there is so little in the individual aspects of the argumentation of the Confutation that is historically defensible, indeed *"Valde pueriliter,"* as Melanchthon wrote to Luther on Aug. 6, 1530,[67] it does, however, in general outline correctly reflect the historical development.

The theological interest of the Confutation is directed toward making certain that in the sacrament "Christ has not been divided, but that the entire Christ is present under both forms." [68] In the negotiations this concern for correct doctrine also made the Catholic side hesitant in granting the chalice in Communion. It was made dependent on the precondition that the congregation receive prior instruction concerning the fact that the entire Christ was present under each kind and that freedom be given to receive the sacrament under only one kind. As the positions became increasingly more fixed during the course of the negotiations, the Protestants were no longer content with the compromise over the second kind, but demanded it as nonnegotiable because it alone was in accordance with the institution of Christ. To be sure, they allowed for the continued recognition of requests to receive only one kind, but refused to declare this in their preaching out of fear that this would confuse devout people.[69]

If the CA merely established the fact that the second kind had been abolished in lay Communion, without expressing any opinion regarding the motivation or the specific point in time, then the Apology called into question Communion under one kind from the perspective of ecclesial communion. The opponents wanted to make a clear distinction between priests and laity "to elevate the position of the clergy by a religious rite." [70] "For Christ instituted both kinds, and he did not do so only for part of the church, but for all of the church. By divine authority and not by human authority, as we suppose our opponents admit, all of the church uses the sacrament, not only the priests. If Christ instituted it for all of the church, why is one kind taken away from part of the church and its use prohibited?" (Apol. 22, 1-2 [BC 236]) The danger of spilling cannot be considered sufficient ground for withdrawing the chalice from the laity. One dare not make the directive of Christ into an adiophoron, which is, above all, reason why one dare not forbid the second kind.

The separation of the body and blood given in the sign of the sacrament, which otherwise is interpreted as an allusion to the passion of Christ, plays no part for either side. Thus the Catholics did not succeed in making it comprehensible to the evangelical side why both kinds are required for the Mass as *repraesentatio passionis* and should be received by the celebrant, nevertheless for the Communion of the people the second kind can be waived. The Communion of the congregation under both kinds received such heavy stress by the evangelicals that it more and more came to be *the* point of distinction between the two confessions. For this reason, the granting of the chalice to the laity in wide areas of Germany in 1564 under Pius VI only created more confusion rather than helping to win back the Protestants. Therefore this indulgence was withdrawn by Gregory XIII in 1584.[71]

This makes it all the more significant that according to the "Constitution of the Sacred Liturgy" of Vatican II,[72] the Communion of the laity under both kinds again has its place in Roman Catholic worship. In the "General Instruction" of the new Roman Missal approved in

1965, respectively 1974, it states, "The sign of communion is more complete when given under both kinds, since in that form the sign of the eucharistic meal appears more clearly. The intention of Christ that the new and eternal covenant be ratified in His blood is better expressed, as is the relation of the eucharistic banquet to the heavenly banquet." [73] In principle, a unity is thereby established between the two partners, even if Communion under both kinds is not restored as the common form for administration of Holy Communion among Roman Catholics. Even though Communion under both kinds continues to be restricted to certain occasions, such as the marriage service, the Baptism of adults, etc., it is, however, clear that the church continues the practice of Communion under one kind for practical reasons and not as a matter of principle, or indeed because of dogmatic considerations. It is defended with the statement that "they receive the whole Christ and the genuine sacrament when they participate in the sacrament even under one kind and that they are thus not deprived of any grace necessary for salvation." [74]

5.2. The Practice of the So-Called Private Masses

If the evangelical congregations were accused of "having abolished the Mass," (24, 1 [BC 56]), the CA acknowledged this as valid only with regard to "private Masses." The rejection of such Masses was based on holy Scripture and the tradition of the ancient church. The criticism of these private Masses was further developed by raising the accusation that they had come to be observed for "the purpose of gain . . . for revenues or stipends" (24:10). Instead of this practice, in the congregations of those who adhered to the CA the Mass was celebrated only in connection with the Communion of the people, and indeed on the basis of its essential character as a Communion meal. From the beginning on, the restoration of the Communion of the people had been the desire of the Reformation movement.

In the opinion of the CA, the private Masses could only destroy that dimension of the Mass which establishes and preserves community.[75] According to the CA, private Masses are a novelty of the Latin church of the Middle Ages, whereas the Mass with the Communion of the people is in no way "contrary to the church catholic (*nihil fit contra catholicam ecclesiam*). . . . Even today, Greek parishes have no private Masses but only one public Mass" (Apol. 24, 6 [BC 250]).

The history of the private Masses and the abuses which resulted from them in the Middle Ages have been clearly demonstrated in the current research in liturgical history.[76] The superstitious ideas of the unenlightened people which accompanied these private Masses led to the spread of financial abuses; and for this reason the CA can maintain that "hardly any private Masses were held except for the sake of gain" (24, 13 [BC 57]). The effort of the authors of the Confutation to defend this practice by using scripture references to justify the view that "those who wait at the altar live of the altar," [77] hardly sounds like a truly earnest effort to examine the actual abuses, which then were later corrected by the Council of Trent itself. It is against this background that we must understand the strong declarations of the CA and the Apology, which follow Luther's bitter battle against the Mass "business."

Historians of dogma can today contribute much to the understanding of the practice of that time, which calls in question the imprecise and generalized criticism of the authors of the CA. In the conflict over the private Masses and the accompanying Mass stipends for the institution of a chancel priest or Mass priest or, one could say, beneficiary of a Mass, the issue was not purely theological; rather, it centered around the question of the livelihood of the clergy.[78] The objections to these conditions were perhaps presented in an all too polemical manner in the literature of that period. It is to be regretted that it was not until a later period that these conditions were cleared up by the Roman Catholic Church. Today the tragedy of this schism in the church can be rethought with more objective arguments.

Connected to the practice of the private Mass is the question of whether the application of the Mass to those who are not present during its celebration can be theologically defended. The fundamental Reformation concern as stated in the CA and in the Apology is expressed in the assertion that faith is necessary for an effective use of the sacrament. In what way, then, can the grace which has been offered be applied to the living and the dead through the Mass? It has already been noted that in its article on the Mass the CA based its criticism on an opinion which had not been represented by its opponents. Yet even without such an opinion, it is an established fact that a Roman Catholic Mass can be celebrated for the living and the dead, and also for various other purposes.

Since in Reformation theology the Mass is represented only as Communion, the sacrament can only be distributed to the communicants who are present and can only be received by them. The faith of the communicants participates in the saving gift of Christ's sacrifice on the cross through the sacramental eating and drinking. The view of the Reformation applies not only to the private Masses which were rejected, but also to the Mass with the Communion of the people in its insistence that the saving grace offered through this sacrament cannot be communicated to others who are not present.[79]

Catholic theology, however, can argue from another direction. Namely, if the accent rests on Communion, indeed, if the Mass merely becomes a celebration of Communion, then what is meant by the application for the living and the dead cannot be understood. Even as one cannot allow one's self to be baptized for another, neither can one carry out the sacramental eating and drinking for another. To be sure, Communion with Christ also has significance for my Communion with my neighbor, and I can include that person in prayer. However, if the Mass is first and foremost *repraesentatio passionis,* if the priest functions in the name of the church, and if the church is represented by the priest and at least by the acolyte, then the Mass in its grace-giving effect is not limited to the congregation of those present; those who are absent, living and dead, can be included. That does not mean, however, that they are automatically granted the fruits of salvation—as is mistakenly understood in the Apology.

The CA (and its Apology) cannot bring itself to separate Communion from the celebration of the Lord's Supper in this way. To be sure, the living and the dead are included together in the hymn of praise and in the intercession of the worshiping congregation; and, therefore, "the fruits of the eucharist extend beyond the circle of those present at a celebration." [80] But the sacrament of the body and blood of Christ can only be offered for those who in the Communion are united in faith with the one who himself is the only true propitiatory sacrifice. Therein lies the Reformation's reservation regarding the so-called private Masses.[81]

The liturgical forms of both parties involved in the conflicts of 1530 have changed considerably in our time. Theological reflections on both sides are evident in this change. The two "Masses" no longer stand in such sharp opposition to each other, as was originally the case. The liturgical movement in both traditions has resulted in a considerable broadening of the Lutheran eucharistic order into a more complete liturgy. At the same time, the Roman Mass has also experienced very substantial changes. Increased dependence on the liturgical traditions of the early church has meant that Roman Catholics and Lutherans have drawn closer to each other.

An ecumenical movement is drawing both groups closer together. The Roman Catholic/Lutheran dialogs of recent years have resulted in significant clarifications. In view of the fact that until recently Lutheran theology had avoided any discussion of a "sacrifice of the Mass," such a theological convergence is especially noteworthy. So we stand today—in spite of terminological differences—closer to each other than did the formulators of the CA and the Confutation, assuming that on both sides the essential theological substance and not the polemically charged concepts predominate.

Notes

1. Cf. *ministerium spiritus,* Apol. 14, 59 (BC 260).
2. E. Schlink, *The Theology of the Lutheran Confessions,* trans. by Paul Koehneke and Herbert Bouman (Philadelphia: Muhlenberg, 1961), p. 182 notes with regard to this that "the interest in a general sacramental concept recedes rather strikingly into the background." See also W. Maurer, *Historischer Kommentar zur Confessio Augustana,* vol. 2 (Gütersloh: 1967-77), pp. 175-176.
3. H. Fagerberg, *A New Look at the Lutheran Confessions 1529-1537,* trans. by Jean Lund (St. Louis: Concordia, 1972), pp. 185ff.; W. P. Schwab, *Entwicklung und Gestalt der Sakramententheologie bei Martin Luther* (Frankfurt-Bern: 1977), pp. 269ff. and 329ff.
4. H. Fagerberg, *op. cit.,* pp. 167-171. Cf. also E. Iserloh, *Die Eucharistie in der Darstellung des Joh. Eck* (Münster: 1950), pp. 174-175, and V. Pfnür, *Einig in der Rechtfertigungslehre* (Wiesbaden: 1970), pp. 45ff.
5. For more specifics, refer to V. Vajta, "Participation in Salvation: The Relation of Sacrament and Faith" *Lutheran World* 15 (1965): 122-123.
6. AE 36, 56; WA 6, 526.
7. In Apol. 4, 73 (BC 117) the Catholic objection that the *"sola fide"* excludes the sacraments is refuted.
8. See V. Vajta, *Evangile et sacrament* (Paris: 1973), pp. 123ff.
9. Apol. 24, 70 (BC 262). E. Schlink, *op. cit.,* pp. 185-186. R. Prenter, *Kirkens lutherske bekendelse* (Fredericia: 1978), p. 134 writes: "In the word of the sacrament, God's promise is *given.* This promise *awakens* faith. In the elements of the sacrament, the promise is *made visible* and perceptible. This process of making the promise visible strengthens the faith which had been awakened through the promise." See also E. W. Gritsch and R. W. Jenson, *Lutheranism: The Theological Movement and Its Confessional Writings* (Philadelphia: Fortress, 1976), pp. 70ff., where the sacraments are portrayed in connection with Augustine's concept of *verbum visibile* (quoted in Apol. 13, 5 [BC 211-212]). Something similar occurs in R. W. Jenson, *Visible Words: The Interpretation and Practice of Christian Sacraments* (Fortress: 1978), esp. pp. 3-28.

228   Erwin Iserloh and Vilmos Vajta

10. For this reason, the Apology in Articles 13 and 24 always uses *signum* in connection with *ritus* and *ceremonia*.

11. Due to the significance of the sign, Luther gave preference to *immersio* in Baptism (AE 36, 68; WA 6, 534; BC 444-445).

12. For this reason, Luther suggested in the German Mass (1526) that the bread should be distributed immediately after it is consecrated, and that after that the consecration and distribution of the wine should take place (AE 53, 81-82, WA 19, 99).

13. BC 440. P. Brunner speaks of a "spiritual suitability of the sign" in *Leiturgia: Handbuch des Evangelischen Gottesdienst. . .*, ed. by Ferdinand Müller and Walter Blankenburg, vol. 1 (Kassel: 1954), pp. 276ff. Regarding the concept of the *Signum* in CA 13, refer also to W. Maurer, *op. cit.*, pp. 200ff.

14. Against the inclusion of penance among the sacraments the argument cannot be raised, as is so often done, that the CA does not specifically designate penance as a sacrament; for Baptism and the Lord's Supper are also not explicitly listed as sacraments in the CA. What is determinative is the relationship outlined above.

15. At the beginning of the *Babylonian Captivity*, Luther spoke of *one sacramentum* (Christ) and *three* sacramental signs *(signa sacramentalia)*, namely Baptism, absolution, and the Lord's Supper. At the end of the same writing, however, he no longer holds to the view that absolution is a sacrament (AE 36, 18, 124; WA 6, 501 and 572). See also V. Vajta, *Evangile et sacrement*, pp. 145ff. and 151ff., and the essay by Fagerberg-Jorissen in this volume, note 17 (pp. 256-257).

16. Immenkötter 98-99.

17. BC 348-349.

18. CA 27, 11-17 (BC 72-73).

19. BC 449.

20. Immenkötter 100-101.

21. H. Immenkötter, *Um die Einheit im Glauben: Die Unionsverhandlungen des Augsburger Reichstages im August und September 1530* (Münster: 1973), p. 40.

22. *"Et comperimus non tantum romanam ecclesiam affirmare corporalem praesentiam Christi, sed idem et nunc sentire et olim sensisse graecam ecclesiam. Id enim testatur canon missae apud illos, in quo aperte orat sacerdos, ut mutato pane ipsum corpus Christi fiat. Et Vulgarius, scriptor ut nobis videtur non stultus, diserte inquit, panem non tantum figuram esse, sed vere in carnem mutari* (We know that not only the Roman Church affirms the bodily presence of Christ, but that the Greek Church has taken and still takes this position. Evidence for this is their canon of the Mass, in which the priest clearly prays that the bread may be changed and become the very body of Christ. And Vulgarius, who seems to us to be a sensible writer, says distinctly that 'the bread is not merely a figure but is truly changed into flesh')" (Apol. 10, 2 [BC 179]).

23. See J. Betz, *Die Eucharistie in der Zeit der griechischen Väter*, vol. 1 (Freiburg: 1955), esp. pp. 197ff. and 300ff.

24. Evidence for this can be found in V. Vajta, *Luther on Worship* (Phila-

delphia: Muhlenberg, 1958), pp. 100-101. Cf. also R. Prenter, *op. cit.*. 110-111.

25. It is unfair of L. Grane to accuse Melanchthon of "a conscious camouflage" (*Die Confessio Augustana: Einführung in die Hauptgedanken der lutherischen Reformation* [Göttingen: 1970], p. 83). Quite to the contrary, in ecumenical dialogues this terminological variability is perceived as an asset. This is evident in the document, "Catholic-Lutheran Agreed Statement on the Eucharist," *Origins*. vol. 8, no. 30 (1979), pp. 465ff. Cf. also the documents from the U.S. dialogues, *The Eucharist as Sacrifice*. Lutherans and Catholics in Dialogue III (Minneapolis: Augsburg, 1967), pp. 195ff., and *Eucharist and Ministry*, Lutherans and Catholics in Dialogue IV (Minneapolis: Augsburg, 1979), pp. 62-63.

26. B. Möller, *"Das Innocentianum von 1215 in der CA."* *Zeitschrift für Kirchengeschichte* 75 (1964): 156-158.

27. For a historical understanding of the articles on the Lord's Supper in the CA, refer to *Festschrift für G. Ritter* (Göttingen: 1950), pp. 161-209, esp. p. 163.

28. *Ibid.,* p. 164.

29. The two versions of CA stand side by side: the German version more strongly Lutheran, in wording almost reflecting the dogma of the Middle Ages; the Latin version almost devoid of Lutheran character, all but totally stripped of it, born out of Melanchthon's humanistic mediation theology. *Ibid.,* p. 209. Cf. also Maurer, *Historischer Kommentar*, vol. 2, *op. cit.,* pp. 187-195.

30. B. Möller, *"Augustana-Studien,"* *Archiv für Reformationsgeschichte* 57 (1966): 91, note 83.

31. E. Schlink, *op. cit.,* p. 170, speaks in a nuanced way about the difference between the Latin and the German version of CA 10.

32. An example of this would be the chapter on the Eucharist in the document from the W.C.C. Faith and Order Commission Meeting in Accra, "One Baptism, One Eucharist, and a Mutually Recognized Ministry," Faith and Order Paper No. 73 (Geneva: W.C.C. Publications Office), pp. 18-28. See also *The Eucharist as Sacrifice, op. cit.,* pp. 194-195.

33. The Formula of Concord quotes the "useful rule" of Melanchthon: *"Nihil habet rationem sacramenti extra usum a Christo institutum oder extra actionem divinitus institutam* (Nothing has the character of a sacrament apart from the use instituted by Christ, or apart from the divinely instituted action. . . . In this context 'use' or 'action' does not primarily mean faith, or the oral eating alone, but the entire external and visible action of the Supper as ordained by Christ)." Solid Declaration 12, 85-86 (BC 584).

34. Cf. Apol. 24, 70 (BC 262). In the text quoted here, one should observe the allusion to CA 13, 2 (BC 36). The intimate connection between presence and offering (distribution) is evident in the various preliminary formulations of the final text of CA 10, as demonstrated by W. Maurer, *Historischer Kommentar,* vol. 2, *op. cit.,* pp. 181-182.

35. R. Prenter, *op. cit.,* p. 103.

36. WA 6, 538 (AE 36, 735). For further explanation, refer to W. Schwab, *op. cit.,* p. 320, note 50.

37. WA 19, 537 (AE 53, 101). See also BSLK 63, note 1.
38. WA 6, 363 (AE 35, 91).
39. Smalcald Articles 2, 10 (BC 294).
40. Cf. E. Iserloh, *"Der Wert der Messe in der Diskussion der Theologen vom Mittelalter bis zum 16. Jhdt."* Zeitschrift für katholische Theologie 83 (1961):44-79.
41. "For this has never been heard by Catholics, and very many others who are now asked most constantly deny that they have so taught" (Immenkötter 162). In the *"Responsio catholica,"* the early form of the Confutation, the further remark is made that, "They may show us those who hold this view that Christ through his suffering only made satisfaction for original sin, and we will resist them just as emphatically as Luther" (J. Ficker, *Die Konfutatio des Augsburgischen Bekenntnisses* [Leipzig: Barth, 1891], p. 100. Regarding the Apology's repeated reproach (24, 62 [BC 260]) that it had been taught that the sacrifice of the cross had only atoned for original sin, see E. Iserloh, *Die Eucharistie in der Darstellung des Johannes Eck* (Münster: 1950), p. 185.
42. Immenkötter 162. The *Responsio catholica* (Article 24) states: *"Sed eque falsum imponunt hic concionatores catholicis. Nam missa non delet peccata, sed delet reatum seu penam pro peccatis debitam. Quomodo enim mortuis posset peccata delere! Proderit ergo missa ad penarum pro peccatis exsolutionem et gratie augmentum ac salutarem protectionem in vivis"* (Ficker, *op. cit.,* p. 100).
43. *Lexikon für Theologie und Kirche,* vol. 1 (Freiburg: Herder, 1966), p. 156.
44. Immenkötter 162; *"quam eucharistia mundissima in altaris sacrificio"* (Immenkötter 163).
45. Immenkötter 168-169.
46. Immenkötter 169.
47. Immenkötter 170-171.
48. Immenkötter 172-173.
49. Immenkötter 173.
50. R. Prenter has raised the question in an essay whether the Reformation polemic against the sacrifice of the Mass is still defensible. Although he does not consider the manner in which CA 24 criticizes the teaching about the sacrifice of the Mass as any longer valid, he nevertheless is of the opinion that the view expressed in the CA is still right because of the Roman doctrine regarding the sacrifice of the Mass which seeks to retain the propitiatory sacrifice alongside the sacrifice of thanks. (*"Das Augsburgische Bekenntnis und die römische Messopferlehre,"* in *Kerygma und Dogma,* vol. 1 [1957], pp. 42ff.) In the discussion with H. Messerschmidt which follows the essay *(Lumen* 7-8, Copenhagen, 1960), Prenter established the basis for his Reformation criticism on the primitive Christian tradition since Hippolytus. In this sense he represents a corrective to the Lutheran tradition in favor of a doctrine of eucharistic sacrifice which at least makes a distinction between the sacrifice of thanks and praise and the propitiatory sacrifice. For example: "Luther on Word and Sacraments" in *More About Luther,* Martin Luther Lectures, vol. 2 (Decorah, Iowa: 1958), pp. 100ff.; "A Lutheran Doctrine of Eucharistic Sacrifice?" in *Studia Theologica* 19 (1965):189ff.; *Creation and Redemption* (Phila-

delphia: Fortress, 1967), pp. 503ff. (the chapter on "The Sacrificial Meal of the Consummation").

51. Here both the present authors wish to stress explicitly that there is no theological difference of opinion behind this difference in interpretation; rather it has to do with a difference in the interpretaton of the historical text of the Apology to the Augsburg Confession.

52. V. Pfnür, "Beyond an Old Polemic: *sola fide/opus operatum,*" in the "Catholic-Lutheran Statement on the Eucharist," *op. cit.,* p. 480. Apol. 4, 210 [BC 136] explicitly cites Gabriel Biel as the authority regarding the controversial doctrine of the sacrifice of the Mass (cf. Apol. 21, 23 [BC 232]).

53. *Enchiridion, symbolorum,* 33rd ed., H. Denzinger and A. Schönmetzer, eds. (Freiburg: Herder, 1965), 1608. (Hereafter cited as DS).

54. *Ibid.,* 1606.

55. Session 22 (1962), *"Decretum de observandis et vitandis in celebratione missarum,"* *Concilium Tridentinum,* vol. 8 (Freiburg: Herder, 1901-1929), 963, 20-22; *Conciliorum Oecumenicorum, Decreta,* Joseph Alberigo, ed. (Freiburg: Herder, 1962), 713, 15-17. Cf. also A. Franz, *Die Messe im deutschen Mittelalter* (Freiburg: 1902), p. 329, and E. Iserloh, *Die Eucharistie, op. cit.,* pp. 227-228.

56. Apol. 4, 72-74 (BC 117; BSLK 175). Cf. V. Pfnür, "Beyond an Old Polemic," *op. cit.,* p. 478, and *Einig in der Rechtfertigungslehre?* (Wiesbaden: 1970), pp. 45-63.

57. Pfnür, "Beyond an Old Polemic," *op. cit.,* p. 480.

58. Cf., among others, Kasper Schatzgeyer, *Examen novarum doctrinarum* (1523): *"In sacramentis divinitus institutis necessario requiritur fides in actu secundo in suscipiente. . . . Claret haec, cum sacramenta signa sint. . . . Signa etenim solis fidelibus sunt. Ob hoc nullus infidelis recipere potest sacramentum ut sacramentum, quia ipsum non credit alicuius effectus spiritualis signum. Est ergo infidelitas obex principalis in effectu et fructu sacramenti"* (*Opera omnia* [Ingolstadt: 1545], p. 126).

59. H. Henning, *"Die Lehre vom opus operatum in den lutherischen Bekenntnisschriften."* *Una Sancta* 13 (1958):135.

60. Cf. Bartholomaei Arnoldi de Usingen o.s.a., *Responsio contra Apologiam Philippi Melanchthonis* (1532), Primoz Simoniti, ed. (Würzburg: 1978). Regarding Apol. 24, 9 (BC 250-251): *"nos nec dicimus missam ex opere operato conferre gratiam ut tu nobis falso et migaciter ascribis"* (p. 552). Regarding Apol. 24, 31 (BC 255): *"nullus nostrum dicit missam ex opere operato justificare aut illam applicatam aliis mereri eis remissionem peccatorum"* (p. 569). Regarding Apol. 24, 60 (BC 260): *"Nemo fidelium dicit missam iustificare ex opere operato . . . . Num cum larvis pugnas et nescis quid impugnes"* (p. 590; cf. p. 591). Regarding Apol. 24, 78 (BC 263): *"Tu autem nequiter et malitiose nobis hoc crebro ascribis"* (p. 601; cf. p. 613).

61. DS 1753.

62. K. Rahner and A. Haeussling, *The Celebration of the Eucharist* (New York: Herder, 1968), p. 63.

63. *Ibid.,* p. 77.

64. G. Müller, *"Um die Einheit der Kirche: Zu den Verhandlungen über den*

Laienkelch während des Augsburger Reichstages 1530," in *Reformata Reformanda, Festgabe für H. Jedin,* E. Iserloh and K. Repgen (Münster: 1965), pp. 392-427ff.; E. Honée, *"Die römische Kurie und der 22. Artikel der Confessio Augustana: Kardinal Lorenzo Campeggios Verhalten zur protestantischen Forderung des Laienkelches während des Augsburger Reichstages 1530,"* Nederlands archief voor kerkeschiedenis, Nieuwe Serie 50 (1969-70): 140-196; E. Honee, *"Die Theologische Diskussion über den Laienkelch auf dem Augsburger Reichstag 1530: Versuch einer historischen Rekonstruktion 1,"* Nieuwe Serie 53 (1972-73):1-96.

65. BC 49-51.

66. *"Et licet liberum fuerit olim vel una vel utraque specie uti in eucharistia, insurgente tamen haeresi, quae docebat utramque speciem esse necessariam, ecclesia sancta, quae a spiritu dirigitur, interdixit utramque speciem laicis* (And although it was formerly a matter of freedom to use either one or both forms in the Eucharist, nevertheless when the heresy arose which taught that both forms were necessary, the Holy Church, which is directed by the Holy Ghost, forbade both forms to laymen)." Immenkötter 139; Reu 363.

67. *Corpus Reformatorum,* C. G. Bretschneider and H. E. Bindseil, eds., vol. 2 (Halle: C. A. Schwetschke and Son, 1834-60), p. 253; WA Br., vol. 5, p. 537.

68. Reu 364; Immenkötter 142-153.

69. H. Immenkötter, *Um die Einheit . . . , op. cit.,* p. 99.

70. Apol. 22, 9 (BSLK 330; BC 237).

71. *Lexikon für Theologie und Kirche,* vol. 6 (Freiburg: Herder, 1957-66), p. 744.

72. *Vatican Council II: The Conciliar and Post-Conciliar Documents,* Austin Flannery, O.P., ed. (Northport, N.Y.: Costello, 1975), pp. 1ff.

73. *The Roman Missal (The Sacrementary),* no. 20 (Collegeville, Minn.: The Liturgical Press, 1974), p. 37. See also *Vatican Council II . . . , op. cit.,* p. 186.

74. *The Roman Missal, ibid.,* no. 241, p. 37. See also Vatican Council II . . . , *op. cit.,* pp. 186-187.

75. Luther naturally already recognized that "private Masses" were theoretically being placed into the social structures of the church; but an acolyte ("bystander") is still no fulfillment of the communal character of the Mass and of the reception of the sacrament (AE 34, 31; WA 30, 307).

76. A. Franz, *Die Messe im deutschen Mittelalter* (Freiburg i. Br.: 1902); J. A. Jungmann, *The Mass of the Roman Rite: Its Origin and Development,* vol. 2 (New York: Benziger, 1951-55) makes a clear distinction between "domestic celebration of the eucharist" in the primitive church and the private Masses, pp. 212ff. *(missa solitaria, missae privatae/speciales/peculiares);* O. Nussbaum, *"Kloster, Priestmönch und Privatmesse,"* Theophaneia 14 (Bonn: 1961); H. B. Mayer, *Luther und die Messe* (Paderborn: 1965); etc.

77. Reu 30; Immenkötter p. 161.

78. W. Schwab, *op. cit.,* pp. 207, 222.

79. *Ibid.,* pp. 195ff.

80. "Catholic-Lutheran Agreed Statement on the Eucharist," *op. cit.,* no. 61,

p. 475. Cf. also no. 71, p. 476 of the same article and the article, *"Die Eucharistie als Gemeindschaftsmahl"* in *Dokument der Gemeinsame lutherisch-katholischen Kommission* (Frankfort-Paderborn: 1978), pp. 105ff.
81. For example, R. Prenter, *Creation and Redemption. op. cit.,* pp. 524-525.

9

Penance and Confession

by Holsten Fagerberg and Hans Jorissen

translated by James L. Schaaf

1. Background and Presuppositions

1.1. The Medieval Theology of Penance

The precise delineation of the Lutheran position on the question of penance demands a brief look at the pre-Reformation medieval theology of penance, which was far from being a uniform theory. The central problem consisted of the question of how the subjective-personal efforts of the individual work together in the sacrament of penance with the objective-ecclesiastical intervention. There was agreement about the necessity for sorrow, confession of sins, and satisfaction on the part of the penitent. However, there were different interpretations of the nature of the required sorrow *(attritio* or *contritio)*, and about the precise relation of the actions of the penitent to the priestly absolution, but chiefly about the function of the priestly absolution (whose necessity was undisputed). In what follows the essential stages of the development of the theology of penance will be sketched briefly.[1]

1.1.1. The point of departure is the early scholastic theory of the sorrow that blots out sin *(contritio)*, which was established through

Peter Lombard (d. 1160). According to it the forgiveness of the guilt of sin took place in *contritio* even before the priestly absolution. This sorrow, however, was true sorrow, i.e., sorrow that really blotted out sin, only if it was connected with the determination *(votum)* to submit one's self to the ecclesiastical power of the keys, i.e., with the determination to confess *(confessio)* and to understake the satisfaction *(satisfactio)* imposed. Without this determination the sorrow is ineffective, merely *attritio*.[2] The foundation or the basic act of subjective penitence thus became located in the sorrow of contrition. It implicitly contained the two other elements—*confessio* and *satisfactio*.

1.1.2. Combined with this "contritionism"—and affected also by Peter Lombard—was an at first merely declaratory understanding of priestly absolution as the authoritative declaration announced to the individual that in sorrow *(contritio)* God has already forgiven sins (declaratory theory). The essence of this theory was also not overcome by the attempts of the school of the Victorines (Hugh of St. Victor, d. 1141, and Richard of St. Victor, d. 1173), which, with the help of the distinction between the guilt of sin *(culpa)* and the punishment of sin *(poena),* ascribed at least a real effect of priestly absolution on the blotting out of the punishment of sin.

1.1.3. The decisive change was first accomplished by Thomas Aquinas (d. 1274) when he applied to the sacrament of penance[3] the Aristotelian concepts of "matter" and "form," which had first been used this way only recently, and worked this out in a thoroughgoing way. The acts of the penitent *(contritio, confessio, satisfactio)* are the "matter" of the sacrament of penance; the priestly absolution, the "form." The two, "matter" and "form," are strictly related to one another as correlative constitutional principles. In this way Thomas combined subjective penance and priestly absolution into a dynamic unity in which the whole, composed of "matter" and "form," accomplishes the blotting out of sin. Within this whole the efficacy *(efficacia)* flows principally *(principaliter)* from the "form," absolution, and the sign-character *(significatio)* flows chiefly from the "matter," the personal penance in sorrow, confession of sin, and (the will to accomplish) satisfaction. Now this means that, according to Thomas, absolution exercises of real, causal influence on the forgiveness of sin occuring in *contritio*. That is further underscored by his theory of the real prior working of the power of the keys, according to which the power of the sacramental absolution is already effective in the *contritio* which precedes the actual reception of the sacrament of penance. It is also the rule, according to Thomas, that a person receives the sacrament of penance as one already justified through contrition.

Though the theory of the prior working of absolution is not tenable in this form, Thomas' epoch-making achievement still consists in the inner connection of the sacrament of penance to the personal process of conversion and justification brought about and sustained by the grace of God, inasmuch as the grace which justifies in the sacrament of penance is precisely the grace of *contritio,* the grace of personal conversion.

1.1.4.   At the end of the period of high scholasticism this unity of the personal and the sacramental which was characteristic of the Thomistic doctrine of penance was abandoned again by Duns Scotus (d. 1308). He emphasized, as Thomas did, the causal working of priestly absolution on the eradication of the guilt of sin. But the penitent's acts (contrition, sorrow, will to accomplish satisfaction) were for him no longer a constitutive part ("matter") of the sacrament of penance itself, as they had been for Thomas, but only a necessary precondition *(conditio sine qua non)* for its reception. The essence of the sacrament of penance, according to him, consists exclusively in priestly absolution. Consequently the justification which could take place in the sorrow for sin prior to the sacramental absolution is not related internally to the sacrament of penance. The obligation of confession, which was retained by Scotus, is based purely positivistically on the divine command. Consequently Scotus taught two ways of justification—extrasacramental and sacramental.

His doctrine of sorrow for sin is also determined by this. The extrasacramental way requires a more intense degree of sorrow *(contritio),* one which merits grace *de congruo* (on the basis of a claim of appropriateness, not a claim of justice). It is therefore more difficult and uncertain than the sacramental way, which does not make such great demands. Hand in hand with this goes a reevaluation of *attritio* as a true sorrow sufficient for the reception of the sacrament *(attritio sufficiens).* The extrasacramental justifying contrition and the merely sufficient attrition are different only in degree, according to Scotus, while the nature of the act of penitence itself is the same in both.

1.1.5.   Gabriel Biel (d. 1495), relying on William of Occam (d. 1347), developed his understanding of penitence in express opposition to Duns Scotus. He did indeed see, as did Scotus, that the real essence of the sacrament of penance was in the absolution. Nevertheless, he criticized Scotus' "attritionism," though according to recent scholarship

he misinterpreted this. Against Scotus he held that *contritio* was necessary, and in his separation of the two sorts of sorrow he chiefly placed
the consideration of the goal and the motive of the sorrow in the
foreground. Consistent with his presuppositions, Biel, as Occam before
him, revived Peter Lombard's declaratory theory of absolution and
expressly appealed to him.[4] The effect of absolution relates not to the
eradication of guilt *coram Deo,* but only *in facie ecclesiae.*

1.2. The Reformation Objection

The Reformation-Lutheran doctrine of justification, as will be made
clear below, is directed with equal passion against the theology of
penance in late medieval Nominalism, especially as expressed by Gabriel Biel, as against the deficient attitudes and abuses in the practice
of penance and their legalization and externalization.[5] One will have
to pay close attention to this *"Sitz im Leben"* in order not to miss the
exact point of the questioning, the intention and purpose of the statements and attacks. Thus we cannot play down and trivialize the incorrect developments in the theology and practice on the one side (i.e.,
the Catholic side), and evaluate the objections and attacks of the
Reformation side, removed from their context, as abstract doctrinal
statements. Therefore the proper discussion of the question before us
does not demand only a moving away from outdated positions, but
also (by the Catholic side) the express and positive recognition of the
validity and the significance of the Reformation objection—this for
the sake of the truth of the gospel.[6] The fathers at the Council of
Trent examined the Reformation concept of the doctrine of penance
only in the form of theses or lists of errors and in this sense *in ab-
stracto,*[7] and we must take this into consideration in evaluating Trent.

1.3. Luther's Rediscovery of the Promise of Matthew 16:19

1.3.1.   The Lutheran Reformation was ignited by the critique of the
contemporary Catholic practice of penance, especially the practice of
the traffic in indulgences. This critique was gradually deepened to the
point where not only the theological place and significance of satisfaction, but especially contrition and absolution were subjected to a
thorough discussion. Here Luther confronted the word of promise in
Matt. 16:19 to which he had previously paid no attention: "I will
give you the keys of the kingdom of heaven . . . and whatsoever you
loose on earth shall be loosed in heaven." He understood that these
words of Jesus had to do with the church's practice of penance. This

discovery and the new understanding of the central role of the power of the keys *(potestas clavium)* connected with it signified the breakthrough to a radically changed understanding of penance.[8] From now on the main burden no longer lay on the human activity of contrition, but on God's activity in absolution. The result of the process of development which then began is present in the CA and in the Apology.

1.3.2.   Luther too at first had a simply declaratory understanding of absolution and could appeal to Occam and Biel.[9] But now through his discovery of the word of promise of Matt. 16:19 (Matt. 18:18; John 20:23) he understood the meaning of absolution more and more as an effective word of forgiveness addressed to the believer. With this the inner connection of promise and faith dawned on him. As a consequence of this new understanding, faith from then on became a necessary element of the act of penance.

Whether this bipartite nature of the act of penitence *(contritio et fides)*—which was so strongly emphasized from then on—contradicts the traditional tripartite nature of the act of penitence *(tres partes poenitentiae: contritio, confessio, satisfactio)* will be discussed at length below.

1.4. Penance and Justification

The development of the Reformation understanding of the act of penance and the word of absolution is very closely associated with the new understanding of *iustitia Dei,* the righteousness of God, and justification. This insight is clearly expressed in the Apology. There Melanchthon emphatically, even passionately, presented the inner connection between the doctrine of justification and the doctrine of penance: "For this [that man obtains the forgiveness of sins through grace] is the chief issue [*praecipuus*] on which we clash with our opponents and which we believe all Christians must understand. . . . For the doctrine of . . . [penance] and the doctrine of justification are very closely related *(Sunt enim loci maxime cognati, doctrina poenitentiae et doctrina justificationis)."* [10] "Yet the issue at hand is a great one, the chief doctrine of the Gospel, the forgiveness of sins *(agitur de re maxima, de praecipuo evangelii loco: de remissione peccatorum)."* [11]

The relationship between penance and justification as background for the understanding of the Reformation doctrine of penance makes necessary some clarification. When penance is spoken of, sometimes it is the act of repentance and sometimes the sacrament of penance which is meant. The two cannot be separated from one another, but they are also not identical. The act of repentance goes into the sacrament of penance as a prerequisite.

By the act of repentance *(poenitentia proprie)* the CA understands sorrow and faith, and by the sacrament of penance it understands absolution: "Properly speaking . . . [penance] consists of these two parts: one is contrition, that is, terror smiting the conscience with a knowledge of sin, and the other is faith, which is born of the Gospel, or of absolution, believes that sins are forgiven for Christ's sake. . . ." [12] The Apology states: "There are, then, two chief parts here, contrition and faith." [13] Penance as a sacrament is absolution.[14]

1.5. Sorrow and Faith: Law and Gospel

Since the sorrow and faith of the act of penance are conceived of as dying and rising again with Christ, they are closely connected with Baptism and thus also with the central Reformation conception of law and gospel. Sorrow is God's work in human beings and an expression that God puts the old person to death through the law, in order to let the new arise to life. Faith is also God's work. But while in sorrow God destroys and terrifies, in faith he quickens terrified consciences. An important biblical point of departure for this way of looking at things is Isa. 28:21 with its distinction between God's foreign work *(opus alienum)* and his proper work *(opus proprium)*. The foreign work of God is in the work of the law through which human beings are terrified in their consciences over their sins. That is contrition; but since it is God's work it can also be said that God kills *(mortificat)* the old person. God's proper work *(opus proprium) is faith,* which is accomplished through the word of promise of the gospel. Through faith the broken hearts are raised up, preserved, and made alive. The words of 1 Sam. 2:6, "The Lord kills [*mortificat*] and brings to life; he brings down to Sheol and raises up," or the statements of Romans 6 about death and resurrection in Baptism are biblical evidence for what now takes place in Christians in penance.[15]

God's work through law and gospel corresponds to the chief parts of penance, i.e., the act of penance—contrition and faith. This action marks the total existence of the Christian. It is connected with Baptism and justification and it also occurs in connection with the sacrament of penance.[16]

2. The Sacrament of Penance and the Act of Penance

2.1. The Nature of the Sacrament of Penance: Absolution

Article 13, 4 of the Apology includes penance among the genuine sacraments *(proprie dicta sacramenta)*. In the CA the sacramentality of penance is expressed sufficiently by the location of CA 11 and 12 after the articles on Baptism (CA 9) and the Lord's Supper (CA 10) and before CA 13 (the use of the sacraments).[17]

The essence of the sacrament of penance is seen in the absolution, "which is the sacrament of . . . [penance]." [18] "Absolution may properly [*proprie*] be called a sacrament of . . . [penance]." [19] As we have shown above, this description of the essence of penance corresponds to the Scotistic and Occamistic scholastic tradition. But the formal correspondence must not be allowed to obscure the more basic differences. The presupposition for the Apology's statements concerning the sacramental significance of absolution is the chief article *(praecipuus evangelii locus;* Apol. 12, 3) of justification through faith, the doctrine of law and gospel. There it is said that contrition as God's work in human beings is the indispensable prerequisite of absolution.

The concept of the sacramentality of penance expressed in the CA and the Apology can be held without contradicting the Tridentine teaching, according to which the "form of the sacrament of penance in which its power principally lies" is given by the word of absolution *("Docet . . . synodus, sacramenti paenitentiae formam, in qua praecipue ipsius vis sita est, in illis ministri verbis positam esse: Ego te absolvo . . . ."* DS 1673). According to the evidence of the acts of the Council, the Council of Trent did not want to decide the Thomistic-Scotistic scholastic controversy concerning the nature of the sacrament of penance.

2.2. The Effect of Absolution

According to CA 12 the sacrament of penance has its special meaning for those who have lapsed after Baptism and are returning to repentance. Through absolution they receive the forgiveness of sins (cf. Apol. 12, 1). In absolution the power of the keys given by God through Christ to the church is active. "The power of the keys administers and offers the Gospel through absolution, which is the true voice of the Gospel [*vera vox evangelii*]," [20] and "It is not the voice or word of the man who speaks it, but it is the Word of God, who forgives sin, for it is spoken in God's stead and by God's command." [21] "Therefore this absolution is to be believed no less than if we heard God's clear voice coming from heaven," [22] "according to the statement (Luke 10:16), 'He who hears you, hears me.' " [23] For "it is God's Word through which the power of the keys absolves us from sins," [24] and so "It would therefore be wicked to remove private absolution from the church . . . [for] those who despise private absolution understand neither the forgiveness of sins nor the power of the keys." [25] Accordingly absolution is God's undeceitful word itself, mediated by the church.

Even though the *vera vox evangelii* sounds in the absolution, the confessional writings do not on this basis identify absolution with the sermon. Absolution and sermon are different activities.[26] In this context it must especially be noted that the CA and the Apology (as well as Luther's writing of 1530, *The Keys*)[27] more decisively express the efficacy *(vis)* of the absolution in blotting out sin before God than do the opponents against whom they are writing (especially Gabriel Biel): "The keys truly forgive sins before him" *(vere coram Deo)*.[28] With decisiveness and passion the "vicious error" is repudiated, according to which the power of the keys extends indirectly only to the forgiveness of sins before the church, but not before God, or it relates only to the transformation of eternal punishment into temporal punishment or to partial remission of temporal punishment.[29] The background in the history of theology of the theory of penance which is here attacked—one which does not go beyond ascribing a mere declaratory function to the absolution in forgiving sins, and therefore ascribes to absolution the chief function of imposing penitential or punitory acts of satisfaction—has been briefly described above (1.1).

It appears important to us that in this context the decisive and theologically justified objection against trivializing or obscuring the benefit *(beneficium)* and power *(vis)* of absolution—of the power of the keys [30]—is directly connected with the preservation of the forgiveness of sins freely offered for Christ's sake through faith, the *iustitia fidei*, and also with the equally decisive rejection of any self-obtained works-righteousness. Cf. Apol. 11, 2: "Previously the whole power of absolution had been smothered by teachings about works, since the scholastics and monks teach nothing about faith and free forgiveness." [31] This shows, first, that obtaining the forgiveness of sins through faith is not in competition with the forgiveness before God through the working of absolution;[32] and, second, that the main force of the protest is directly addressed to even the slightest appearance of a forgiveness of sins on the basis of our merits and works.[33] The Reformation objection to an understanding of "satisfaction" *(satisfactio)* as a meritorius accomplishment has its objective basis here. In contrast to this, Luther's new discovery of the word *absolution,* which is determinative for the Confessions' doctrine of penance, is "not only the discovery of the free grace of God," but is rather "the discovery of the concretely expressed, tangibly manifested, and undeceitfully enduring word of forgiveness which gives certainty. . . . Because the word is so addressed concretely, a person can give up all need to trust in his own work." [34]

2.3. The Act of Penance

The absolutely indispensable and necessary prerequisites for obtaining the forgiveness of sins on the part of the penitent, according to CA 12 and Apol. 12, are contrition *(contritio)* and faith *(fides).* This faith which must necessarily be added to contrition—the faith that first makes contrition to be salvific contrition—is not, as Apol. 12, 60 expressly emphasizes against the misunderstanding of the Confutation,[35] the faith preceding the act of penance *(fides praecedens* or *fides praevia),* but rather the *fides specialis* in Christ's promise *(promissio)* of forgiveness [36]—the justifying, life-giving, comforting, and consoling faith.[37] This faith distinguishes the sorrow of Peter from that of Judas.[38] Therefore *contritio* and *fides,* as is shown through the Scriptures, are the *partes praecipuae,*[39] the *praecipua membra* of the act of penance.[40] The sacrament of penance is not thus excluded, but it is expressly included in justification through faith. "In speaking of faith, therefore, we also include absolution *(Ita et absolutionem complectimur, cum de fide dicimus)."* [41] Indeed, faith is received and strengthened through the word of absolution, "which is the true voice of the Gospel." [42] This clear and plain doctrine of penance adds to the honor of the power of the keys and the sacraments, illumines the blessing of Christ, and teaches us why and how Christ is our mediator *("Haec ratio poenitentiae plana et perspicua est, et auget dignitatem potestatis clavium et sacramentorum, et illustrat beneficium Christi, docet not uti mediatore ac propitiatore Christo").*[43]

The necessity of faith in the totality of the Christian life and the direction of the "acts of the penitent" toward the sacrament of penance is again presented clearly in the dispute with the opponents, i.e., the Confutation. The opponents are asked whether the reception of absolution is a part of penance *(utrum absolutionem accipere sit pars poeni-*

tentiae). In case they wish to separate the confession of sins from the absolution with the aid of subtle distinctions, it must then still be asked what is the value of a confession without absolution. Otherwise they would have to acknowledge that faith is a part of penance *(pars poenitentiae),* since without faith one cannot receive absolution, the promise of the forgiveness of sins.[44]

From the passages cited (which must be interpreted within the entire context), we derive three conclusions: first, the sacrament of penance, absolution, belongs to complete Christian penance (to *tota poenitentia*).[45] Second, from the perspective of the sinner contrition and faith are indispensable prerequisites for obtaining the forgiveness of sins through absolution. To these must be added a third: contrition and faith are not self-generated works, but God's activity in human beings *(opera Dei in hominibus).*[46] Therefore the forgiveness of sins does not take place *"ex opere operato* because of contrition, but by that personal faith *(fide illa speciali)* by which each individual believes that his sins are forgiven." [47] Precisely in order to exclude the idea that a self-generated contrition is the "cause" of the forgiveness of sins, Melanchthon emphasizes so strongly the necessity of faith: "We insist that this faith is really necessary for the forgiveness of sins." [48]

That in this sense faith, as the "second part of penance," [49] belongs necessarily to contrition is also maintained without qualification by the Catholic side and was also expressly affirmed in the discussions at the Council of Trent by some council fathers in referring to the virtue of penance (active contrition).[50]

2.4. Contrition and Faith: The Chief Parts of the Act of Penance

Apology 12, 98 introduces the section concerning confession and satisfaction with the note that it is very important to preserve the true teaching about the *superiores partes* of penitence, contrition, and faith. The entire effort has been concentrated on this, while there was no separate disagreement about confession and satisfaction. The *superiores partes* can be interpreted both as superior in the sense of order of appearance (i.e., the parts mentioned above), as well as superior in the sense of order of importance. It is precisely the second interpretation—the dominant one, at least in terms of the subject matter—which gives the whole a theological significance and thus interprets the second remark (for, in fact, there were very serious disputes about confession and satisfaction). Two consequences follow. First, there is a "hierarchy" among the "acts of the penitent" (which is also to be recognized and has been recognized by the Catholic side). Over against confession and satisfaction which, under certain circumstances, may be missing (e.g., because of physical impossibility), contrition and faith are absolutely indispensable. Second, confession and satisfaction are not excluded from the complete act of penance (the *tota poenitentia*). Contrition and faith are indeed the *praecipuae partes,* the chief and foremost parts—therefore, according to CA 12, penance *proprie,* in the strict sense, consists of these two parts—but they are not thereby the only parts (in an exclusive sense).[51]

2.5. Confession and Satisfaction

2.5.1. Expressly for the sake of absolution the confession of sins was retained: "Nevertheless, confession is retained among us on account of the great benefit of absolution *(propter maximum absolutionis beneficium)* and because it is otherwise useful to consciences." [52] The Apology expresses the same thought: "For we also keep confession, especially because of absolution, which is the Word of God that the power of the keys proclaims to individuals by divine authority *(Nam et nos confessionem retinemus praecipue propter absolutionem, quae est verbum Dei, quod de singulis auctoritate divina pronuntiat potestas clavium)." [53] Confession and absolution therefore "complement one another." [54] The value and use of confession are emphasized everywhere in the CA and in the Apology in agreement with Luther, and the faithful are admonished to receive absolution frequently.[55]

As the passages already cited show, it would be a truncation of the doctrine of the CA and the Apology to understand the retention of confession exclusively with reference to the comforting of consciences or for pastoral-pedagogical reasons (even though this is no small thing). When confession is related to absolution, that inner confession in which one recognizes and acknowledges oneself before God as this actual sinner is explicit and open. With this one should compare Apol. 12, 107: "Such confession, made to God, is itself contrition. For when confession is made to God, it must come from the heart and not just from the voice, as in a play." [56] Compare this also with the citation attributed to Chrysostom in Apol. 12, 170: "In the heart contrition *(contritio),* in the mouth confession *(confessio),* in the deed complete humility *(tota humilitas)." [57] Rejected is a mere external confession, understood as an external work without inner contrition before God and without faith.[58] Subsequently we must deal more carefully with confession and the questions related to it, some of which are still open.

2.5.2.   As was mentioned above (2.2), the late medieval theory of absolution which was attacked by Luther and Melanchthon saw the primary function of the power of the keys residing in the imposition of works of satisfaction for the purpose of blotting out the temporal punishment of sins. A misunderstanding of "satisfaction" as merit was thereby not excluded, at least in practice. It now appears to us that the vehement rejection of the imposition of penance *(satisfactio)*[59] must be evaluated as a pointed rejection of this opposing theory of the power of the keys, which obscured righteousness by faith and the power of absolution, and its negative influence on the practice of the "keys."

Yet if we look at the subject itself and substitute "penance" or "repentance" for the easily misunderstood word "satisfaction," then there exist no serious differences on this matter. We must proceed from the fundamental statement that Christ's death is the real satisfaction for sin and for the penalties of sin.[60] The satisfaction of Christ is made ours through faith and the sacraments *in remissionem peccatorum*— not through our own meritorious works. Nevertheless penance is and remains a perpetual task of living the Christian life. But penance must bring forth good works as fruits of repentance *(parere)*.[61] There can be no true repentance or contrition without other works of penance *(mortificationes carnis)* and good fruits. Inner repentance demands its expression in a living, concrete way.[62] What is demanded is penance in deed which proves itself in an improvement of life, in a new way of living, one that may not be understood as "Platonic" in the sense of a mere hypocritical change of mind.[63] That is—building on the citation ascribed to Augustine—the "true satisfaction" *(vera satisfactio)*, which consists of "cutting off the causes of sins" *(peccatorum causas excidere)* and "mortifying and restraining the flesh." [64] The "condemnation" of sins, the judgment of ourselves mentioned in 1 Cor. 11:31, must express itself in active contrition, i.e., in the improvement of life and in the good works demanded by the gospel.[65] "Satisfaction" is thus embodied in the process of daily, lifelong penance.

In this sense Melanchthon was also prepared to admit "fruits worthy of . . . [repentance] and an improvement of the whole life and character" (Apol. 12, 28, 45) as the third part of penance (in addition to the two chief parts of *contritio* and *fides*),[66] even though he himself preferred to maintain the twofold division, not in order again to downplay "good works," but rather to illuminate clearly in this way what is absolutely indispensible on the sinner's part for obtaining forgiveness of sins and what thus are the "real" parts of penance *(quae propriae sunt in conversione seu regeneratione et remissione peccati),* and to emphasize more fully the faith demanded in penance *(ut majis conspici fides possit, quam in poenitentia requirimus),* while "good works" are the results of regeneration and the forgiveness of sins.[67] This faith originates and is displayed in penance and it grows and becomes stronger through the good works of penance. "For this purpose we are reborn and receive the Holy Spirit, that this new life might have new works and new impulses, the fear and love of God, hatred of lust, etc. The faith we speak of has its existence in . . . [penance]. It ought to grow and become firmer amid good works as well as temptations and dangers. . . . From these statements the fair-minded reader can judge that we very definitely require good works, since we teach that this faith arises in . . . [penance] and ought to grow continually in . . . [penance]." [68]

The character of punishment is also not excluded from penance: "We grant that punishment is necessary in penance *(vindictam seu poenam in poenitentia necessariam esse),* but not as a merit or reward *(non tamquam meritum seu pretium)*. . . . But punishment belongs essentially to penance *(sed vindicta formaliter est in poenitentia)* because regeneration itself takes place by constantly mortifying the old life *(quia ipsa regeneratio fit perpetua mortificatione vetustatis),*" which is then explained "etymologically" as *poenitentia quasi poenae tenentia.*[69] A reduction of punishment through penance (Apol. 12, 164) is excluded just as much as is the veneration of God by means of good works and divine reward for these works.[70]

When one observes all of this, it becomes clear that in this doctrine of penance there is no "cheap" forgiveness of sins and that it lacks none of the deeds (contrition, confession, satisfaction) that the Catholic theology of penance demands of the penitent. In the active penance that we sketched out, the essential element of *satisfactio,* the thing itself, is fully present.[71]

Furthermore the question of the "punishment" of sins, in distinction to the "guilt" of sins, must also be newly thought through by the Catholic side and purified of all external, vindictive understandings. The punishments of sin are not to be thought of as "punishment" additionally and externally imposed, but rather as conatural (i.e., founded in the inner nature of sin itself) results of sin, in which one's efforts—made possible by the grace of forgiveness—are supported by the church's intercessory prayer.[72]

In the following we must examine individual questions in which, at least at first glance, serious differences of a dogmatic nature appear to exist.

3. Critical Questions Concerning Confession

3.1. Human or Divine Law?

The CA and the Apology distinguish between absolution as sacrament and—in connection with the private *absolutio,* the absolution of an individual—individual confession. Absolution, called *sacramentum poenitentiae* in the Apology, is commanded by God in the Holy Scriptures and is therefore *iuris divini* (Apol. 12, 12: *absolutio quae vere est iuris divini*).[73] The same thing cannot be said of individual confession. It is not, as the *Glossa ordinaria* to Gratian's Decretal established,[74] supported in the New Testament; therefore, it is *iuris humani.*[75]

In reference to the sacraments, the Reformers maintained only those things which could be traced back directly to an institution by Jesus Christ testified to in the Scriptures. Therefore absolution, in which the office of the keys is effective, is a sacrament; therefore public confession *(confessio publica)* is also a sacrament and a "divine law," but not secret confession *(confessio occulta),* since it cannot be proved by the Scriptures—despite its uncontested value.[76]

Now, however, a new theological situation has arisen today, insofar as theology on both sides cannot trace the church, Baptism, the power of the keys, and even the Lord's Supper back to a direct institution by the historical Jesus with the same apodictic certainty that prevailed in earlier times.[77] Therefore we must inquire together in a new way about the criteria for recognition of the *ius divinum* and the institution by Jesus Christ. Here a hermeneutical key concept appears to be offered by the *consensus ecclesiae,* a consensus which is fundamentally based on the equally primitive origin of the church, the kerygma, and the office of sending on the basis of the self-revelation of the resurrected and glorified Lord which historically unfolded—with the assistance of the Holy Spirit—in the process of comprehending interpretation and appropriation of the revelation of Christ. This process of the appropriate interpretation—one that remains faithful to the "subject"—is not a mechanical process, but a continuing task of the church(es) led by the Spirit.

In the light of recent exegetical research a revision of the traditional evangelical understanding of the relationship of Scripture and tradition may be appropriate. To no other "part of the Christian faith" did Luther himself hold so decidedly and uncompromisingly "without a clear foundation in the Scriptures" as he did to confession.[78] The reason lies in his new discovery of the divine word of forgiveness that in absolution is efficaciously and unmistakably pronounced over the sinner. Confession and absolution thereby enter into the center of the event of justification.

In the chief article mentioned again and again in the Apology, "that we obtain the forgiveness of sins not by our own works, but for the sake of Christ," a consensus between the churches exists today. On the basis of this central point the Apology bases its insistence on preserving confession too.[79] The recognition of an essential agreement in the doctrine of justification will therefore involve at least the supposition that also in the doctrine of penance (including the doctrine of confession) no insurmountable differences exist. On the other hand, the doctrine of penance will provide a means of testing whether there is a real agreement on the doctrine of justification.

The Council of Trent based the recognition of the *ius divinum* of the confession of sins on the *consensus ecclesiae,* as the fundamental investigation of K.-J. Becker shows.[80] The magisterial decision in the strict sense relates to the sacramental confession in general *(in genere)* and does not mention the two "subdivisions"—public or private. Of private confession it is said only that it does not contradict the institution by Jesus Christ (DS 1706). This is in complete agreement with the CA, the Apology, and the other confessions, as was proved by the practice of confession that was retained.

According to the Council of Trent, confession must be made of all mortal sins of which a person is aware *(omnia et singula peccata mortalia;* DA 1707). On this point an agreement should not be difficult. For according to the CA the possibility that a justified person can lapse after Baptism and lose the Holy Spirit is a completely real possibility, and it is precisely for those who have lapsed after Baptism that the sacrament of penitence has its special significance.[81]

As for the requirement to confess secret sins (or sins of the heart), the relevant statement of the Council of Trent (DS 1007) is not in itself a definition,[82] but is part of the magisterial statement about the requirement to confess mortal sins. In this context, saying that the confessional obligation is established exclusively for the purpose of imposing ecclesiastical penalties *(tantum ad satisfactionem canonicam imponendam)* is expressly rejected.

Also concerning the connection of the power of absolution with the ministerial office there is in principle no distinction between the view of Luther and the CA,[83] although the role of the ecclesiastical minister is conceived somewhat differently. He should pronounce the absolution, but he has no authority to demand from the penitent a complete enumeration of his sins. Contrition is a matter between God and the penitent. Through the law God, the true judge, works genuine contrition. Since pastors therefore have no commission to judge, they also do not need to know all sins in order to be able to pronounce the absolution.[84] "The ministry of absolution is in the area of blessing or grace, not of judgment or law (*ministerium absolutionis beneficium est seu gratia, non est iudicium seu lex*)." [85]

3.2. Completeness of the Confession?

Therefore, according to the CA and the Apology, the completeness of the confession of sins is neither necessary nor commanded. It is not *iuris divini*. The CA emphasizes, "that private absolution should be retained and not allowed to fall into disuse. However, in confession it is not necessary to enumerate all trespasses and sins." [86] This viewpoint is repeated throughout the Reformation period in every confessional writing that contains statements about confession.[87] It is impossible to demand a complete enumeration of all sins in confession. If the demand for a complete confession of sins were maintained, then the forgiveness of sins would always remain only conditional, since it would then depend on the completeness of the confession. Then it would not be the absolution which stands at the center, but human confession, something that would lead again to oppression of conscience and works-righteousness. No one knows to the last detail how often he sins (Ps. 19:12). For "our wretched human nature is so deeply submerged in sins that it is unable to perceive or know them all, and if we were to be absolved only from those which we can enumerate we would be helped but little." [88]

This rejection is directed precisely against the decree on penance of the Fourth Lateran Council of 1215 (DS 812), in which "every believer (*omnis fidelis*)" who has reached the age of reason is obligated to confess "all his sins (*omnia sua peccata*)" at least once a year. Now 13th-century theology (Thomas Aquinas) had indeed already understood this in the more precise and limited sense of "all sins which one remembers." [89] With this modification and a further one (instead of "*omnis fidelis*" it now read "*peccator*"), and without mentioning the annual requirement, this was picked up by the Council of Florence (1439) which, notwithstanding this limitation, especially emphasized the duty of making a complete confession: "It belongs [to oral confession] that the sinner confess completely *(integraliter)* all sins which he remembers" (DS 1323). On this the authors of the Confutation can rest when over against CA 11 they maintain the complete confession *(confessio integra)* of all sins which come to mind after a thorough searching of one's conscience.[90] With this the point of contention could theoretically have been decided.

As the response in the Apology nevertheless shows, Melanchthon is not dealing here with a theoretical question, but rather with a highly practical and pastoral concern which at the same time challenges the heart of the gospel, the message of divine forgiveness.[91] The objection is not so much directed against the Fourth Lateran Council's definition "as such," but more so against the casuistry which the "Summists," the authors of the canonical penitential manuals, had developed out of it.[92] "The whole church throughout Europe knows how consciences have been ensnared. . . . What labyrinths *(labyrinthi)*! What great tortures *(carnificina)* for the most pious minds!" For "these terrors" *(terriculamenta)* had made no impression on "wild and profane men." [93] All of this would have been less unbearable, however, if the opponents had added only a single word about the comfort and consolation of faith. But in the entire mass of constitutions, glosses, summae, penitential and indulgence letters not one syllable speaks about this. There we read not a word about Christ; instead there are only lists of sins.[94]

All of this is associated by Luther and Melanchthon with the phrase "enumeration of all sins *(enumeratio omnium delictorum)*." To use the words of the first draft of the Apology: "Although men should have been taught about absolution and faith, it was the sole concern of the writers and teachers to accustom men to enumerate sins, while the deepest silence reigned over faith." [95] Here the cardinal point of the discussion becomes clear and from here the continually repeated accusation of mere works-righteousness becomes understandable.

It would be wrong and also not in accord with the historical truth if, in reference to the "theoretical" exploration of the Confutation, one would here impute to Melanchthon only an extreme form of exaggeration in order stubbornly to maintain his position. The attack is directed against coarse grievances in the practical administration of the sacrament of penance. This is evident also in the fact that, in the unity negotiations at the Diet of Augsburg, CA 11 was removed from the discussion concerning the doctrinal articles of the first part and dealt with in the discussion about the second part (on abuses; cf. CA 25).[96]

In summary we can conclude: what is rejected is the obligation of a self-torturing, scrupulous, mathematically-precise *enumeratio omnium peccatorum,* something which places impossibly excessive demands on one, never releases one from doubts and terrors of conscience, and finally drives one to despair—an obligation which (and this is the decisive objection) does not even have the counterpoint of a comforting and liberating message of God's gracious forgiveness for Christ's sake, based on faith and not based on our merits and works. In opposition to this the joyous message of confession and absolution is brought forward.[97]

3.3. Rejection of the CA and Apology's Doctrine of Penance by the Council of Trent?

Melanchthon therefore in several places in the Apology decidedly rejects the *ius divinum* and the necessity of the *enumeratio peccatorum* for salvation.[98] Becker believes that this formulation of Melanchthon is condemned almost verbatim by the Council of Trent (DS 1707).[99] In our opinion that is only partially correct. It is correct if one separates the statements of the Apology from their context and thus regards them as abstract doctrinal statements. But if one remembers what is associated for Melanchthon with the phrase—one might call it a red flag—*"enumeratio,"* which (as the following will show) was not included by the Council of Trent in its condemnation of the clearly recognized abuses connected with it, and one thus leaves the statements in their actual historical context, then Becker's opinion must be considerably modified. This will be demonstrated with two important texts.

In Apol. 12, 11-12, Melanchthon opposes the "endless enumeration of sins" *(infinita enumeratio peccatorum)* with absolution, which is truly a divine law *(quae vere est iuris divini).* Thus he critically attacks the penitential handbooks' demands which were required under the pretext of divine law *(praetextu iuris divini),* although they chiefly lost themselves in human ordinances. They spoke only incidentally and "very coldly *(frigide)"* about absolution. The contrast between the imagined divine law *(fingunt, hanc enumerationem esse iuris divini)* and the neglect of real divine law is sharpened even more through the accusation that the opponents "pretend that the sacrament grants grace *ex opere operato,* without a right attitude in the recipient *(sine bono motu utentis),"* while they do not once mention faith which grasps the absolution and consoles the conscience.[100]

In Apol. 12, 110-111 Melanchthon expressly takes a stand against the Confutation. After he has conceded the value and usefulness of confession, he continues: "Still it [confession] must be controlled, lest consciences be ensnared; for they will never be at rest if they suppose that they cannot obtain the forgiveness of sins without . . . [a scrupulous enumeration of] all their sins *(si existemabunt se non posse consequi remissionem peccatorum, nisi facta illa scrupulosa enumeratione).* In the Confutation our opponents have maintained that complete confession is necessary for salvation; this is completely false, as well as being impossible *(Hoc certe falsissimum est, quod adversarii posuerunt in Confutatione, quod confessio integra sit necessaria ad salutem. Est enim impossibilis).* What snares this requirement of complete confession has cast upon consciences! When will the conscience be sure that its confession is complete?" [101] Here it is completely clear in what way Melanchthon understands the *confessio integra* demanded by the Confutation—as self-tormenting introspection and never-ending cataloging and enumeration of sins.

Melanchthon is correct in saying that such an understanding of the enumeration of sins cannot rest on a *ius divinum;* similarly CA 25, 10 says, "such an enumeration is not necessary." [102] In this connection it is well to pay close attention to the melody and the harmony that here combine to make music.

As far as the penitential discipline of the ancient church is concerned, which is what Melanchthon is discussing in this context, the competent judgment of H. Jedin may be cited here: "It is hardly a matter for discussion that certain historical claims of the reformers were closer to the truth than were those of the Catholics." [103]

The Confutation had claimed that "complete confession *(confessio integra)"* was not only necessary for salvation, but that it was also the "nerve of Christian discipline and complete obedience *(sed etiam nervus existat christianae disciplina et totius quoque oboedientiae)."* Therefore the princes and cities are exhorted to conform to the orthodox churches *(ut ecclesiae othodoxae se conforment).*[104] Do we not see here at the very least something dangerously close to an abusive instrument of domination, and do not the Reformers' impassioned attacks on the "tyranny of conscience"—precisely on account of the high evaluation of the sacrament of penance—thereby gain their concrete form and authenticity?

In this context a twofold observation with reference to the Council of Trent is significant. During the concluding consultation on the completeness of the confession of sins, the council fathers in their doctrinal declaration intentionally did not use the term *"enumeratio peccatorum,"* which was contained in the list of errors, in order to avoid misunderstandings (instead of *enumerari* they used *confiteri,* DS 1707). In addition, they made the limitation of the Council of Florence even more precise by applying the obligation to confess to "all mortal sins which one remembers after obligatory and painstaking consideration," and not indeed "in order to warn against a laxity in interpreting the decision of Florence, but rather to say that a serious and conscious preparation is intended in the searching of one's memory, not the attitude of a scrupulous person." [105]

If we now once again compare the statement of the Apology with those of the Council of Trent, this can be established: exactly what Melanchthon opposed is not condemned in that form by Trent, and what Trent anathamatized was not meant in that way by Melanchthon.

4. Comments on CA 12

W. Pannenberg proposes as a way of solving the "most difficult difference which is not yet overcome" in the doctrine of penance—namely, that CA 12 speaks of only "two parts" of penance (contrition and faith) instead of the traditional "three parts" (contrition, confession, and satisfaction), which the Council of Trent also demanded—that CA 12 be interpreted "so that it does not speak about the institutional arrangement of the sacrament, but about the theological content of penance." [106] With this we agree entirely. For in fact confession is not here replaced by faith, as our discussion has already shown, but here we are dealing with subjective penance, the act of penance (contrition), to which faith necessarily belongs as an absolutely indispensable "component." The "two parts" of penance (contrition and faith), about which CA 12 speaks, are therefore not at all opposed to the "three parts" or three acts of the penitent (contrition, confession, and satisfaction). The "two parts" belong rather—if we hold to the traditional tripartite division—constitutively to the "first act" of the penitent, i.e., to contrition. For this, two further reasons can be added to what has already been said. First, the Apology itself in defending CA 12 relates the *duae partes,* especially the necessity of faith, to the "first step" of the penitent. It concludes the pertinent discussion with the statement, "All this happens in the first step," [107] and following this explains confession and satisfaction. Second, at the unity negotiations at the Diet of Augsburg, in which Melanchthon himself participated, complete agreement was achieved about the necessary relationship of faith to contrition, as well as about the "three elements of penance" (contrition together with faith, confession, and satisfaction).[108]

On the side of the Confutation, as well as of the Council of Trent, we are dealing with a terminological misunderstanding that was chiefly occasioned by the "snare of language," inasmuch as the CA's way of speaking about the "two parts of penance *(duae partes poenitentiae)*" almost inevitably had to evoke the association with the traditional way of speaking about the "three parts *(tres partes)*" which was commonly used to designate the "three acts of the penitent *(tres actus poenitentis)*" in the church's theology of penitence (cf. Council of Florence; DS 1323). The matter itself was already clarified in the unity negotiations —with John Eck's specific approval. The reason the meaning of the statement in CA 12 escaped the Council of Trent is that the deliberations at the Council had as "proof texts" only the list of errors containing isolated sentences taken out of context.[109] Nevertheless some fathers, as mentioned, expressly emphasized the correctness of the statement with regard to the virtue of penance (the active contrition).

Therefore it is certain that the anathema of the Council of Trent (DS 1704) does not apply to the matter intended in CA 12 and in the Apology. Accordingly the notes in Denzinger should be revised. The corresponding doctrinal decisions of the Council of Trent no longer need to be viewed as "the most difficult difference in the doctrine of the sacraments which is not yet overcome" and need not stand as an obstacle in the way of possible recognition of the CA.

With regard to satisfaction *(satisfactio)*, no agreement could be achieved in the unity negotiations of 1530 on "whether satisfaction is necessary for the eradication of the penalty of sin." [110] This disputed question has primarily a historically-conditioned background. The distinction between the guilt of sin and the punishment of sin *(culpa* and *poena)* first appeared, as was said above (1.1.2), in the school of the Victorines in the 12th century in order—on the basis of the early medieval contritionism (according to which the forgiveness of sins already took place in contrition)—to be able to ascribe still a real function to the power of absolution. In view of the full recognition of the true nature of satisfaction in the sense of *fructus poenitentiae* displayed by Luther, the CA, and the Apology, this disputed question has no dogmatic relevance.

5. Conclusion and Results

Our discussion should have shown—after a sober analysis that considers the historical context—that in the question of the sacrament of penance and confession no essential difference exists between the CA and the Apology on the one side and the Catholic interpretation on the other. Rather, the view of the CA and the Apology as they are influenced by Luther has brought significant aspects back into focus, especially the value of absolution, the preparation of man to receive divine forgiveness as a "being prepared by God," the rejection of every form of self-generated satisfaction and works-righteousness in confession and contrition ("satisfaction"). The sacrament of penance and confession has been newly understood from the central theme of justification. That is completely acceptable to the Catholic side.

However, the high evaluation of the sacrament of penance and of confession did not last in the history and practice of the churches of the Reformation, the practice of private confession being almost completely extinguished with the rise of Pietism. "Out of sacramental penance came the penitential feeling of the piety of Pietism." [111] Luther's optimism was not fulfilled, that if confession were only rightly taught "such a desire and love for it would be aroused that people would come running after us to get it, more than we would like." [112] On the other hand, the ecclesiastical requirement about confession could not prevent the crisis of the sacrament of penitence in the contemporary Catholic Church. From this emerges a common theological and pastoral task. Both churches are thereby directed to the common way of the gospel.

The possible objection that the way to a renewal of the sacramental "private" penance ("private" confession) may lead anew into a privatism and subjectivistic narrowing down of piety can be countered with the following consideration: where one recognizes oneself realistically as a sinner before God and confesses it, any sort of "fatal delusion of innocence" which separates one not only from God, but also from one's fellow human beings, is radically shattered and God bestows a new freedom that grants openness for others as well.

The common theological and pastoral task which we have indicated may be the way to a full agreement.

Notes

1. Cf. Herbert Vorgrimler, *Busse and Krankensalbung* (Freiburg, Basel, and Vienna: 1978) = HDG 4/3.
2. Toward the end of early scholasticism and continuing on into late scholasticism, a distinction was made between the two types of contrition according to their relation to the grace of justification. The *contritio* which is connected with the intention to confess and perform satisfaction is informed by justifying grace and is therefore an effective sorrow, the *paenitentia per gratiam formata; attritio,* on the contrary, is *paenitentia informis* and therefore is an ineffective sorrow in eradicating the guilt of sin. The distinction according to the motives of the sorrow was first established in late scholasticism (Gabriel Biel).
3. Hugo of St. Cher, O.P. (d. 1263), is considered the creator of the hylomorphic structure of the sacraments (matter and form as correlative principles in the sense of Aristotelian philosophy). Through this it was now possible to apply the dual concepts of matter and form to those sacraments which contained no material, physical element, such as penance.
4. Wolfgang Schwab, *Entwicklung und Gestalt der Sakramententheologie bei Martin Luther* (Frankfurt and Bern: 1977), pp. 81-84; Vinzenz Pfnür, *Einig in der Rechtfertigungslehre?* (Wiesbaden: 1970), pp. 77-82.
5. Cf. Pfnür, *op. cit.,* pp. 29-88.
6. Cf. Pfnür, *op. cit.,* p. 386.
7. *Concilium Tridentium,* vol. 7/1, ed. by the Görres-Gesellschaft (Freiburg: 1961), pp. 133-139.
8. Schwab, *op. cit.,* pp. 84-105, 365-366. Ingemar Oberg, *Himmelrikets nycklar och kyrklig bot* (Uppsala: 1970).
9. Schwab, *op. cit.,* pp. 83-84.
10. Apol. 12, 59 (BC 190; for the Latin text see BSLK 263 or CT 266). In quoting from the BC we shall consistently depart from Tappert by translating *"poenitentia"* as "penance" rather than as "penitence."
11. Apol. 12, 10 (BC 184; for the Latin text see BSLK 254 or CT 254).
12. CA 12, 3-4 (BC 34-35).
13. Apol. 12, 45 (BC 187).
14. Apol. 13, 4 (BC 211).
15. Apol. 12, 49-54 (BC 188-189).
16. Holsten Fagerberg, *A New Look at the Lutheran Confessions (1529-1537)* (St. Louis: Concordia, 1972), pp. 72-74, 95, 211-217.
17. In the question about the sacramentality of penance the CA and the Apology are not in essential opposition to Luther, although in *De capt. babyl.* (AE 36, 124; WA 6, 572) he wanted to regard only Baptism and the Lord's Supper as sacraments in the strict sense *(si rigide loqui volumus).* Here he excludes penance from the list of "real" sacraments because, in distinction to the two others, it lacks a visible sign. Yet this is only a terminological question—the question of the concept or definition of a sacrament, which as such is not given in the Holy Scriptures, although they certainly bring the principles of revelation to bear on the concept. According to *De capt. babyl.,* the constitutive element of this "strict concept" of the sacraments (which was inspired by Augustine) includes

the "visible" earthly element (but cf. note 3 above). Nevertheless this is not a substantial theological problem. For according to Luther exactly the same conditions apply to the power of the keys and to absolution as he otherwise ascribed preeminently to the sacramentality of Baptism and the Lord's Supper—the institution of Jesus Christ and the divine promise *(promissio)*. This is not an "empty" promise, but in the case of absolution is a justifying declaration, effectively mediating grace as it is spoken. Luther never wavered on this subject. Cf. Schwab, *op. cit.*, pp. 370-374.

18. Apol. 13, 4 (BC 211).
19. Apol. 12, 41 (BC 187).
20. Apol. 12, 39 (BC 187); cf. Apol. 11, 2 (BC 180).
21. CA 25, 3, German (BC 61-62).
22. Apol. 12, 42, German (BSLK 259; CT 260).
23. Apol. 12, 40 (BC 187).
24. Apol. 12, 103, German (BSLK 273; CT 280).
25. Apol. 12, 101-102 (BC 197).
26. Fagerberg, *op. cit.,* p. 98, note 35; cf. Pfnür, *op. cit.,* pp. 159-160.
27. Cf. Pfnür, *op. cit.,* pp. 82, 217-218.
28. Apol. 12, 40 (BC 187; for the Latin text see BSLK 259 or CT 260).
29. Apol. 12, 6-8, 21-22, 118, 139 (BC 183, 185, 199, 203-204).
30. Apol. 11, 2; 12, 10 (BC 180, 184).
31. Apol. 11, 2 (BC 180); cf. also Apol. 12, 65, 116, 118 (BC 191, 199-200) and CA 12, 10 (BC 50).
32. Cf. especially Apol. 12, 39-43 (BC 187).
33. Cf. especially Apol. 12, 116-117 (BC 199-200).
34. Schwab, *op. cit.,* p. 129.
35. Immenkötter 107.
36. Apol. 12, 60, Latin (BSLK 263; CT 266-267); cf. also Apol. 12, 35, 44, 54 (BSLK 258, 259-260, 261-262; CT 260, 261, 264).
37. Apol. 12, 36, 52 (BC 186, 189; BSLK 258; 261; CT 260, 264).
38. Apol. 12, 8, 36 (BC 183, 186; BSLK 254, 261; CT 254, 260).
39. Apol. 12, 44ff. (BSLK 259-260; CT 262-263).
40. Apol. 12, 52 (BSLK 261, CT 264).
41. Apol. 12, 39 (BC 187; for the Latin text see BSLK 259 or CT 260).
42. Apol. 12, 39 (BC 187). Cf. Apol. 12, 42: *"Ita fides concipitur et confirmatur per absolutionem, per auditum evangelii, per usum sacramentorum"* (BSLK 259; CT 262).
43. Apol. 12, 43 (BSLK 259; CT 262; for Eng. trans. see BC 187).
44. Apol. 12, 61, Latin (BSLK 263-264; CT 268; for Eng. trans. see BC 190).
45. Apol. 12, 132, 163 (BSLK 280, 287; CT 290-291, 302).
46. Apol. 12, 53 (BSLK 261; CT 264; for Eng. trans. see BC 189).
47. Apol. 12, 59 (BC 190; for the Latin text see BSLK 263 or CT 266). On the understanding of *opus operatum* rejected here, cf. Pfnür, *op. cit.,* pp. 45-77.
48. Apol. 12, 60 (BC 190); cf. especially also Apol. 12, 91-93 (BC 195-196).
49. Cf. CA 12, 3-5, Latin (BSLK 67; CT 48; for Eng. trans. see BC 34); cf. also Apol. 12, 35, German or Latin (BSLK 258; CT 260).
50. *Concilium Tridentium,* vol. 7/1, p. 296, 11. 37-41; p. 308, 1. 31.

51. Cf. Apol. 12, 98 (BC 197; BSLK 272; CT 280) and CA 12 (BC 34-35; BSLK 66-67; CT 48). Luther and the Confessions emphatically demand a holistic understanding of the act of penance, in which the internal self-accusation before God (*accusatio sui* in sorrow and trusting faith) is not separated from its concrete expression in external penitential acts; cf. Luther's strong attack in the Smalcald Articles against the dismemberment and splitting up of penance (BC 304ff., 308-309). In this holistic view the so-called "three parts" of penance (contrition, confession, and satisfaction which is equivalent to renewal and improvement of life or "fruits of repentance") are integrated into the unity of the fundamentally single act of penance (cf. Smalcald Articles, BC 308-309).

52. CA 25, 13 (BC 63; for the Latin text see BSLK 99-100 or CT 70).

53. Apol. 12, 99 (BC 197; for the Latin text see BSLK 272 or CT 280); cf. Apol. 11, 2 (BC 180).

54. W. Maurer, *Historischer Kommentar zur Confessio Augustana,* vol. 2 (Gütersloh: 1979), p. 198.

55. CA 2 (BC 61ff.) and Apol. 11, 3 (BC 180).

56. BC 198.

57. BC 209; for the Latin text see BSLK 289 or CT 304.

58. Cf. also Apol. 12, 95 (BC 196).

59. Cf. especially Apol. 12, 116-123, 131, 138 (BC 199-200, 202, 203).

60. Apol. 12, 140, 146-147. (BC 204-205).

61. CA 12, 6; Apol. 12, 174 (BC 35; 210).

62. Apol. 12, 131, 148 (BC 202, 205).

63. Apol. 12, 45-46, 164, 169-170. (BC 187-188, 208, 209).

64. Apol. 12, 168 (BC 209; for the Latin text see BSLK 288 or CT 304).

65. Apol. 12, 163-164 (BC 208).

66. Apol. 12, 28 (BC 185; here we have translated *"poenitentia"* as "repentance" as the context seems to demand). Cf. Apol. 12, 45 (BC 187-188).

67. Apol. 12, 58 (BSLK 262; CT 266; for the Eng. trans. see BC 189-190). Cf. Apol. 12, 131 (BC 202).

68. Apol. 4, 349-350, 353 (BC 160-161).

69. Apol. 12, 148 (BSLK 284; CT 298; for Tappert's translation, from which we depart sharply, see BC 205).

70. Apol. 12, 139, 164, 174 (BC 203-204, 208, 210).

71. In this context it must be noted that the corresponding expressions of the Council of Trent about the imposition of penance and absolution (Session 14, especially canon 15 with the chapter connected with it; DS 1715, cf. 1692) do not present a dogmatic definition and, as should have become clear in the preceding, do not exactly apply to the position of the CA and Apology.

72. On this cf. especially Karl Rahner, *Theological Investigations,* vol. 10 (London: Farton, Longman, and Todd, 1973), pp. 150-198. Here Rahner also presents a theological interpretation of "indulgence" with which even evangelical Christians could agree. Cf. also Vorgrimler, *op. cit.,* pp. 212-214. On the contemporary official teaching of the church of the doctrine of indulgences see *Apostolische Konstitution "Indulgentiarum doctrina",* in AAS 59 (1967):5-24; Latin and German text in *Nach-*

konziliare Dokumentation, vol. 2 (Trier: 1967), pp. 72-127, with a commentary by O. Semmelroth, *ibid.*, pp. 51-71. Indulgences are briefly mentioned only in CA 25, 6, German (BC 62) in connection with the rejected meritorious understanding of satisfaction, without more detailed treatment.

73. BSLK 255; CT 256.

74. *Glossa ad Decr. Grat. De paenitentia* d. 5, c. 1: "*Sed melius dicitur eam (sc. oris confessionem) institutam fuisse a quadam universalis ecclesiae traditione potius quam ex novi vel veteris testamenti auctoritate. Et traditio ecclesiae obligatoria est us praeceptum . . . ergo necessaria est confessio in mortalibus apud nos; apud Graecos non: quia non emanavit apud illos traditio talis.*" *Decretum Gratiani . . . una cum Glossis* (Rome: 1582), p. 2363.

75. CA 25, 12 (BSLK 99; CT 70; for Eng. trans. see BC 63).

76. Cf. *Defensio* (WA 2, 645) and *De capt. Babyl.* (AE 36, 86-87; WA 6, 546).

77. Cf. Hans Jorissen, "*Die Begründung der Eucharistie im nachösterlichen Offenbarungsgeschehen,*" in Hans Georg Geyer, ed., *Freispruch und Freiheit: Festschrift Walter Kreck* (Münich: 1973), pp. 206-228. Cf. also K. Rahner, *op. cit.,* vol. 14, pp. 135-136.

78. Bernard Lohse, "*Die Privatbeichte bei Luther,*" KuD 14 (1968):224.

79. Apol. 12, 99 (BC 197); for the text, see section 2.5.1 above.

80. Karl-Josef Becker, "*Die Notwendigkeit des vollständigen Bekenntnisses in der Beichte nach dem Konzil von Trient,*" ThPh 47 (1972): 161-228, especially pp. 221-224.

81. CA 12, 1-2, 7-9 (BC 34-35). Cf. Luther's corresponding expressions: Sins should be confessed "that are manifestly [*manifeste*] mortal sins" (WA 1, 329) and "we can readily call to mind" (AE 36, 85; WA 6, 545); cf. AE 36, 86; WA 6, 546), which "gnaw and oppress the conscience" (WA 8, 182). Cf. also the introduction to confession in the Small Catechism (BC 349-351). Schwabach Articles 11 (BSLK 66, 1): "which bite the heart and make it restless." On the concept of "mortal sin" in Luther and Melanchthon, cf. Pfnür, *op. cit.,* pp. 182-193.

82. H. Becker, "*Die Notwendigkeit,*" *loc. cit.,* p. 219.

83. Cf. Peter Manns, in *Amt und Eucharistie* (Paderborn: 1973), p. 107, note 10-11; p. 26, note 118. On lay confession cf. also Hans Jorissen, "*Beichte oder Busse?*" in Karl Delahaye, Erwin Gatz, and Hans Jorissen, eds., *Bestellt zum Zeugnis: Festgabe für Bischof Pohlschneider* (Aachen: 1974), pp. 224-225.

84. CA 25, 10 (BC 63). The Council of Trent defined priestly absolution as *actus iudicialis* in can. 9, sess. 14 (DS 1709). Thereby *nothing* was decided about whether this was to be understood as an act of judging in a professional technical sense or (corresponding to the character of the sacrament as a disposition toward the *beneficium mortis Christi,* DS 1668, and the character of absolution as *alieni beneficii dispensatio,* DS 1685) as a royal act of pardon, i.e., one authoritatively addressed toward the individual. Although the question remains open, the latter interpretation seems to be more appropriate. For the understanding of absolution as an *actus iudicialis* is an understanding of absolution in the sense—expressly

rejected in can. 9—of a *nudum ministerium pronuntiandi et declarandi. remissa esse peccata confitenti*, i.e., in the sense of a mere declaratory understanding. This rejection does not apply at all to the position of the CA and the Apology. Can. 9, with its statement about the *actus iudicialis*, intends primarily to defend the efficacy of absolution. Cf. also Becker, *"Die Notwendigkeit,"* *loc cit.*, pp. 212, 219.

85. Apol. 12, 103 (BC 197; for the Latin text see BSLK 273 or CT 280). The CA and the Apology (and Luther too) recognized in addition to the loosing power (absolution) also the binding power of the keys; (twofold power of the keys; cf. Matt. 16:19; 18:18; John 20:23). However, unlike the strongly juridical view of the opposing theory they are attacking, the binding is not related to the imposition of atoning penalties *(satisfactiones; poenae)*. Based on Matt. 16:19, it is rather related to the "not loosing" of sins, to the reproving *(arguere)*, and to the exclusion *(excommunicare)* of the impenitent (CA 28, 5, 21 [BC 81, 84; BSLK 121, 124; CT 84, 86]; Apol. 12, 138, 176 [BC 203, 210; BSLK 281, 290-291; CT 292, 306]). But otherwise, "God's command is that the ministers of the gospel *(ministri evangelii)* absolve those who are converted, according to the statement (2 Cor. 10:8), 'Our authority, which the Lord gave for building you up.' " (Apol. 12, 176 [BC 210; BSLK 291; CT 306]; cf. CA 12, 2, 5 [BC 34-35; BSLK 66-67; CT 48]).

86. CA 11, 1, German (BC 34).

87. CA 25, 7ff. (BC 62-63); Apol. 11, 6ff. (BC 181-182); Apol. 12, 11 (BC 184); Apol. 12, 102-103 (BC 197).

88. CA 25, 9, German (BC 62-63); cf. Apol. 11, 8 (BC 181).

89. Cf. Becker, *"Die Notwendigkeit,"* *loc. cit.*, pp. 204-205.

90. Immenkötter 103-104.

91. Cf. Apol. 11, 1-2 (BC 180).

92. Apol. 11, 7, 9 (BC 181-182); cf. Apol. 7, 32 (BC 174).

93. Apol. 11, 7-8 (BC 181; for the Latin text see BSLK 251 or CT 250).

94. Apol. 11, 9 (BC 181-182); cf. Apol. 12, 12 (BC 184).

95. BSLK 249, 11; cf. BSLK 326, 11.

96. Cf. Pfnür, *op. cit.*, pp. 264, 267-268. H. Immenkötter, *Um die Einheit im Glauben: Die Unionsverhandlungen des Augsburger Reichstages im August und September 1530* (2nd ed.; Münster; 1974), p. 41.

97. Cf. Apol. 11, 1-2; Apol. 12, 3-4, 35-36, 39-43, 98-101 (BC 180; 182-183, 186-187, 197).

98. Apol. 11, 6-8, 10; Apol. 12, 11-12, 23, 102, 110-111 (BC 181-182; 184f-185, 197ff.).

99. Becker, *"Die Notwendigkeit,"* *loc. cit.*, p. 205.

100. Apol. 12, 11-12 (BC 184; for the Latin text see BSLK, 255 or CT 254-255).

101. Apol. 12, 110-111 (BC 198; we have departed from Tappert's translation of *"facta illa scrupulosa enumeratione"* as simply "enumerating"; for the Latin text see BSLK 274 or CT 284).

102. CA 25, 10 (BC 63).

103. Hubert Jedin, *"La nécessité de la confession privée selon le Concile de Trente,"* *La Maison-Dieu* 104 (1970):115.

104. Immenkötter 175-176.

105. Becker, *"Die Notwendigkeit,"* loc. cit., p. 205.
106. W. Pannenberg, *"Die Augsburgische Konfession als katholisches Bekenntnis,"* in H. Meyer, H. Schütte, and H. J. Mund, eds., *Katholische Anerkennung des Augsburgischen Bekenntnisses?* (Frankfurt: 1977), p. 33.
107. Apol. 12, 1-11 (BC 182-184).
108. Pfnür, *op. cit.,* pp. 264-268; Immenkötter, *Einheit im Glauben,* pp. 41-42.
109. *Concilium Tridentinum,* vol. 7/1, pp. 233-234.
110. Pfnür, *op. cit.,* pp. 266-267; Immenkötter, *Einheit im Glauben,* p. 42.
111. Pannenberg, *"Die Augsburgische Konfession,"* loc. cit., p. 33.
112. Large Catechism, A Brief Exhortation to Confession, 34 (BC 461).

10

The Cult of the Saints

by Georg Kretschmar and René Laurentin

translated by Ralph Gehrke

1. The Origin of the Article

1. The veneration of the saints was not originally one of the central topics under dispute in the 16th century, at least not for the Wittenberg Reformation. Luther wrote in his 1528 "Augsburg Confession in connection with the exposition of the Third Article, as an appendix to the question of prayer for the dead, "The invocation of the saints is something that others attacked before I did. And I am also happy to believe that Christ alone is to be invoked as our mediator. That is scriptural and is certain. The Scripture says nothing about invoking the saints; therefore it must be uncertain and is not to be believed." [1] Taken as a whole, that is also the import of the appendix Luther added in his own handwriting to the section on the Mass in the Smalcald Articles in December 1536, an appendix which, to be sure, also takes into consideration the 1530 discussions at Augsburg. It was preceded by a more sharply defined paragraph which was added by the Wittenberg Theological Commission that examined these articles at the end of 1536 and the beginning of 1537, calling the invocation of the saints one of the

"abuses of the Antichrist." Luther approved the addition and it was
included in the official text (Part 2, Article 3, 25-28).[2] Neither the
Schwabach nor the Marburg Articles had treated the subject; because it
was not a fundamental part of Christian faith, it did not seem necessary
to treat it in texts which were directed to the South Germans or the
Swiss, with whom there seemed to be no disagreement on this question.

2. Yet no matter how the dogmatic importance of the conflict is
evaluated, the veneration of the saints had assumed such an important
place not only in the medieval worship but also in practical piety (and
even in ecclesiastical law) that taking a position toward it in the second
half of the '20s was unavoidable. The topic, therefore, often occurs in
the Church Orders; also the *Instruction for the Visitations in Electoral
Saxony,* which Melanchthon composed in 1527 and which Luther
examined, contains a rather long paragraph about the veneration of
the saints at the end of the chapter "On Human Church Order." [3] In
line with the purpose of this document, the point is not the removal of
abuses but a positive exposition of the correct way of revering the
saints. In preparation for the Diet of Augsburg in 1530 the electoral
court prompted its theologians to prepare a defense of the innovations
that had resulted from the visitations, i.e., a defense of the specific
ecclesiastical reforms in Saxony. These *Torgau Articles* became the ante-
cedents of the second part of the CA. In a later phase of their elaboration, one for which Melanchthon was responsible, they contain a section
on the veneration of the saints.[4] Accordingly the topic stands in the
context of the complex of "Abuses That Have Been Corrected." During
the continued elaboration at Augsburg itself, however, it was omitted
by Melanchthon from "The Articles on Matters Under Dispute," [5] and
appears instead among "The Articles of Doctrine" in Part One. As is
well known, Luther still sharply criticized this shift on July 21st and
attributed it to Magister Philippus' pussyfooting.[6] But this explanation
is not very convincing; at least it is not sufficient. Obviously Melanchthon was concerned in the Augsburg Confession, as he had been in the
Instruction for the Visitations, primarily with promoting a correct
stance toward the saints, and was convinced that here he was in agreement with the orthodox church of all ages. These doctrinal statements
were later developed in the Apology in opposition to the Confutation.
Here Melanchthon went back to the initial points that occurred already
in the Visitation Articles; both texts ought therefore to be consulted
when CA 21 is being explained.

That we are here dealing with a topic of doctrine is clear from the placement of the article in the structure of the confession. Shortly before June 15 it had been placed ahead of the later Article 20, the tract on "Faith and Good Works" [7]; but finally it was placed after it. That the saints are examples in faith and good works is the red thread that runs through all of Melanchthon's statements after 1527. But, as we shall see, he was saying more than that. In any case the CA places the proper veneration of the saints in the context of the doctrine of justification and of Christian ethics. Also, the rejection of false worship of the saints is connected with justification, as is more clearly elaborated in Apol. 21, 14ff. (BC, 230-231) than in CA 21, and as is likewise in keeping with the perspective of those who treat special abuses under this rubric: the opponents of the Reformation position are accused of viewing the saints as mediators and propitiators who take the place of Christ on the basis of the merits that they have gained.

In the negotiations in Augsburg on the 16th and 17th of August, in which positions were compared, the chief question was whether there was a biblical basis for invoking the saints and angels as intercessors before God.[8] Luther received detailed reports at the Coburg on these disputations—even though this information reached him only after decisions had been made in Augsburg. He took a position on all of this as late as September 1530 in two writings.[9] In the foreground again stands the rejection of abuses in invoking the saints; indirectly, however, one learns something of how the reformer himself dealt with the figures he had in mind when he used the category "saints."

3. From this it follows that the wording of CA 21 was fixed only later, after June 15, when Charles V entered Augsburg. It is particularly this article which addresses the emperor directly and advises him in his war against the Turks to refer to the example of King David.[10] The two versions of the confession differ from one another; the German is more extensive than the Latin. Melanchthon practically rewrote the article anew in the *Variata* of 1540. In it he dealt no longer with the cult of saints ("service of the saints" according to the German version), but with their invocation. The point under dispute in August 1530 has become the real topic. Such invocation is of course condemned; but that it is worthwhile to read historically reliable stories about pious people is conceded at the very end in a codicil. But in 1542 Melanchthon again abandoned this version. Apparently it appeared to him to be insufficient and merely polemical. The new version, the final formulation which he gave to CA 21, returns to the positive approaches of 1527 and 1530 and elaborates them, since viewpoints were now intro-

duced which the Augsburg Confession did not yet include but which were included for the first time in its *Apology*.[11] Curiously, the Greek translation of 1559 follows the German version of 1530, also no doubt because it is fuller than the more succinct Latin text and therefore more understandable to Greek Christians.[12]

2. Background

1. The dispute about invoking the saints as well as the doctrinal statements of CA 21 are understandable only against the background of medieval liturgical practice and piety. Of course the veneration of the saints is a heritage from the ancient church.[13] If we understand the saints as the members of the people of God who have died, whom various churches or regions regularly remember in public worship, then we can begin by saying that this conception was present at the end of the fourth century. Such a description is, of course, only an attempt at formulating the conviction which was implicit in the calendars and prayers of that day about the relation of the church in the heavenly realm to the church on earth. In fact, neither the ancient nor the medieval church defined who the saints were; neither did Melanchthon in CA 21. What veneration of the saints means can really be attested only from liturgical traditions and from reports about piety and legal practice. Conflicts about excesses in the cult of the martyrs and other saints occurred already in the fourth and fifth centuries. But we know of no conflict in connection with the elaboration of the concept itself. The practice of remembering martyrs at their graves certainly goes back to the second century. In Asia Minor already in the first century Christians may well have cared for the places where the apostolic witnesses of the earliest period awaited their resurrection. But it was a long way from here to the cult of the saints at the end of the fourth century. And the Middle Ages were to introduce a number of genuinely new features.

2. One of these was that church buildings, and later, individual altars, were routinely dedicated to saints, a practice which was usually strengthened by the transfer of relics to these places. As propriators and guardians, the saints thus protected church property from the grasp of the powerful in society.[14] Also, they were patrons of specific areas of life, like certain vocations, cities, and countries. As saints for specific days they regulated the flow of the year. Thus they left their imprint on daily life. One may understand this as an expression of that mutual

interpenetration of church and society that was so characteristic of the Middle Ages. The Wittenberg reformers did not view this, in retrospect, in a positive light, but as endangering the very center of the Christian faith. Luther wrote at the Coburg, "It was for me personally a difficult thing to tear myself from the saints, because I had been extremely involved in this and had in fact almost drowned in it." [15] He gave reasons for this in the same connection: "First of all, you ought to know that under the papacy we not only learned that the saints in heaven pray for us—which is something we cannot know for sure because Scripture does not tell us—but also we learned that they were to be made into divinities, that they were supposed to be our patrons whom we were to invoke, including some who never existed. Each saint had a special power and authority; one over fire, one over water, one over pestilence, fever, and all plagues, so that God himself had to be inactive and let the saints work and act in his place." [16] This biographical recollection is accurate, as it attested by the Wittenberg reformer's writings and sermons until 1523.[17] Also his polemical statements about life "under the papacy" describe widespread customs of popular piety which were not sharply separated from ecclesiastical practice and which were too deeply embedded in theology to be put aside as mere superstitions. That this does not uncover everything that is to be said on the topic of "the saints in the Middle Ages" is something Luther also knew. But every form of invocation of the saints, even his own attempts before 1523 to hold God and his saints together without idolatory, now appeared to him to be indefensible.

The combination of the invocation of the saints and the cult of relics also extends back into the ancient church. The desire to be certain of salvation through the perceptible nearness of the divine accelerated the growth of the practice of collecting relics in the late Middle Ages. Clear examples of this were the relics Frederick the Wise had collected in the Castle Church; here too we can see the connection with the traffic in indulgences.[18] The exhibition of these relics on All Saints Day, 1517, is part of the historical context of the 95 theses, which Luther had completed on the vigil of that feast and whose publication initiated the conflict on indulgences, and with it the Reformation movement in Germany.

The medieval West was acquainted with very different types of saints; great rulers and warriors and princesses were numbered among the *sancti* (saints) after their death, along with scholars, bishops, and monks. Common to all of them was the ascetic feature, often added subsequently in legendary form, but indisputably also an important aspect of their life; at least this stands out clearly from Gothic times on.[19] From the Reformation viewpoint this moved them into the circle of "self-chosen piety."

The naming of holy women and men in public worship appeared also to be qualified by the above-mentioned aspects of the cult of the saints; for the Wittenberg Reformation, however, it was also thereby disqualified—at least in its previous formulation. In the canon of the Mass individual names were recited as representatives of "all of God's saints," and then mention was made of their "merits" and "prayers"— with the qualification, however, that God should "respect their merits and prayers, so that we may be preserved in all things by the aid of his (God's) protection." In any case the invocation of the saints in litanies permitted them to appear as patrons and intercessors, whose number was infinitely great and who, together with the angels, fill the space between Christians on earth and the triune God. The heightened piety of the late Middle Ages let the exaggerated features of the world of the saints stand forth even more boldly as mediators of salvation.

3. This description certainly does not reveal the full scope of medieval piety. In liturgically-ordered worship the ancient church's structure of prayer continued to be the norm; prayer is directed to God "through our Lord Jesus Christ (. . . *per dominum nostrum Jesum Christum, qui . . .),*" something to which Melanchthon specifically referred in the Apology.[20] In fact, it was in the late Middle Ages that a type of piety existed which directed itself entirely to Christ and put his suffering at its center. Thus a basis for gaining control of unrestricted abuses in the cult of the saints was available, which could and did become effective, also outside the Reformation.[21]

But, to repeat, in spite of the significance of the veneration of the saints in the Middle Ages, at no place do we encounter dogmatic definitions before the 16th century. They are not to be found in expositions of the phrase in the Apostles' Creed, "the communion of saints *(sanctorum communionem),*" not even when it was taken with a personal meaning as in apposition to "the holy catholic church" and as expressing a connection with the heavenly world.[22] The first attempt in the West at formulating what is meant by the veneration of the saints in doctrinal terms is indeed found in CA 21. Melanchthon proceeded from the fact that, despite all abuses and perversions, there exists a common conviction about a legitimate cult of the saints, and that conviction is in accord with the gospel.

3. The Doctrinal Statements of CA 21

1. This article deals with the "Cult of the Saints" (*"de cultu sanc-torum,"* in German, "On the Service of the Saints"). In place of that expression Melanchthon spoke in the *Instruction to the Visitors* and later in the Apology of "honoring" the saints. What Melanchthon had in mind was not only the position of the saints in worship but in the entire breadth of daily life, especially in those areas where the saints had been believed to have been actively engaged. But they are not to be invoked; instead they are to be remembered. This seems to mean the same as the Torgau Articles when they speak of "their serving to re-mind us." The goal of "their reminding us" is described briefly and succinctly in the CA's Latin text as "to imitate their faith and good works according to our calling." The visitation article and the Torgau text spoke of "the example of the saints." But the German version of the CA develops a bit more fully the significance which the saints have for faith as examples and so deepens the statement; looking to the saints strengthens our faith because we see "what grace they received and how they were sustained by faith." This must be understood, as it had been formulated in the Visitation Articles, not as consolation based on the experience of success of God's people in the past; rather "just as Peter and Paul and other saints with our flesh and blood and weak-ness were saved by God's grace through faith, thus we receive the comfort through these examples that God will bear with our weakness and pardon us, if we, like them, trust, believe, and call on him in our weakness." Precisely the fact that the saints are not heavenly persons but humans as we, helps us believe in the God who justifies the ungodly. Although the scripture passage itself is not cited, it seems likely that we are to think of the "cloud of witnesses" of Hebrews 11; at any rate Melanchthon cited Heb. 13:7 in the *Instruction to the Visitors.*[23]

Reference to the Articles of Visitation helps clarify how the reference to the example of the saints is to be understood in relation to their respective callings. As it stands, it still contains the rejected medieval conception that the saints can be patrons of specific callings; at the same time, however, holiness is moved from the realm of monastic asceticism and placed into the worldly service in which God has placed each one. This is a conscious adoption of Luther's vocation ethic and is certainly more important than the concrete example in which King David is mentioned as the specific model for the Emperor Charles in his war against the Turks. Moreover, the German text is also in this case much more extensive and clarifies what was involved in such warfare: the office of a king demands that he protect his subjects. The example is, nevertheless, a bit troublesome because a contemporary example was therewith introduced which later was not to be sustained. At that time, any rate, the signers of the CA thus defended themselves against the charge that they refused to serve the emperor in the war against the Turks. Similarly in the Visitation Articles, in connection with 1 Peter 3:5-6, women are referred to the example of their mother Sarah: here the family is their God-given station. Though this exhortation cannot be transposed unchanged into contemporary instruction, it corroborates the fact that the example of the saints is aimed primarily at strengthening us in daily life, since daily life is the place in the world where God has put Christians.

All the examples Melanchthon used show that by "saints" he understood first of all biblical persons, the fathers and mothers of the Old and New Testaments. Obviously they are exclusively people of the past, people who have died and whom we can only remember.

But this is not all that Melanchthon means. In the *Apology* he makes it clear that such remembering always takes place in the presence of God: we honor the saints by thanking God for having showed in them examples of that mercy of his which is directed toward rescuing humans. This thanks includes the praise of the saints themselves, those who have faithfully used God's gifts, as indeed Christ also praises his faithful servants (Matt. 25:21, 23). Thus "the saints" also include teachers of the church and other postbiblical persons who can be understood as God's gifts to his church (cf. most likely Eph. 4:7ff.). Only after that is reference made to other ways in which to honor the saints: "letting ourselves be strengthened in faith" and following them with good works in our callings (*Apol.* 21, 4-7 [BC, 229-230]). Saints who are praised in Christendom as faithful servants of Christ are not only figures of the past who are remembered, and their work is not only a matter of history. Perhaps one grasps Melanchthon's point better if one formulates it in reverse: to relate oneself rightly to the history of salvation and the history of the church is the proper veneration of the saints. Such a relationship with history and with the saints can only occur *coram Deo,* in the presence of God. This is what "serving the saints" means in everyday life and in worship.

2. The invocation of the saints is something entirely different. It is a false service of the saints. This position is supported by arguments

that go in two directions: (1) Scripture knows nothing of such *invocatio;* (2) on the contrary, it shows us Christ as sole mediator, propitiator, high priest, and intercessor.

"Invocation" *("invocatio")* means prayer that is directed to a specific saint or perhaps to a group of saints, in order to "seek help" from them, a prayer which seeks to move them to intercede with God or Christ.[24] This is to be clearly distinguished from "praising the saints" in God's presence. The emphasis in the reference to Scripture is on the positive argument that only calling on Christ has God's promise. What is stressed is not so much that a prayer to saints diminishes Christ's honor, but that such praying is on the wrong track, i.e., it misses God's relation to us in Christ. The *Apology* clarifies (21, 15): persons who cling to such invocation "suppose that Christ is more severe and the saints more approachable. . . . Thus they actually make them mediators of redemption."[25] What is thus put aside is the *Confutation's* theological distinction between Christ as the sole mediator of salvation *(mediator redemptionis)* and the many mediators of prayer *(mediatores intercessionis).*[26] Here prayer-mediation and salvation-mediation belong together. It is the *Apology* which will for the first time make specific reference to the doctrine of the merits of the saints as the basis of their mediatorship and, naturally, reject it *(Apol.* 21, 14-15, 29-30 [BC 230-231, 233]).

In the intervening discussion at Augsburg (mentioned above, p. 264) the question at stake was whether there were scriptural attestations of intercession by angels or saints. Here Melanchthon was very open to persuasion.[27] But that angels and saints pray for the church never establishes that we should invoke them as patrons *(Apol.* 21, 10-11 [BC 230]). At this point the discussions broke off. The fact that the Confutators were not prepared to abandon even the unquestionably obvious abuses embittered Melanchthon *(Apol.* 21, 39 [BC 235]) and explains the subsequent broad enumeration of such practices and disastrous preaching, an enumeration developed under the general notion that pious folk were ever and again misled by foolish or covetous monks to invoke the saints, to go on pilgrimages, to venerate relics of the saints. This attempt to trace the origin of the false veneration of the saints (an attempt which is, of course, impossible in historical terms) is nevertheless in keeping with the firm conviction that such veneration is a historically late innovation (a fact which is well attested); whoever therefore rejects and removes such invocation of the saints returns to Scripture and to the ancient church.

4. Liturgical Practice

Article 21 of the Augsburg Confession expresses a broad consensus of theological conviction by the Wittenberg Reformers. This can be shown for Luther, but for many others as well. It is also true of Melanchthon's positive doctrinal statements.[28] The Church Orders also confirm this. At first polemics against the invocation of the saints occurred in them here and there; but later this topic disappeared; the practice had obviously disappeared. The traditional saints' days for the biblical saints continued, however, to be celebrated.[29] Moreover, Bugenhagen's Church Orders enable us to see that such a limitation to biblical saints was not compelling; in all three of the cities involved, the day of St. Lawrence continued to be observed with a reference to Ambrose's praise of him. In Braunschweig the day of the local patron St. Autor was modified so that, instead of the saint, God was thanked for protecting the city; but in Hamburg and Lübeck the preacher of the day was to exhort the people on the Sunday after the anniversary of St. Ansgar's death "to thank God through Christ most heartily for the first revelation of the name of Christ in these territories and in the good city by Willehad, Bishop Ansgar, and other pious people who were sent here to preach to the heathen." [30] Also the Feast of All Saints continued to be celebrated in many regions, especially in Scandinavia. Luther's German version of the Te Deum continued this: "The twelve apostles praise you, and all the faithful prophets; all the noble martyrs raise their voices to you in songs of praise. All Christendom on earth glorifies you unceasingly."

In contrast to the Middle Ages, the saints have here moved to the edge of piety. Faith deals only with the Triune God. But the heavenly world of those members of God's people who have been perfected indicates the goal of the Christians' earthly pilgrimage, and already now the praise of God in the church militant on earth joins their hymn of praise. Biblical figures from the New Testament are proclaimed as examples of God's gracious activity on the traditional days of commemoration (Mary Magdalene included!); remembrance is also made of the apostles as being, above all, witnesses to the gospel. In the age of religious wars especially those saints of the earlier church who had contended for the true faith moved into the foreground. This chain was not terminated but led to anniversary celebrations of events of the Reformation. Though it was not thought about in the categories of the old hagiography, Luther himself became a saint as a witness to the faith and as a church Father.[31] This in itself is already "a venerating of the saints," being mindful of them in God's presence without invoking them in prayer.

5. Critical Evaluation

1. If the teaching and practice of the Wittenberg Reformation with regard to persons who had traditionally been called saints is to be evaluated, it would be in keeping with the Reformation understanding to consider its scriptural basis. That it became customary in the church after the 3rd-5th centuries to speak of departed members of God's people as *hagioi* (holy ones) or *sancti* (saints) is even linguistically understandable only on the basis of the Old Testament, especially of the Psalter, where God and the saints are always mentioned together (Pss. 16:3; 21:4 [LXX]; 68:36 [LXX]; 89:6). Whether these Old Testament *aedoshim* referred originally to angelic beings or to humans on earth, it is fitting that Christians understand such expressions in the light of the Lord's saying about the resurrection from the dead as it is given in Mark's gospel: "Have you not read in the book of Moses, in the passage about the bush, how God said to him, 'I am the God of Abraham, and the God of Isaac, and the God of Jacob' (Exod. 3:6)? He is not God of the dead, but of the living" (Mark 12:26). Luke added, "For all (the dead) live to him (Luke 20:38)."

If God condescends to be characterized by human names, and if the history of God's people is shaped by such names because of the election and mercy of God, then it is appropriate for us to remember them. And what is legitimate for the fathers and mothers of the Old Testament is no less appropriate for the people of God which gathers about the confession of Christ.

2. In the history of the Christian veneration of the saints, the Reformation marks a turning point insofar as "the saints" ceased to be demigods, or even divine figures, such as medieval piety often made them. They became human beings again.[32] This tendency certainly was in keeping with humanism's discovery of historical criticism. The demand that fictitious, unverifiable figures be removed from the lists of saints had been heard already in the ancient church,[33] and it is also self-evident in the contemporary Roman Catholic Church, which has recently sharply pruned its calendar of saints for this reason.[34] This demand is legitimate; indeed it is necessary, because in the case of the saints we are dealing not with ciphers for experiences of salvation nor with starting

points for edifying narratives, but with persons from the history of God's people.

This demand does, of course, encounter limits when the history of the people of God has been elaborated by means of biblical names which are not comprehensible for us in the same historical sense as are the men and women of church history. Jesus Christ does not cease to be the new Adam as the apostle Paul interprets him (Romans 5; 1 Corinthians 15) if Adam is no longer comprehensible for us as an individual person. Therefore the name *Adam* can also be named in prayer directed to God. This is especially the case with Abraham, Isaac, and Jacob. Precisely when we investigate the origin of the veneration of the saints, we come upon marginal areas in which our normal categories are inadequate. This certainly has nothing to do with confessional differences between our churches.

3. If the saints have their place in history and with God, their remembrance is not dependent on relics. It is natural and in keeping with the matter with which we are dealing that traces of their lives in our midst (graves, memorials, momentos) remind us of God's work in and through these men and women. Church history knows of experiences of the spiritual force of such signs and also of relics; there may be theological traditions and cultic practices which even incorporate particles of saints' bones in an appropriate manner as they are remembered before God. However, here also there are dangers and limits, theologically and on the level of what is humane (when certain ways of treating relics appear to us as lacking in piety).[35] Legitimate veneration of the saints is not bound to the cult of relics. Also the Council of Trent did indeed defend the legitimacy of such practices which the Reformation rejected, but it did not make them obligatory.[36]

4. In the Smalcald Articles Luther accented matters differently than Melanchthon had in CA 21 and in the *Apology*. He expressed the opinion that once the abuse of invoking angels or saints as patrons (something that contradicts the honor of God) was removed, then all further veneration of the saints would sink into oblivion, for "When spiritual and physical benefit and help are no longer expected, the saints will cease to be molested in their graves and in heaven, for no one will long remember, esteem, or honor them out of love when there is no expectation of return" (SA 2, 28 [BC 297]).[37] No matter whether this was said with sarcasm or with resignation (for as long as he lived Luther, despite everything, knew himself to be close to the saints),[38] he was largely right: without the invocation of the saints, their remembrance lived on

in evangelical piety only here and there. To evaluate this development critically does not mean abandoning Melanchthon's distinction between "veneration" and "invocation," the most important dogmatic judgment of this article of the Augsburg Confession. But a criticism of this development can include questions about the theological framework in this article for establishing what is veneration of the saints. The following three lines of questioning seem necessary:

5. That God is the God of the living and not of the dead, because they all live in him, not only underlines a basic aspect of all ecclesiology; this promise belongs to the basis of the church. The people of God have a unity not merely in the empirical present; but they include, as Hebrews explains, the wandering band of mothers and fathers in the faith from Old Testament times to Judgment Day. The Apostles' Creed's "communion of saints *(sanctorum communio)*" is referred by CA 7 to the one church that "will always continue *(ecclesia perpetua mansura),*" which is gathered through word and sacrament. That this *communio* includes also the *sancti in patria* ("the saints in their homeland," as the Middle Ages liked to describe the saints in heaven), is certainly presupposed in CA 7 (though not elaborated, since there was actually no reason for doing that). On the other hand, the article on the veneration of the saints does not speak of its ecclesial-eschatological context. A. F. C. Vilmar wrote in 1853, "The subject matter which is at both the center and in all parts of what we are dealing with here, the relation of the this-worldly world of faith to the saints in Paradise (or better, in the state of complete blessedness in heaven), has not yet been exhausted either by the Augsburg Confession or by the Confutation or by the Apology; and indeed, it could not be exhausted at that time, because a doctrine of the church was rather far removed from both parties." [39] This thesis provides important pointers, no matter how one evaluates the philosophy-of-history context in which it is presented.

As noted above, communion with the saints in heaven, especially with the biblical ones, appears to be more casual in Luther as he deals with Scripture and history than in Melanchthon.[40] This topic points to problems and tasks which are burning issues today, though they were not yet such in the 16th century. Among them is a new question in the secularized societies of Europe and of North America concerning death and of personal human existence. In other cultures there is the as-yet-uncompleted related task that arises because of confrontation with the cult of ancestors and with animism.[41] Our Lord's promise, "all live to him," frees people from anxieties and opens up their horizons. The certainty that grows from this promise dares to and should take concrete form in prayer; for those who live in him are those who praise him; they live in the praise of the true God. It is particularly the Lord's Supper which has fostered the conviction that the church on earth joins in the hymn of praise with the church of all ages.[42] In Lutheran congregations too the heavenly host's threefold cry of "Holy, holy, holy" has not ceased during eucharistic service.

6. The certitude that God's encompassing promise has broken through what experience tells us is possible makes questionable too close an identification of holiness and "calling." To be sure, Christian ethics is concerned with strengthening life in the world; however, we are to do this not only by fitting ourselves into existing structures but also by breaking through, extending, and transforming them. If it is through humans that God opens up new paths for following Christ, then it is not enough (and is indeed contrary to the Reformation) to speak of "homemade" holiness, as examples let the names of Francis of Assisi and of Dietrich Bonhoeffer be mentioned. Saints are mirrors of God's promise that humanity will be perfected. Such divine promise that is realized in human experience is not to be played off over against perseverance in the work of everyday life. Rather, God's call is not exhausted in our callings. If the veneration of the saints and church history have something to do with one another, as Melanchthon taught, then we are here dealing with the reality of God's transforming power in history.[43]

7. Finally, a peculiar silence in the CA is to be noted. Mary, the mother of the Lord, is mentioned only in CA 3, the article "On the Son of God," and then only because the wording of the Creed is being followed. In the light of the dogmatization of the Immaculate Conception (1854) and of Mary's Bodily Assumption to Heaven (1950) during the last century and a half, this reticent silence might appear wholesome to a Lutheran theologian. However, precisely for this reason reticence is no longer sufficient, now that differing church traditions are again confronting one another. Of course, one can, on the one hand, find more than this about Mary in Luther's writings [44] provided one notes that his 1521 exposition of the Magnificat, which is often cited in this connection, most likely appears "pre-Reformation" when viewed from the perspective of 1530 (it was written before the reformer's above-mentioned 1524 turn). Yet on the other hand, nothing forces us to attribute any dogmatic binding force to Luther's personal views.

Theological reflection on the Mother of God's place in the church which wishes to be true to the Reformation's insights would have to combine the viewpoints which result from both CA 3 and CA 21: Mary has a unique place, and she is an *exemplum fidei,* a model for faith.[45] This is in keeping with the New Testament testimony concerning this woman. On this basis a discussion of Mary, our Lord's mother, is possible with the doctrine and traditions of both the Orthodox Church and contemporary Roman Catholicism. CA 21 is silent about Mary, but it leaves the way open for a deepened understanding; and at the same time it forces us to ask critical questions about the new dogmas of the 19th and 20th centuries.

6. Veneration of the Saints and Church Communion

1. The Augsburg Confession's comments on invoking the saints and on their intercession are extremely restrictive (it was on this that conversations with the Orthodox floundered in the 16th century).[46] At first sight it seems that with regard to the saints, the Augsburg Confession knows only the categories of "remembrance" and "example." Although the inclusion of the Apology may modify this impression, still the curious example of legitimate relationship to the saints (King David as a model for the Emperor in his war against the Turks) indicates the historical relativity of this text.

But even after we take into consideration this historical limitation as well as the motivations for the CA's position—the silence of the New Testament concerning the intercession of the saints, and the concern to make unambiguously certain that Christ is our only mediator and deliverer—is there, we ask, some bridge or even a narrow footpath we might construct across the gulf which seems to separate a Protestantism which is heir to the Augsburg Confession from Eastern Orthodoxy and a Catholicism which knows itself bound to the Council of Trent as well as to the Second Vatican Council?

The difficulty is concentrated more on what the texts call "invocation" *("invocatio")* and less on "intercession." If both mutual aid and mutual intercession are part of "the communion of saints" (as is our common teaching and practice),[47] then there is no dispute about the fact that death cannot destroy or diminish the unity that already exists on earth, the unity between Christ and Christians, the unity of God's people in the communion of saints.[48] When seen thus, there can be no diminution of the intercession which those who have been brought to perfection in

Christ make (through the glory which has already been given to them) on behalf of the church militant on earth.

The invocation of the saints as an obligatory ordinance is rejected by the CA. But does it not leave the question open as to whether such invocation is a possibility, if that invocation occurs in Christ, if it addresses itself fundamentally to God? The latter is, of course, the basic rule of Catholic prayer; it has been the rule of prayer *(lex orandi)* since the days of the Fathers: prayer is to address itself to God through Christ. Such is the structure of all eucharistic prayers and of all petitions in the western Catholic Mass—with the exception of the very rare and late petitions which directly address Christ who rules with God the Father. Not a single liturgical prayer ever addresses itself to the saints, as Melanchthon already noted (Apol. 21, 13 [BC 230]). And saints are not mentioned as mediators of prayer before the 3rd or even the 4th centuries. Even today the saints do not appear in the official collects except in the reasons for praying: "O God, who hast glorified your servant N N . . . grant us according to his example. . . ." In this respect we not only come out of the same liturgical tradition, but the official ordinances of our churches by and large also agree. What is commonly called "the invocation of the saints" and what is rejected in the churches of the Augsburg Confession can in Catholic understanding refer only to asking the saints to intercede before God through Christ in the unity of the body of Christ.

Do Catholics always sufficiently understand this fundamental law that is the norm for their prayers, and therefore also the relativity of prayers addressed to saints? And have Lutherans understood sufficiently that such prayer, which actualizes the interconnection in the one family of God consisting of the church militant on earth and of the church of those who have been made perfect, nevertheless has only secondary and relative character?

From this perspective the points that obviously remain in dispute between us can be relativized by appeal to the Second Vatican Council's concept of "the hierarchy of truths." [49] The word *hierarchy* may be inappropriate (it is at least not unambiguous); but the idea behind it is undeniable and fruitful. The expression invites us to distinguish between what is essential and what is supplementary, between the center and the periphery. This ordering of things to what is central was expressed clearly by the Second Vatican Council when it said, "Every genuine witness of our love for the saints is therefore by nature directed in the end to Christ, who is the 'crown of all saints' (Invitatory for All

Saints in the Roman Breviary), and through him to God, who is marvelous in his saints and who is glorified in them." [50]

From this perspective the question is addressed to Lutherans whether they are able to recognize that a veneration of the saints thus understood is not intended to obscure God's sovereignty and the sole mediatorship of Jesus Christ, and also whether they are in a position to understand the Augsburg Confession in such a way that it indeed opposes the necessity of invoking the saints but allows it if "invocation" in this sense has its place in Christ, in the communion of saints living and dead, which the Holy Spirit sent by Christ unifies and makes alive.

2. Viewed theologically then, such invocation of the saints does not seem all too far removed from the remembering and praising which the Apology of the Augsburg Confession describes.[51] Yet differences remain, as the liturgical practice and piety of our two churches indicate. What we ask, however, is how far these differences can be interpreted as differences of perspective and of spirituality.

These differences are connected with our experience and our historical traditions. The grave abuses in the veneration of the saints in the 16th century evoked from the Reformation a reaction that, with its emphasis on "Christ alone," was not without its rigidity and which led to a deep mistrust toward every liturgical practice that undertakes to help us express the communion of the saints that spans even the chasm of death. The hardening of the boundaries proceeded far beyond the statements of the Augsburg Confession, of its Apology, and of the Reformation-age Church Orders. The Protestant concerns that were expressed in them have, of course, themselves lost much of their *raison d'être* now that Vatican II has brought Catholics back to a sobriety in the cult of the saints. It has not only underlined the relativity of their veneration, but has also diminished the number and significance of their festivals.[52] In the wake of the Council even very popular saints (like St. George) have been dropped from the calendar; the number of statues has been reduced to the point where in some churches they have disappeared entirely. These reforms have been so decisive and were put into practice so radically that many Catholics have been deeply wounded. What is evident then is that this development within Catholicism has not been a matter of theoretical protestations which were supposed to guard against continued abuses; these have been genuine reforms which influence the actual practice of the Roman Church.

Is it then not possible to interpret the remaining differences (whose existence ought not be denied) in large measure as differences of spirituality? No individual Christian, no particular group of Christians, exhausts all the possibilities of the gospel. Therefore a legitimate plurality has existed from the beginning among individual churches. From this perspective one could view the Lutheran, Catholic, and Orthodox traditions as successors to three tendencies which are attested in the New Testament itself.[53]

The Protestants have worked out the heritage of Pauline spirituality in concrete terms: its stress on faith, its distrust of works of which one could boast before God as did that Pharisee whom Jesus stigmatized. Together with the apostle Paul Lutheran theology stresses God's condescension, his self-humiliation in the incarnation of his Son for the salvation of human beings, and also adopts the Pauline contrast between the glory of the preexistence and resurrection and the lowliness of the earthly Jesus (2 Cor. 8:9; Gal. 4:4). In line with the apostle to the Gentile's battle against all temptations to include heavenly mediators of the Gnostic sort in the gospel, Protestants insist, to the point of making it exclusive, that Christ is the sole mediator—an insistence which is now shared by Vatican II.

The Orthodox evaluate the incarnation from the perspective of the evangelist John, "The Word became flesh . . . we have beheld his glory" (John 1:14). They lay hold of his glory in the flesh—so to speak, in human weakness; it is there that the mediation of this glory occurs for those "who were born . . . of God (1:13)." From this perspective Orthodox Christians attribute great significance to the Mother of God, the virginal symbol and instrument of the incarnation. They highlight her intercession and her intimacy with her son as they were manifested in the mystery of Cana; despite Christ's negative response, Mary considered her prayer heard and invited the servants to cooperate in this first sign in which Jesus, anticipating the future, "revealed his glory," and according to this view, she thus laid the foundation of the faith of the disciples (John 2:11). Thus the mother of Jesus appeared to them as the witness of revelation, as herself Christ's disciple, and as the mother of that disciple whom she accepted as son at the foot of the cross (19:25-27).

The Roman Catholic perspective is best seen to be a continuation of Luke 1-2. Mary is not merely God's instrument; nor is she a woman as function and object (as alsewhere in the Gospels), but she is a person, loved by God and filled with the gift of grace (1:28-30), chosen as a partner in freedom, in dialog (1:29-34), herself agreeing (1:34-35). Whereas Zechariah's doubt and unbelief was censured, "blessed is she who believed" (1:45); and she is praised as blessed by all generations (1:48). But all of this came to her—that is clear—solely by God's grace and the power of the Holy Spirit (1:35; Acts 1:14). Luke is the only author in the New Testament who includes something like a hagiography in his accounts of Stephen, Paul, and Peter. The unique feature of these figures, which we could call their holiness, is something Luke conceived of as coming from that identification of Christians with Christ which the Lord himself expressed when he threw the future apostle to the Gentiles to the ground, saying, "Saul, Saul, why do you persecute me?" (Acts 9:4). Has Catholicism not followed an authentic Christian path when it has taken this work of the risen Lord seriously and included in its life the communion of the saints in Christ, a communion not destroyed but only deepened by death?

Differing forms of spirituality have a place in the one church if they urge us to hold fast to the unity and community of God's people, the church, from its beginnings with the ancestors of the Old Testament, and the unity and community of the saints on earth and in glory, who look forward to the fulfilment of all God's promises and are one in adoration and praise. They have their place if they remind us that Jesus Christ alone is the one who has fulfilled the promises and who is bringing them to their goal, the one who in the Holy Spirit remains sole mediator of all salvation and of all prayers.

Notes

1. WA 26,508. The quotation (like the ones following) has been slightly modernized by G. Kretschmar.
2. BSLK 424-425; BC 297.
3. *Unterricht der Visitatoren an die Pfarhern ym Churfurstenthum zu Sachssen,* 1528 (CR 26,77; cf. WA 26, 224-225; AE 40, 263ff.).
4. Torgauer Article 9 in Förstemann, *Urkundenbuch* 1, 82-83; cf. BSLK 83b App. On the historical details see W. Maurer, *Historischer Kommentar,* 1, 29-31.
5. It is missing in the version of May 31 which went to Nürnberg on June 3 and was there translated into German (Na), cf. Maurer, *Hist. Comm.,* 1, 26.
6. WA Br 5, Nr 1657, 2ff., 8-9 (to Justus Jonas). Luther here speaks of a *"dissimulare";* if one does not wish to interpret this as referring to the shift from articles under controversy to articles in which there was agreement, one must assume that Luther has misread CA 21 or did not distinguish between the preliminary drafts and the final version of the text.

7. Cf. the version as Spalatin copied and translated it (BSLK, 83 App.); see also Maurer, *Hist. Comm., op. cit.,* pp. 48-49.
8. Concerning the course of the discussions see H. Immenkötter, *Um die Einheit im Glauben. Die Unionsverhandlungen des Augsburger Reichstages in August und September 1530* (Münster: 1972), p. 43.
9. *Sendbrief vom Dolmetschen,* ms. sent to Nürnberg on Sept. 12, 1530 (WA 30, 632-646); on the invocation of the saints cf. WA 30, 643ff.; *Warnungen D. Martini Luther an seine lieben Deutschen,* ms. Oct. 1530, published 1531 (WA 30, II 276-320); on the invocation of the saints. cf. WA 30, 312-313). In the first writing from the Coburg *(An die gantze Geislichkeit zu Augsburg versammelt auff den Reichstag, Anno 1530. Vermahnung Martini Luther),* ms. sent to Wittenberg on May 5 for printing, a special discussion of the topic of saints is missing; the listing of "the articles which are being practiced in the hypocritical church" includes, of course, also: "12. Cult of saints, some of which were never born; 13. Countless saint's days. 14. Mary made a common idol with all sort of worship, celebration, songs, and antiphons" (WA 30, II 348).
10. Bernd Moeller, "Augustana-Studien," in *ARG* 57 (1966): 76-95; here 83, note 33.
11. The version of the article in *Corpus Doctrinae Christianae* (Leipzig: 1560) still agrees verbally with that of the Wittenberg Printing of Rhau, 1542.
12. Cf. Kretschmar, "Confessio Augustana graeca," in *Kirche im Osten* 20 (1977): 11-39.
13. Alongside the classical presentations, esp. the Bollandists; for this I refer to the collection *Aspekte frühchristlicher Heiligenverehrung, Oikonomia* (Erlangen: 1977), Kretschmar, "*Die Theologie der Heiligen in der frühen Kirche*" (pp. 77-125).
14. Cf., among others, Ulrich Stutz, "*Eigenkirche, Eigenkloster*" in RE[3] 23 (1913), reprinted in the same author's *Die Eigenkirche als Element des mittelalterlich-germanischen Kirchenrechts* (Darmstadt: 1955), p. 69.
15. WA 30, II 644; This statement by Luther is certainly to be viewed in connection with the fact that the Confutators had referred specifically to earlier writings of the Wittenberg reformer. Melanchthon, of course, could hardly have written in this fashion. Reuchlin's humanistically educated nephew did not grow up in the same world of piety out of which Luther came and in which he remained caught, also in his polemics.
16. WA 30, III 643; Cl 4, 190.
17. Attestation of this in L. Pinomaa, *Luther und die Heiligen (Schrift der Luther-Agricola-Gesellschaft),* A 16 (Helsinki: 1977), pp. 64ff. The shift becomes clear, above all, in the writing, *Vom Abgott zu Halle* (1524).
18. *Theologie des Heiligen,* pp. 77-78.
19. Examples are, among others, those of Saint Elizabeth of Thuringia and of Saint Hedwig of Silesia.
20. *Apol.* 21,13 (BSLK 319; BC 230): ". . . this is a novel custom in the church. The ancient prayers mention the saints, but they do not invoke them."
21. That is why one can sometimes find, particularly in recent Catholic saintly figures, statements which are in keeping with the convictions of the Reformers. Thus, for example, Bernadette writes, "I find that one ought

to point out the mistakes which the saints have made and to indicate the means that they have employed to correct themselves. This aids us. We will understand how this must be understood. But one does not say that about their revelations or about the prophecies that they have made. That is not able to serve our progress" *(Logia* 2, p. 118).

22. A survey in F. Kattenbusch, *Das Apostolische Symbol II* (Leipzig: 1900 [Reprint: Darmstadt: 1962]) pp. 941ff; cf. also St. Benko, *The Meaning of "Sanctorum Communio,"* Stud. of Hist. Theol. 3 (London: 1964), pp. 109ff.

23. Cf. note 3.

24. August Vilmar worked this out particularly clearly. He wrote, "Therefore, as far as the invocation itself is concerned, every misunderstanding, as if the invocation included a *prayer,* must be entirely obviated, something which has not been successfully accomplished, neither in the Augsburg Confession, which expressed itself entirely too carefully and therefore unclearly, nor in the Confutatio, which was still caught in deep error, nor in the Apology, which let itself be blinded by error." *Die Augsburgische Confession erklärt* (Gütersloh: 1870), pp. 168ff.

25. BSLK 319, 39-40 (BC 231).

26. *Cath. resp.* p. 73, 4-14 Ficker, ed.; *Conf.* p. 129, 14-15., Immenkötter, ed. Luther had opposed this distinction already in 1524, *Wider den neuen Abgott . . .* (WA 15, 197).

27. According to the minutes of the discussion for the 16/17th of August, "They agree in the first place that all the saints and angels in heaven intercede for us with God. Secondly, that it is both pious and right to remember the saints and observe festivals on which we pray God to let the intercession of the saints avail for us. But whether the saints are to be invoked by us was not agreed on. Indeed, they say that they do not prohibit it, but since Scripture does not teach the invocation of the saints, they themselves do not wish to invoke them, not only because Scripture does not teach it, but also because it seems to them to be a dangerous abuse" (F. W. Schirrmacher, ed., *Briefe und Acten zu der Geschichte des Religionsgespräches zu Marburg 1529 und des Reichstages zu Augsburg 1530* [Gotha: 1876; reprint, Amsterdam: 1968], p. 222).

28. On Luther cf. Pinomaa (note 17) and Maurer, *Hist. Komm.* 2, pp. 156-160; further esp. Robert Lansemann, *Die Heiligentage, besonders die Marien- Apostel- und Engeltage in der Reformationszeit* (Göttingen: 1939), pp. 93ff.

29. *Ibid.,* pp. 106-107; Marientage, pp. 123ff; Aposteltage, pp. 135ff; otherwise pp. 145ff.

30. *Braunschweig* 1528: EKO 6, 1 (Tübingen: 1955), pp. 348-455; esp. pp. 398-399. *Hamburg* 1529: EKO 5 (Leipzig: 1913), pp. 488-540; esp. p. 515; *Lübeck* 1531: EKO 5, pp. 334-368; esp. p. 358; also "The Wittenberg Reformation" of 1545 could be mentioned here: EKO 1,1 (Leipzig: 1902), pp. 209-222, esp. pp. 214-215; but it follows largely the *Instruction to the Visitors* of 1527; after the Interim it was obviously necessary to reiterate the old Church Orders.

31. Cf. Karl Dienst, *"Reformationsfest"* in RGG[3] 5 (1961), Columns 873.

874, and Ernst Walter Zeeden, *Martin Luther und die Reformation im Urteil des deutschen Luthertums,* vols. 1-2 (Freiburg: 1950/51).

32. Pinomaa (note 17) particularly elaborates this. Gerhard Müller calls attention to a remarkable memorandum by Andreas Osiander, the Nürnberg reformer, of April (?) 1525: the ancient oath-formula of this imperial city (as of other cities), "by God and all his saints" was considered by Osiander as unexceptionable, because " 'the saints of God' are understood to be the believing Christians as is the common expression of the holy apostles and indeed of the whole Christian church. . . ." The council did not, however, adopt his opinion but removed the oath by the saints. *Andreas Osiander und d. A. Gesamtausgabe,* vol. 2, G. Müller, ed. (Gütersloh: 1977), pp. 71-78 (esp. 74, 5-7).

33. A classical example of this is Sulpicius Severus, *Vita s. Martini,* c. 11.

34. How deeply this affected the sensibilities of many Christians shows the importance that veneration of the saints still possesses today. This observation is not a criticism, but shows that the question about the true and false cult of the saints continues to be posed.

35. In any case the dismemberment of corpses, to gain relics, was not ancient custom among Semites, Greeks, or Romans of classical times. Such customs arose first in connection with the Christian cult of relics.

36. Sess. XXV, Dec. 3-4, 1563, *"De invocatione, veneratione et reliquiis sanctorum et de sacris imaginibus."*

37. BSLK 425, 20-25. SA II, 28 (BC 297).

38. We see an indication of this in the well-known sentences which were found after Luther's death on a piece of paper, "Let no one imagine that he has had a sufficient taste of the Holy Scripture unless he has spent a hundred years in charge of congregations together with the prophets, like Elijah and Elisha, John the Baptist, Christ, and the Apostles. . . . We are beggars; that is true!"

39. *Die Augsburgische Confession erklärt* (cf. note 24), pp. 167-168.

40. Peter Manns rightly referred to this in his contribution to the symposium, *"Der Augsburger Reichstag 1530 und die Einheit der Kirche: 450 Jahre Confessio Augustana und Confutatio"* held by the Society for the Publication of the Corpus Catholicorum, Sept. 3-7, 1979, in Augsburg, a contribution entitled *"Die Heiligenverehrung bei Luther." Confessio Augustana und Confutatio,* E. Iserloh and B. Hallensleben, eds. (Münster: 1980).

41. Cf. on this, for example, the 1951 Confession of the Batak Church (which belongs to the Lutheran World Federation), Article 16, "Remembering the Dead." English text: G. Forell, *The Protestant Faith* (Philadelphia: 1975), pp. 290-298. and Edward W. Fasholé-Luke, "Ancestor Veneration and the Communion of Saints" in *New Testament Christianity for Africa and the World* (London: F.S.H. Sawyers, 1974), pp. 211-235.

42. Cf. on this the recent document of the Joint Roman Catholic-Evangelical Lutheran Commission, *Das Herrenmahl* (Paderborn and Frankfurt: 1978), c. 27, pp. 21-22.

43. For this reason it was not inappropriate that the experience of the existence of Christian nations since the early Middle Ages was theologically understood to mean that their saints represented the true identity of the nation

before God. That is an appropriation and historicizing of the Jewish conception that each nation has its own angel.

44. Horst Dietrich Preuss, *Maria bei Luther* (SVR 172) (Gütersloh: 1954); Hans Düfel, *Luthers Stellung zur Marienverehrung* (KuK 13) (Göttingen: 1968).

45. The Formula of Concord of 1577 contains no section on the veneration of the saints, because there was no controversy on that within Lutheran theology. It does, however, contain a section, "On the Person of Christ," and in that connection it again speaks correctly of Mary as "the mother of God." Epit. 8, 7 (BSLK 806, 12; BC 488) and 8, 24 (BSLK 1024; BC 595).

46. It is perhaps not unimportant that Patriarch Jeremias II in his first theological message received CA 21 in the Greek translation favorably (it had been authorized, if not translated, by Melanchthon.). It was only the opposition of his Tübingen partner-in-dialog which began a controversy which continued until the exchange of letters ceased and which had special significance for the failure of the talks. The polemic against invoking the saints is something which the Patriarch would have been able to understand if reference had been made to the categories that had been formulated in the Iconoclastic Controversy: invocation in the strict sense belongs to God alone; in the case of the saints, it occurs only *"schetikos."*

47. Cf. on this Dietrich Bonhoeffer in his Summer Semester 1932 lecture, "The Nature of the Church," reconstructed by Otto Dudzus: "the limits to intercession are to be placed where the limits of the community are located. Intercession for all people brings them into the community. . . . Intercession is based on the realization that the community carries the individual's guilt, that every one is guilty of Christ's death. Thus each one can become Christ for his neighbor, even if he is not even acquainted with that neighbor." *Gesammelte Schriften,* vol. 5, Eberhard Bethge, ed. (Munich: 1972, p. 266); cf. also *Sanctorum Communio: Eine dogmatische Untersuchung zur Sozialogie der Kirche* (1930) (Munich: 1969⁴), pp. 133-137.

48. For evangelical theology and piety, one would have to point out that, when mutual intercession for a dead person is spoken of, the topic of prayer for the dead is posed, a topic historically burdened by the doctrine of purgatory. The early church discovered, with reference to intercession for the dead, the distinction between "the saints" and "the blessed" (in the sense of all Christians who have died). We would indeed all have to ask again what death means for communion in word and sacrament. The ancient church gave an answer insofar as it introduced intercession for the living and the dead ever more forcefully into the Eucharistic prayer: the sacrifice of Golgotha unifies the church militant and the church of those who have been perfected.

49. "When comparing teachings with one another, it should not be forgotten that there is an order or hierarchy of truths in Catholic teaching, according to the different way in which they are connected with the foundation of the Christian faith." *UR* 11.

50. From *Lumen gentium.* The "invocation" is based on a quotation from the Council of Trent. Evangelical theology would also have questions for

this chapter of the *Lumen Gentium*, but the title of the chapter already shows that these would be questions in the context of common conviction: *"De indole eschatologica ecclesiae peregrinantis eiusque unione cum ecclesia coelesti"* (Concerning the eschatological nature of the pilgrim church and its union with the heavenly church). "How much needs still to be done, in the opinion of a Catholic theologian, is shown by Karl Rahner's *"Warum und wie können wir die Heiligen verehren?"* in *Schriften zur Theologie VII* (Einsiedeln: 1966), pp. 283-303; cf. also *"Der eine Mittler und die Vielfalt der Vermittelungen"* in *Schriften zur Theologie VIII* (Einsiedeln: 1967), pp. 218-235. For further select German-language Catholic literature on the topic cf. P. Molinari, *Die Heiligen und ihre Verehrung* (Freiburg: 1964); Hans Urs von Balthasar, *"Gemeinschaft der Heiligen"* in *Klarstellungen*, Herderbücherei 393, (Freiburg: 1972³), pp. 59ff; *"Ueber Stellvertretung"* in *Pneuma und Institution: Skizzen zur Theologie IV* (Einsiedeln: 1974), pp. 401-409.

51. This is clear from *Lumen gentium* 50, but also from *The Constitution on the Liturgy*, which should be cited. It speaks of the remembrance of the martyrs in the church year: "The church has furthermore placed into the annual cycle remembrance of the martyrs and of other saints, who, having been brought to perfection by the multiform grace of God and having already attained salvation, sing perfect praise to God in heaven and intercede for us. For on the saints' heavenly birthdays the church preaches the paschal mystery in the saints who suffered with Christ and were glorified together with him, and it proposes their examples to the faithful, examples which draw all through Christ to the Father; and by their merits it begs God's blessings," SC 104. Evangelical theology would not speak of the martyr's "merits"; but the Constitution's inclusion of their path in the communion of Christ and of the Easter mystery is solid. This goes far beyond Apol. 21, but in a direction which should unite us dogmatically rather than separate us.

52. These statements are not to be referred to the cult of the mother of God without qualification. The topic of Mariology should be treated separately, as in part 7 of section 5 of this essay.

53. The following sketch could appear ambiguous, but it goes in the direction pointed out in Ernst Käsemann's well-known dictum that the New Testament establishes not the unity of the church but the diversity of its confessional groups. Presupposed in these considerations is the fact that the indisputable plurality of thought-forms and theological structures in the many writings collected in the New Testament takes firm hold of a legitimate difference of ways of expressing what is Christian in the unity of the confession of Christ, as was obviously characteristic of primitive Christianity, esp. according to the Apostle Paul (Gal. 1:18—2:10; 1 Cor. 15:3-8). It is undeniable that misleading, heretical extensions of such tendencies can occur from roots which can be traced back into the New Testament. The following typology, which requires a more extended exegetical discussion, naturally includes the fact that the entire church is to take its bearings from the entire New Testament; unilateral isolation of such tendencies of spirituality is thereby rejected.

11

Monasticism

by Bernhard Lohse, Karl Suso Frank,
Johannes Halkenhäuser, and Friedrich Wulf

translated by Richard W. Schoenleber

1. Toward an Understanding of CA 27 (Bernhard Lohse)

The CA deals with the question of monastic vows in Article 27. This article belongs to the second part of the CA, i.e., to those articles which concern the elimination of abuses rather than to those articles which concern issues of faith and doctrine. However, practical piety and doctrine are so closely intertwined in this article that in a certain respect it still must be considered with the articles of doctrine. At any rate, because of the doctrinal perspective of the CA the rejection of monastic vows is stronger than would be accounted for by the practical abuses alone, and that circumstance reflects the development of Luther's attitude toward monasticism. Among the numerous questions which became contested between Luther and Rome after 1517—which extended from the proper understanding of repentance and faith to the concept of freedom of the will and sin, and from the authority of the pope and of Councils to the question of the priesthood of all believers and sacramental doctrine—the problem of monastic vows was the last thing in which Luther broke with Rome. Perhaps that was due to the fact that Luther himself was a monk and with the repudiation of monastic vows, to a greater degree than with other controversial questions, his own existence in the monastery was also called into question. Without a doubt the development of Luther's critique of monasticism was in part an attempt to come to terms with his own past; however, the theological problems that monasticism posed for Luther and the Reformation were probably decisive.

Nevertheless, the theological conflict must be seen against the background of the role which monasticism played at the time of the waning Middle Ages. It is important to note that at that time monasticism was in part only a caricature of what it originally had wanted to be and also of what it formerly had been. Thus the conflict between Luther and the monasticism of his day did not fundamentally concern monasticism's spiritual contribution to the church; instead, it concerned the definite forms and shapes which monasticism had assumed in the late Middle Ages. In both the church and the public, and not least in the universities, monasticism presented itself as one of the most powerful realities. A significant percentage of the population lived in cloisters or was at least professionally and economically bound to them. Of course, there were always many who entered the cloisters in order to obey the evangelical counsels. The cloisters were also sought as secure places of care, especially for unmarried women. The monastic orders had at one time accomplished much in the colonization of the land, but their task had changed in the waning Middle Ages: the theologians of the orders occupied chairs of philosophy and theology and often played decisive roles in the universities. In particular, the Dominicans acted as preachers in the cities and frequently had great influence as inquisitors and peddlers of indulgences. The cloisters were a significant economic factor nearly everywhere because of their special tax status, and their privileges aroused the envy of the guilds and of city governments. With the growing wealth and influence of the orders in the waning Middle Ages, many of them exhibited the symptoms of decay, and the mendicant orders were no exception in that regard. Already in the late Middle Ages many orders and cloisters were reformed, often with the help or through the initiative of secular lords. Indeed, such cloister reform had by no means been completed before the onset of the Reformation. The question of the special economic status of the cloisters remained unanswered. The theological question of the relationship between monk and lay person was also unsolved. It was, of course, understood that a lay person could attain salvation, but entry into a cloister was considered a shorter and more certain way to that goal. Especially in the case of a grave sin, the path into the cloister freed one from performing the penance which had been imposed. The higher value of monastic life before God served as a justification of its privileged position in the world.[1]

This higher value had been described carefully and cautiously by the great theologians of monasticism such as Augustine or Thomas Aquinas. In everyday life, however, cruder ideas were prevalent. The comparison of the taking of monastic vows with a second baptism, which already occurs in Jerome although Augustine did not use it, allowed monasticism to appear as a class of the perfect, even if, as a matter of fact, it was considered merely a better place to strive for perfection. Johann Paltz (d. 1511), who was entrusted with the instruction of the novices at the Augustinian monastery in Erfurt, had instructed Luther concerning the monastic ideal. In his *Supplementum Coelifodinae* he interpreted monasticism entirely in the context of Mariology. He claimed that Mary, by virtue of her humility, "drew down" the Lord of heaven, established by three vows and all cloisters, and as a matter of fact founded the entire Christian faith. Thus for Paltz, Mary furnishes the example for monks through her humility and chastity.[2] Such a far-reaching view cannot be seen as an occasional aberration but appears to be the consequence of a theologically irresponsible assessment of monasticism. Paltz, himself, always sought to place the benefits of monasticism very clearly before the eyes of the novices.

Out of concern for the salvation of his soul Luther became a monk in 1505. The "assaults" *("Anfechtungen")* which he experienced when thinking of standing before God at the Last Judgment must have been further intensified by ideas such as Paltz represented them. Nevertheless, Luther never used the comparison between taking vows and a second baptism in his earlier period (1513-1515).[3] At that time Luther did not polemicize against monasticism as such, but he recast his ideas on the subject. He saw in the baptismal vow the decisive vow of a person. It stands above the monastic vow and is at most reasserted, but not revalidated, by the monastic vow. From that point of view humility no longer appears as a virtue but is fundamentally identical to faith, which takes hold of the judgment of God pronounced in Christ and is reckoned by God as righteousness. From this point of view Luther sharply criticized the works-righteousness of many monks, even in his early period.

In the *Lectures on Romans* (1515/1516) the criticism became even stronger. On the other hand, Luther maintained in an excursus on Rom. 14:1 that although everything in itself is free according to the "new Law," one can legitimately bind one's self in freedom through a vow. Not only is Luther's understanding of freedom expressed here interesting, but also his opinion that vows stand on the side of the law.[4] In spite of this theological reconsideration of monasticism, Luther said as late as 1519 in a sermon on Baptism that in order for a person to achieve "the completion of his Baptism" he might bind himself to an order and there devote himself to the realization of the dying which had happened symbolically in Baptism.[5]

The year 1520 brought a sharpening of Luther's criticism of monasticism. In *To the Christian Nobility of the German Nation* Luther unfolded his conception of the priesthood of all the baptized—from that point on no place remained for a special value of monasticism. In addition Luther made numerous proposals for reforms in order to end the draining of Germany's resources by means of monasteries and to avoid a binding through vows before the thirtieth year of a person's life. In *The Babylonian Captivity of the Church* he maintained on the basis of his theology of Baptism that actually all vows should be cancelled. He hoped it would happen through a general edict which at the same time would call people back to their baptismal vows.

During Luther's stay at the Wartburg (1521/1522) the development came to a head. Many monks and nuns left their cloisters. In June of 1521, Karlstadt claimed in theses for disputation that a monk who suffered from lust could break the vow of chastity because the sin of breaking the vow was less serious than the sin of inner resistance to the vow. Melanchthon found no fault with that argumentation.[6]

Luther did not agree with giving monks such a blank check. In the fall of 1521, he wrote first his *Theses Concerning Vows (Themata de votis)* and then his *Judgment Concerning Monastic Vows (De votis monasticis iudicium)*.[7] In the latter book, which is constructed very systematically, the following topics are presented: (1) vows do not rest in God's Word but much more oppose it, (2) vows oppose faith, (3) vows oppose the freedom of the gospel, (4) vows oppose the commandments of God, and (5) monasticism opposes reason *(ratio)*. A significant issue is the question of which vows are proper and in what sense monastic vows are fulfilled. The freedom which vows oppose is the freedom of the conscience from dependence on works on the basis of "by faith alone *(sola fide)*". According to Luther, eternally binding vows are not valid. Thus Luther dared to declare all monks free from their vows. Certainly Luther granted the possibility that someone "in godly conviction," not for the sake of reward, might choose the monastic life, just as another might become some type of craftsman.[8] But in no case may the vows be made into a law. Monks and nuns must be free to leave the cloister and to marry. In any case virginity must not be considered to stand higher than the married estate.

This book strengthened the movement, already in progress, to leave the cloisters. Many cloisters dissolved, indeed, in large parts of Germany many orders nearly ceased to exist. But there were also monks and nuns who remained in the cloisters. Thus the reorganization of cloisters became a major task during the construction of an evangelical church organization in the time after the Diet of Speyer in 1526. Most often cloister possessions were secularized, and the cloister income was used for the support of pastors, schools, and the poor. In most cases old monks and nuns were allowed to end their days in a cloister. Still, cloister life gradually ceased in the territory of the Reformation. The new valuation of secular vocations by the Reformation gave the necessary justification to this far-reaching transformation of social life.[9] Among the many tasks which were necessary for the realization of the Reformation hardly another was so irreversible as the secularization of the cloisters: the social structure was decisively changed. A restoration of the earlier conditions was, in fact, quite impossible.

Due to the imperial citation to appear at the Diet of Augsburg, the Evangelicals were faced with the necessity of defending and justifying the changes that had been effected. As early as the so-called Torgau Articles at the end of March, 1530, there was a section "Concerning Monastic Life *(Vom Klosterleben)*." Appropriate to the apologetic purpose of that article, it was emphasized that the Elector of Saxony did not command the monks to leave the cloisters. Thus the article maintains that it must be asked why the situation of monks and nuns leaving the cloisters arose. The article then gives three reasons why the monastic life, as practiced until then, was wrong and against God: (1) the belief that one could atone for sin and earn grace through entry into the cloister, as Thomas taught, (2) it is against God's commandment to vow celibacy if one suffers from lust, and (3) the monks were forced to practice the abuse of Masses for the dead and other improper religious services, especially the invocation of saints.

In the CA these thoughts were taken up and put into a comprehensive context. Here Melanchthon drew, to a large degree, on Luther's *Judgment Concerning Monastic Vows,* taking essential thoughts from it.

In CA 23, just as in the Torgau Articles, priestly celibacy had been disputed. Melanchthon had pointed out that Scripture did not know priestly celibacy, that only a few people were suited for celibacy, that in the ancient church priests were often married, and that in Germany celibacy had been enforced only since about 1100. But on account of priestly celibacy the danger existed that soon recruits for the ministry would no longer be available. Melanchthon concluded that no human law could cancel God's commandment; therefore vows were invalid.

Similarly, CA 27 argues chiefly concerning practical abuses. The CA holds the factually incorrect view that the cloisters had been at one time free associations (*collegia*) and that vows first came after a decline of discipline. Still other rites were added later.[10] Often people entered cloisters mistakenly, i.e., in ignorance of their capabilities, and then had no opportunity to revise their decision. Such abuses were worse in the nunneries than in the monasteries.[11] Idealizing the past to a certain degree, the CA claims that the cloisters had once been schools of Holy Scripture and other branches of knowledge, which had furnished a welcome supply of pastors and bishops.[12]

But more important than the mention of such abuses was, for the CA, the false doctrines and opinions connected with monasticism and especially with vows. Essentially, the following views were contested: (1) vows are of equal worth with Baptism, and one could merit forgiveness of sin and justification as a monk.[13] (2) Monks keep not only the commandments but also the evangelical counsels. Thus to the monastic estate was given a higher value than to Baptism. In addition, monastic life was considered of greater value and preferred to service in government, as pastors, and in other occupations.[14] The distinction between commandments and counsels led the common people to consider the counsels as not binding.[15] Yet monastic piety is only an "invented spirituality." [16] (3) Monasticism is called the "state of perfection," as the CA, following Luther, claims in a somewhat overstated formulation.[17] (4) The opponents are inconsistent insofar as they defend the eternally-binding character of vows while the popes themselves have in certain cases dispensed from vows.[18] (5) The thesis of the opponents that vows can be fulfilled does not conform to reality; in addition, the vow of chastity opposes God's creation and order of marriage. Vows (*votum*) are against the commandment (*mandatum*) of God.[19] (6) Even if the breaking of vows should be a sin, still it does not follow that the opponents should dissolve already completed marriages on account of previously taken vows.[20]

Against the claims of monasticism, the CA advocated the principle that vows are invalid because every service of God which does not rest upon God's commandment and serves self-justification is godless.[21] Moreover, God's commandment with regard to marriage frees most people from vows. For the CA, as for Luther since 1516, vows forced a falling-back under the dominion of the law; the assertion of Paul that the attempt at self-justification through the law means a fall from grace applies to the making of eternally-binding vows.[22] Monasticism is not the "state of perfection *(status perfectionis)*"; instead, that state consists much more in fearing God with seriousness, having strong faith for Christ's sake, expecting help from God in all things in accordance with one's calling, and in the meantime conscientiously doing good works and serving one's vocation.[23]

The CA appealed to the fact that even Gerson had rejected the assertion that monks were in the state of perfection. In short, the godless opinions concerning monasticism were so numerous, and moreover were so closely connected with vows, that vows must be viewed as false and vain.[24]

It must be granted that many of the judgments which are given in the CA are not warranted. The picture of early monasticism is not correct. Monasticism did not consider itself as a state of perfection but as the effort of attaining perfection. In general, monasticism cannot be accused of attempting self-justification, even at the time of the waning Middle Ages. Here the CA came to some unjustified wholesale condemnations based on embittered controversies.

On the other hand, the distinction between commandments and counsels, as well as the exceedingly dangerous comparison of vows with Baptism, and the assertion of monasticism as of a higher value than the secular life, were all criticized with good reason. In fairness it must be noted that the specific theological questions of monasticism were considered far too little by scholarly theology in the high and late Middle Ages. Indeed, theology in the waning Middle Ages practiced its critical function only inadequately or not at all in view of the excrescences of piety experienced by the church. In all fairness it must be admitted that the Reformation criticism of indefensible and extremely dangerous assertions concerning monasticism pointed toward deficiencies that urgently needed reexamination. Yet the Reformers did not see that theologians of monasticism had made some helpful beginnings which, as a consequence of the Reformation criticism, became increasingly meaningful.

The Confutation corrected many assertions of the CA concerning the early period of monasticism and concerning the "state of perfection," but in the main restricted itself to a defense of certain specific positions. Above all, it heavily emphasized that monastic vows were based on the Old and New Testaments. Certainly, the texts were unable to prove what the Confutation wanted them to prove: Scripture knows many vows, but definitely not eternally binding ones.

Among the different items which were contested by the opposing religious parties at the Diet of Augsburg, the question of monastic vows was also touched upon; however, other controversial questions such as the marriage of priests, giving the cup to the laity, or the authority of bishops were considered more important at the time. With regard to monasticism, the problems of property rights were debated, but the real theological questions were not thoroughly addressed. An opinion of Melanchthon from Sept. 7, 1530, in which he again brought together the Protestant reproach, is interesting. According to him the following blasphemies are present in monasticism: (1) our own works make us pious before God; (2) our own works suffice to atone for sin and to take away sin; (3) Masses make all those for whom they are celebrated pious before God, even when they add no good thoughts; (4) monastic life is equal to Baptism, takes away all sins, is Christian perfection, is above the estate of marriage, the princely estate, etc.; (5) one should invoke the saints; (6) the merit of the saints atones and pays God not alone for the saints themselves but also for us just as the merit of Christ.[25]

In the Apology to the CA Melanchthon expounded the most important thoughts in juxtaposition with the Confutation once more. In Apol. 23 he first of all called attention to the numerous violations of the vow of chastity by priests, monks, and nuns. He excoriated the admonition, which the Confutation directed to the emperor and the princes, that they should not tolerate the marriage of priests. When the Confutation described the marriage of priests as an "infamy to the Roman Empire *(infamia romani imperii),*" it thereby disgraced the holy estate of matrimony, which after all was considered a sacrament in the Catholic Church.[26] For his side, Melanchthon asserted that "we" could not recognize celibacy because it was against divine and natural law, against Scripture, and against the canons of the Councils. Marriage, however, is certainly ordained by God.[27] For the rest, Melanchthon invoked 1 Cor. 7:2.

In Apol. 27 Melanchthon reported first of all about a Franciscan monk, Johannes Hilten, at Eisenach, who on account of his criticism of abuses in cloister life was held in confinement by his brothers and kept in a monastery for his whole life.[28] Melanchthon asserted again that the cloisters at one time were schools but that now indolence and hypocrisy were said to reign in them, especially since the cloisters were generally very rich. Naturally, there were some good men in the cloisters, who placed their confidence in the gospel of Christ and not in self-invented services to God. From Luther's book on monasticism Melanchthon borrowed again the decisive formulation of the issue: it is not a question of whether properly made vows should be kept, but rather which vows are proper.[29] Once again Melanchthon accused his opponents of equating vows and Baptism.[30] After a discussion of the three monastic vows, he concerned himself with the "state of perfection." The authors of the Confutation said that monasticism should merely serve as an opportunity to strive toward perfection. Melanchthon admitted that such a view was met already in Gerson, but Melanchthon held firm to the heart of the Reformation protest when he wanted to force his opponents to admit that monasticism is in no manner superior to any other vocation, in which one strives also toward perfection.[31] Indeed, differences in the evaluation of secular work in comparison to the spiritual estate and monasticism persisted in the 16th century and probably to some degree into the 20th century, in spite of the overly sharp criticism of the "state of perfection."

Both the radical criticism of monasticism and especially the rejection of eternally binding vows in light of the Reformation doctrine of justification as well as the denial of any special value to monasticism resulted in the extinction of monasticism in the region of the Reformation. Only a few cloisters, with, however, other descriptions of purpose, continued to exist. To some extent they retained the name "cloister," but they had nothing in common with earlier monasticism and with Catholic cloisters. Where something of the idea of celibacy was retained in a modified form, there were no vows and celibacy was not viewed as a lifelong obligation.

This situation completely changed in the 20th century. From approximately the beginning of this century, and again from the 1920s, and since the 1940s at an increased rate, many brotherhoods and sisterhoods have been founded, which, although they have their distinctive character, are on the whole comparable to the old monasticism.[32] Generally, it may be said for this movement that the binding character of the Christian faith to determine and involve all of life has been newly recognized. The value of a spiritual community living together has been newly experienced, and the necessity of discipline, poverty, and obedience has been newly discovered. On the whole, these communities strive to take into account the conflict which occurred in the Reformation period in regard to monasticism. They emphasize that life in such community is not something better than life in the world. Celibacy is not particularly praised, although there is certainly no rejection of its value. Marriage and celibacy are understood as the two possibilities which Christians are given and into which, at some point, they enter according to their own decision in obedience to God's command. In the numerous communities a lively spiritual life has developed. Some of these communities, especially that of Taizé, have exerted considerable influence on the whole of Christendom and even far beyond the limits of the Christian movement. Thus one can say that the blessing which for a long time has been part of monasticism has become newly effective in evangelical Christianity.

Indeed, the theological questions in regard to monasticism which present themselves to us in the light of the Reformation have not always been thought through with the necessary clarity and self-criticism, just as, on the other hand, many prejudices and resentments against the evangelical communities are still found in the major Reformation denominations and need further study. Questions such as these need further clarification: (1) the relation of such communities to the church in the light of Baptism and the complete community of one Christendom; (2) the question of obligation, especially of vows, as well as the possibility of leaving such a community; and (3) the question of the differentiated realization of the obedience and discipleship required of all Christians, whether they live in community or in the world. Even today there can be no doubt that both the Christians in the world and the members of communities can learn much from each other if they recognize their interdependence. Thus the multifaceted charisms and the unity of grace should find new expression in the association of the communities and the church in the world.

It follows that the harsh judgment of CA 27 concerning Catholic monasticism cannot be sustained. Both the practical experience in the evangelical communities and the theological examination of the questions of monasticism have made it clear that the evangelical church and theology cannot stop with the statements of CA 27. Properly understood, monasticism is a legitimate path for Christians.

2. The Catholic Reaction (Karl Suso Frank)

2.1. The Confutation

The Reformation attack against the estate of orders and the monastic establishment provoked a Catholic defense. Since the early 1520s the points of attack were all known and had led to the dissolution of the cloisters in those territories which had adopted the Reformation. For the believers in the old order all this was especially distressing. The territorial church authorities had followed an established precedent in their procedures. The Catholic reform of the 15th century (observance movement) had also been supported by the territorial authorities. The monasteries in cities and territories were now "reformed" for the same basic reasons. Now, however, this meant the dissolution of these institutions. The very theological argumentation, which in the 15th century lead to an improvement of the life in orders and to the abolition of abuses and the correction of erroneous developments, was now, as a matter of principle, built on a basic no to the life in orders. As a result the old alliance between theological argumentation and princely power now meant the end of the cloisters in the territories of the Reformation. Therefore the Catholic reply had to address both parties. In its concluding remark to the territorial rulers the Confutation very appropriately advised the rulers to take care to see to it that the cloisters are reformed instead of dissolved and that monks who broke their discipline are punished and recalled to good discipline.[33] It is the exact reverse of the Reformation demand of the princes.[34] However, to a decisive degree, the theological argumentation had to be taken into account. The no of the Reformation had to be theologically rejected in order to win back the cloisters which had already been lost and to strengthen and preserve floundering monks and nuns in their vocation.

The authors of the Confutation had recognized the dangerous nature of CA 27. Among them was an impressive number of theologians who were members of orders, familiar with traditional teaching about their own form of life, yet honest enough to confess abuses and the need for correction.[35] But at this point in the development the mere advocacy of reforms would no longer do. Nevertheless the authors of the Confutation were apparently unwilling to enter into a detailed discussion of the statements of CA 27—an observation which applies to other parts of the Confutation as well and is easily explained by the intention of the rebuttal.[36] Above its rebuttal stands briefly and succinctly the assertion: everything that CA 27 maintains is to be flatly rejected *("Reiicienda sunt omnia!")*. The definitive no of the CA to a life in the estate of orders under a pledge to monastic vows was opposed by the Confutation's equally definitive affirmation of such a life: monastic vows are founded in the Holy Scriptures of the Old and New Testaments sanctified through the lives of so many people, and recognized in the church for thousands of years. Thus Scripture and tradition support monastic vows.[37]

The CA had denied that the life under vows was in accordance with Scripture. Therefore, the Confutation had to remind its readers that the life in orders was a "life in accord with Scripture." A detailed discussion of the relationship of vows and Holy Scripture was not to be expected. For the authors of the Confutation that was not an issue. They were sure of their cause. A few references to biblical texts, which for a long time had been interpreted as referring to cloister vows, were assembled: the vows of the Nazirites (Num. 6:1-4) and the Rechabites (Jer. 35:6, 8, 14, and a few texts which demonstrate that vows are pleasing to God (Deut. 23:21; Prov. 15:8 and 20:25; Isa. 56:4). These Old Testament texts had already been used by the apologists for monasticism. The old monasticism had quite commonly discovered its forerunners in the prophets Elijah, Elisha, and the "sons of prophets."[38] Obviously, no unbroken line can be drawn from these Old Testament words and figures to Christian monasticism. Only the ascetic-monastic experience with its self-made hermeneutic could discover such a genealogy. But with that genealogy the defenders of monasticism in the early 16th century had tradition on their side.

The same holds for the arguments that were extracted from the New Testament: Matt. 19:12; Luke 9:23; 1 Cor. 7:38; 1 Cor. 7:40.[39] No one would want to maintain that the only possible consequence of these words of Scripture is life in orders. But just as little is it to be denied that these words can legitimate such a life.

History, which according to the CA is hardly suitable as proof material, appears different in the eyes of the authors of the Confutation. The list of monastic fathers and founders of orders—Paul, Basil, Antony, Bernard, Dominic, Francis, William, Augustine, and also Clara and Brigitte—was cited.[40] In using the oldest names in this line the argumentation goes back to early monasticism; in the course of time it was enlarged and probably grew to this number in the time of the Reformation. The special mention of the two holy women might have been a direct answer to the CA, which saw greater injustice in the nunneries than in monasteries. Not in vain did the authors of the Confutation devote special attention to the "cloisters of virgins" and— not without reason—point out that these communities really wanted to hold fast to their life and vows.[41]

The CA read history to show that the cloisters originally were "voluntary associations." Only later were vows introduced as protection against general decadence.[42] The CA also claimed that the cloisters had been originally schools and seedbeds of good pastors.[43] The Confutation answered both claims. In the first assertion the Confutation saw a blunt reversal of the historical events. First there were vows and only later cloisters.[44] The proof for this would be difficult to produce. The voluntary ascetic life of the single Christian in and at the fringes of Christian society in all likelihood preceded the ordered life in a community, the beginnings of which belong in the fourth century. However, the decision for the ascetic life must not be too quickly equated with an explicit vow. When from the third century on the decision for such a life became bound up with the concept of the vow (perhaps *homologia* and *votum*), then first and foremost the celibate, virginal life is meant with such a pledge which has been made to God. Certainly that is inseparably bound up with the remaining basic requirements of an ascetic life.[45] The first organizers of the communal life also demonstrate this fact. In the rules of Basil the object of vows is explicitly the virginal life; but the *Koinobiarch* (the head of the community) views this pledge as being realized in the well-ordered cloister with all its demands and claims on the individual. The conviction, which has been present from the beginnings of monasticism, that the conversion to the ascetic-monastic life is irrevocable, results in the view that the monastic life with its essential elements is explicitly included in the vow. Thus one can neither agree with the assertions of the CA nor simply repeat the Confutation in its opposition to them. Both positions overlook the effective power and obviousness of historical development.

It is not much different with the second assertion of the CA concerning the original school character of the cloisters. The authors of the Confutation wanted to meet this assertion on friendly terms: it was not denied. But with good reason they pointed out that the monasteries were schools of spiritual life (virtue, good discipline, Holy Scripture, and other arts), as in fact it was programmatically formulated from the Master rule and the Rule of St. Benedict: we want to establish a school for the service of the Lord![46] Real school and educational activities developed only later in the cloisters. With both of these arguments drawn from history the CA believed it would be able to legitimate a widely adopted solution to the question of the cloisters: their acceptance as voluntary institutions or their conversion into public schools.

History was brought into the discussion in still other connections by the CA. It advances examples of the inconsistencies of the Catholic practice. Vows are seen as valid pledges which have been given to God and are binding for the entire life. On the other hand, there is the practice of ecclesiastical dispensation. The case of King Ramir II of Aragon, who was released from his vows because of reasons of state, is referred to. The possibility of papal dispensation from vows once taken had for a long time been the subject of learned discussion, but up until then a unified answer had not been found.[47] The Confutation justified that well-known dispensation with an allusion to the higher interests of the state. Yet for the normal situation this dispensation means nothing at all: here the vow which once has been entered into remains forever valid.[48]

And with that the Confutation returned to the basic question of vows. Vows must not be viewed as inherently impossible. Scripture does not permit this: Wisd. Sol. 8:21; Luke 11:9; Matt. 18:19; 1 Cor. 10:13. In the eyes of the authors of the Confutation these words of Scripture give clear evidence that it is God himself who makes the apparently impossible possible. The many thousands of men and women, who, in accordance with their vows, have even to this day lived continent lives, are proof of the effective power of God's gift.[49] For the Confutation leaves no doubt that a life according to vows is a life based on a special grace. Thus the character of the life in orders as a life "of works," so steadfastly maintained in the CA, is rejected. The life in orders stands also under grace and was even in its very beginnings not a human invention but a legitimate deduction from the gospel: people in orders make an effort to live faithfully according to the gospel; what they take upon themselves in orders happens for Christ's sake and in discipleship to him.[50] Here, again, the authors of the Confutation demonstrate a harmony with the entire tradition. From its beginnings the ascetic-monastic life understood itself as "life according to the gospel," as a form of life that has biblical legitimation. Thus they omit a long controversy with the Reformation position which had ruled out the biblical legitimate of orders. They also paid no attention to the danger revealed in the history of monastic orders that this biblical legitimation became occasionally the claim to be the sole possessors of the gospel. This often caused misunderstandings and confusion, the crude claims which the CA justifiably denounced: monks also taught and preached.[51]

To the authors of the Confutation one point appears to be worth special refutation: the false assertion that the estate of orders is a "state of perfection." [52] With good reason they can reject such a proposition. Not a state of achieved perfection but the effort to achieve perfection was at issue. The people in orders did not claim perfection: with their form of life, freely chosen under God's grace, they hoped—again, under God's grace—to achieve eternal blessedness. With this explanation the authors of the Confutation undersood themselves in no way as innovators. To the reference which the CA had made to Jean Gerson they could have added Thomas Aquinas and even long passages of monastic literature which show that also in the estate of orders salvation can be effected "only with fear and hope in God's grace." The novice prayed (and prays) "for God's mercy" when he is admitted to profession!

Striking is the fact that talk of profession as a second baptism—a serious accusation of CA 27—is ignored. This was a central concern of Reformation polemic against the estate of orders. Why did the authors of the Confutation fail to address this challenge? That it was not taken seriously does not make sense in light of the obstinancy with which the opposing side proposed it. The authors of the Confutation may have thought that this false understanding of orders had been implicitly rejected by their constant emphasis that vows are not human work but God's work and that the justification of the Christian in the monastery is not the result of consecration but of grace. On the other hand, the authors of the Confutation could not have been unaware of the fact that there was a long tradition which has related profession and Baptism.[53] The main point in this manner of speaking, which ranged from an edifying analogy to the insistence that profession equals second baptism, was the understanding of monastic life as permanent repentance. But because repentance was understood as a "second baptism" in the ancient church, the beginning of the monastic life of repentance could be so described. The authors of the Confutation probably did not realize that Luther's own conception of Baptism and repentance stood behind the sharp rejection of this Catholic tradition. The conception of profession as second baptism remained credible in the later Catholic claims concerning the life in orders; R. Bellarmine called it a *"pie creden-dum."* [54]The Catholic reply could not see the contradiction which the Reformers had discovered: "But I know that the grace of forgiveness is given through Baptism and repentance alone." To the Catholics the talk of profession as a second baptism was compatible with this funda-mental confession.

2.2. Bartholomew Arnold von Usingen, *Responsio contra Apologiam Philippi Melanchthoni* (1531)[55]

Bartholomew von Usingen (1465-1532) formulated the confession just cited above. This educated Augustinian had been encouraged by Martin Luther himself to enter into the order.[56] He was among the authors of the Confutation [57] and reacted afterward, in his own re-sponse, very sharply to Melanchthon's Apology to the CA. The reply (Article 4 concerns monastic vows [58]) follows the Apology sentence by sentence and is also closely related to the Confutation, from which it takes verbatim the fundamental claim concerning the legitimacy of monastic vows.[59]

Bartholomew cites the Franciscan Johannes Hilten of Eisenach, who was mentioned by Melanchthon at the beginning of the Apology, with a blunt denial: Bartholomew was in Eisenach forty years ago and visited frequently after that, but he never heard anything about Hilten or his life.[60] If Melanchthon emphasizes the degeneration of the cloisters, Bartholomew agrees with him: what estate could be so steadfast and firm that with time it would not suffer loss and become negligent. But that alone does not justify the dissolution and destruction of the cloisters but demands their correction and reform.[61] This happens fundamentally within the context of tradition. For in tradition Bar-tholomew, like the Confutation, sees no contradiction to the gospel whatsoever. What Melanchthon ascertains to be a contradiction to the gospel is really the result of his own misunderstanding and distorted picture: no man in orders is so foolish as to think that through his vow he earns remission of sin or justification for sin.[62] We too do not claim perfection on the basis of our estate, but all the more we recog-nize in humility that we are sinners and live in a state of eternal re-pentance.[63] When believers take vows, they do not do it in order to be justified through the law or the vows but in order to fulfill the com-mandments of God more easily and without hindrances. Thus they preserve the justification which happens out of grace and thus they grow in grace. And these believers also know that one earns eternal life only through grace and a life according to the gospel, whether one is a monk or a lay person.[64]

Bartholomew was of one mind with the claims of the Confutation. The Christian validity of the life in orders and its full congruence with the gospel are unshakable facts. The renewed attack of Melanchthon certainly sharpened the conflict in comparison with the Confutation. Any remnant of a mild and restrained tone had been abandoned by Bartholomew. Hard confrontation and hostile polemic guide his pen.[65] The *Responsio* clearly shows that in the matter of monastic vows agreement was no longer possible. The Apology had ignored the Confutation's explicit affirmation that no one can earn eternal life by his own power and without grace,[66] and thus it was not able to rethink the matter of monastic vows. In the lands of the Reformation the no to vows now dictated the law of action. In the Catholic lands one sought to give the people in orders new trust and self-confidence.

2.3. The Council of Trent

To the Reformation's no to the life in orders the Catholic camp opposed a fundamental yes. Yet this yes was bound to a criticism of the status quo. Basic programs for reform were proposed. The colorful multiplicity of the orders should be radically reduced: the organization of all orders in three basic types, perhaps Benedictine, Augustinian, and Franciscan. These daring plans wanted to continue the unfinished reform of orders of the 15th century and were a reaction to the radical critique of life in orders from the camp of the Reformers. These demands show a great deal of unhappiness with the actual life in orders at the time. Such decisive measures certainly were not put into practice. The orders themselves wanted to preserve their properties and wealth, which were still secure in the Catholic territories. The Roman Curia refused to bless such an artificial reform. Finally, medieval theology had acknowledged all the many individual orders and communities as proof of the multifaceted operation of the Holy Spirit in the church. Why should one just now renounce these visible signs and vessels of the diverse gifts of the Spirit? [67]

Thus the Council of Trent also remained on a moderate course of reform when it took up the question of orders in its twenty-fifth session (Dec. 3 and 4, 1563). The motto of the reform plan of the Council can be paraphrased with the statement: "They should not be eliminated but reformed." In its general law concerning the reform of orders, the Council stated that the existing orders contribute to the splendor of the church and accomplish a special service in her *(utilitas)*. In order to preserve and renew this special service for the future church, every order is asked to recover a historical conscious-ness of its own origins. Faithfulness to the eternally binding pledges of a communal life in obedience, poverty, and chastity and to the special laws of each individual community is impressed upon the people in orders. The Council reminded them of proven systems of control through general and provincial chapters and regular visitation. These medieval reforms had been repeatedly used to consolidate institutional reform. They now hoped they would have the power to accomplish the desired results. The decretal turned into an imploring admonition to the people in orders to grasp the essence of their life *(substantia regularis vitae)* and to adhere to the foundations of this life in un-conditional faithfulness *(bases et fundamenta)*. Bitter experience from the errant developments of the past was expressed in the lapidary pro-nouncement, where the foundations are not considered, the entire structure must collapse *(totum corruat aedificium necesse est)*.[68]

The Council did not see itself obligated to produce a complete theological justification of the estate of orders. For the fathers of the Council the theological legitimacy of orders was not debatable. When speaking earlier concerning the sacrament of marriage (Session 24), the fathers of the Council had reaffirmed the old conviction that the estate of virginity as such was more perfect than the estate of mar-riage *(melius ac beatius,* Canon 10)—a pronouncement about which it must always be remembered that it does not intend to say anything in regard to the individual perfection or imperfection of those who live in these estates.

The obvious deficiency of the Council in offering theological-spiritual statements in regard to orders was perhaps counterbalanced by the living powers of reform in the orders themselves. From Spain the reforms of the Carmelites influenced the church and the cloisters; the Society of Jesus, which was regarded with special favor by the council fathers, ex-panded tremendously in the post-Tridentine period and had a lasting influence on the different religious communities with its own spirituality and practice of piety. In the Franciscan family the reform group of the Capuchins took root. The composite effect of these forces led to the de-sired renewal of the estate of orders. The numerically strong growth of the cloisters and federations of orders and also the origin of new fami-lies of orders returned to the people in orders their self-confidence. One knew what one was about: "Vows, profession, the striving for perfection" retained their acknowledged and uncontested place in the life of the church.

"The estate of monasticism is that high mountain [of transfiguration.]. To it the Lord in all truth has led those, whom he has accepted as his chosen; he sets them apart, whom he has chosen from so many thousands." That is the pious confession of G. Buzelin (d. 1681), a monk of Weingarten;[69] it is representative of the rediscovered self-confidence. It finally found its structural expression in the representative Baroque cloister—indeed for all communities of any rule. The end of the Baroque culture certainly brought a forcible end to renewed monasticism. The far-reaching church renewal of the 19th century led again, for rather different motives, to a revivification of the existence in orders. It was marked by a great number of new religious communities and a surprising enlargement of the activities of the orders.[70]

3. Toward an Assessment and Judgment of CA 27 from the Perspective of Evangelical Communities (Johannes Halkenhäuser)

"With his book *Concerning Monastic Vows (De votis monasticis)* of 1522, Luther declared monastic vows invalid because they oppose the New Testament. Since then all Protestant parties are united in the rejection of monasticism." [71]

This apodictic judgment, which denies biblical legitimacy to the monastic life-style, is typical of the traditional Protestant writings on church history and of the evangelical sense of the church. Obviously, it can appeal not only to Luther's harsh critique of the abuses in the monasticism of his day and to his several hundred remarks concerning his own time in the monastery but above all to his theological critique of the basic premises of the life in orders. If one adds the remarks of the Lutheran Confessions, especially the CA (27, but also 15, 16, and 23) and the corresponding articles of the Apology, then the rejection of monasticism appears to belong to the irrevocable basis of Reformation doctrine and proclamation. Against this background it must be considered a strong challenge for the Lutheran Church and for the whole of Protestantism if, after long centuries of "cloister oblivion *(Klostervergessenheit)*," it sees itself confronted with the rediscovery and renewal of life in communities, especially after World War II and the decades which followed. In this context one can properly point out that here "a Protestant taboo has crumbled." [72] But it seems more important that these communities, which want to realize discipleship to Christ by means of spiritual group existence, are increasingly being recognized and accepted by the official churches as a form of Christian faith, life, and service community which is defensible in the light of the gospel. In 1976, the Conferences of Bishops of the United Evangelical Lutheran Church of Germany *(VELKD)* directed a word to the congregations that stated (among other things): ". . . we recommend to the congregations, as they reflect upon church renewal, that they affirm the communities as possible forms of Christian life." [73] With that word is the judgment of CA 27, which sounds so definite, *via facti* left behind? Here it cannot be demonstrated in detail that the assertions of Luther and the Confessions concerning the life in orders are by no means so totally negative as later Protestantism supposed. An impartial examination of these comments reveals that in spite of conditional rejection a monasticism which has been renewed by the spirit of the gospel can have a legitimate place within the context of the whole church.[74] It seems more significant that the members of the evangelical communities do not understand themselves in their Christian life as existing at the fringes of the church with sectarian inclinations; rather, they consciously want to live in and with their churches. Thus they will take all the more seriously the questions which were advanced by the Reformation critique of the cloisters, especially where it concerns a biblical justification of its communal life-style and the definition of its place in the light of the doctrine of the church. In our opinion the following main theological insights are important and deserve our attention now in order to bring about a continuing and successful dialogue between the communities and CA 27:

3.1.   For the CA, the mean and measure of all theological judgments of the life in orders is the understanding of the gospel of the justifying grace of God in Christ, which had been newly won in the Reformation. Therefore CA 27 vehemently protests against a monasticism which, with an overdeveloped salvific claim to be an "estate of perfection," [75] wanted to understand itself as Christianity of a higher power and thereby violated and endangered the primacy of grace and the exclusive salvific meaning of faith at their very roots.[76] Every form of being a Christian in a community must allow itself to be measured by the intactness and clarity of the "evangelical reservation," the chief article of justification. The communities acknowledge the continuing legitimacy of this biblical-prophetic protest against all thoughts of merit.[77] They know that the communal life is also (and especially) founded in the experience of unconditional grace, understands itself as an obedient answer of thankful love to the call of God, and has to prove itself in the exercise of the new freedom for witness and service to which Christ frees (Gal. 5:1).

3.2   The CA directs the attention of the communities always again to the fact that discipleship is not the exceptional, privileged, or special achievement of "religious virtuosos" [78] but the primordial form of every Christian life, which is founded by Baptism and challenges every-one to the total decision of faith. Over against an ascetic-monastic ab-breviation of the gospel the CA (16, 4-5 and 27, 49-50 [BC 37-38 and 78-79]) properly underscores that everyone who seriously wants to be a Christian is obliged in his vocation, estate, and sphere of life to love God, to show love to his neighbor, and to do good works. But if the primacy of grace is kept in focus, the Christian existence in communities is a possible manifestation of faith, alongside other (dif-ferent but equally valuable) forms of existence and types of organiza-tion of the Christian life which are complementary within the body of Christ. It remains, at least from the point of view of the communities, an open question to what degree the ecclesiastical tradition of Luther-anism, by eliminating the life in orders from evangelical sociology, restricted all avenues of communication and action within the church to the structure of the parish. This may have resulted in an "impulse towards homogenization," [79] which became ever stronger and which eventually lead to the uniformity of a single type of Christian life. In this context the communities, with their consciously ecclesial self-understanding, make, in our opinion, a decisive contribution to the living renewal and realization of the church as the body of Christ, whose charismatic reality becomes visible as "multiplicity in unity." [80]

3.3.   The particular significance of the communal life-style is the realization of the gospel in community as a particular form of the social-ization of faith. This life-style has its basis in personally experienced guidance and bestowal of grace by God (Phil. 3:12; Eph. 4:7); it un-derstands the evangelical counsels as constitutive and stabilizing factors in the communal life and, having come under the spell of the kingdom of God (Matt. 6:33), knows of the goal—the possibility of living for God and the world as "people of a single love." [81] Thus for the com-munal Christians the living-out of the evangelical counsels is not a work of supererogation,[82] nor a meritorious way *to* salvation,[83] but a way *in* salvation, i.e., a representative and symbolic expression for the total devotion of faith, which is exemplarily concretized in three far-reaching existential possibilities for human existence without limiting itself to them. Put differently, communities are places of the obedient practice of a discipleship inspired by and oriented to the love of Christ.

3.4. The communities leave no doubt that the evangelical counsels, ratified through "profession," can legitimately become institutionalized as voluntarily taken vows (CA 27, 27 [BC 75]) for a lifetime in a special pattern of life.[84] Also if these communities generally avoid the term *vow* in their literature (because since the days of the Reformation critique of vows it smacks of merit) and rather speak of engagement, binding, pledging, or devotion, the fact remains that a person can give to the call of Jesus (John 21:22) a final and unconditional answer which binds further life in its totality. Against the critique of vows of the Reformation and the Confessions, which must be evaluated entirely within the context of the history of theology,[85] the communities draw our attention to the following viewpoints in a constructive and future-oriented manner:

3.4.1. All "special" vows—also the vow to orders—have their possibility and prerogative grounded in the baptismal vow. Through this subordination they are seen not as an expression of a higher grade of Christian perfection—as perhaps on the basis of a "second baptism" which has been assumed to supply effective power for making satisfaction [86]—but are seen as the much more concrete form of an affirmative development and intensification of the baptismal vow involving every Christian.

3.4.2. The vows of profession are (in the sense of having been charismatically grasped) a binding personal answer of the person to the preceding call of Christ, which is heard and taken up in faith. Exactly in their character as a response they preserve the sovereignty of the work of God and thus the primacy of his transcendence and freedom.

3.4.3. Because the vow of profession is based on the unconditional character of the call of God (Isa. 45:23), the person who has been caught up by God's call can live out his engagement only in the same unconditional and irrevocable manner.

3.4.4. The complete and final vow of the person who has been so called is, however, not an act undertaken once-and-for-all and complete in itself; rather, in the context of justification and sanctification (CA 4 and 6) it becomes a dynamic yes which must remain ever open to God's guidance. Thus the vow points beyond itself to the coming aeon, i.e., to the coming Lord, whose gifts and call are irrevocable (Rom. 11:29).

3.4.5.   While Luther and, following him, the Confessions reject eternally binding vows as "null and void" [87] from their understanding of law and freedom, the communities see in them neither an expression of nomological existence nor a limitation of freedom but rather a divinely commissioned and vital manner of the practice and preservation of Christian freedom, which comes to a full development where it is taken up in a free and unforced decision for a lifelong commitment under vows.

Such statements, which probe behind the critique of vows in the CA, certainly are not simply the result of abstract theological reflections, but rather are the guiding insights of the contemporary Christian existence in communities, which have been derived from existential experience, have proved their worth in the communality *(Gemeinschaftlichkeit)* of the communal life-style, and have been verified by the witness of Scripture and in ecumenical dialog. Precisely at this place, in our opinion, the theological dialog between the CA and the evangelical communities must be intensified in order to lead to a systematic clarification of the questions which have now been raised in a changed historical setting for theology and the church.

As "Christ's bondservant" (E. von Tiele-Winckler) the evangelical communities want to be places of responsible spiritual life, of living brotherhood, and of committed service of Christ in church and world. If they credibly live the authenticity of their vocation, they can, in spite of all realistic estimates of the gulf between claim and reality which will only be dissolved in the eschaton, be a beacon for the freedom of the Christian, in the knowledge "that through faith they were accounted righteous and had a gracious God because of Christ.[88]

4. Toward a Catholic Evaluation of CA 27 from a Contemporary Perspective (Friedrich Wulf)

The following theses are offered in the hope that the response to the criticism of churchly monasticism, as presented in CA 27, may now turn out differently from the Catholic side than it did in 1530 in the so-called Confutation. We have gained distance from the actual conflict; we have learned to understand the different "word-games"

("Sprachspiele") better and so do not so easily talk past each other. We have penetrated more deeply into the appropriate problems through a more exact knowledge of the historical development of monasticism, its self-understanding and its constitutive elements, and also through a better knowledge of the controversial theological questions (such as justification by faith alone, faith and works, gospel and law, grace and merit, etc.) which were posed under the heading of CA 27, "Monastic Vows." Furthermore—and this is very decisive—in both churches within the last decade something has taken place which has led to a new situation in which to deal with this issue.

4.1. Theology and Self-Understanding of Orders in the Contemporary Catholic Church

The present renewal of monastic life [89] in the Catholic Church has a long prehistory. It owes its deeper impulse to the new theological movement which broke through the strongly rationalistic neoscholastic thought and had its roots in Scripture and patristics but which also did not keep aloof from a recognition of modern anthropology with its philosophical and psychological implications. Direct and concrete incentives for a renewal came immediately after World War II from Pope Pius XII and his associates. Pope John XXIII later coined the expression *"aggiornamento"* for these concerns. Thus the preconditions for a fruitful discussion at the Second Vatican Council were given. Where, in the declarations of the Council, is the theological and spiritual essence of the Catholic understanding of orders and its place (task) among the people of God (in the church) seen? [90]

4.1.1. A religious (theologically expressed: graceful) call must precede the decision of a Christian to enter the life in orders. For the form of life of the so-called "evangelical counsels," which is essential to orders, is considered "a divine gift, which the church has received from her Lord." [91] The decision to enter the life in orders thus has its origin not in the will of the person, however pious that will might be, but in the call of God, in a charismatic call. The state of having been called *(Gerufensein)* can, and even must, manifest itself in a number of ways: in addition to an inclination to this Christian form of life and a psychophysical aptitude for it (especially for celibacy), it involves above all an inner, lasting encounter with God, Jesus Christ, the message of the gospel, the need of people, and the redeemed and unredeemed situation of the world and its history.[92] Where such an encounter is experienced as having come from God (which, perhaps over the ensuing years, must be tested for its authenticity), the person who is called at the same time experiences himself as being challenged to respond in obedience and trust in God's grace and promise. It occurs in a solemn pledge (profession) to a life in poverty, celibacy, and obedience. This promise is not private but is made before the church, *in facie ecclesiae*. It is accepted by one who holds office in the church [93] and has, therefore, a public-ecclesial character in both a theological and a legal sense.

In the documents of the Council, the act of profession is still more precisely characterized: the meaning, essence, and goal of profession is the loving and total submission to God, the complete assignment to him, the surrender to his service.[94] Honor of God, love of God, and service of God are the primary and noblest things to which the monastic vocation *(Ordensberuf)* is directed. But because God's will is essentially a saving will and his love has been finally and irrevocably turned toward humankind, by his free decision, in Jesus Christ, the monastic vocation contains simultaneously within itself the service for people and to people.[95] The path to this double goal, which in view of the commandment of love is only one goal, consequently is "a following of Christ as proposed by the gospel." It is called the "fundamental norm" and the "supreme law" of the religious life *(Ordensleben)*.[96] From this point of view, monks and people under vows like to see the model of their vocation in the special vocation of the disciples in the gospel.[97]

4.1.2.   At the Council, in accord with the ancient monastic tradition, profession has been related to Baptism.[98] In what sense? It is stated there: "It is true that through baptism he [the Christian] has died to sin and has been consecrated to God. However, in order to derive more abundant fruit from this baptismal grace, he intends, by the profession of the evangelical counsels in the Church, to become free from those obstacles which might draw him away from the fervor of charity and the perfection of divine worship. Thus he is more intimately consecrated to divine service.[99] The authors of this text were familiar with the monastic typology of profession as a "second baptism." They knew that it had played an unhappy role in the controversies of the Reformation period.[100] Therefore they formulated the text with foresight and discretion. First of all the text concerns justification through Baptism ("through Baptism he has died to sin and has been consecrated to God"). One must live out of the grace of Baptism in order to reach perfection in honoring God and in love. The commitment to the evangelical counsels (and profession is precisely that) is seen as a great help in the life aimed at perfection. It does not appear to be entirely clear what is theologically meant when it is stated that the person who is under vows, through profession, becomes "intimately consecrated *(intimius consecratur)*" to divine service. Does not this term attribute a consecratory effect of its own to profession (on account of its similarity with the baptismal vow") which somehow adds something to the baptismal vow? The second text of the Council gives the answer concerning the relationship between profession and Baptism. It reads: "The members of each community should recall above everything else that by their profession of the evangelical counsels they have given answer to a divine call to live for God alone not only by dying to sin (cf. Rom. 6:11) but also by renouncing the world. They have handed over their entire lives to God's service in an act of special consecration *(peculiaris quaedam consecratio)* which is deeply rooted in their baptismal consecration and provides an ampler manifestation of it." [101] Here God is explicitly the prime mover, not the human being. God calls and gives the vocation; human beings answer and follow the vocation. God offers the gracious gift of a conception of life according to the gospel and the example of Christ the first witness (Phil. 2:6ff), in which the three evangelical counsels have become visible and tangible, and human beings open themselves to this calling. In the submission to God, who calls and gives the vocation, God lays his hand on the person who consigns himself to God, and God equips that person with his own Spirit, in a similar manner as he did the prophets, for the service which has been entrusted to him. This event is called "an act of special consecration." However, the consecration involved in profession does not stand by itself, but is to be seen in an inner connection with the grace of Baptism. Consecration is based, rooted, and planted in the grace of Baptism. From this perspective consecration has only *one* meaning: to provide "an ampler manifestation" of the baptismal consecration, i.e., to make it clearer in the manner of a "sign" [102] so that the justified believer is totally and irrevocably consigned to God and his service, or, formulated more christologically in the language of Paul's Epistle to the Romans (6:3-11), to have been united with the death of the Lord to a new life. In such an understanding of the consecration involved with profession, the uniqueness of baptismal grace and consecration remains unviolated. Baptismal grace is unsurpassable. There is no greater grace. All the graces which a person is given in the course of his life, including the gifts of the Spirit *(charisms)*, serve only to allow him to live the baptismal grace and to make it fruitful in the person's own heart, in praise and service of God and of our fellow humans, for the people of God and the whole world.

4.1.3.   However, in spite of the rooting of profession in baptismal grace, which is equal and unsurpassable in all Christians, do not the Christians who are under vows in the Catholic Church still become elevated to a privileged class through a certain emphatic prominence of their special gifts of grace, and thus are they not again educated to have an elitist attitude, and do they not tend to separate themselves from the congregations? Two facts oppose such a charge. First, the more than a thousand-year-old tradition of a distinction of rank in Christian conduct of "commandments" and "counsels," in the sense of a common and a higher class of Christians, has not been mentioned in the declarations of the Council. That tradition, as it was commonly understood, has no basis in Scripture.[103] Accordingly, the consequences of this recognition were also drawn. All ethical and religious comparatives with regard to a higher perfection on the basis of a class, such as "greater love," "stricter discipleship," etc., were avoided. The tenor of the assertions amounts to this: all Christians have to live the gospel completely, and there is no cheaper discipleship than that of the Crucified; the obedience to the law knows no measure because all commandments have their meaning in love, and so the evangelical counsels, such as those of the Sermon on the Mount, are binding for all Christians. Secondly, with the change of consciousness that has arisen, together with the newly awakened baptismal piety (based upon a newly emphasized uniqueness of baptismal grace) the emphasis of the spirituality of the persons under vows is beginning to shift noticeably from the extraordinary duties of their vocation to the common duties of all Christians to such a degree that for many people the orders have lost their power of attraction, and recently at a conference of women religious superiors the cry was heard: "Let us first of all be Christian women!"[104] This is the dilemma: if one emphasizes preeminently the extraordinary duties of the vocation to orders, i.e., the gracious gifts which distinguish it, the foundation on which everything rests threatens to disappear from view, and vice versa. One must always see both together, in a living and dynamic dialectic, and one must live this dialectic in order to grasp the reality of vocation which has its source in the guiding and enticing love of our Lord, who gave up his privileges for our salvation.

4.1.4.   Today, as always, the striving for holiness and perfect love still validly remains the essential goal of the life in orders. Traditionally, this goal may have often been understood too individualistically (in the sense of the salvation of one's own soul). Thus a certain undercurrent of Semi-Pelagianism (or in the language of the 19th century, *"Aszetismus"*) always threatened monastic spirituality, and that was quite justifiably, although with some exaggeration, exposed by the Reformation. In order to meet this reproach and its corollaries, above all, the preeminence of grace and faith over religious and ethical efforts has been so strongly, so directly, and so comprehensively emphasized in Chapter V of the "Dogmatic Constitution of the Church *(Lumen gentium)*" concerning "The Call of the Whole Church to Holiness," that no sort of suspicion of any kind of a works-righteousness can arise any more. Even the concept of the "state of perfection," which has been used since the 13th century, has been abandoned because of its tendency to lead to misunderstanding.[105] In this connection it is noteworthy that today the three evangelical counsels are not primarily understood as "means to perfection" (Thomas Aquinas), but more as aids for "becoming free for service" to God and to people and also, on account of their character of renunciation, as repentance in the discipleship to the Lord. With this emphasis on "discipleship" and the idea of "service," Christians under vows should be forced even more out of a self-centered circle. Their vocation pledges them to other people, wherever they need their help, and pledges them to the people of God and to the church as the lasting mystery, which has become visible, of the salvific presence and action of Christ in this world. According to contemporary theological understanding, the religious community of orders as a whole, which understands itself as a community of disciples in a special sense, symbolically represents the church; it *"is* the church and should manifest the church in such a way that one can believe that the Lord is in her midst (1 Cor. 14:25)." [106] Thus the societal place, i.e., the special "function" or orders in the diversely organized church (ecclesiastical offices, churchly service to the laity, worldly service to the laity, charismatic service), is described. Nobody is a Christian in orders in isolation but they are what they are in communion and thus in the church as church.

4.2. What Judgment of CA 27 Results from this View of Orders?

4.2.1.   Whoever reads CA 27 as a Catholic theologian in light of the above exposition must come to the judgment that the accusations of the Reformation, so far as they were argued theologically and did not simply protest concrete abuses, essentially are, for the greatest part,

314   *Lohse, Frank, Halkenhäuser, and Wulf*

no longer applicable. He comes to such a judgment all the more, the deeper he has confidence in and affirms the concerns of the Reformation. (Whether and how far these accusations at one time—above all with regard to the opposing theology of the Catholic side—were justified is not the subject of this contribution.) Thus many people in recent years—on all sides of the issue—have expressed the view that if the contemporary theological and spiritual self-understanding of orders would have been offered in the first decade of the 16th century, and if a corresponding reality would have stood behind it, then the hard and unconditional protest of the Reformation against monasticism and vows probably would not have occurred.

4.2.2. On the other hand, however, some on the Catholic side will gladly concede that the theses of Luther concerning monasticism and vows, *Theses Concerning Vows (Themata de votis)* and *Judgment Concerning Monastic Vows (De votis monasticis iudicium)*, as they found their upshot in the CA, still have their significance for the theological and spiritual penetration of the life in orders and can be profitably reconsidered if one disregards their polemics. We shall single out two examples: the proposition of justification by faith alone, repeated nearly to the point of a frenzy, and the proposition of the freedom for which "Christ has set us free" (Gal. 5:1), the freedom from a legalistic conception of the path to salvation. Where the charisma of vocation to orders, vocation to a life according to expressly stated counsels, is institutionalized and becomes part of ecclesiastical law, attitudes may develop which could obscure one or the other basic utterance of the message of the gospel. On the one hand, in line with the goal and the life in orders, the individual's own religious striving and effort can dominate his consciousness so much, that the unconditional preeminence and irreplaceable precedence of grace is no longer present; on the other hand the effort to realize the evangelical counsels, with their overregulation, can lead to the danger of legalism. Even a vow which has been entered into in freedom can become a law which is unfruitful of salvation if the original freedom is not continually regained.

Thus the CA can be and may remain a point of departure for a fruitful Catholic-Lutheran dialog even concerning monasticism.

5. Conclusion

5.1. There is *agreement* that the CA's critique of monasticism essentially concerned faithfulness to the message of the gospel and dealt only secondarily with the actual historic abuses which were to be condemned. Thus the CA expressed its own character as a confessional document which wanted to articulate the common faith of the one church. The ecumenical dialog has to begin at this point in the interpretation of the text.

There is apparently extensive agreement that the criticism of the CA which was theologically argued was too wholesale and too absolute and did not do justice to the monastic tradition of the ancient church.

A last point of agreement is that in light of the contemporary self-understanding and observance of the life in orders in the Catholic Church (especially since Vatican II), the judgment of the CA can no longer be maintained. Nevertheless, the cardinal point of CA 27, the assertion of justification by faith alone, should continue to remain a critical norm of the ecumenical dialog concerning monasticism.

The result: "monasticism" as a communal form of an unconditional realization of the gospel is a legitimate path for Christians, although with the present state of the dialog (even within Lutheranism itself) the interpretation in particulars remains open. Thus one great step in not only the understanding of CA 27 but also far beyond it has been taken.

5.2.   However, in the investigations *(Untersuchungen)* different viewpoints and judgments among the partners in dialog have also become apparent. The two most important should be mentioned here:

5.2.1.   The monastic tradition (from the beginnings of monasticism up to the Reformation), which plays a significant role in the CA, is interpreted very differently in the Catholic and Lutheran contributions respectively. This difference shows more than a controversy among historians—it reveals itself in every case as depending on a presupposition concerning the historical development of monasticism. While Lutheran historians read the development and self-description of monasticism, in accordance with the CA, with the eyes of the basic Reformation assertion of justification, Catholic historians (as also the *Confutatio*) see the continuous tradition of the origin of monasticism in a self-understanding appropriate to the gospel as a decisive theological fact.

5.2.2.   The consensus has been reached that there is no higher form of Christianity, no higher perfection based on a certain estate *(Stand)* in the church. But the consequences which are drawn from that consensus are very different according to the various authors. According to the Lutheran tradition it is above all granted to the freedom of individuals to decide for themselves for one of the two possibilities for

Christian existence—for marriage or celibacy, for the life in the world or life in a community, and to serve God in either state, according to the gifts which the individuals have been given. Both possibilities are equally valid in terms of their relationship to salvation, although the Apology (23, 38-39 [BC 244]), following Paul, still concedes to virginity the status of a higher gift over against marriage. The Catholic tradition proceeds here primarily from God's call and vocation which is issued to the individual. From this point of view the vocation in orders is seen as a very special gift of grace. Those who stand under this call and believe that they recognize the call as having come from God cannot remain neutral and make their choice according to their own discretion but must at least face the call. When they follow the call, they are neither a better nor a more highly exalted Christian than the others, but in a special way they know themselves to be persons who have been called by the gospel and challenged to discipleship. On this issue the Lutheran communities converge generally more closely with the Catholic orders than with the general opinion in Lutheranism. The ecumenical dialog which is due here will have to go in different directions on this issue, but because it proceeds from a far-reaching agreement on the central questions, the answers to the questions that present themselves here will be more easily found.

5.3. There still remain a number of *open questions*, which need to be further clarified.

5.3.1.   Are the Lutheran communities (brotherhoods and sisterhoods) to be understood as communities of the church like the Catholic orders and in what sense? Is the ecclesial character of these communities, where it is accepted, only a question of sociology of the church, or also of theology in the proper sense?

5.3.2.   Do both churches recognize the possibility of vows or other forms of a binding pledge for life? Can such pledges be revised, and if so, by whom can the disavowal of a pledge become legitimized?

5.3.3.   Concerning questions of controversy such as "justification and works" and "works of satisfaction" (the correct understanding and limits of these terms), see the respective contributions to this volume by G. Müller and V. Pfnür ("Justification—Faith—Works") and by H. Fagerberg and H. Jorissen ("Penance and Confession"). *Summary:* If the basic gospel-oriented assertion of the Reformers is affirmed with respect to monasticism in the church (leaving the one-sidedness and polemics of the concrete controversies aside), the road has been cleared to find solutions to the open questions. These solutions will, however, bring a greater multiplicity of forms and of understandings of "monastic life."

Notes

1. On the history of the monastic ideal and Luther's attitude see Bernhard Lohse, *Mönchtum und Reformation: Luthers Auseinandersetzung mit dem Mönchsideal des Mittelalters,* in *Forschungen zur Kirchen- und Dogmengeschichte* 12 (Göttingen: 1963), which is the source for the following statements. Cf. also Bernhard Lohse, *Askese und Mönchtum in der Antike und in der alten Kirche,* in *Religion und Kultur der alten Mittelmeerwelt in Parallelforschungen* 1 (Münich-Vienna: 1969). On Luther see also Heinz-Meinolf Stamm O.F.M., *Luther und das Ordensleben* (Rome: 1977).

2. B. Lohse, *Mönchtum und Reformation,* pp. 160-171; on the tradition of the conception of monastic profession as a second baptism see also Heinrich Bacht, *Die Mönchsprofess als zweite Taufe,* in *Catholica* 23 (1969): 240-277.

3. B. Lohse, *Mönchtum und Reformation,* pp. 227-278.

4. *Ibid.,* pp. 278-311.

5. AE 35, 41 (WA 2, 736); cf. Lohse, *Mönchtum und Reformation,* pp. 325-343.

6. See the description of these events in Bernhard Lohse, *Die Kritik am Mönchtum bei Luther und Melanchthon,* in Vilmos Vajta, ed., *Luther und Melanchthon: Referate und Berichte des Zweiten Internationalen Kongresses für Lutherforschung,* Münster, 8.-13. August, 1960 (Göttingen: 1961), pp. 129-145.

7. On these works see esp. René-H. Esnault, *Le "De Votis Monasticis" de Martin Luther,* in *Etudes Théologiques et Religieuses* 31 (1956): 1, 19-56; 31 (1956): 3, 58-91; Bernhard Lohse, *Luthers Kritik am Mönchtum,* in *Evangelische Theologie* 20 (1960): 413-432; a Catholic assessment of Luther's "attack on monastic vows" in Otto Pesch O.P., *Luthers Kritik am Mönchtum in katholischer Sicht,* in H. Schlier, E. v. Severus, J. Sudbrack, and A. Pereira, eds., *Strukturen christlicher Existenz: Beiträge zur Erneuerung des geistlichen Lebens. Festgabe für Friedrich Wulf S.J. zum 60. Geburtstag* (Würzburg: 1968), pp. 81-96, 371-374.

8. AE 44, 294-295 (WA 8, 604); AE 44, 305-306 (WA 8, 611-612).

9. On the spiritual and theological aspects in the reorganization of the cloisters and other spiritual houses see above all Nicolaus C. Heutger, *Evangelische Konvente in den welfischen Landen und der Grafschaft Schaumburg: Studien über ein Nachleben klösterlicher und stiftischer Formen seit Einführung der Reformation* (Hildesheim: 1961); N. Heutger, *Das Stift Möllenbeck an der Weser* (Hildesheim: 1962); Robert Stupperich, *Luther und das Fraterhaus in Herford,* in *Geist und Geschichte der Reformation: Festgabe Hanns Rückert zum 65. Geburtstag, Arbeiten zur Kirchengeschichte* 38 (Berlin, 1966): 219-238; R. Stupperich, *Das Herforder*

Fraterhaus und die Reformation, in *Jahrbuch des Vereins für Westfälische Kirchengeschichte* 64 (1971): 7-37.

10. CA 27, 2 (BC 71).
11. CA 27, 5-8 (BC 71-72).
12. CA 27, 15-17 (BC 73).
13. CA 27, 11 (BC 72).
14. CA 27, 12-14 (BC 72-73).
15. CA 27, 54 (BC 79).
16. CA 27, 13 (BC 73).
17. CA 27, 16 (BC 73).
18. CA 27, 24-26 (BC 74-75).
19. CA 27, 18-23 (BC 73-74).
20. CA 27, 34-35 (BC 76).
21. CA 27, 36 (BC 76).
22. CA 27, 41-48 (BC 77-78).
23. CA 27, 49-50 (BC 78-79).
24. CA 27, 60-62 (BC 80).
25. See Karl Eduard Förstemann, *Urkundenbuch zu der Geschichte des Reichstages zu Augsburg im Jahre 1530,* vol. 2 (Halle: 1835; new printing Osnabrück, 1966), pp. 402-403.
26. Apol. 23, 1-3 (BC 239).
27. Apol. 23, 6-8 (BC 240).
28. Apol. 27, 1-4 (BC 268-269).
29. Apol. 27, 5-9 (BC 269-270).
30. Apol. 27, 20 (BC 272).
31. Apol. 27, 36-37 (BC 275).
32. See Lydia Präger, ed., *Frei für Gott und die Menschen: Evangelische Bruder- und Schwesternschaften der Gegenwart in Selbstdarstellungen* (Stuttgart: First edition, 1959); Johannes Halkenhäuser, *Kirche und Kommunität: Ein Beitrag zur Geschichte und zum Auftrag der kommunitären Bewegung in den Kirchen der Reformation,* in *Konfessionskundliche und kontroverstheologische Studien XLII* (Paderborn: 1978).
33. Immenkötter, pp. 196-197.
34. See, for example, J. Eberlin von Günzburg, *Vermahnungen an den Ulmer Rat,* L. Endres, J. E. von Günzburg, *Sämtliche Schriften* (Halle: 1900).
35. Immenkötter, pp. 17-23.
36. *Ibid.,* p. 24
37. *Ibid.,* pp. 186-187.
38. Representative of early monasticism: Jerome, ep. 58,5 (CSEL 54, pp. 534-535).
39. Immenkötter, pp. 188-189.
40. *Ibid.*
41. *Ibid.,* pp. 190-191.
42. CA 27, 2 (BC 71).
43. CA 27, 15 (BC 73).
44. Immenkötter, pp. 188-189.
45. Impressively in Cyprian, *De habitu virginum;* on vows in the ancient church see B. Kötting's article *"Gelübde"* in RAC 9, pp. 1084-1099.
46. Immenkötter, pp. 190-191.

47. *Ibid.,* p. 192, note 21.
48. *Ibid.,* pp. 192-193.
49. *Ibid.,* pp. 192-193.
50. *Ibid.,* pp. 194-195.
51. CA 27, 15 (BC 73).
52. Immenkötter, pp. 194-197.
53. Described in detail by H. Bacht, *Die Mönchsprofess als Zweite Taufe,* in *Catholica* 23 (1969): 240-277.
54. *Ibid.,* p. 273; cf. as an example from a more recent time, G. Morin, *Mönchtum und Urkirche* (Munich: 1922), pp. 53-69: *Taufe und Profess* (French original: Maredsous: 1912).
55. P. Simoniti, ed. (Würzburg: 1978).
56. Simoniti, p. XII, note 3.
57. Immenkötter, p. 19.
58. Simoniti, pp. 616-654.
59. *Ibid.,* p. 634.
60. *Ibid.,* p. 617.
61. *Ibid.,* p. 619.
62. *Ibid.,* p. 622.
63. *Ibid.,* p. 636.
64. *Ibid.,* p. 623.
65. The polemic is expressed in Art. 4: "Melanchthon's objections are defamations, coverups, nit-pickings, battologies, and Melanchthon himself is a battologist, miserable sophist, and trickster."
66. Immenkötter, pp. 84-85.
67. H. Jedin, *Zur Vorgeschichte der Regularenreform Trid. Sess. XXV,* in *RQ* 44 (1936): 231-281 (=*Kirche des Glaubens II,* pp. 360-397).
68. *Concilium Tridentium* IX, pp. 1036-1044.
69. As cited by R. Reinhardt, *Restauration, Visitation, Inspiration: Die Reformbestrebungen in der Benediktinerabtei Weingarten von 1567-1827* (Stuttgart: 1960), pp. 21-22.
70. K. S. Frank, *Grundzüge der Geschichte des christlichen Mönchtums* (Darmstadt: 1978).
71. P. Kawerau, *Geschichte der alten Kirche* (Marburg, 1967), p. 145.
72. See von Kortzfleisch, *Mitten im Herzen der Massen* (Stuttgart: 1963), p. 15.
73. Complete text in L. Mohaupt, ed., *Modelle gelebten Glaubens* (Hamburg: 1976), pp. 142-144.
74. Full documentation in J. Halkenhäuser, *Kirche und Kommunität* (Paderborn: 1978), pp. 13-81. H. Asmussen correctly summarizes: "The hostility to the cloisters in the evangelical camp does not have its origin in the CA. Much more, it is rooted in a history which preceded and followed the CA." (in *Warum noch Lutherische Kirche?* [Stuttgart: 1949], p. 296). In the rest, in our opinion, it belongs to ecumenical integrity to reconsider the often ideologically excessive assertions of the CA (such as concerning the origin of monasticism, monastic profession as a second baptism, and the eschatological dimension of life in orders) in light of statements of monastic theology in the Reformation period that have to be judged in a more differentiated manner. In addition in the present changed ecumenical situation, the official pronouncements of Vatican II (and also

the documents concerning orders of the Würzburg Catholic Synod) concerning a timely renewal of the life in orders signal a remarkable convergence in the theology of the life in communities.

75. CA 27, 16 and 46-47; Apol. 27, 9 (BC 73, 78, 270).
76. CA 27, 38-44 (BC 77-78).
77. CA 27, 11 and 38 (BC 72 and 77).
78. M. Weber, *Wirtschaft und Gesellschaft* (Cologne and Berlin: 1964; after the 4th edition: Tübingen: 1956) p. 885 and passim.
79. H. Asmussen, in H. Asmussen and Th. Sartory, *Gespräch zwischen den Konfessionen* (Frankfurt and Hamburg: 1959), p. 198.
80. Cf. H. -D. Wendland in L. Präger, ed., *Frei für Gott und die Menschen* (Stuttgart: 1959), p. 15: "Unity, but not uniformity, rules in the Body of Christ, communion in the Holy Ghost, in love, but not the uniformity of a single form of life."
81. R. Schultz, *Das Heute Gottes* (Gütersloh: 1961), p. 90.
82. CA 27, 44 and 61 (BC 78 and 80).
83. CA 27, 11-12, 61 (BC 72, 80).
84. CA 27, 27 (BC 75).
85. See J. Halkenhäuser, *op. cit.,* pp. 46-59, 320-331.
86. CA 27, 11 (BC 72).
87. CA 27, 36 and 62 (BC 76 and 80). Cf. the index in Tappert under "vows" (BC 713).
88. Apol. 4, 211 (BC 136).
89. The "renewal of life in orders" which has been meant here, unlike the reform of orders of the 15th century or also of the Reformation period, does not have abuses as its cause but is more deeply rooted and more creative. It wants to rethink the whole of life in orders, theologically and from present exingencies, and in that respect it bears a certain analogy to the claims of the Reformation without being directly influenced by them.
90. The fundamental assertions of Vatican II concerning the life in orders are found in the "Dogmatic Constitution of the Church *(Lumen gentium),"* chapters 5 and 6, and in the "Decree on Appropriate Renewal of the Religious Life *(Perfectae caritatis),"* available in English translation in Walter M. Abbott, s.j., ed., *The Documents of Vatican II* (New York: Herder and Herder, 1966), pp. 65-78 and 466-482, respectively. Note: the German translation of these documents (LThK[2], *Das Zweite Vat. Konzil* [Freiburg: 1966-1967] contains an extensive commentary by F. Wulf.
91. *"Lumen gentium,"* chap. 6, art. 43,1 (Eng. trans., *op. cit.,* p. 73). The individual receives the gift of grace in and through the church.
92. Cf. to F. Wulf, *Theologische Phänomenologie des Ordenslebens,* in *Mysterium Salutis, Grundriss heilgeschichtlicher Dogmatik,* 4,2 (Einseideln-Zurich-Cologne: 1973), pp. 457-467.
93. *"Perfectae caritatis,"* art. 5 (Eng. trans., *op. cit.,* p. 470).
94. *"Lumen gentium,"* chap. 6, art. 44, and *"Perfectae caritatis,"* art. 5 (Eng. trans., *op. cit.,* pp. 74-75 and 470, respectively).
95. *"Perfectae caritatis,"* art. 6, and *"Lumen gentium,"* chapter 6, art. 44 and 45 (Eng. trans., *op. cit.,* pp. 470-471 and 74-77, respectively).
96. *"Perfectae caritatis,"* art 2a (Eng. trans., *op. cit.,* p. 468); in many other places the act of profession is closely related to the discipleship of Christ,

the assignment to Christ, the relationship to Christ, the union with Christ, etc.

97. For a justification of the model by modern exegesis compare H. Schürmann, *Der Jüngerkreis Jesu als Zeichen für Israel (und als Urbild des kirchlichen Rätestandes)*, in *Ursprung und Gestalt: Erörterungen und Besinnungen zum Neuen Testament* (Düsseldorf: 1970), pp. 45-60; for the basis of this model see also M. Hengel, *Nachfolge und Charisma: Eine exegetisch-religionsgeschichtliche Studie zu Mt 8,21f und Jesu Ruf in die Nachfolge* (Berlin: 1968).

98. Cf. for the following the historically and theologically very refined and weighed study of H. Bacht, *Die Mönchsprofess als Zweite Taufe,* in *Catholica* 23 (1969): 240-277.

99. *"Lumen gentium,"* chap. 6, art. 44 (Eng. trans., *op. cit.,* p. 74).

100. Luther was convinced out of his own experience that generally in monastic circles monastic profession was made equal to Baptism with respect to remission of sin and justification, and he incorrectly believed that this doctrine went back to Thomas Aquinas (*"Die kleine Antwort auf Herzog Georgs nähestes Buch,"* WA 38, 148). Melanchthon took up the critique in the CA (27, 11 [BC 270]), and he made Thomas responsible for it (CA 27, 20 [BC 272]), as already had been done in the Torgau Articles.

101. *"Perfectae caritatis,"* art. 5 (Eng. trans., *op. cit.,* p. 470).

102. "Sign" is understood here *"theologically* as something which makes the central message of the gospel visible and tangible and which shapes the church." This conception of "sign" was entirely crucial for the decision of the general synod of the dioceses in West Germany concerning "Orders and Other Spiritual Communities" on a theological-spiritual distinguishing mark of a life according to the three evangelical counsels in a community. Cf. the commentary volume to this decision *Nachfolge als Zeichen* (F. Wulf, O. Bamberg, and A. Schultz, eds. [Würzburg: 1978]), above all what is said there in Chapter 1 concerning the "basic commission" to the order.

103. Demonstrated with respect to the pericope of the "rich young man" (Mark 10:17-31 and par.) by S. Legasse, *L'appel du riche: Contribution a l'étude des fondements scripturaires de l'état religieux* (Paris: 1966).

104. Thus according to an address of Pope John Paul II, who seized upon and fundamentally affirmed this rallying cry of the women in orders (French original text in: *La Documentation catholique* from Nov. 19, 1978, no. 20, pp. 1005-1006).

105. Compare the introduction of Wulf's commentary in: LThK², *Das Zweite Vatik. Konzil,* Bd. I, pp. 284-285. For the sake of correctness it should be added that in the *"Lumen gentium"* (chapter 6, art. 45—Eng. trans., *op. cit.,* p. 76) the expression *"quodcumque perfectionis Institutum"* ("any institute of perfection") is found; it probably has remained as an oversight—meanwhile everyone knows how the term is to be understood.

106. *Nachfolge als Zeichen,* p. 33.

12

Political Order and Vocation
in the Augsburg Confession

by George Wolfgang Forell and James F. McCue

1. Introduction

The topics of "political order *(Weltliches Regiment)*" and "vocation" *("Beruf")* differ from all the other topics treated in this commentary at least in this: they were not viewed by the Catholic party at Augsburg as matter for debate and disagreement. CA 16 was "gladly accepted *(libenter acceptatur)*" by the authors of the *Confutatio* for its polemic against what was taken to be the Anabaptist refusal of political responsibility.[1] And Melanchthon acknowledges this agreement: "Our opponents approve Article XVI without exception *(sine ulla exceptione)*."[2] And if CA 16 is to be understood as teaching a doctrine of vocation, this either eluded the authors of the *Confutatio* or seemed to them thoroughly orthodox. Furthermore, not only did the *Confutatio* not take issue with the CA on political order and vocation, throughout the subsequent discussion at Augsburg, these never became matters for debate.[3]

As for the passing reference to the distinction between the ecclesiastical power and the power of the sword in CA 28, the *Confutatio*

322

does not address this but passes immediately to more detailed questions.

It is therefore tempting, in a Lutheran-Catholic commentary on the CA, simply to take note of this harmony and pass on to other matters. What we shall attempt to do, however, is first to explore the extent to which this apparent consensus really expresses agreement. Is it, for example, undermined by Luther's understanding of the "two kingdoms"? Then we shall consider briefly some of the ways in which the CA's teachings on political order have become problematic for *both* the Lutheran and Roman Catholic communities. Finally, we shall try to identify what the CA still can teach the church in our own day.

2. The CA on Political Order

Civil government or civil affairs, what the CA calls *res civiles (weltliches Regiment),* are so central to the life and concerns of all of us in the last quarter of the 20th century that we may at first be surprised, even disconcerted, by the brevity with which the CA treats these matters. The author, signers, dissenters, and official respondents apparently did not feel that they were dealing with a central theological topic or one central to their conflict. Thomas Aquinas had observed: "When we consider all that is necessary to human life it becomes quite clear that man is naturally a social and political animal, destined more than all other animals to live in community." [4] Those in attendance at Augsburg, whatever their disagreements, would have found this cogent, even rather obvious.

Though the CA thus treats civil affairs with surprising brevity, this should not lead Roman Catholics and Lutherans in their conversations to consider issues of political theology to be of minor importance in our day. No regulative conclusions should be drawn from the emphasis given to these issues in the controversies of the 16th century.

It is noteworthy, however, that at that time Roman Catholics and Lutherans were aware that the political situation had changed drastically since New Testament times, and that they addressed themselves to the questions of vocation and political authority in the light of their own historical experience. Roman Catholics as well as Lutherans were aware of their responsibilities for civil government and the political order. That was why they came to Augsburg. They were in agreement that "it is right for Christians to hold civil office, to sit as judges, to decide matters by the imperial and other existing laws, to award just punishments, to engage in just wars, to serve as soldiers, to make legal contracts, to hold property, to swear oaths when required by magistrates, to marry, and be given in marriage." [5] The confession was a call to participate responsibly in the public life of men and women of their time. Those who were involved in the formulation and initial debate over the CA were not as focused on the challenges and responsibilities of the common life as would be their descendants 450 years later, but they clearly took their political responsibilities seriously. It is this attitude, so evident in CA, that should guide efforts to interpret CA 450 years later.

In order to define more precisely the extent of agreement and areas of possible disagreement we begin by simply asking what it is that CA (16 and 28) is asserting about the socio-political order and about the relation to it of the Christian's calling. A straightforward reading of the text yields the following:

1. Legitimate political structures are good works of God, and it is proper for Christians to exercise political responsibility according to presently existing laws. (CA 16)

2. It is the Christian's responsibility to obey civil laws and authorities except where these command sin. (CA 16)

3. It is within the structures of political and family *(Oeconomiam)* life that one exercises charity; and evangelical perfection consists in fear of God and faith, not in flight from such life. (CA 16)

4. The civil magistrates and the political order are autonomous over against the ecclesiastical power. (CA 28)

The authors of the *Confutatio* not only accepted CA 16, they "accepted it gladly." They refer, however, only to CA 16, 1-3, apparently overlooking the antimonastic polemic of CA 16, 4-7. Since the attack on monasticism is concentrated elsewhere in CA, perhaps the issue is passed over here because it would be more fully addressed elsewhere. There was then apparent agreement—even vigorous agreement—on the first two propositions stated above. The third, however, would seem to present a thesis unacceptable to the opponents of CA. As to the fourth, it is interesting to note that the *Confutatio* never really addresses what we have identified as the point at issue relative to political authority. The *Confutatio* instead discusses the legitimacy of clerical immunities and the right of bishops to use coercion. Indeed, our fourth proposition expresses a widely held though surely not uncontested late medieval view, and it is not unlikely that there was some disagreement on this issue among those who were united in opposing CA.

In what follows we shall first explore the four propositions to see to what extent they expressed a common ground in 1530, or, where this is not the case (No. 3), to what extent subsequent events have created a common tradition. Secondly, we shall consider some of the limitations of CA relative to political authority and vocation, limitations which should be clearly seen and which must be overcome if the church is to be guided by CA 16 in times to come.

2.1. On Political Responsibility

Anyone who is aware of Luther's teaching conventionally designated with the words "two kingdoms" will recognize in CA 16 and 28 certain ideas and expressions that in Luther's writings are part of that teaching. It is therefore necessary to ask whether, to begin, our first two propositions above are so much a part of that teaching that they can neither be understood nor affirmed without it. Another way of putting the question is to ask whether CA 16 proposes the specifically Lutheran teaching of the two kingdoms as part of the church's confession of faith.

It seems to us that CA 16 does not and does not intend to include Luther's views about the "two kingdoms," even though this is doubtless the context out of which the text evolves.[6] CA is intended to be, so far as possible, a formula of concord, and here as in many other places it affirms positions that could be arrived at from a number of different theological starting points. When the authors of the *Confutatio* greet the first sections of CA 16 "gladly," they correctly understand it as expressing an old and common tradition. What they would have done if confronted with a summary statement of the doctrine of the "two kingdoms" we can only imagine. What the contemporary Roman Catholic theological community would make of the "two kingdoms" is something we can likewise only imagine, since that tradition has long been informed by a different, less dichotomous way of relating Christian life and the socio-political order.

But it is important to be clear that in CA 16 one is not confronted with that teaching.[7] In determining whether theologians (or whatever) coming out of two different traditions agree on a particular matter, it is always tempting to argue that if one only presses on far enough one will find that apparent agreement can be turned into a disagreement. Neither the authors of the *Confutatio* nor the author of the Apology did this: the former received the assertions under consideration here with joy; the latter simply acknowledges this.

2.2. The Worldly Versus the Monastic Calling

The third of our propositions, however, does pose problems. That it is within the setting of the worldly calling rather than in withdrawal from it that the Christian life is to be lived—this clearly was a polemical assertion in 1530; and if the authors of the *Confutatio* passed over the assertion in their discussion of CA 16, in substance they responded to it in their discussion of CA 27.

Our understanding of the setting of this assertion is as follows: For centuries prior to the Reformation, the Latin church had tended to view some version of the celibate-ascetic-contemplative life as the highest form of Christian living. It was, of course, possible to be a Christian and to be saved in other ways of life, but except in quite extraordinary circumstances this was second best. Gratian's *"Duo sunt genera christianorum"*—there are two kinds of Christians—is only the most quotable expression of this. It is illustrative of the staying power of this view within Roman Catholicism that the writer who did as much as anyone else to help Roman Catholicism move beyond this view of things, Yves Congar, could still write: "Only at the expense of ignoring the whole of history can it be denied that this idea is in conformity with the nature of things. Christian life led integrally and without compromise in accordance with its proper requirements to what is traditionally called the angelic or apostolic life, that is, the monastic life (in the wider sense)." [8]

However, it should be recognized that during the three decades since that was written, important though ill-defined changes have taken place in Roman Catholicism. Whatever the causes, monastic life has largely ceased to be honored as the paradigm of Christian life; so much is this the case that it seems quite possible that the coming generation may be the first in a millennium and a half in which the western church will function without a substantial monastic component. In such a setting will the churches wish to say the same things about the worldly calling and monasticism that were said when monasticism so dominated the thought of western Christendom that it was difficult to take seriously any other form of Christian life? Under changed circumstances, some Catholic theologians have begun thinking differently about the monastic life and its relationship to the worldly calling. [9] Developments in our own day within the churches of the Lutheran and the Reformed traditions suggest that CA 16 and 27 do not represent the final word on monasticism and the Christian calling.

Though the doctrine of the calling is an important one in Luther and in Lutheranism, it is touched on only in passing in the CA. It is in one's calling that the Christian is to exercise charity on behalf of others. While we should recognize the rightness and the importance of the insistence on the worldliness of the Christian calling, we should also acknowledge that the doctrine of the calling as developed by Luther and by classical Lutheranism presupposes a world which we no longer inhabit. It was a more or less static world, in which there were a number of well-defined roles to be played; the role that one was to take up was largely (never entirely) a matter of inheritance and circumstances. The Christian was to see the social and economic necessities as mediating a calling.

Though the church today may take the older conception of calling as a point of departure, it must recognize that we are separated from the world in which that conception was born by a series of social and economic revolutions. The character of one's task in the world is less clearly and obviously given, once and for all. The orders of creation are not fixed. They change; and it may at times be the Christian's calling to participate in the work of changing them.

2.3. On the Distinction Between Civil and Ecclesiastical Authority

The fourth assertion, asserting the separation and autonomy of the civil and religious authorities or powers (*potestates, Gewalten, Regiment*), poses many problems. CA 28 itself is not focused on precisely this issue. Its title and subject is *de potestate ecclesiastica,* and it affirms the distinction and autonomy of the civil authority only en route to its proper subject, the *potestas clavium seu episcoporum.*[10] The *Confutatio* focuses on the question of clerical immunities and on the right of bishops to use coercion for spiritual ends. This has a double disadvantage: as Melanchthon (*Apol.* 28, 1) points out these were not under attack;[11] and with the gradual destruction of the churches of the *ancien régime,* these immunities have by now largely ceased to exist. Accordingly, we here abstract from these issues.

As the opening lines of CA 28 suggest, the issue of the relationship between political and ecclesiastical authority had already been much discussed, and a confusion of opinions had been expressed. Some writers had argued for the autonomy of the political order, others for its derivation from the ecclesiastical authority. No consensus in theory had been reached, though in practice few if any kings or princes were willing to acknowledge themselves vassals of the ecclesiastical authority.

328   *George Wolfgang Forell and James F. McCue*

Though it is sometimes suggested that the territorial church was a peculiar outcome of Lutheranism, it should be noted that some form of territorial church was common throughout the Middle Ages and persisted in Catholic Europe until the French Revolution and its attendant aftershocks. The Christian Roman Empire, especially by the time of Theodosius, the Visigothic Kingdom, the Frankish Kingdom first of Clovis and then of the Carolingians, and the Ottonian empire, are all part of the background of the 16th-century territorial church. The episode between Gregory VII and Henry IV at Canossa, important though it is, does not mark the end of imperial or monarchical claim to and exercise of an important role in the affairs of the church in a given territory. Though the papacy grew steadily in power and authority for 200 years after Gregory VII, the political authorities would never acknowledge the extreme papal claims of the *Dictatus Papae,* and will never simply turn over the control of the church in their domains to the ecclesiastical establishment. The CA does not, of course, challenge the territorial church, but neither does it invent it. The position taken here is directly opposed to assertions of Gregory VII and Boniface VIII;[12] but to suppose that it ran counter to "the Catholic view" of the pre-Reformation era is to interpret that period too much on the model of Roman Catholicism of 1870-1960.

The issue of the relationship of the two powers is, moreover, a question posed within a Christian society: it is a question of the relationship between two orders or structures within a single society. Events have largely destroyed that setting: and once again the French Revolution rather than the Reformation would seem to be the watershed. In our own day it may well be that popes and bishops have (wisely or unwisely, properly or improperly) tried to influence voters; this is a very different thing from claiming the *right* to replace governments. The relationship between Christian faith and Christian decision is a complex and difficult issue; and CA 28 ought not be understood as *settling that issue;* but what it does say about the autonomy of the civil-political authority has become so much a matter of everyday experience that we must enter imaginatively into another world even to argue about it.

It should also be pointed out here that though the vocabulary of the German text of CA 28 (esp. 28, 12) may suggest Luther's teaching on the two kingdoms—*die zwei Regiment, das geistlich und weltlich*—the Latin is more traditionally medieval, the language of what was by then a more than 200-year-old dispute *de potestate ecclesiastica et civili.*[13]

Though the teaching on the "two kingdoms" is presumably the context out of which the autonomy of the political order is asserted, this autonomy is proposed here as something that can be arrived at from other starting points.

3. The CA and the Limitations of Its Perspective

In situating CA 16 and 28 it is important that we see not only what was positive in the way in which it addressed the issues of its own day. We must also see the ways in which it bore the limitations of its own time, and some of the negative consequences of these limitations in the subsequent history of the church. CA does not present a well-rounded theological analysis of the state and of life in the world, and should not be used as though it did.

We limit ourselves to two observations: CA antedates the rise of modern democratic practice and theory; and in its discussion of the state it seems to presuppose a simple view of sin and justice which, one might reasonably argue, is quite "un-Lutheran."

3.1. The CA and the Democratic Tradition

In saying that CA is predemocratic, we wish to be careful not to suggest that democratic political theory is God's final gift to humankind. There is, however, a way of thinking about politics and the state which has become commonplace in the traditions associated with the major 18th and 20th-century revolutions. Within these traditions political authority is seen as arising from the people ruled; it has legitimacy from them, and at least in theory it is subject to their judgment. Christians living and thinking in these traditions have not found it impossible to reconcile these ideas with Romans 13 and 1 Peter 2. Not surprisingly, CA 16 and 28 ascribe an unmediated divine authority to rulers; and it is easy to infer, especially if one is familiar with Luther's writings on the subject, that it is for God alone to judge whether they rule well or ill; further that it is God's right alone to punish or replace, and that for people so to act is to usurp the divine prerogative.

Ernst Troeltsch was neither the first nor the last—simply one of the most long-winded—to argue that this has often led the church of the CA to supineness before authoritarian, sometime quite cynical, regimes, and surely events since Troeltsch's day have not lessened the force of this kind of criticism.

Political manipulation of ecclesiastical affairs was indeed a serious problem in the 16th century, as it has been in every century since Constantine. Charles V's role at Augsburg, in the shaping both of the CA and the *Confutatio,* might appear as a significant "confusion of ecclesiastical authority and the power of the sword." Yet the purpose of the distinction between these two in CA 28 is exclusively to keep ecclesiastics from overstepping the proper limits of their order. There is no concomitant effort to safeguard the proper autonomy of the church.

The authors of the *Confutatio* did not find this striking. They shared with Melanchthon a rather generous view of the authority of the emperor and of the lesser rulers in the church; and given the fact that the argument at Augsburg was an argument over the shape of Christianity that would be legal within the emperor's domain, it is not surprising that neither side used the occasion to caution against abuses of political power in ecclesiastical affairs.

Today, however, we seem faced with the threat of the disappearance of the church into the omnivorous, omnicompetent state and its civic piety. The church will presumably want to stand by what was said in 1530 in regard to Christian political responsibility, but it might find that other political-theological concerns are more vital to it today than those discussed at Augsburg.

3.2 The CA and the Sinful State

CA 16 speaks of legitimate civil ordinances *(legitimae ordinationes civiles),* of the Christian's right *(liceat)* to award just punishments *(supplicio iure constituere),* to engage in just wars *(iure bellare),* of the obligation to obey magistrates and their laws except when they command sin *(nisi cum iubent peccare).* The German text adds a troubling detail not in the Latin: Christians may also punish evildoers with the sword.[14] There is, however, no discussion of what constitutes legitimacy in law, of what is the *ius* in punishment or in war, of what sin might be in this domain. It is accordingly natural to suppose that all of this is unproblematic, that ordinarily law is legitimate, that ordinarily war and punishment are just, that being commanded to sin would be altogether extraordinary and thus recognizable.

The consequence of this would seem to be to reinforce the tendency already noted by granting to the powers that be the benefit of the doubt, the assumption of legitimacy. Participation in war is legitimate, indeed of obligation, unless the contrary is absolutely clear (which is rarely possible in an era of mass propaganda). Sin will be construed in as narrow and legalistic (sic!) a way as possible in judging what the state requires of me.

The comfortable acquiescence of patriotic Christians in most of the major atrocities of the 20th century ought, if nothing had previously, to force us to recognize that CA 16, while it had something important to say vis-a-vis "anabaptist" withdrawal and monastic otherworldly perfectionism, does not confront the entire range of challenges posed to the church by *das weltliche Regiment*. Only if this is recognized, and only if this recognition leads us to work our way through the challenges of our day with all the resources of the Christian tradition, can CA 16 and 28 function in a healthy and fruitful way in the church.

4. The Positive Value of the CA Today

But granted the dangers concerning the Christian calling and political authority which can be created by a nonhistorical reading of CA, there is an important positive lesson to be learned from the willingness of the signers of the CA to accept change and to deal with the problems and structures of their own age. As we indicated earlier they were not in any way interested in reconstructing or more accurately constructing a society which would use the examples of the Old and New Testament as the model. They were neither interested in a theocracy nor in a separation which would establish a perfect and isolated religious community using the Sermon on the Mount as a blueprint. They were prepared to live responsibly in the world of the 16th century.

By taking their historical setting so very seriously, with all the problems that such a stance might involve for us (e.g., "just war" in the age of the atom bomb or private property in the age of the multinational corporation) they have provided an example of the manner in which Christians should address themselves to the constantly changing political and social questions which are posed to them in a rapidly changing world. What has to be avoided is the pretension and self-righteousness of "theocracy" and "separatism." In our own day theocracy has come to be more and more simply impossible, and therefore a less seductive alternative than it was in 1530. However, as political life grows ever more complex, brutal, and apparently unmanageable, the temptation of separation becomes more attractive. At this point CA 16 still has much to say to us. It is not so much the specific answers to the political issues of 1530 which make CA so useful as the manner in which it has chosen to address the political issues of its time.

5. Summary

We have concluded that in our judgment no basic disagreement in the understanding and evaluation of CA 16 separates Roman Catholics and Lutherans today. Relative to the value of the monastic life and its relationship to the Christian's worldly calling, differences that have existed in the past are called into question by developments in our own time. Furthermore, the church/state issues under discussion in CA 28 (the power of bishops/ecclesiastical power) presuppose a political situation which has not existed for centuries. The changes in the pervasiveness and sophistication of the power of political rulers in our age confront us with a profoundly different set of problems than those facing the Christians at Augsburg in 1530. We agree that the political developments of the past 400 years make a much more subtle understanding of the relation of church and state imperative for all Christians than could possibly be envisioned by the participant at the Diet of Augsburg in 1530. It is of some significance that the word *"Staat"* does not even occur in CA. Yet this *"Staat"* is the reality which tends to dominate the lives of women and men in our time and is likely to do so for the foreseeable future. It is the task of the church in the present to come to a theological understanding of "Civil Government," "the Political Order," "the temporal sword," "the Two Authorities, the Spiritual and the Temporal" in their relationship to each other. In the CA we see not so much ready-made answers to our questions, but an important and valuable point of orientation which, if considered with care, may prove helpful to Lutherans and Roman Catholics in their efforts to draw a course in a radically different political environment.

Notes

1. Immenkötter 114-115. It is perhaps worth noting that the *Confutatio* bases its agreement with CA 16 on Rom. 13:1. The CA had referred only to Acts 5:29, which presupposes the limitation of political authority over the human conscience.
2. Apol. 16, 1 (BC 222; for the Latin text see BSLK 307 or CT 328).
3. See H. Immenkötter, *Um die Einheit im Glauben: Die Unionsverhandlungen des Augsburger Reichstages im August und September 1530* (Münster: 1973). This is especially remarkable since it was political pressure by the emperor that was decisive for the presentation of the CA and the *Confutatio* and for the irenic tone of both documents. This political involvement of the secular power constitutes the essential background for the conversations at Augsburg. Thus the political authority exercises

considerable influence in spiritual matters, and the two powers are not as clearly separated as one might infer from CA 28, 12 (BC 52-53).

4. *De regimine principium ad regem Cypri,* c. 1, n. 741, in R. Spiazzi, ed., *Opuscula philosophica* (Rome: 1954), p. 257. Translation in J. G. Dawson, *Aquinas: Selected Political Writings* (Oxford: 1948), p. 3.
5. CA 16, Latin (BC 37).
6. See Wilhelm Maurer, *Historischer Kommentar zur Confessio Augustana,* vol. 1, *Einleitung und Ordnungsfragen* (Gütersloh: 1976), pp. 78-124.
7. The "two-kingdoms doctrine" has been the focus of heated debate in the 20th century. We do not enter into a discussion of the doctrine, not because we wish to avoid that debate or because we side with those who think that the church would be better off without the doctrine, but simply because in our judgment it was not confessed at Augsburg.
8. Y. Congar, *Lay People in the Church* (Westminster: 1957), p. 10 *(=Jalons pour une théologie du laicat)*. For medieval texts, see pp. 7-10.
9. See, for example, the early work of Karl Rahner, "The Ignatian Mysticism of Joy in the World" (1937), "Passion and Asceticism" (1949), and "Reflections on the Theology of Renunciation" (1953), all of which are included in: *Theological Investigations* (London: Darton, Longman & Todd, 1967), vol. 3.
10. CA 28, 5 (BSLK 121; CT 84; for the Eng. trans., see BC 81).
11. Apol. 28, 1-2 (BC 281).
12. For the *Dictatus papae* of Gregory VII, see Mirbt-Aland, *Quellen zur Geschichte des Papsttums und des römischen Katholicizmus* (6th ed., Tübingen: 1967), p. 282. For *Unam sanctam* of Boniface VIII see pp. 458-460.
13. CA 28, 12 (BSLK 122; CT 84).
14. CA 16 (BSLK 70-71; CT 50).

Confessio Augustana - Confessing One Faith

1. It was a presupposition of our common work with the CA of 1530 that this document is a binding foundation of doctrine for the Lutheran churches. Of course, the Lutheran churches recognize other confessional writings, which (aside from Luther's Catechisms) were formed after 1530, but they all understand themselves as expositions or continuations of the CA or have been so evaluated. An agreement concerning the CA has a fundamental significance for an agreement concerning the other confessional writings and should form the basis for a clarification of the further questions posed therein. Because the CA has this status, the endeavor to understand or comment on it could not only be of the philological-historical variety but must also orient itself to the goal of an agreement concerning the Christian faith, the faith to which the Confession of 1530 wanted to bear witness.

2. It is a conclusion of our common work that the CA not only had the intention of bearing witness to the common catholic faith but that to a large degree its assertions must actually be understood as an expression of that catholicity. Even where questions still remain open, con-

vergences can be seen. That is, in reaching back to the CA we have arrived at a common understanding of the center of the Christian faith.

3. This consensus was especially evident where the beliefs in the Triune God and the saving work of Jesus Christ, which unite all Christendom, were concerned. Thus we have again become aware that the church division of the 16th century had not gone to the roots. We consider it noteworthy that the profound agreement already includes areas which were always considered matters of controversy between our churches: the doctrine of justification as an unfolding and applying of faith in Christ; the doctrine of original sin; and the understanding of the sacraments, especially with respect to penance, Baptism, and in a large measure the Lord's Supper as well.

4. Today we see the real difference that led to division more in the conception of the church than in these topics viewed in themselves and apart from the question of the church. But here, too, there is a fundamental commonality, although unmastered problems and open questions still remain, especially with respect to ecclesial offices. The assertions of the CA concerning the church bind rather than separate us. They provide the basis for a common understanding of the holiness, catholicity, apostolicity and, with that, unity of the church. The constitutive marks of the church are founded on the right proclamation of the gospel and in an administration of the sacraments that is in keeping with Christ's institution, as well as in the office of ministry, which has been given to the church for the sake of those functions.

5. This large measure of agreement is possible because of a deepened insight into Holy Scripture, a more impartial historical evaluation of the controversies of that time, and sometimes a new assessment of the consensus which already was achieved in the unity discussions at Augsburg in 1530, and which the Confutation expressed or prepared the way for in the fundamental theological questions. The present agreement cannot be understood apart from the fact that the shaping conditions for both the life and theology of our churches have changed since the 16th century, even if this is reflected in only a preliminary way in the individual investigations. These include the change on every continent of the position of the church and its officeholders in society. Related to this are the challenges common to Christendom, even if they are not always identical in every region. Included also are the renewal

movements. These have left their impression on our churches since the 16th century. In particular they have led to a renewed practice of divine worship and sacramental piety in the Roman Catholic Church, while in Lutheranism they have led to new forms of community in sister- and brotherhoods of service and to the communities that have originated in our time. All of this facilitates our approach to the critical articles of the second part of the CA.

6. The questions that are still open between us today can be defined on the basis of a common point of departure: if the church is understood as the "congregation of all believers," "the saints," or a "communion" in the Holy Spirit because of its participation in Christ through his gospel and the sacraments, then we can ask as a test what consequences that view has for the understanding and form of the office of ministry in the church. In particular, what meaning does this "communion" impart to the doctrine of apostolic succession? Further: It is possible to achieve a common understanding of the Mass, even as a sacrifice,[1] which retains both the "communion" in the Holy Spirit with Christ present in the sacrament, and the abiding face to face encounter between Christ and his church? Here then we can add the convictions that distinguish us which were not treated in the CA: in particular the papacy (for here also new possibilities for understanding suggest themselves [2]), the doctrinal assertions concerning Mary, the Mother of our Lord, which were dogmatized in the 19th and 20th centuries, and the doctrine of purgatory. It is yet to be tested what importance these still open questions have for the path of our churches toward each other and whether it is significant that some of them attained their present sharpness only in the last centuries.

7. Not only between but also within our churches we have different forms of piety, in which we experience crises and renewals. That applies, for example, to penance and the Lord's Supper. There are new forms of Christian development which at times we are still unable to evaluate with certainty, such as the charismatic movement or the communities in the churches of the CA. It remains to be seen what variety of forms of eucharistic piety or veneration of the saints is possible in the one church. The CA will have a critical weight in these matters because it reminds us that all forms of piety and ecclesial practice remain subordinate to the fundamental norm of the common Christian faith. That includes a criticism not only of a questionable hypertrophy,

but also of a legalistic narrowness that does not want to allow any room for the fullness and freedom of true catholicity.

8. The common understanding of justification in the CA is a common understanding of the center of the Christian faith, of the salvation which God has effected for the world through Jesus Christ in the Holy Spirit. It is the duty of our churches to hold fast to this center in our proclamation and in the practice of divine worship. This agreement at the center gives a basis for hope that it will also be possible to answer with the necessary degree of agreement the difficult questions of the papacy and of the place of Mary, the mother of our Lord, in the whole of Christian doctrine of salvation. In addition, beyond the study of the CA a further and new listening to Holy Scripture and the witness of the Fathers and brothers (i.e., to the ancient church), to other Christian traditions, especially eastern Christendom, and not least, to the questions and answers of the churches in Asia, Africa, and Latin America will be necessary. We are still on the way to unity, but the fact that this goal has not yet been reached should not obscure the deep consensus which we have on the basis of the CA. On the contrary, on both sides we must take responsibility for this consensus in the practical life of the church; indeed we must introduce it there.

9. The fact that the CA unites us (the Roman Catholic and Evangelical-Lutheran churches) far more than it separates us has significance that goes beyond the relationship of both our churches. The CA is also highly regarded in Reformed churches which have not accepted it as a binding norm of doctrine. Just as the consensus which has been discovered in this study, even if it is not complete, has its place within the framework of the intensive dialog of churches of different traditions in the ecumenical movement of our day, so it will have significance beyond the circle of the confessions which have not as yet been mentioned, including the dialogs of both the Roman Catholic and Lutheran churches with Eastern Orthodoxy. It would be a fulfillment of the hope of the confessors at Augsburg in 1530 if God used their Confession as an instrument to advance the common growth of Christendom into the one *ecclesia catholica*.

10. The common commentary on the CA which has been presented in this collective volume is our contribution to the discussion of the question of whether the appropriate organ of the Roman Catholic

338 Confessing One Faith

Church can recognize this doctrinal document as an expression of the Catholic faith and how the Evangelical-Lutheran church is to conduct itself in relation to such an eventuality. The unity of the church is not something that human beings need to produce. However, the separated ecclesial communities can recognize each other again in the antedently given unity of the one church which "is to continue forever" (*perpetuo mansura*). That obliges them to take steps toward a reconciliation and to ask whether the continuing separation can be justified before God. Such a recognition has itself occurred time and again in this study. To that extend we have found the CA to be "confessing one faith," even if open questions still remain and we cannot speak of the CA as a common confession of this one catholic faith. We hope that our churches will find forms to manifest this acknowledged community as a sign and a help for our congregations and before the world.

Notes

1. Compare also the document of the Evangelical Lutheran-Roman Catholic study commission, *"Das Herrenmahl"* (1980), nos. 37, 56-61 (pp. 27, 35-39).
2. See the "Malta Report" of the Roman Catholic-Evangelical Lutheran study commission, *"Das Evangelium und die Kirche"* (1972), nos. 66f., and the American studies of the Petrine office: *Papal Primacy and the Universal Church* (Minneapolis: Augsburg, 1975), and *Teaching Authority and Infallibility in the Church* (Minneapolis: Augsburg, 1980).

Index

Contributors

Wilhelm Breuning
Professor of Dogmatics, University of Bonn

Avery Dulles
Professor of Systematic Theology, Catholic University
of America

Holsten Fagerberg
Professor of Systematic Theology, University of Uppsala

George Wolfgang Forell
Professor of Religion, University of Iowa

Karl Suso Frank
Professor of Ancient Church History and Patristics,
University of Freiburg

Bengt Hägglund
Professor of Systematic Theology, University of Lund

Johannes Halkenhäuser
Pastor, Casteller Ring Community

Erwin Iserloh
Professor of Medieval and Modern Church History,
University of Münster

Hans Jorissen
Professor of Dogmatics and Introduction to Theology,
University of Bonn

Walter Kasper
Professor of Dogmatic Theology, University of Tübingen;
Consultant, Secretariat for Promoting Christian Unity, Rome

Georg Kretschmar
Professor of Church History and New Testament, University
of Munich

René Laurentin
Professor and Member, Mariological Academy of Rome

Karl Lehmann
Professor of Dogmatics and Ecumenical Theologie,
University of Freiburg

George A. Lindbeck
Professor of Theology, Yale University

Wenzel Lohff
Professor of Systematic Theology,
University of Hamburg (and Göttingen)

Bernhard Lohse
Professor of Church and Dogmatic History,
University of Hamburg

James F. McCue
Professor of Religion, University of Iowa

Harding Meyer
Research Professor, Institute for Ecumenical Research,
Strasbourg

Gerhard Müller
Professor of Historical Theology, University of Erlangen-
Nuremberg

Vinzenz Pfnür
Chief Academic Advisor for Church History and Its Didactics,
University of Münster

Horst Georg Pöhlmann
Professor of Systematic Theology, University of Osnabrück

Heinz Schütte
Professor of Systematic Theology, University of Bonn; Director,
Johann-Adam-Möhler Institute for Ecumenism, Paderborn

Vilmos Vajta
Research Professor, Institute for Ecumenical Research,
Strasbourg

Friedrich Wulf
Editor-in-Chief, *Geist und Leben*